REFORMING CORPORATE RETAIL INVESTOR PROTECTION

The spate of mis-selling episodes that have plagued the financial services industries in recent years has caused widespread detriment to investors. Notwithstanding numerous regulatory interventions, curtailing the incidence of poor investment advice remains a challenge for regulators, particularly because these measures are taken in a 'fire-fighting' fashion without adequate consideration being given to the root causes of mis-selling.

Against this backdrop, this book focuses on the sale of complex investment products to corporate retail investors by drawing upon the widespread mis-selling of interest rate hedging products (IRHP) in the UK and beyond. It brings to the fore the relatively understudied field concerning the different degrees of investor protection mechanisms applicable to individual retail investors – as opposed to corporate retail investors – by taking stock of past regulatory reforms and forthcoming regulatory initiatives as well as, more importantly, the conclusions reached by the judiciary in IRHP mis-selling claims. The conclusions are particularly interesting: corporate retail investors are in a vulnerable position when compared to individual retail investors. The former are exposed to a heightened risk of mis-selling, meaning that regulatory intervention should be targeted accordingly. The recommendations made as a result of these findings are further supported by insights emerging from behavioural law and economic theories.

This book is aimed at researchers, lawyers and students with an interest in the financial regulation field who are keen to explore potential regulatory reforms to the investment services regime that address the root causes of mis-selling, and restore a level playing field amongst all retail investors.

Hart Studies in Commercial and Financial Law: Volume 3

Hart Studies in Commercial and Financial Law
Series Editor: John Linarelli

This series offers a venue for publishing works on commercial law as well as on the regulation of banking and finance and the law on insolvency and bankruptcy. It publishes works on the law on secured credit, the regulatory and transactional aspects of banking and finance, the transactional and regulatory institutions for financial markets, legal and policy aspects associated with access to commercial and consumer credit, new generation subjects having to do with the institutional architecture associated with innovation and the digital economy including works on blockchain technology, work on the relationship of law to economic growth, the harmonisation or unification of commercial law, transnational commercial law and the global financial order. The series promotes interdisciplinary work. It publishes research on the law using the methods of empirical legal studies, behavioural economics, political economy, normative welfare economics, law and society inquiry, socio-legal studies, political theory and historical methods. Its coverage includes international and comparative investigations of areas of law within its remit.

Volume 1: *The Financialisation of the Citizen: Social and Financial Inclusion through European Private Law*
Guido Comparato

Volume 2: *MiFID II and Private Law: Enforcing EU Conduct of Business Rules*
Federico Della Negra

Reforming Corporate Retail Investor Protection

Regulating to Avert Mis-Selling

Diane Bugeja

•HART•
OXFORD • LONDON • NEW YORK • NEW DELHI • SYDNEY

HART PUBLISHING

Bloomsbury Publishing Plc

Kemp House, Chawley Park, Cumnor Hill, Oxford, OX2 9PH, UK

First published in Great Britain 2019

A catalogue record for this book is available from the British Library.

Library of Congress Cataloging-in-Publication data

Names: Bugeja, Diane, author.

Title: Reforming corporate retail investor protection : regulating to avert mis-selling / Diane Bugeja.

Description: Oxford ; New York : Hart 2019. | Series: Hart studies in commercial and financial law ; volume 3 | Based on author's dissertation (doctoral – King's College London, Dickson Poon School of Law, 2018) issued under title: An analysis of the UK corporate retail investor protection framework regulating the sale of complex investment products. | Includes bibliographical references and index.

Identifiers: LCCN 2019031387 (print) | LCCN 2019031388 (ebook) | ISBN 9781509925865 (hardback) | ISBN 9781509925889 (Epub)

Subjects: LCSH: Securities—Great Britain. | Individual investors—Legal status, laws, etc.—Great Britain. | Consumer protection—Law and legislation—Great Britain.

Classification: LCC KD1774 .B84 2019 (print) | LCC KD1774 (ebook) | DDC 346.41/092—dc23

LC record available at https://lccn.loc.gov/2019031387

LC ebook record available at https://lccn.loc.gov/2019031388

ISBN: HB: 978-1-50992-586-5
ePDF: 978-1-50992-587-2
ePub: 978-1-50992-588-9

Typeset by Compuscript Ltd, Shannon

PREFACE AND ACKNOWLEDGEMENTS

Regulation has, in many cases, failed to prevent mis-selling

Treasury Committee, *Conduct and competition in SME lending* (HC 204, 2015) Eleventh Report para 172

Mis-selling and poor advice are recognised as inherent risks for the investment services industry. Corporate retail investors emerge in a particularly vulnerable position, and are hence exposed to a heightened risk of mis-selling, especially when transacting in complex investment products. The widespread mis-selling of interest rate hedging products to this category of investors in the United Kingdom and beyond clearly supports this view, as do insights emerging from behavioural law and economics theories.

The exposure of corporate retail investors to the risk of mis-selling derives from the limited redress options available to this category of investors. More specifically, case law has shown that English courts tend prioritise the parties' agreement as expressed in the contractual documents which they execute, which thinking is grounded in the unchallenged principles of contractual freedom and legal certainty underpinning the English common law framework. This triggers the need for regulatory intervention in establishing enhanced investor protection measures for corporate retail investors, which should take the form of ex-ante and ex-post regulatory reforms to the investment services regime with the objective of restoring a balance to the position of corporate retail investors vis-à-vis investment firms. The reforms being contemplated in this book purport to mitigate the extent to which the restricted knowledge and experience of corporate retail investors is exploited by the more powerful investment firms before entering into an investment transaction, especially when this relates to complex products; post-transaction reforms, on the other hand, aim to secure adequate channels for these investors when seeking redress for losses incurred as a consequence of being mis-sold an investment product.

I would like to thank the many people who have supported me on this venture. In particular, I am grateful to Professor Eva Lomnicka and Mr James Lee whose continuous encouragement was instrumental throughout the completion of my doctorate at King's College London, from which this book derives. I also owe thanks to Professor Niamh Moloney and Professor Iain MacNeil who have examined my doctoral thesis and have provided invaluable advice. I remain indebted to my mother, Brigitte, and my husband, George, for their incessant love and support.

Finally, this book is dedicated to my two guardian angels who I miss dearly but who I am confident would be immensely proud of my achievements – my late grandparents, Charlotte and Joseph.

TABLE OF CONTENTS

PART II
THE REGULATORY AND LEGAL INTERPRETATION OF 'INFORMATION' AND 'INVESTMENT ADVICE'

PART III
CONCLUDING REMARKS AND RECOMMENDATIONS

LIST OF ACRONYMS AND ABBREVIATIONS

ACP	Autorité de contrôle prudentiel
AFM	Authority for the Financial Markets
AMF	Autorité des Marchés Financiers
APER	Approved Persons Regime
ASIC	Australian Securities and Investments Commission
BaFIN	Bundesanstalt für Finanzdienstleistungsaufsicht
BBA	British Bankers' Association
BIS	Department for Business Innovation and Skills
CCA 1974	Consumer Credit Act 1974
CCA 2006	Consumer Credit Act 2006
CCD	Consumer Credit Directive
CESR	Committee of European Securities Regulators
CFD	Contract for Difference
CFPB	Consumer Financial Protection Bureau
CII	Chartered Insurance Institute
CJEU	Court of Justice of the European Union
CMA	Competition and Markets Authority
CMVM	Comissão do Mercado de Valores Mobiliários
COB/COBS	Conduct of Business Sourcebook
CONSOB	Commissione Nazionale per le Società e la Borsa
CPUTR	Consumer Protection from Unfair Trading Regulations 2008
CRA 2015	Consumer Rights Act 2015
CRD	Consumer Rights Directive
DISP	Dispute Resolution: Complaints Sourcebook

DTI	Department of Trade and Industry
ECON	Committee on Economic and Monetary Affairs
EFER	Economics for Effective Regulation
ESMA	European Securities and Markets Authority
EU	European Union
FAMR	Financial Advice Market Review
FCA	Financial Conduct Authority
FCAC	Financial Consumer Agency of Canada
FIN-USE	Forum of User Experts in the Area of Financial Services
FINRA	Financial Industry Regulatory Authority
FMA	Financial Markets Authority of Austria
FOS	Financial Ombudsman Service
FSA	Financial Services Authority
FSA 1986	Financial Services Act 1986
FSA 2012	Financial Services Act 2012
FSCP	Financial Services Consumer Panel
FSCS	Financial Services Compensation Scheme
FSMA	Financial Services and Markets Act 2000 (original and current versions)
FSUG	Financial Services User Group
HKSFC	Hong Kong Securities and Futures Commission
IBIP	Insurance-Based Investment Product
IDD	Insurance Distribution Directive
IMD	Insurance Mediation Directive
IRHP	Interest Rate Hedging Product
ISD	Investment Services Directive
KID	Key Information Document
LAUTRO	Life Assurance and Unit Trust Regulatory Organisation
LIBOR	London Interbank Offered Rate
MAS	Money Advice Service

MiFID	Markets in Financial Instruments Directive I and II (as applicable)
MiFIR	Markets in Financial Instruments Regulation
NAO	National Audit Office
NCA	National Competent Authority
OFT	Office of Fair Trading
PCBS	Parliamentary Commission on Banking Standards
PERG	Perimeter Guidance Manual
PFS	Personal Finance Society
PIA	Personal Investment Authority
PPI	Payment Protection Insurance
PRA	Prudential Regulatory Authority
PRIIP	Packaged Retail Investment and Insurance-Based Investment Product
PROD	Product Governance and Product Intervention Sourcebook
RAO	Financial Services and Markets Act 2000 (Regulated Activities) Order
RDR	Retail Distribution Review
RPPD	Responsibilities of Providers and Distributors for the Fair Treatment of Customers Sourcebook
SEC	Securities and Exchange Commission
SFA	Securities and Futures Authority
SFC	Securities and Futures Commission
SIB	Securities and Investments Board
SMCR	Senior Managers and Certification Regime
SME	Small and Medium-Sized Entity
SMSG	Securities and Markets Stakeholder Group
SRO	Self-Regulatory Organisation
TBL	Tailored Business Loan
TCF	Treating Customers Fairly
TPIR	Temporary Product Intervention Rule

UAE	United Arab Emirates
UCITS	Undertakings for the Collective Investment in Transferable Securities
UCPD	Unfair Corporate Practices Directive
UCTA	Unfair Contract Terms Act 1977
UK	United Kingdom
US	United States
UTCCD	Unfair Terms in Consumer Contracts Directive
UTCCR	Unfair Terms in Consumer Contracts Regulations 1994 and 1999 (as applicable)

TABLE OF CASES

Australia

Canada

Court of Justice of the European Union

Judgements

Opinions

Germany

Hong Kong

Italy

Netherlands

Spain

United Kingdom

TABLE OF LEGISLATION

Australia

Belgium

European Union

Directives

Commission Recommendations

Regulations

Hong Kong

Netherlands

United Kingdom

PART I

The Illusion of Uniformity

The regulatory model ... failed. The standard orthodoxy was that... people make rational decisions when given sufficient information; that markets are self-correcting organisms; and ... that if you oversee distribution channels ... the right products get to the right people. All three orthodoxies failed.[1]

[1] FSA, 'My vision for the FCA' Speech by Martin Wheatley (British Bankers' Association, London, 25 January 2012): www.fsa.gov.uk/library/communication/speeches/2012/0125-mw.shtml, accessed 25 August 2015.

1

Breadth of Investor Protection Regulation

I. Why Regulate to Protect Retail Investors?

The history of financial services regulation has shown, albeit with the benefit of hindsight, that law and regulation are unlikely to evolve as rapidly as market practices and therefore swiftly become obsolete. This, together with the magnitude of investor detriment that has been registered in recent years, suggests that the need for more effective investor protection regulation has become 'self-evident'.[2]

Both the common law and the regulatory framework for investment services are rooted in the neo-classical economic theory. This model is based on the assumption that investors act rationally such that, as long as they are supplied with accurate information, investors are presumed 'willing and able to use it wisely'.[3] Seen from this perspective, investor protection only becomes necessary where market failures arise, which failures are commonly attributed to information asymmetries such that disclosure is used as a central regulatory tool to support better decision-making and stronger market-based investing.[4] The effectiveness of this approach, which is founded on the notion of *caveat emptor*,[5] is dampened in the present climate marked due to the ever-increasing number of mis-selling scandals that have caused widespread investor detriment. Although regulators seem to

[2] Joseph Stiglitz, 'Regulation and Failure' in David Moss and John Cisternino (eds), *New Perspectives on Regulation* (The Tobin Project 2009) 22. The Parliamentary Commission on Banking Standards (PCBS) also commented on a 'widespread appetite' for measures to constrain the misconduct, complacency and recklessness that fuelled the past mis-selling incidents (PCBS, *Changing banking for good: Report of the Parliamentary Commission on Banking Standards, Volume I* (HL Paper 27-I, HC 175-I, 2013) 16).

[3] Donald C Langevoort, 'Selling Hope, Selling Risk: Some Lessons for Law from Behavioural Economics about Stockbrokers and Sophisticated Customers' (1996) 84 California Law Review 627, 699.

[4] European Securities and Markets Authority (ESMA), Opening statement of Steven Maijoor (ESMA Investor Day, Paris, 12 December 2012): www.esma.europa.eu/system/files/2012-_818.pdf, accessed 29 June 2015.

[5] The doctrine of *caveat emptor* has its origin in the famous case of *Chandelor v Lopus* [1603] 79 ER 3 (KB). In its purest form, *caveat emptor* ('let the buyer beware') suggests that it is incumbent upon the buyer alone to assess the quality of a purchase (see further Patrick S Atiyah, *The Rise and Fall of Freedom of Contract* (Clarendon Press 1979) 178–79; Gerrit De Geest, 'The Death of Caveat Emptor' (2014) University of Chicago Law School, Law and Economics Workshop).

have acknowledged the need for more paternalistic interventionist tools, elements of *caveat emptor* are still evident in the UK's regulatory framework as well as in the deliberations of the English judiciary, particularly where certain categories of investors are concerned.

At a macroeconomic level, mis-selling poses a risk to financial stability and can have a de-stabilising effect on the balance sheets of investment firms, which in turn makes the economy prone to systemic risk.[6] At a micro level, retail investors may also suffer from significant financial detriment. Indeed, since the pensions mis-selling scandal in the late 1980s, the UK has witnessed numerous incidences of investment products' mis-selling.[7] These episodes have caused widespread investor detriment and have contributed towards driving the overhaul of the UK's regulatory system throughout the years. Amongst these reforms, one finds the abolition of the concept of self-regulation in the wake of structural changes that led to the establishment of the Financial Services Authority (FSA) in the late 1990s, and, subsequently, the restructuring of the FSA that resulted in the adoption of a 'twin peaks' model of regulation during 2013. The latter was implemented by the Financial Services Act 2012 (FSA 2012) and had the effect of splitting the then FSA into the FCA and the Prudential Regulatory Authority (PRA). The establishment of the FCA meant that investor protection concerns took on a more prominent role on the agenda of a regulator that focuses on conduct regulation and pursues objectives which include the protection of consumers and, therefore, retail investors.[8] More recently, the increasing use of new interventionist tools by the FCA suggests that the regulatory mind-set that previously promoted *caveat emptor* is shifting towards a more paternalistic approach.

Reforms were also evident at an EU level to the MiFID regime,[9] in response to the investor detriment caused by the global financial crisis as well as numerous other incidences of retail market detriment. These measures were dominated by

[6] The financial crisis of 2007/08 has shown that certain financial products can be a destabilising factor and contribute significantly to global financial and economic instability when these are inappropriately sold to investors. This trend is also noted in mis-selling of payment protection insurance (PPI) and interest rate hedging products (IRHPs), with the latter being used as a case study. These cases have cost banks and building societies in the UK over £50 billion in fines and other penalties since 2000 (see further European Parliament, 'Consumer Protection Aspects of Financial Services' (2014); FCA, 'Annual Report and Accounts 2016/17' (2017).

[7] These include pensions; the marketing of home income plans or equity release mortgages to consumers considered to be vulnerable; endowment policies in the retail mortgage sector; 'with profits' life insurance products; PPI-related products; and IRHPs.

[8] The FCA's consumer protection objective is set out under s 1C of the Financial Services and Markets Act 2000 (FSMA), as inserted by the FSA 2012. Whilst responsibility for conduct regulation rests with the FCA, the PRA's focus lies in addressing systemic and prudential regulatory concerns, including those related to financial stability, as set out in FSMA, s 2B and. 2C, and as inserted by the FSA 2012.

[9] The EU regime for the provision of investment services is set out in the MiFID framework, which is composed MiFID II (Directive 2014/65/EU, repealing the original MiFID I, Directive 2004/39/EC) and MiFIR (Regulation (EU) No 600/2014).

the introduction of regulatory reforms aimed at enhancing the safety of financial products as well as improving their transparency and accessibility.

Despite these regulatory reforms and the imposition of hefty penalties on the industry the familiar cycle of investment product mis-selling, massive investor detriment, and the problems of securing redress for corporate retail investors, has proved particularly hard to break. Rather than simply being reduced to 'coincidental cocktail of circumstances',[10] these events can be described as classic characteristics of mis-selling driven by the complexities of regulation and the novelty surrounding certain intricate investment products. Further, these episodes also have one common fact at their core – the retail investor being sold a product that could place him at an actual or potential financial disadvantage primarily triggered by a mismatch between the product's complexity and the investor's financial acumen, circumstances, and risk appetite.

Investor protection, as one of the core objectives of investment services regulation, remains dominated by a 'complex blend of statutory and non-statutory'[11] instruments, primarily inspired by reactions to major market events. These measures however do not fully address the disparities between investor protection frameworks applicable to different categories of retail investors (and which render corporate retail investors more vulnerable to registering financial losses as a result of mis-selling, in comparison to individual retail investors). Indeed, as also acknowledged by the FCA itself, these regulatory developments have come about as a 'mechanistic response'[12] to scandals and crises, as regulators were more concerned with fighting fires rather than analysing the root causes giving rise to mis-selling. In consequence, the combination of opaque products, a competitive selling environment, and increasing retail investor participation in financial markets, remains an intractable challenge that requires the regulators' attention and that has put to the test the robustness of past and present regulatory frameworks, particularly insofar as corporate retail investors are concerned.

Against this backdrop, the diverging treatment of different categories of retail investors emerges as one of the primary root causes of the mis-selling of complex investment products. Indeed, the position of corporate retail investors underlines a number of lacunae in the application of the investor protection framework to the needs and circumstances of this category of retail investors, as their exposure to the risk of mis-selling is further exacerbated by the principles underpinning the common law regime.

[10] Julia Black and Richard Nobles, 'Personal Pensions Misselling: The Causes and Lessons of Regulatory Failure' (1998) 61 The Modern Law Review 789, 817.

[11] Julia Black, *Rules and Regulators* (Clarendon Press 1997) 46.

[12] FCA, 'Building on experience' Speech by Martin Wheatley (The future of financial services conference, Lansons, London 17 April 2013): www.fca.org.uk/news/speeches/building-experience, accessed 5 May 2015.

II. Categorising Retail Investors

A. Individual v Corporate Retail Investors

A 'retail' investor' is defined in MiFID II by opposition to, or exclusion of, a 'professional investor'.[13] For the purposes of this definition, retail investors include both natural persons (what this book terms 'individual retail investors') as well as corporate entities (referred to in this book as 'corporate retail investors'), unless these fall within the de facto definition of 'professional' investor,[14] or otherwise request to waive some of the protections afforded by the conduct of business rules by electing to be treated as professional investors subject to meeting certain criteria (known as 'elective professional investors').[15]

Professional investors typically include institutional investors whose main activity is to invest in financial instruments, as well as large undertakings meeting specific size requirements. The size-based thresholds set out in the MiFID definition of 'professional investors' are lower than those set out in the Commission's definition of micro, small and medium-sized enterprises (SMEs),[16] meaning that corporate entities that do not meet the thresholds attached to the 'professional investor' definition under MiFID are small, unsophisticated entities that are presumed to have the same (relatively low) level of financial acumen and sophistication, that generally lack access to financial and professional resources, and that do not engage in complex investment transactions on a regular and habitual basis.

It is pertinent to note that, prior to the MiFID regime coming into force in the UK on 1 November 2007,[17] UK investors were categorised in a different manner. The client classification provisions in the then FSA's Conduct of Business Sourcebook (COB)[18] provided for three categories of clients, being private customers, intermediate customers, and market counterparties. Private customers included the least sophisticated investors who were accordingly entitled to the greatest degree of regulatory protection; intermediate customers comprised the more experienced investors generally having either appropriate expertise in-house or the means to

[13] MiFID II, Art 4(1). This definition replicates the MiFID I definition and is also mirrored in the definition of 'retail' client set out in the FCA Handbook Glossary.

[14] As defined under MiFID II, Annex II, Section I.

[15] As prescribed by MiFID II, Annex II, Section II.

[16] The EU definition of 'SME' is set out in European Commission Recommendation 2003/361/EC of 6 May 2003 concerning the definition of micro, small and medium-sized enterprises, and has been replicated in ss 382 and 465 of the UK Companies Act 2006. The definition adopts upper-most thresholds for balance sheet total and net turnover of €43,000,000 and €50,000,000 respectively. The related MiFID thresholds tied to the 'professional' investor definition are of €20,000,000 and €40,000,000 respectively. As a third test to these definitions, MiFID uses the 'own funds' amount, whereas the European Commission Recommendation uses 'staff headcount' and hence this third limb is not directly comparable.

[17] In the UK, MiFID was implemented through the Conduct of Business Sourcebook (COBS).

[18] COB 4.1.

pay for professional advice when needed;[19] and market counterparties included those investors who were experienced in financial products and markets (and hence sufficiently sophisticated to operate within a 'light-touch' regime without the application of most regulatory protections) as well as authorised counterparties operating within the inter-professional regime. Once the MiFID classification took effect, private customers were generally grandfathered to the retail category under MiFID; intermediate customers were classified as either retail or professional clients depending on the applicable quantitative thresholds; and market counterparties were mapped onto the eligible counterparty category under MiFID[20] (with some being classified as professional clients in certain circumstances).

B. Uneven Retail Investor Protection

It has been established that the MiFID regime only distinguishes between the broad categories of 'retail' investors and 'professional' investors and does not provide for more granular sub-divisions within the 'retail' category itself. Any investor falling within the definition of 'retail' investor is hence entitled to the same level of protection irrespective of whether the investor is an individual or a corporate. Yet, the protection extended to the corporate sub-set of retail investors through the MiFID regime is diluted by domestic UK legislation that exists alongside the MiFID framework and which has a restricted scope that operates to the exclusion of corporate retail investors.

When individual retail investors purchase investment products, they enjoy certain rights and protections under the UK general consumer protection legislation and also under financial services-specific regulation, which are designed to help these investors make investment decisions without fear of exploitation or misrepresentation. The level of protection that corporate retail investors are entitled to is generally significantly lower, amidst a prevailing *caveat emptor* culture reflective of the view that corporate entities ought to be in a position to look after their own interests, which view is evidently shared by English courts. As a result, relatively small businesses falling within the definition of 'retail' investor under MiFID are treated no differently from larger businesses classified as 'professional'

[19] Body corporates which had called-up share capital or net assets of at least £5 million qualified as an 'intermediate customer'.

[20] According to MiFID II, Art 30(2) eligible counterparties include investment firms, credit institutions, insurance companies, Undertakings for the Collective Investment in Transferable Securities (UCITS) and their management companies, pension funds and their management companies, other financial institutions authorised or regulated under EU law or under the national law of a Member State, national governments and their corresponding offices including public bodies that deal with public debt at national level, central banks, and supranational organisations. In addition to these categories, Art 71 of the European Commission Delegated Regulation supplementing Directive 2014/65/EU of the European Parliament and of the Council as regards organisational requirements and operating conditions for investment firms and defined terms for the purposes of that Directive (C(2016) 2398 final) (MiFID II Delegated Regulation), allows for certain specific professional clients to be re-categorised as eligible counterparties, subject to these investors fulfilling specific criteria.

investors, such that corporate retail investors do not have recourse to the domestic protection mechanisms that individual retail investors are entitled to and hence receive substantially less protection in comparison to individual retail investors.

Where the transaction relates to complex investment products, the vulnerable position of corporate retail investors becomes even more precarious.[21] Numerous episodes of mis-selling suggest that these products are increasingly being marketed to retail investors, and the market for these types of products is likely to continue to grow unless measures are taken to contain their proliferation. Complex investment products typically present a convoluted interaction of risks, costs and expected returns with a high probability of causing detriment to retail investors, be they natural persons or corporate entities, in view of their limited financial acumen and experience. Faced with an infinite number of variations of complex investment products, often designed to intensify the obscurity of these products, corporate retail investors are likely to struggle to understand their intricate features and must place reliance on the judgement of investment firms, such that the choice of product is, in reality, made by the latter.[22] Therefore, even though additional responsibilities for the assessment of appropriateness or suitability of the product for the retail investor are incumbent upon the investment firm when marketing and selling complex investment products, the importance of more robust investor protection measures especially for corporate retail investors lacking access to alternative redress avenues should not be under-estimated.

III. The IRHPs Mis-selling Scandal

IRHPs are one example of a complex investment product, the purpose of which is purportedly to enable the customer to manage fluctuations in interest rates. These products can be grouped into four broad categories: swaps (allow for a 'fix' in the interest rate); caps (place a limit on any interest rate rises); collars (enable interest rate fluctuations to be limited to a simple range); and structured collars (enable interest rate fluctuations to be limited to a specified range but involve arrangements where, if the reference rate falls below the bottom of the range, the interest rate payable by the investor may increase above the bottom of the range).[23] IRHPs were typically sold separate to, but as a pre-condition of, a loan, with the

[21] The term 'complex' is not specifically defined in the investment services regulatory regime, however ESMA has provided guidance on the characteristics that investment products typically exhibit when considered as 'complex' (see further: ESMA, 'Opinion: MiFID practices for firms selling complex products' ESMA/2014/146 (2014) 2–3; ESMA, 'Guidelines on complex debt instruments and structured deposits' ESMA/2015/1787 (2016); see also MiFID II Delegated Regulation, Art 57, which lists the criteria that must be satisfied in order for financial instruments to be considered as 'non-complex' in terms of MiFID II, Art 25(4)).

[22] Kit Jebens, *LAUTRO: A Pioneer Regulator 1986 to 1994* (C E Jebens 1997) 25–26.

[23] As defined by the FCA (see further www.fca.org.uk/consumers/interest-rate-hedging-products/background-review, accessed 22 October 2016).

objective of enabling the investor to manage future fluctuations in interest rates in connection with the said loan. In this sense, they were marketed as a risk mitigation tool to protect investors against loan interest rate movements.[24]

IRHPs may therefore be appropriate when properly sold in the right circumstances. Due to their complex nature, however, they require a very finely balanced judgement on the part of the investor and the investment firm as they introduce a degree of interest rate speculation, such that an investor risks paying more in interest if base rates fall below an agreed level. Claims alleging the mis-selling of IRHPs in the UK surfaced during 2012, when it appeared that, since 2001, many corporate retail investors had been mis-sold complex IRHPs by banks (acting in their capacity as investment firms).

Using the 'rising market' as a coercive sales tactic, these products were promoted as protecting corporate retail investors from rising interest rates, since a standalone IRHP creates a separate set of payments to and from the business that aims to offset the variability of the interest rate paid on the underlying loan; allegedly, however, without providing a full explanation of associated risks, particularly in the case of a potential dip in interest rates. Thus, when interest rates plunged in the wake of the global financial crisis, most corporate retail investors that had been coerced into investing in IRHPs ended up paying significantly more in interest than they had originally envisaged. These changes in the economic climate were exacerbated by the complexity of IRHPs, which made them susceptible to mis-selling. It later emerged that investment firms consistently failed to ascertain the investors' understanding of risk, whilst it also became evident that corporate retail investors were advised to engage in IRHP transactions without investment firms taking contractual responsibility for their advice. Hence, although IRHPs may have appeared attractive to borrowers in fixing or limiting interest rate fluctuations within a certain range, their sheer complexity meant that the overall impact was difficult to assess, thereby creating unexpected adverse effects for investors.[25] In particular, the widespread sale of IRHPs, coupled with their intricate complexities, meant that a product which was traditionally offered to wholesale market participants was extensively distributed to less experienced investors with largely conservative risk profiles. Against this backdrop, an increasing number of corporate retail investors brought claims against investment firms (the majority of which were also credit institutions) alleging the mis-selling of IRHPs, as a result of which they purportedly suffered considerable financial losses.

The mis-selling of IRHPs is a particularly relevant case because it allows for an analysis of the redress opportunities that corporate retail investors have sought to draw upon with limited success and hence brings to the fore the legal and regulatory obstacles that prevent corporate retail investors from securing adequate compensation. The circumstances surrounding the mis-selling of IRHPs expose

[24] FSA, 'Interest rate hedging products: Information about our work and findings' (2013) 1.

[25] Rodrigo Momberg, 'Beyond the Risk: Swaps, Financial Crisis and Change of Circumstances; Comparative Case Note: Supreme Court of Portugal – 10.10.2013' (2015) 23 *European Review of Private Law* 81, 81.

evident gaps in the UK's corporate retail investor protection framework and provide a practical dimension to the more abstract and theoretical discussions on mis-selling and investor protection.

IV. The Case for Reform

It is acknowledged that the 'regulatory blindness'[26] which has generally exacerbated the factors giving rise to mis-selling is slowly being addressed through a number of regulatory reforms. Yet, the regulatory responses to date are insufficient and generally ineffective, particularly since they are largely short-term in nature and only targeted at a limited category of retail investors (namely individuals), whilst neglecting other equally vulnerable retail investors (including corporate retail investors). Historically, such reforms have been largely piecemeal and *ad hoc*, and have generally been triggered in reaction to crises, scandals and political pressure. Moreover, regulators seem to have been keen to strengthen governance, disclosure, and enforcement stages of the interactions been investment firms at their clients,[27] whilst little has been done to enhance the regulatory framework around the middle tier of the product development and distribution chain, that is, the verbal communications and contractual arrangements between the investment firm and the corporate retail investor purchasing the complex investment product, hence remaining an under-regulated area which presents a breathing space for mis-selling.

The assumption of investor rationality has 'the virtue of a myth',[28] given that numerous behavioural biases undermine the effectiveness of the investment decisions taken by corporate retail investors and their ability to digest the relevant information. This means that the effectiveness of traditional regulatory tools, such as risk disclosures, is undermined by the risk of information overload and other factors, including biases, which affect the investment decisions of these investors. Such conventional tools are unlikely to overcome biases and competence failures on the part of retail investors and should hence not be envisaged as the panacea for investor protection.[29] Similarly, financial capability initiatives are unlikely to have

[26] Julia Black and Richard Nobles, 'Personal Pensions Misselling: The Causes and Lessons of Regulatory Failure' (1998) 61 *The Modern Law Review* 789, 789.

[27] MiFID II has introduced measures around product approval processes (MiFID II, Art 16(3) and Art 24(2)) as well as involvement and accountability of the management body of investment firms (MiFID II, Art 9). Disclosures have also been enhanced including as a result of the PRIIPs Regulation (Regulation (EU) No 1286/2014).

[28] Donald C Langevoort, 'Selling Hope, Selling Risk: Some Lessons for Law from Behavioural Economics about Stockbrokers and Sophisticated Customers' (1996) 84 *California Law Review* 627, 699.

[29] See eg FSA, 'Consumer Research 5: Informed Decisions? How Consumers use Key Features: a synthesis of research on the use of product information at the point of sale' (2000); Joanna Gray and Jenny Hamilton, *Implementing Financial Regulation: Theory and Practice* (John Wiley & Sons Ltd 2006) 212; FSA, 'Discussion Paper DP07/01, A Review of Retail Distribution' (2007); Niamh Moloney, *How to Protect Investors: Lessons from the EC and the UK* (Cambridge University Press, 2010) 292; Daniel Kahneman, *Thinking Fast and Slow* (Penguin Books Ltd, 2011); Commonwealth of Australia Financial System Inquiry, 'Final Report' (2014) 9.

major lasting effects on retail investors' knowledge and behaviour, and hence should not substitute tougher regulatory interventions.[30] In other words, traditional 'softer' approaches to regulation need to be reinforced through more interventionist tools, which are more effective in 'nudging'[31] corporate retail investors towards investment products and services that are best suited to their needs and circumstances.

Notably, the behavioural biases that the regulator has attributed to individual retail investors are equally experienced by corporate retail investors. In light of these behavioural limitations, corporate retail investors should not be treated in the same way as sophisticated contractual parties of equal bargaining power to investment firms simply because they are acting in a business context and irrespective of their circumstances, size, knowledge and experience, as seems to be implied by the regulator and by the English courts. Rather, a distinction between non-financial services corporate entities that invest, say, to hedge risk (that would typically fall within the definition of 'retail' in terms of MiFID), and larger institutional corporate entities that may be transacting on behalf of their clients (which would generally be categorised as 'professional' for the purposes of MiFID) is promoted based on the MiFID classification. In consonance with the spirit of MiFID, corporate investors are viewed as residing on a spectrum – while corporate professional investors may have sufficient experience and access to expertise (hence justifying a lower degree of regulatory protection), smaller businesses falling within the 'retail' category of MiFID have more in common with individual investors by virtue of their MiFID 'retail' classification and should hence qualify for the same level of regulatory protection to which individual retail investors are entitled; in other words, the principle of *caveat emptor* should not dictate the level of protection offered to corporate retail investors.

Whilst the FCA acknowledged the need to assess the extent to which corporate retail investors should benefit from the investor protection measures afforded to individual retail investors as well as the extent to which these investors should be expected to behave like larger, more sophisticated businesses,[32] there has generally been little debate over how the domestic investor protection regime operates to secure an appropriate level of protection to all retail investors, and whether any category of retail investors is being impeded from obtaining adequate redress by

[30] David T Llewellyn, 'Regulation of Retail Investment Services' (1995) 15 *Economic Affairs* 12, 14; OECD, 'Improving Financial Literacy: Analysis of Issues and Policy' (2005); OECD, 'Recommendation of Principles and Good Practices for Financial Education and Awareness' (2005); FSA, 'Financial capability in the UK: Delivering change' (2006); FSA, 'Consumer Research Paper 69, Financial Capability, A Behavioural Economics Perspective' (2008) 2; Parliamentary Joint Committee on Corporations and Financial Services, 'Inquiry into financial products and services in Australia' (2009); World Bank, 'Policy Research Working Paper, Consumer Protection and Financial Literacy: Lessons From Nine Country Studies' (2010).

[31] A 'nudge' is defined by Sunstein and Thaler as 'an aspect of choice architecture that alters people's behaviour in a predictable way without forbidding any options or significantly changing their economic incentives' (Cass Sunstein and Richard Thaler, *Nudge: Improving Decisions About Health, Wealth and Happiness* (Penguin Books, 2008) 6).

[32] Treasury Committee, *Conduct and competition in SME lending: Written Evidence* (17 June 2014) FCA Written submission SME0140.

national legislation which operates in parallel to the broader regulatory framework, or is otherwise hampered from securing compensation by the interpretation of the UK judiciary of such domestic statutes. To this end, this book challenges the presumption that corporate retail investors are more sophisticated than individual retail investors and therefore less in need of protection and sets out to demonstrate that corporate retail investors not only display vulnerabilities and limitations but also face restrictions in terms of inadequate redress options which cause them extensive detriment, thereby justifying the need for the establishment of suitable safeguards targeted at protecting these investors.

V. Brexit Considerations

On 23 June 2016, the UK voted to exit the European Union (EU) – 'BREXIT' – and, on 29 March 2017, Article 50 of the Treaty on European Union was triggered.

The UK's decision to exit the EU is not believed to impact the ongoing implementation of the EU MiFID regime, not least because MiFID II is based, in part, on the G20 commitments and reform agenda stemming from the financial crisis to which the UK, as a G20 member, is committed.[33] The UK, as a member of the G20, opted to tackle these reforms by adopting a European-wide policy (instead of acting in isolation) – a decision which is highly likely to be upheld post-BREXIT.

Furthermore, BREXIT is not likely to lead to a deviation from the standards and obligations imposed by the MiFID II regime since, for the investment services industry to continue doing business in the EU after BREXIT, it will need 'equivalency' of regulation. This can be achieved by implementing MiFID II-like regulation in the UK, with equivalent surveillance, investor protection, and enforcement mechanisms. More importantly, the European Union (Withdrawal) Act 2018 converts existing direct EU legislation into UK law, and preserve existing UK laws which implement EU obligations. The UK Government has also been given powers to amend this retained EU legislation so that it works effectively when the UK leaves the EU. The government's intention is that the same rules and laws will apply after exit as before, as far as possible. As part of this process, the FCA will amend and maintain EU binding technical standards, as well as amend the FCA Handbook to ensure it is consistent with changes the government is making to EU law. All in all, therefore, close correspondence of UK and EU financial services regulation will be maintained, such that there is no reason to believe that the observations, conclusions, and recommendations made and presented in this book will no longer be relevant once the UK exits the EU or once the transitional period terminates.

[33] See eg European Commission, 'More transparent and safer financial markets: European Commission welcomes European Parliament vote on updated rules for Markets in Financial Instruments (MiFID II)' Statement 14/129 (2014); Bloomberg, 'MiFID still happens with "Brexit"' (2016); Weston, 'Brexit: What Does This Mean for MiFID II' (2016).

2

Understanding Corporate Retail Investors and their Behavioural Biases

I. Defining Investor 'Vulnerability'

Investment services regulation is known to use a differentiated approach to investor protection and, due to investors being heterogeneous, regulators must be able to draw upon a variety of regulatory tools to address their different needs and vulnerabilities.[1] To this end, calibration is one of the 'undercutting themes'[2] of the MiFID conduct of business regime, which distinguishes between the levels of regulatory protection applicable to retail and professional investors. Yet, notwithstanding the 'retail' classification of certain corporate investors under MiFID, UK policymakers have historically considered these investors less in need of regulatory protection and investor protection efforts have consequently been channelled predominantly towards individual retail investors, to the detriment of corporate entities and their shareholders.

Despite acknowledging that the needs, behaviour and expertise of corporate and individual retail investors are 'often similar', the FCA admitted that corporate retail investors have 'traditionally been treated as having greater self-sufficiency and bargaining power than individual consumers', and are therefore 'seen by regulators as requiring less assistance'.[3] This clearly transpires from the FCA's definition of 'vulnerable consumers', which refers exclusively to individuals (as opposed to corporate entities) who, due to their personal circumstances, are 'especially susceptible to detriment, particularly when a firm is not acting with appropriate levels of care'.[4] In this sense, the FCA considers corporate entities taking on financial risks as less vulnerable than individuals, given that the former are viewed as being more experienced than the latter in assessing the implications

[1] Lorna Fox O'Mahony, Christian Twigg-Flesner and Folarin Akinbami, 'Conceptualizing the Consumer of Financial Services: a New Approach?' (2015) 38 *Journal of Consumer Policy* 111, 117.

[2] Niamh Moloney, 'Large-Scale Reform of Investor Protection Regulation: The European Union Experience' (2007) 4 *Macquarie Journal of Business Law* 147, 169.

[3] FCA, 'Discussion Paper DP15/7, Our approach to SMEs as users of financial services' (2015) para 2.5.

[4] Such personal circumstances include physical/mental illness, disability, loss of a close family member, old age, caring responsibilities and illiteracy. Investment firms are expected to be mindful of these situations and take on a heavier burden of responsibility when such conditions are present (see further FCA, 'Occasional Paper No 8: Consumer Vulnerability' (2015) 20).

of contractual terms, in determining their product needs, in supporting themselves financially, and in having access to professionals for assistance and advice.[5] The FCA's perception of the extent to which corporate retail investors need regulatory intervention also affects the manner in which the FCA applies its investor responsibility principle to these investors, such that it is more likely to hold corporate retail investors responsible for 'mis-buying', than would have been the case if an individual retail investor were party to the same investment transaction.

Broadly speaking, therefore, the UK regulator's approach to vulnerability, apart from being directed at individuals only, is excessively focused on an investor's personal characteristics, without any consideration of the characteristics of markets and the products which impact on decision-making. In so doing, the FCA however dismisses the susceptibility of corporate retail investors to detriment due to the characteristics of a particular product or transaction; even though corporate retail investors may not have deficiencies which are immediately apparent, their lack of experience and knowledge, coupled with the behavioural biases influencing the investment decisions of the individuals who run them, still makes them vulnerable to mis-selling. Hence, although corporate retail investors purchasing complex investment products may not be illiterate or suffering from physical impairment, the interplay of market factors, such as inadequate information, complex product characteristics, poor access to resources and an inability to secure redress, heightens their vulnerable position and makes them dependent on regulatory protection.[6]

Notwithstanding a clear acknowledgement that 'small business may also be "consumers" in [retail] markets',[7] the FCA still excludes corporate retail investors from the more paternalistic regulatory protection measures, thereby equating corporate retail investors to wholesale market participants. Wholesale markets are characterised by experienced institutional investors and there is therefore greater scope for *quasi* self-regulation as well as the adoption of a more substantive, purposive, and flexible regulatory approach based on principles.[8] In a wholesale market context, prescriptive rules are feared to stifle innovation and competitiveness, and investor protection concerns are 'outweighed by concerns for market efficiency'[9] as fears of regulatory arbitrage and over-regulation driving business outside of the jurisdiction take over. Despite the FCA's commitment for a 'renewed

[5] FCA, 'Discussion Paper DP15/7, Our approach to SMEs as users of financial services' (2015) para 4.6.

[6] See eg Omri Ben-Shahar, 'The Myth of "Opportunity to Read" in Contract Law' (2009) 5 *European Review of Contract Law* 1, 2; Law Commission, 'Unfair Terms in Consumer Contracts: a new approach?' (2012) para 3.54.

[7] FCA, 'Our Future Mission' (2016) 12.

[8] Treasury and Civil Select Committee, *The Regulation of Financial Services in the UK* (HC 1994–95) Sixth Report Vol I, para 86; Cristie Ford, 'New Governance, Compliance, and Principles-Based Securities Regulation' (2008) 45 *American Business Law Journal* 1, 43.

[9] Julia Black, *Rules and Regulators* (Clarendon Press, 1997) 241.

focus on wholesale conduct' as one of its key priorities,[10] market imperfections are predictably more pervasive in the retail sector than in the wholesale sector, suggesting that the case for regulatory intervention will always be stronger in the former than in the latter.[11]

By assimilating corporate retail investors to the more professional wholesale market participants, the regulator completely disregards that corporate retail investors are run by individuals who are investing in the name of an entity for corporate reasons, rather than doing so in their own name. In these circumstances, corporate retail investors (being typically a sole-trading business or a close-knit family operation, as demonstrated by IRHP case law) are equally exposed to cognitive biases and other weaknesses that transpire from behavioural economics literature, and should hence be entitled to a level of regulatory protection which is equivalent to that extended to individual retail investors. In other words, and notwithstanding the 'corporate' status of these investors, investment transactions entered into by corporate retail investors are a result of investment decisions made by individuals acting as, or as agents of, the entity. It follows, therefore, that the assessment of vulnerability should be made with reference to the individuals who have the authority and ability to influence or effect, and benefit from, the investment decision being transacted in the name of the corporate retail investor, and who would, in their own personal capacity, typically be classified as individual retail investors.

The regulator's approach to investor vulnerability thus fails to see through the 'corporate' status of a retail investor, making it less sympathetic towards a sole trader, or a small group of individuals, who generally lack access to resources and who are still exposed to behavioural biases and limitations, thereby wrongly positioning corporate retail investors on an equal footing with professional investors. Whilst accepting that different degrees of investment knowledge and experience exist amongst those acting for corporate retail investors, it is only a limited number amongst these investors who have the tools and resources to fully understand the risks associated with complex investment products independently, and, where this is the case, such corporate investors would typically meet the criteria to qualify as de facto or elective 'professional', rather than 'retail', investors. Indeed, the combination of standard terms, lack of negotiating power, behavioural limitations, inexperience, and an urgent need for funding, exposes corporate retail investors to the risk of mis-selling and suggests that the founding principles of private law, namely contractual freedom and legal certainty, hinder the creation of an adequate investor protection framework for corporate retail investors.[12]

[10] Since its inception, the FCA has secured a number of enforcement actions in wholesale markets, including the long-running investigations related to the manipulation of the London Interbank Offered Rate (LIBOR) and other foreign exchange market benchmark rates. These actions have also been extended to areas that were historically unregulated, as in the case of currency markets.

[11] Charles AE Goodhart and others, *Financial Regulation: Why, how and where now?* (Routledge, 1998) 8.

[12] Paul Marshall, 'Novating mis-sold swaps: the poverty of narrowly contractual analysis' (2015) 30 *Journal of International Banking and Financial Law* 11, 11.

II. A Behavioural Law and Economics Perspective

A. Overview of Behavioural Biases in Complex Investment Transactions

Behavioural economics uses insights from psychology to explain the effects of cognitive and behavioural processes on investor behaviour and market outcomes, thereby introducing 'a more human face'[13] to investment services regulation. Behavioural theories have 'crossed from academic book shelves into both the public imagination and policy making',[14] to challenge conventional economic thinking and highlight the behavioural distortions that retail investors suffer from, which make them vulnerable to malfeasance and poor investment decisions. This in turn puts into question the effectiveness of conventional regulatory tools which, to date, have largely constituted the regulators' instinctive answer to mis-selling.[15] Notwithstanding criticisms directed at behavioural law and economics theories,[16] it is here argued that embracing insights from this discipline provides a novel dimension to the retail investor protection framework by enhancing the understanding of the nature and limitations of imperfect investor choices and applicable investor protection mechanisms. Although behavioural economics may not be the 'silver bullet' solution to curbing mis-selling, it may therefore still add value by acting as a 'lens on financial regulation'[17] and consequently assisting in reforming regulation and anticipating problems in a proactive manner.

The most common biases and cognitive limitations experienced by retail investors include procrastination, hyperbolic discounting, framing effects (namely

[13] FCA, 'Human face of regulation' Speech by Martin Wheatley (London School of Economics, London, 10 April 2013): www.fca.org.uk/news/speeches/human-face-of-regulation, accessed 6 December 2014.

[14] Tony Curzon Price and Peter Andrews, 'The game of caps and nudges' (Insight: Opinion and Analysis from the FCA, 27 July 2017): www.fca.org.uk/insight/game-caps-and-nudges, accessed 30 July 2017.

[15] See eg Financial Services Consumer Panel (FSCP), 'Response to FSA Discussion Paper 08/5 on Consumer Responsibility' (2009); Niamh Moloney, 'Regulating the Retail Markets: Law, Policy and the Financial Crisis' in George Letsas and Colm O'Cinnéide (eds) *Current Legal Problems* (Oxford University Press, 2010) 392, 394; Julia Black, 'Financial Markets' in Peter Cane and Herbert M Kritzer (eds), *The Oxford Handbook of Empirical Legal Research* (Oxford University Press, 2010) 156; FCA Practitioner Panel, 'Consumer Responsibility: Identifying and closing the gap' (2013).

[16] Insights from the behavioural law and economics theory have been challenged for, inter alia, being inherently subjective and failing to address biases that regulators themselves may be suffering from (see eg Niamh Moloney, 'Building a retail investment culture through law: the 2004 Markets in Financial Instruments Directive' (2005) 6 *European Business Organization Law Review* 341, 370; Richard A Posner, 'Treating Financial Consumers as Consenting Adults' *Wall Street Journal* (New York, 23 July 2009); James C Cooper and William E Kovacic, 'Behavioral Economics: Implications for Regulatory Behavior' (2012) 41 *Journal of Regulatory Economics* 41, 56; Joshua D Wright and Douglas H Ginsburg, 'Behavioral law and economics: Its origins, fatal flaws, and implications for liberty' (2012) 106 *Northwestern University Law Review* 1033, 1062–66).

[17] Werner DeBondt and others, 'What can behavioural finance teach us about finance?' (2010) 2 *Quantitative Research in Financial Markets* 29, 34 (see also Adair Turner, 'The Turner Review: A Regulatory Response to the Global Banking Crisis' (2009) para 1.4).

attribute framing and anchoring effects), loss aversion, social contagion, regret aversion, mental accounting, status quo bias, egocentric bias (predominantly over-optimism and over-confidence) and confirmation bias. Collectively, these biases contribute to incorrect information processing on the part of retail investors that can be grouped under the heading 'curse of knowledge', since those affected are likely to draw erroneous inferences, focus on inappropriate or unimportant data, become distracted by too much information and choice, over-deliberate, or otherwise misuse information.[18] These behavioural characteristics, coupled with investment firms' incentives, may therefore lead to irrational, time-inconsistent choices and context-dependent preferences, which may in turn give rise to conduct risks.

The aforementioned biases become evident when applied to the manner in which retail investors tend to consider disclosures. Despite being minimally interventionist as a regulatory tool, disclosure is particularly susceptible to the skill and ability of the person receiving the information, and is also open to manipulation by those imparting it. In fact, as a result of their over-confidence bias, investors tend to exhibit behaviours that make them overly credulous and insufficiently sceptical of disclosures. Traditional regulatory measures, namely disclosures, do not address framing effects and, due to confirmation biases, information contained in risk disclosures that conflicts with prior assumptions tends to be discounted. Past performance information is also likely to be over-relied on due to anchoring biases, whilst information overload likewise limits the extent to which disclosures can actually protect investors. Although disclosure may fit the needs of the industry 'like a glove',[19] placing excessive reliance on this as a regulatory tool is also seen as an 'excuse to shift responsibility from firms to financial users',[20] and as being 'too captured by the interests of firms'.[21] In truth, reliance on disclosure as an indispensable weapon of the regulatory arsenal has been stretched beyond its original aim of issuer disclosure and prevention of market abuse.[22] Moreover, the persistent increase in mandatory disclosure further restricts the extent to which this new disclosure and pre-existing disclosure is effective at empowering retail investors

[18] On cognitive biases, see eg Christine Jolls, Cass Sunstein and Richard Thaler, 'A Behavioral Approach to Law and Economics' (1998) 50 *Stanford Law Review* 1471; Richard A Posner, 'Rational Choice, Behavioral Economics, and the Law' (1998) 50 *Stanford Law Review* 1551; FSA, 'Discussion Paper DP08/5, Consumer Responsibility' (2008); Lars Klohn, 'Preventing excessive retail investor trading under MiFID: a behavioural law and economics perspective' (2009) 10 *European Business Organization Law Review* 437; Kent H Baker and John R Nofsinger (eds), *Behavioral Finance: Investors, Corporations, and Markets* (John Wiley & Sons, Inc, 2010).

[19] FCA, 'Building on experience' Speech by Martin Wheatley (The future of financial services conference, Lansons, London 17 April 2013): www.fca.org.uk/news/speeches/building-experience, accessed 5 May 2015.

[20] Financial Services User Group (FSUG), 'Making financial services work for financial users, Paper 1: New model financial regulation' (2012) 6.

[21] See n 19.

[22] Emilious Avgouleas, 'What Future for Disclosure as a Regulatory Technique? Lessons from Behavioural Decision Theory and the Global Financial Crisis' in Iain MacNeil and Justin O'Brien (eds), *The Future of Financial Regulation* (Hart Publishing, 2010) 206.

to make sound decisions.[23] As additional disclosure obligations are imposed on the industry, retail investors are prone to consult with their investment adviser in order to counter-balance the information overload and file the excess information given to them. In so doing, retail investors tend to rely on the advice provided by investment firms.[24] Regulators must therefore not only rethink the disclosure process but should also intervene more actively in order not to depend exclusively on disclosure and other tools of a similar passive nature.[25]

The nature of investment services further exacerbates the effects of the said cognitive limitations. As abstract 'credence' goods, investment products do not carry any warranties and are also unpredictable and volatile, making it difficult for retail investors to understand whether a particular investment product is fit-for-purpose or otherwise.[26] Just as the quality of investments themselves is difficult to assess and becomes apparent, if at all, sometime after purchase, the quality of an investment service can only be assessed with hindsight, particularly because retail investors engage only infrequently in complex investment transactions, which means that they have only limited opportunities to build up experience and, consequently, the products remain unfamiliar and harder to understand.[27] Bad advice thus becomes a ticking 'time-bomb' that will eventually explode to the detriment of retail investors and the industry's credibility.[28]

These concerns become even more pronounced with complex investment products, the distribution of which is becoming increasingly wide. Complexity, coupled with financial innovation, exacerbates information asymmetry and fuels suboptimal contracting, agency cost issues and other opportunistic behaviour, which investment firms are likely to exploit to their benefit.[29] The marketing and sale of complex products to retail investors in particular was also highlighted by

[23] FCA, 'The Financial Conduct Authority's response to the European Commission's call for evidence on the EU regulatory framework for financial services' (2016) para 3.1.

[24] Gerald Spindler, 'Behavioural Finance and Investor Protection Regulations' (2011) 34 *Journal of Consumer Policy* 315, 321–22.

[25] See further Parliamentary Joint Committee on Corporations and Financial Services, 'Inquiry into financial products and services in Australia' (2009) para 5.134; Kern Alexander and Niamh Moloney (eds), *Law Reform and the Financial Markets* (Edward Elgar Publishing Ltd, 2011) xvi.

[26] Philip Nelson, 'Information and consumer behaviour' (1970) 78 *Journal of Political Economy* 311; Dimity Kingsford Smith, 'Regulating investment risk: individuals and the global financial crisis' (2009) 32 *University of New South Wales Law Journal* 514, 526; Dimity Kingsford Smith and Olivia Dixon, 'The Consumer Interest and the Financial Markets' in Niamh Moloney, Eilís Ferran, and Jennifer Payne (eds), *The Oxford Handbook of Financial Regulation* (Oxford University Press, 2015) 697.

[27] Julia Black, *Rules and Regulators* (Clarendon Press, 1997) 141; David T Llewellyn, 'The Economic Rationale for Financial Regulation: FSA Occasional Paper 1' (1999) 26, 38; HM Treasury and FCA, 'Financial Advice Market Review: Call for input' (2015) 8; FSCP, 'Consumers and competition: Delivering more effective consumer power in retail financial markets' (2017) 14.

[28] Jean Eaglesham, 'Making the Watchdogs Come to Heal' *Investors Chronicle* (London, 9 December 1994).

[29] Dan Awrey, 'Complexity, Innovation and the Regulation of Modern Financial Markets' (2012) 2 *Harvard Law Business Review* 235, 238–39 (see also IOSCO, 'Suitability Requirements With Respect To the Distribution of Complex Financial Products' Final Report FR01/13 (2013); ASIC, 'Report 384: Regulating complex products' (2014) 15–16).

ESMA as a 'key concern',[30] since the intrinsic complexity of certain investment products may hinder the understanding by unsophisticated investors of the risks, costs and expected returns. This, according to ESMA, 'hampers their ability to make informed investment decisions, and increases the likelihood of consumer detriment'.[31] The toxic combination of limited investor ability to decrypt complex and detailed disclosures and to assess conflict of interest risk, together with largely unrestricted access to risky and complex products, thus makes all retail investors, including corporate retail investors, particularly susceptible to mis-selling. These circumstances also suggest that investment firms should, by design, be more concerned with the composition and behaviour of investors when a product is selected, in comparison to the providers of many other consumer goods and services.

As retail investors come to appreciate their limitations and the growing complexity of investment products, their need for expert advice becomes almost indispensable.[32] This results in 'relational contracting',[33] as a form of 'social contract',[34] where softer emotions around trust and confidence are likely to play a more fundamental role in characterising the relationship between the parties, than the formal written contractual agreement itself.[35] The 'trusting investor', who is typically 'ill-equipped' to 'navigate [the] competitive waters'[36] of investment services, relies on his investment service provider to guide him towards the product which best suits his needs, objectives, and circumstances.[37] From a regulator's perspective, these concerns portend that any strategy purporting to make any retail investor (irrespective of whether the investor is an individual or corporate retail investor) responsible for his decisions, must be treated with caution. Further, these issues also inspire calls for more active public policy intervention in protecting all retail investors.[38]

[30] ESMA, 'Opinion: MiFID practices for firms selling complex products' ESMA/2014/146 (2014) 1.

[31] ibid.

[32] See eg NMG Consulting, 'Retail Investment Advice Assessment of Ongoing Services – A research report' (2014); CFA Institute & Edelman, 'Investor Trust Study' (2013) 2; Europe Economics, 'Retail Distribution Review: post-implementation review' (2014); Andy Cheng and Angus Young, 'Lack of legal safeguards for investors when buying financial investment products: the need for legal reforms in Hong Kong' (2015) 30 *Journal of International Banking Law and Regulation* 267, 267–68.

[33] Joanna Gray and Jenny Hamilton, *Implementing Financial Regulation: Theory and Practice* (John Wiley & Sons Ltd, 2006).

[34] Iris H-Y Chiu, 'The nature of a financial investment intermediary's duty to his client' (2008) 28 *Legal Studies* 254, 263.

[35] See eg Donald C Langevoort, 'Selling Hope, Selling Risk: Some Lessons for Law from Behavioural Economics about Stockbrokers and Sophisticated Customers' (1996) 84 *California Law Review* 627; Chris Doyle, 'Self Regulation and Statutory Regulation' (1997) 8 *Business Strategy Review* 35.

[36] Julia Black, *Rules and Regulators* (Clarendon Press, 1997) 143.

[37] See eg European Commission, 'Special Eurobarometer 373, Retail Financial Services Report' (2012); Competition and Markets Authority, 'Retail banking market investigation: Summary of provisional findings report' (2015) para 97.

[38] Joint Committee on the draft Financial Services Bill, *Draft Financial Services Bill* (HL 236 HC 1447, 2010–12); House of Commons, Committee of Public Accounts, *Forty-First Report: Financial services mis-selling: regulation and redress* (HC 847, 2016) 11.

B. Behavioural Economics and Corporate Retail Investors

There are several examples of existing EU legislative measures which draw upon behavioural economics theories to consider aspects of the decision-making process of consumers.[39] ESMA has also referred to cognitive psychology literature and behavioural theories in acknowledging that 'investors are very susceptible to how certain choices are presented to them' and that this 'might lead to sub-optimal outcomes for them'.[40] Closer to home, behavioural economics has also been described as a 'game changer'[41] for the FCA, which has seen it 'put at its core a much better way of protecting consumers and making sure they get a fair deal',[42] even if it meant running the risk of 'being accused of reducing personal freedom'.[43] The FCA is also aware of 'mounting evidence'[44] that retail investors are generally irrational in their investment decision-making,[45] such that it has recently recommended to the EU that the latter should prioritise further research into consumer diversity and behaviour.[46] By acknowledging that the incidence and significance of behavioural biases is increasingly being recognised as 'playing an important role in driving poor market outcomes',[47] the FCA has also launched a new methodology for regulatory economic analysis – Economics for Effective Regulation (EFER) – which, inter alia, incorporates more explicit and structured consideration of these biases. The FCA's trajectory towards the incorporation of behavioural economics theories in its regulatory strategy is also supported by a similar broader stance

[39] See eg Consumer Credit Directive (Directive 2008/48/EC); Mortgage Credit Directive (Directive 2014/17/EU); Payment Accounts Directive (Directive 2014/92/EU); Insurance Distribution Directive (Directive 2016/97/EU); and PRIIPs (Regulation (EU) No 1286/2014). These EU legislative measures were instigated by behavioural theories contending that simple information (limited to salient features of products) can greatly improve consumers' financial choices.

[40] ESMA, 'Consultation Paper: Guidelines on certain aspects of the MiFID suitability requirements' ESMA35-43-748 (2017) 9, published as final guidelines on 28 May 2018 (see ESMA, 'Final Report: Guidelines on certain aspects of the MiFID suitability requirements' ESMA35-43-869 (2018).

[41] FCA, 'Making competition king – the rise of behavioural economics at the FCA' Speech by Martin Wheatley (Australian Securities and Investments Commission, Australia, 25 March 2014): www.fca.org.uk/news/making-competition-king, accessed 5 October 2015.

[42] FSA, 'My vision for the FCA' Speech by Martin Wheatley (British Bankers' Association, London, 25 January 2012): www.fsa.gov.uk/library/communication/speeches/2012/0125-mw.shtml, accessed 25 August 2015.

[43] FSA, 'The Future of Banking Regulation in the UK' Speech by Hector Sants (BBA Annual Conference, Guildhall, 29 June 2011): www.fsa.gov.uk/library/communication/speeches/2011/0629_hs.shtml, accessed 15 May 2015.

[44] John Y Campbell and others, 'Consumer Financial Protection' (2011) 25 *Journal of Economic Perspectives* 91, 91–92.

[45] On the use of techniques inspired by behavioural law and economics by the FSA and the FCA, see further FSA, 'Discussion Paper DP11/1, Product Intervention' (2011); FCA, 'Occasional Paper No 1: Applying behavioural economics at the Financial Conduct Authority' (2013) 3; FCA, 'Guidance Consultation GC14/03, Retail Advice: Clarifying the boundaries and exploring the barriers to market development' (2014).

[46] FCA, 'The Financial Conduct Authority's response to the European Commission Green Paper: Retail Financial Services' (2016) 7.

[47] FCA, 'Occasional Paper No 13: Economics for Effective Regulation' (2016) 3.

taken by the UK Government, which is pushing forward the 'nudge agenda' more generally as well as embracing insights of behaviourists.[48]

Despite generally acting on findings from behavioural law and economics, the FCA does not, however, extrapolate and apply these insights to corporate retail investors. The conviction that corporate retail investors are more sophisticated than their individual counterparts, and that hence they do not need consumer protection measures, comes across as being 'largely false'[49] on two main counts – the biases experienced by corporate retail investors, and their limited knowledge of, and experience in, complex investment product transactions. First, the biases considered in this chapter constitute a solid rebuttal to the FCA's approach to corporate retail investors – the IRHP mis-selling episode introduced in chapter one highlights the incidence of a range of biases at the level of corporate retail investors, specifically the egocentric bias, framing effects, as well as elements of loss and regret aversion and mental accounting. IRHP investors came across as particularly over-confident in terms of their expected level of interest rates and were therefore caught unprepared when the drastic and prolonged fall in interest rates hit, causing them significant financial detriment. Additionally, the effect of these biases was exacerbated by investment firms on whom corporate retail investors depended for advice and who often forced the IRHP transaction upon them as a pre-condition of the financing requested by these investors, whilst also strongly suggesting that IRHPs would constitute a feasible risk mitigation tool.

For corporate retail investors, therefore, the justification for a behavioural economics approach is grounded in the individuals running the business of the corporate retail investor and taking investment decisions on behalf of that corporate entity, typically being inexperienced individuals who lack knowledge about the risks associated with complex investment products. Notwithstanding the regulatory expectation for corporate retail investors to take responsible and autonomous investment decisions, corporate retail investors are subject to the biases and vulnerabilities experienced by the individuals controlling them and hence still suffer from 'information vulnerability' as a result of information asymmetry, which makes them powerless against deceptive investment firms, as well as the limited access to financial specialists and other professionals.[50] They are also prone to 'impact vulnerability', since, not only are they likely to make poor choices due to behavioural biases, but they also suffer more as a result of those choices due to them facing financial fragility. Especially in the case of IRHP transactions, corporate retail investors experienced 'pressure vulnerability' in that they had to make

[48] By way of example, the Behavioural Insights Team (or 'Nudge Unit') in the UK helps organisations to apply behavioural insights in support of social purpose goals (see further www.behaviouralinsights.co.uk/about-us, accessed 12 October 2016).

[49] Citizens Advice Bureau, 'The experiences of small businesses as consumers in regulated markets' (2014) 1.

[50] See eg BDRC Continental, 'SME Finance Monitor: Q4 2014' (2015); Money Advice Trust, 'The cost of doing business: Supporting the self-employed and small businesses' (2015); FCA, 'Discussion Paper DP15/7, Our approach to SMEs as users of financial services' (2015) paras 1.13, 3.14–3.15.

decisions under pressure by being coerced into investing in an IRHP in order to secure much-needed business financing. 'Redress vulnerability' is also evident in the case of IRHP cases as these investors have struggled to obtain redress as well as to hold investment firms responsible for the damages they have suffered.

Together, these factors reveal that these investors are clearly victims of mis-selling since they became financially disadvantaged as a result of circumstances that they were neither aware of nor desired.[51] The adverse impact resulting from the causes leading to this detriment is therefore comparable to the reasons underlying the losses suffered by individual retail investors. The business owner who runs a small property-holding company, for example, is similarly at risk of being mis-sold a financial product, in that, as with any individual retail investor, he would typically be completely reliant on the investment firm to guide him through the process, without having access to independent advisers and without having the adequate knowledge and experience to filter what he is being told by the investment firm.[52]

Moreover, the regulator's attitude of indifference towards the vulnerabilities of corporate retail investors does not hold ground in view of the restricted levels of engagement and understanding which characterise these investors' transactions in complex investment products. Corporate retail investors are not necessarily equipped to argue their case when investment transactions go wrong and enjoy fewer protections and less access to third-party redress options than individuals. The limited experience and knowledge of corporate retail investors therefore makes them akin to individual retail investors, as was affirmed by the court in *Les O'Hare & Janet O'Hare v Coutts & Co*,[53] a case concerning a professional negligence action brought by a couple against their former private bankers over its alleged failure to exercise reasonable skill and care when advising them on making investments. In the context of this case, Kerr J declared that, although one of the claimants was an 'astute businessman' and owned a corporate entity through which he invested (thereby making him a corporate retail investor), this did not necessarily make

[51] Julia Black and Richard Nobles, 'Personal Pensions Misselling: The Causes and Lessons of Regulatory Failure' (1998) 61 *The Modern Law Review* 789, 819.

[52] This has been acknowledged by the FOS, when it revealed that in only 8% of the complaints it reviewed did it see evidence that micro-enterprises (which also falls within the definition of corporate retail investors) had legal or accountancy support at the time of the events that led to their complaint. It thus stressed that: 'No one should assume micro-enterprises understand financial products and services better than private customers' (FOS, 'Micro-enterprises and financial services: a review of complaints' (2015) 2). It is contended here that all corporate retail investors face the same difficulties and limitations, not just micro-enterprises. In fact, corporate retail investors' understanding of financial products has also been highlighted as problematic in the Treasury Committee's inquiry into the conduct and competition in SME lending (see further Treasury Committee, *Conduct and competition in SME lending: Minutes of evidence* (10 June 2014) response of Frances Coulson (in his capacity as Managing & Client Services Partner, Moon Beever Solicitors) to Q339; Treasury Committee, *Conduct and competition in SME lending: Written Evidence* (17 June 2014) CBI Written submission SME0080; Treasury Committee, *Conduct and competition in SME lending* (HC 204, 2015) Eleventh Report para 144).

[53] [2016] EWHC 2224 (QB).

him an experienced investor.[54] More importantly, the experience accumulated by corporate retail investors will commonly not be as extensive and sophisticated as that of the investment firm selling the products, hence placing the former in a vulnerable position, which requires reliance on the latter.

These reflections further support the argument that corporate retail investors should not be excluded from paternalistic regulatory protections merely on the basis of their 'corporate' status. Indeed, it is encouraging to note that the MiFID II Delegated Regulation introduces the requirement for investment firms to implement a policy for deciding who the suitability assessment[55] should relate to where, inter alia, the client is a legal person.[56] In the case of elective professional investors it is specified that, where the client is a legal person, the knowledge and experience shall be that of the person authorised to carry out transactions on behalf of the underlying client.[57] If this requirement were to be extrapolated to assessments carried out vis-à-vis corporate retail investors, it would therefore indicate that the regulator, the court, and investment firms, should see through the 'corporate' status of the retail investor and focus on the knowledge, experience, and other relevant characteristics of the individual(s) taking the investment decisions on its behalf.

III. The 'Consumer Responsibility Principle'

The regulatory approach that prevailed well into the first decade of this century was underpinned by the *caveat emptor* principle as 'an important force for market discipline'.[58] This encouraged the regulator not to act as a 'shield'[59] in protecting investors from the consequences of poor decisions, such that 'personal responsibility … [was] encouraged'[60] and the regulatory framework was not conceived as 'a guarantee that nothing can ever go wrong'.[61] Increasingly, there

[54] ibid [62]. Notwithstanding these statements, the court held that, on the evidence before it, all of the investments in question were objectively suitable for the claimants, who should therefore reasonably bear responsibility for their own mistaken investment decisions. The claimants had requested permission to appeal to the Court of Appeal but this was refused as the grounds for appeal were not considered as having real prospect of success (case reference: A2/2016/3773).

[55] ESMA defines the 'suitability assessment' as the whole process of collecting information about an investor and the subsequent assessment by the firm that a given investment product is suitable for him, based also on the firm's solid understanding of the products that it can recommend or invest into on behalf of the investor (see further ESMA, 'Final Report: Guidelines on certain aspects of the MiFID suitability requirements' ESMA35-43-869 (2018)).

[56] MiFID II Delegated Regulation, Art 54(6).

[57] MiFID II Delegated Regulation, Art 54(6).

[58] PCBS, *Changing banking for good: Report of the Parliamentary Commission on Banking Standards, Volume II* (HL Paper 27-II, HC 175-II, 2013) 281.

[59] ibid.

[60] Better Regulation Commission, *Risk, Responsibility, Regulation: Whose Risk is it Anyway?* (Cabinet Office 2006) (see also HM Government, *A Better Deal for Consumers: Delivering Real Help Now and Change for the Future* (Cm 7669, 2009); BIS, 'Empowering and protecting consumers: consultation on institutional changes for provision of consumer information, education, advocacy and enforcement' (2011) 14).

[61] Alan Milburn, Financial Services and Markets Bill Deb 28 June 1999, vol 334 col 40.

seemed to be a 'state-led expectation'[62] of retail investor participation in the investment services market, with financial literacy being promoted as the cornerstone for developing the investor protection policy around individualisation, responsibility and market expansion that would transform retail investors into 'watchful regulatory subjects'.[63] Statutory tools were introduced in response to a spate of regulatory failures and mis-selling scandals in the late 1980s and 1990s, to abolish the concept of self-regulation whilst still retaining a principles-based approach to regulation.[64] Even when the FSA was empowered to act as the single regulator during 2001,[65] it articulated a principles-based approach to pursuing its objectives,[66] which it followed through in its Treating Customers Fairly (TCF) initiative.[67] The FSA, at the time, placed significant importance on investor empowerment by repeatedly emphasising that one of the main elements of an 'effective and efficient retail market' consisted of 'capable and confident consumers' who would be able to 'take greater responsibility for their own actions' as well as to protect themselves better 'through less mis-buying'.[68] Here the then FSA was thus suggesting that, just as investment firms could be held responsible for mis-selling, investors could (and should) also be made accountable for 'mis-buying'.

[62] Michael Clarke, *Citizens' Financial Futures: The regulation of retail investment financial services in Britain* (Ashgate Publishing Ltd, 1999) 1.

[63] Toni Williams, 'Who wants to watch? A comment on the new international paradigm of financial consumer market regulation' (2013) 36 *Seattle University Law Review* 1217, 1224 (see also FSA, 'Building financial capability in the UK' (2003) 2; FSA, 'Towards a National Strategy for Financial Capability' (2003); HM Treasury, 'Financial Capability: The Government's long-term approach' (2007) para 1.12).

[64] The major statutory revamp came through the Financial Services Act 1986 (FSA 1986). For a broader discussion on rules-based and principles-based regulation, see eg Julia Black, *Rules and Regulators* (Clarendon Press, 1997); David Walker, 'Financial Services: The Principles Initiative' (1998) 4 *Journal of International Banking and Financial Law* 51; Martyn Hopper and Jenny Stainsby, 'Principles-based regulation – better regulation?' (2006) 21 *Journal of International Banking Law and Regulation* 387; Julia Black, Martyn Hopper, and Christa Band, 'Making a success of Principles-based regulation' (2007) 1 *Law and Financial Markets Review* 191.

[65] The FSA took over from the Securities and Investments Board (SIB) on 28 October 1997 and it started to exercise statutory powers given to it by the FSMA, which came into force on 1 December 2001. At that time the FSA also took over the role of the Securities and Futures Authority (SFA) which had been a self-regulatory organisation responsible for supervising the trading in shares and futures in the UK.

[66] On the FSA's approach to principles-based regulation, see further FSA, 'Better Regulation Action Plan: What we have done and what we are doing' (2005); FSA, 'Principles-based Regulation: Focusing on the Outcomes that Matter' (2007); Stuart Bazley, 'The Financial Services Authority, risk-based regulation, principles based rules and accountability' (2008) 23 *Journal of International Banking Law and Regulation* 422.

[67] Through its TCF project, the FSA sought to achieve behavioural changes without resorting to writing new rules (on TCF, see further FSA, 'Treating Customers Fairly: Towards Fair Outcomes for Consumers' (2006) para 1.7, 2.1; Julia Black, Martyn Hopper, and Christa Band, 'Making a success of Principles-based regulation' (2007) 1 *Law and Financial Markets Review* 191, 192, 199; Toni Williams, 'Open the Box: An Exploration of the Financial Services Authority's Model of Fairness in Consumer Financial Transactions' in Mel Kenny, James Devenney, and Lorna Fox O'Mahony (eds), *Unconscionability in European Private Financial Transactions: Protecting the Vulnerable* (Cambridge University Press, 2010) 233).

[68] FSA, 'Business Plan 2005/2006' (2005) 23 (see also Joanna Gray and Jenny Hamilton, *Implementing Financial Regulation: Theory and Practice* (John Wiley & Sons Ltd, 2006) 212; FSA, 'Annual Report 2007/2008' (2008) 32).

The current statutory 'consumer responsibility principle', which first featured in the original FSMA, section 2(2), clearly transcended this approach. This principle qualifies the otherwise absolute 'consumer protection objective' of 'securing an appropriate degree of protection for consumers'[69] by requiring the regulator to 'have regard' to 'the general principle that consumers should take responsibility for their decisions'.[70] The first draft of the Financial Services and Markets Bill that introduced the concept of consumer responsibility was met with protests from consumer bodies. Consumer groups felt that the consumer responsibility principle was generally 'unfair' in that it placed 'ultimate responsibility on retail customers who are faced with difficult decisions, often on the basis of little knowledge' and therefore lobbied for an absolute consumer protection objective.[71]

Despite these concerns, however, policymakers at the time still favoured an element of *caveat emptor* to target those situations of mis-buying that the regulator could do nothing to prevent, and to address the public's expectations of the regulator. It was also emphasised that retail investors 'have a role to play in protecting themselves in particular by having a responsibility for decisions about their financial arrangements'.[72] Following further debate, policymakers agreed to abolish any reference to *caveat emptor*, subject to a qualified retail investor protection objective, which accentuated the 'non-zero failure' approach to regulation and the conviction that investor responsibility contributes towards the proper functioning of an effective financial services market.[73] This resulted in a diluted 'consumerist narrative'[74] expressed in the consumer responsibility principle.

The fact that the precise extent of 'consumer responsibility' is not defined renders this consumer responsibility principle 'ambiguous and likely to be interpreted very differently by firms and consumers'.[75] Over the years, the UK regulator attempted to clarify this uncertainty by indicating what it perceived to be the general responsibilities of investors in the context of an investment transaction, as dictated by the principles of common law, as well as encouraging the market to use its rules and guidance to shift the balance of responsibilities between investment

[69] FSMA, s 1C(1).

[70] ibid s 1C(2)(d).

[71] Joint Committee on Financial Services and Markets, *Draft Financial Services and Markets Bill: First Report* (HC 328-I, 1999) para 33.

[72] Joint Committee on Financial Services and Markets, *Draft Financial Services and Markets Bill: Minutes of evidence* (18 March 1999) response of Patricia Hewitt (in her capacity as a Member of the House, Economic Secretary to HM Treasury) to Q101.

[73] See eg FSA, 'Financial Services and Markets Bill Conference' Speech by Howard Davies (Grosvenor House Hotel, London, 24 September 1998): www.fsa.gov.uk/library/communication/speeches/1998/sp11.shtml, accessed 15 May 2015; FSA, 'A new regulator for the new millennium' (2000) paras 4–6; FSA, 'Reasonable expectations: Regulation in a non-zero failure world' (2003) para 1.2; FSA, 'What does caveat emptor mean in the retail market for financial services?' Speech by Callum McCarthy (Financial Services Forum, London, 9 February 2006): www.fsa.gov.uk/pages/Library/Communication/Speeches/2006/0210_cm.shtml, accessed 30 November 2014; HM Treasury, *A new approach to financial regulation: building a stronger system* (Cm 8012, 2011) para 4.51.

[74] Joanna Benjamin, 'The Narratives of Financial Law' (2010) 30 *Oxford Journal of Legal Studies* 787, 799–800.

[75] FSCP, 'Incorporating a Duty of Care into the Financial Services and Markets Act' (2015) 2.

firms and investors. On this basis, the FSA emphasised that the investor should make a reasonable effort to understand products' features and properly evaluate the information provided, whilst reflecting on the definition of the 'average consumer' set by the Court of Justice of the European Union (CJEU),[76] and elsewhere defined by the European Commission as 'a critical person, conscious and circumspect in his market behaviour',[77] which standard is to be considered to determine the extent of remedies that should be awarded to an investor in case of a financial loss as well as to decide the extent to which regulators are expected to intervene to protect certain investors.

Against this backdrop, the interaction between the consumer responsibility principle and the responsibilities incumbent upon retail investors pursuant to their obligations under the common law is worth exploring further. Broadly speaking, both investment firms and investors are expected to contribute towards the successful and effective dealing with one another.[78] Yet, investors are under no strict legal obligation other than to act honestly, and, therefore, the implications of an investor failing to discharge his responsibilities (including whether or not he weakens his rights as a consequence) are still unclear. In fact, while the common law is founded on the principles of *caveat emptor* and freedom of contract, investor responsibilities under the common law are not enforceable as such but are still relevant to the court's determination of the extent of the duty of care owed by the investment firm and may still limit the extent to which a retail investor is able to recover any loss suffered as a result of a transaction where the court concludes that there was contributory negligence on the part of the investor.

It has been submitted that, in the context of professional negligence, a successful plea of contributory negligence by the defendant is less common than in other areas of negligence as the parties often do not stand on equal footing. This is because, in these circumstances, the claimant is generally not in a position to spot mistakes made by the defendant, unless the former is expected to possess the same knowledge as the latter.[79] Case law on mis-selling, however, portrays the exception

[76] The 'average consumer' is defined by the CJEU as a 'reasonably well-informed and reasonably observant and circumspect' investor (since the landmark Case C-210/96 *Gut Springenheide GmbH and Others v Oberkreisdirektor des Kreises Steinfurt Ä Amt für Lebensmittelüberwachung* [1998] ECR I-4657 para 31, a case which dealt with the free movement of goods). Yet, the 'consumer' concept in the free movement of goods regulatory regime may not be appropriate to the EU consumer contract law regime, since the latter uses the 'average consumer' as a starting point but introduces a higher level of protection to differentiate between consumers, depending on the extent to which they are perceived to be vulnerable (see also eg Vanessa Mak, 'Standards of Protection: In Search of the 'Average Consumer' of EU Law in the Proposal for a Consumer Rights Directive' (2011) 19 *European Review of Private Law* 25).

[77] European Commission, 'Guidance on the Implementation/Application of Directive 2005/29/EC on Unfair Corporate Practices' (2009) 25.

[78] See eg, the bank charges case of *The Office of Fair Trading v Abbey National Plc and Others* [2009] UKSC 6 [93], where Lady Hale stressed that: 'As a very general proposition, consumer law … aims to give the consumer an informed choice rather than to protect the consumer from making an unwise choice'.

[79] Rupert M Jackson, Roger Stewart and John Powell, *Jackson & Powell on Professional Liability*, 7th edn (Sweet & Maxwell Ltd, 2012) para 5-146.

to this statement, since English courts have considered corporate retail investors to be sophisticated counterparties and therefore well-placed to spot or correct any mistakes made by the defendant. As a result, English courts have accepted defences based on retail investors' contributory negligence in terms of, inter alia, withholding critical information, providing inaccurate information, failing to read product particulars, or neglecting relevant guidance simultaneously being received from other professional advisers, thereby aggravating the consequences of the defendant's breach of duty (had the court concluded that any such breach had indeed been committed by the defendant).[80]

The legal concept of contributory negligence also underpins the FCA's interpretation of the consumer responsibility principle, and is similarly taken into account by the FOS.[81] From the regulator's perspective, if an investment firm is considered to have fulfilled all its obligations and to have treated the investor fairly, then, if the transaction had to cause a financial loss to the investor, the investment firm should not be held responsible. In this sense, the regulator appears to suggest that retail investors do have responsibilities, albeit not in a strictly legal sense, which responsibilities they have 'a self interest in discharging'.[82] In practice, this approach largely operates to the detriment of corporate retail investors since the regulator decides what level of consumer protection is appropriate primarily on two factors, being the complexity of markets and products, and the capability of the investor to exercise judgements about such markets and products. Since corporate retail investors are typically considered relatively less vulnerable, and hence less in need of regulatory protection, the regulator is likely to expect this category of investors to bear a relatively higher share of responsibility when compared to individual retail investors. While the regulatory powers of the FCA do not extend to investors, the FCA's enforcement of the consumer responsibility principle is still transcended onto investors indirectly as, by virtue of its jurisdiction in regulating investment firms, the FCA sets the boundaries for investment firms' responsibilities and its expectations thereof, thereby implicitly carving out the share of responsibility that different categories of investors are expected to shoulder beyond that boundary.[83]

[80] See eg *Spreadex Ltd v Sekhon* [2008] EWHC 1136 (Ch), [2009] 1 BCLC 102; *Bank Leumi (UK) Plc v Linda Joy Wachner* [2011] EWHC 656 (Comm), [2011] 1 CLC 454; *IG Index Ltd v Aryeh Ehrentreu* [2015] EWHC 3390 (QB) [130].

[81] See eg FOS decisions DRN0695327, DRN1405790, and DRN8516283, and FOS, 'Boundaries of responsibility in financial services' Speech by Walter Merricks (Financial Services Research Forum, London, 7 November 2006): www.financial-ombudsman.org.uk/news/speech/WM-research-forum.html, accessed 2 October 2016.

[82] FSA, 'What does caveat emptor mean in the retail market for financial services?' Speech by Callum McCarthy (Financial Services Forum, London, 9 February 2006): www.fsa.gov.uk/pages/Library/Communication/Speeches/2006/0210_cm.shtml, accessed 30 November 2014.

[83] In considering the extent to which it must have due regard to the consumer responsibility principle, the FCA also takes into account, inter alia, the extent of consumer vulnerability, such that a higher element of vulnerability (which is typically attributed to certain individual retail investors as discussed in Section 2.1) equates to lower responsibilities being expected out of the consumers. The converse would apply to corporate retail investors, in virtue of these being considered less susceptible to mis-selling.

Faced by these sensitive and intricate considerations, consumer bodies contested the use of the term 'responsibilities' as referred to in the consumer responsibility principle. Arguing that no 'responsibilities' are, in effect, owed by the investor, consumer bodies claimed that this principle encourages investment firms to continue 'providing reams of documents for each product as a means of discharging disclosure requirements, in the hope that thereafter responsibility is transferred to consumers, as they 'should have read' these documents'.[84] This, they contended, places unrealistic expectations on retail investors and implicitly enables investment firms to use the consumer responsibility principle as a way of negotiating the limits of consumer protection whilst arguably reducing their own liabilities.[85] It was therefore suggested that the spirit of this general principle should lean more towards the outcomes-based TCF-type regime, reflecting what investment firms are expected to achieve, rather than asserting at the outset that investors should bear a share of responsibility for mis-buying.[86]

These observations were considered in deliberations on the Financial Services Bill in 2012, during which the FSCP lobbied in favour of the introduction of a specific requirement for firms engaged in financial services to owe their customers the same duty of care as a lawyer and other professionals, through the inclusion of a duty on firms to 'act honestly, fairly and professionally in the best interest of their customers and to manage conflicts of interest'.[87] In so stating, the FSCP also recognised the vulnerabilities of corporate retail investors when it remarked that the primary intention of this statutory duty would be to 'protect retail and small business customers'.[88] Proposals relating to the implementation of this general duty of care were however not taken forward by the UK Government at the time,[89] as it alternatively opted to supplement the consumer responsibility principle by additional 'have regard to' regulatory principles aimed at placing an increased burden

[84] Consumer Focus, 'Response to HM Treasury on the Draft Financial Services Bill' (2011) para 62. This concern reflects what has been concluded by English courts in mis-selling litigation, as discussed further in ch 5.

[85] Consumer Focus, Which? And Citizens Advice were all in favour of the deletion of the consumer responsibility principle (see further Financial Services Consumer Panel (FSCP), 'Response to FSA Discussion Paper 08/5 on Consumer Responsibility' (2009); Joint Committee on the draft Financial Services Bill, *Draft Financial Services Bill* (HL 236 HC 1447, 2010-12) paras 111–120).

[86] Joint Committee on the draft Financial Services Bill, *Draft Financial Services Bill* (HL 236 HC 1447, 2010–12) para 120.

[87] FSCP, 'Annual Report 2012/2013' (2013) 59 (see further FSCP, 'Position Paper on Fiduciary Duty' (2012) paras 1.2, 2.1–2.3, 3.9; FSCP, 'Position Paper on Consumer Responsibility' (2012) para 1.3; FSCP, 'Position Paper – Banking Culture' (2016)). Similarly, the FSUG recommended the imposition of explicit fiduciary duties of care on investment firms as a measure to curb mis-selling and undue risk-taking (FSUG, 'Making financial services work for financial users, Paper 1: New model financial regulation' (2012) 40).

[88] FSCP, 'Incorporating a Duty of Care into the Financial Services and Markets Act' (2015) 1.

[89] The Netherlands has introduced such a general duty of care relatively recently through its Amendment Act Financial Markets 2016.

of responsibility on investment firms and at addressing some of the inherent limitations of retail investors.[90]

More recently, the FCA has reiterated that, on balance, it does not believe that the introduction of such a duty of care rule is necessary, noting that, in its view, the most effective way to strengthen the requirements for governance bodies of investment firms to act in the best interest of investors is through regulatory reform rather than through the implementation of a statutory fiduciary duty or duty of care.[91] Further, the FCA observed that a statutory duty would still not provide the necessary clarity around its expectations of investment firms and has, as an alternative, proposed to consult on the introduction of a new Prescribed Responsibility under its Senior Managers and Certification Regime (SMCR) to act in the best interests of investors including consideration of value for money.[92] Yet, in light of the differing views and the strength of the concerns expressed by some stakeholders on this topic, the FCA decided to keep alive the debate about the potential merits of a duty of care and launched a consultation process around what it is terming the 'New Duty'.[93] At present, the position is still very fluid as the FCA is now in the process of assessing responses to confirm whether the general view is that there do exist gaps in the existing regulatory framework that could be addressed by the introduction of a New Duty and, if so, what would be the most appropriate solution to make this work in practice (for example through a revision in its Principles for Business).

The position of corporate retail investors thus appears to be undermined by the consumer responsibility principle, which principle has enabled the reminiscence of *caveat emptor* to seep through the UK investment services rulebook. The investor responsibility principle also finds no equivalent under the common law. At common law, whether an investor has acted responsibly or otherwise will not, by itself, determine whether a remedy for a loss suffered is available to a party to the contract. It is the breach of a common law duty of care that will give rise to a claim in the first place and any negligence on the part of the investor will be brought into play in defence of the investment firm to allege contributory negligence and argue

[90] In terms of these new 'have regard to' principles, the FCA is required to consider the general principle that those providing regulated financial services are expected to provide an appropriate level of care (FSMA, s 1C(2)(e)). Moreover, the former principle covering the need for accurate information (former FSMA, s 5(2)(c)) has been replaced with one explicitly setting out investors' need for advice and information that is accurate, timely and fit for purpose (FSMA, s 1C(2)(c)). A further amendment to the senior management responsibility principle has also been introduced (FSMA, s 3B(1)(e)). These additional principles were introduced pursuant to a recommendation of the Joint Committee, which advocated a balance between investment firms' and consumers' responsibilities (Joint Committee on the draft Financial Services Bill, *Draft Financial Services Bill* (HL 236 HC 1447, 2010–12) para 126).

[91] FCA, 'Asset Management Market Study: Final Report MS15/2.3' (2017) 71–72 (see also FCA, 'Our Future Mission' (2016) 24; FCA, 'Our Mission 2017: How we regulate financial services' (2017) 28).

[92] FCA, 'Asset Management Market Study: Final Report MS15/2.3' (2017) 71–72.

[93] FCA, 'Discussion Paper DP18/5, on a duty of care and potential alternative approaches' (2018).

that its liability in damages for breach of duty should bear a reasonable relationship to the extent of its error or culpability.[94]

In light of the foregoing, retail investors' actions should be conceptualised as 'sensible steps'[95] to be taken by investors in protecting their own interests. This book proposes to achieve this by abolishing the consumer responsibility principle and replacing this with a 'Retail Investor Charter', which is aimed at guiding retail investors through their investment decision-making process.[96]

IV. Addressing Vulnerabilities and Biases

Insights from behavioural economics theories show that the preferences of corporate retail investors are often ill-informed by capability barriers and behavioural biases as well as being founded on relationships of trust, which lure these investors into accepting sub-optimal terms designed to appear more attractive than they really are.[97] Indeed, 'SMEs are viewed as sophisticated customers by regulators when, in reality, many are not',[98] as corporate retail investors still suffer from most biases typically reserved for individual retail investors not least because these investors are simply an entity formed and operated by one individual retail investor or a small group of individual retail investors.

Particularly in light of the findings from behavioural law and economics, regulators are encouraged to develop a 'libertarian paternalist' strategy in an attempt to steer retail investors' choices in the right direction, that is towards products that fit their knowledge, experience, risk profile and investment objectives, without completely eliminating freedom of choice.[99] Despite certain reservations,[100] this

[94] Whilst there is consensus around the fact that investors should provide truthful answers to questions and generally behave as a 'responsible citizen', the statutory principle of consumer responsibility seems to imply that a lower regulatory protection will be afforded to 'irresponsible' consumers who fail to do so (Consumer Focus, 'Response to HM Treasury on the Draft Financial Services Bill' (2011) 10–11). In fact, in *IG Index Ltd v Aryeh Ehrentreu* [2015] EWHC 3390 (QB) [130], the court drew upon the FSMA regime, particularly the consumer responsibility principle, in determining the extent of contributory negligence. This led Supperstone J to conclude that the defendant was responsible for his loss to the extent of 95% on the basis of, inter alia, 'the general principle that consumers should take responsibility for their decisions'.

[95] Elizabeth Ovey, 'Balancing the scales: firms v consumers' (2009) 24 *Journal of International Banking and Financial Law* 330, 330.

[96] See further Section 7.2.3.

[97] Bar-Gill calls this process 'seduction by contract' (see further Oren Bar-Gill, 'Seduction by Contract: Law, Economics and Psychology in Consumer Markets – Introduction' (2012) NYU Center for Law, Economics and Organization, Law and Economics Research Paper Series, Working Paper No 12-33, 2).

[98] Andrew Tyrie, 'Evidence session on small and medium sized enterprises lending' (2014).

[99] On libertarian paternalism, see further Cass Sunstein and Richard Thaler, 'Libertarian Paternalism Is Not an Oxymoron' (2003) 70 *University of Chicago Law Review* 1159, 1162.

[100] See eg Joshua D Wright and Douglas H Ginsburg, 'Behavioral law and economics: Its origins, fatal flaws, and implications for liberty' (2012) 106 *Northwestern University Law Review* 1033, 1085–87; Karen Yeung, 'Nudge as Fudge' (2012) 75 *The Modern Law Review* 122, 148.

form of intervention is desirable as a form of 'nonintrusive type of paternalism'[101] since it preserves choice for investors whilst refuting the unfounded assumption that all retail investors make rational decisions that are in their best interest. Insofar as investor vulnerability is concerned, a broader notion of 'vulnerability' should be considered in devising regulatory reforms, such that it incorporates the market context whilst taking into account aspects related to the structure of particular transactions and products. This would also support the view that corporate retail investors merit enhanced regulatory protection when engaging in complex investment transactions, with their position being comparable to that of individual retail investors.[102]

Whilst building retail investors' financial capabilities are important, regulators must still recognise limits to retail investor responsibility, which limitation brings into question the validity of the statutory consumer responsibility principle. Regulators must therefore pitch paternalistic intervention accordingly, ideally, through a 'cocktail of measures'[103] as recommended in chapter seven.

[101] Cass Sunstein and Richard Thaler, 'Libertarian Paternalism Is Not an Oxymoron' (2003) 70 *University of Chicago Law Review* 1159, 1162 (see also Jeffrey J Rachlinski, 'The Uncertain Psychological Case for Paternalism' (2003) 97 *Northwestern Law Review* 1165, 1219).

[102] This is also in line with the legal principle of 'normative coherence' (or 'treating cases alike'), which suggests that if corporate retail investors behave more like individual retail investors rather than like professional investors, it would therefore be coherent for the legal and regulatory framework to treat corporate retail investors and individual retail investors equally.

[103] FSA, 'UK Financial Regulation: After the Crisis' Speech by Hector Sants (Annual Lubbock Lecture in Management Studies, London, 12 March 2010): www.fsa.gov.uk/pages/Library/Communication/Speeches/2010/0312_hs.shtml, accessed 8 April 2015.

3

Applying Regulatory Reforms and Redress Avenues to the Case of Corporate Retail Investors

I. The Regulatory Response to Retail Investor Protection Concerns

The scandals that have destabilised the financial system in the last decade, namely the global financial crisis and persistent mis-selling practices, inevitably brought into question the capacity of the regulatory framework to act preventatively or otherwise react quickly to apparent warning signs.[1] Specifically in the context of conduct regulation, which is directed at the client-facing risks generated by financial market intermediation, conduct of business rules are pivotal in protecting retail investors from risks arising from a client detriment perspective.[2] The retail investor protection objective is a chief concern of the investment services regulatory framework given the 'disparity between the knowledge and capability of the provider … and of the user',[3] namely as a result of the limited ability and opportunity on the part of investors to acquire the necessary skills to enter into complex financial contracts and to assess information thereon. Collectively, these factors present a compelling case for the use of the regulatory framework in achieving this objective.[4]

The issue of securities to the public has been regulated in the UK since 1900.[5] Dealing in securities, however, was not regulated by statute until 1939, when the first Prevention of Fraud (Investments) Act came into force to regulate the

[1] Iain MacNeil and Justin O'Brien (eds), *The Future of Financial Regulation* (Hart Publishing, 2010) 7.

[2] Niamh Moloney, 'Conduct Rules and Investor Protection: The Evolution of the EU's Approach' in Matthias Casper and others (eds), *Festschrift für Johannes Köndgen* (RWS Vlg Kommunikationsforum, 2016) 398.

[3] FSA, 'Mansion House speech' Speech by Callum McCarthy (London, 20 September 2005): aid:cstyle="WEBlink">www.fsa.gov.uk/library/communication/speeches/2005/0920_cm.shtml, accessed 30 October 2014.

[4] Julia Black, *Rules and Regulators* (Clarendon Press, 1997) 241 (see also Peter Cartwright, 'Understanding and Protecting Vulnerable Financial Consumers' (2015) 38 *Journal of Consumer Policy* 119).

[5] The Companies Act 1900 was the first to regulate this activity.

proliferation of new companies following an increase in business activity in the 1930s, and made it an offence for a person to carry on the business of dealing in securities without being licensed. Conduct of business rules were then developed in the 1960s[6] and given more structure under the FSA 1986.[7] In those years, the investment services regulatory regime was generally 'light-touch' as policymakers allowed market forces to operate largely undisturbed and attempted to mould retail investors into 'financial citizens'.[8]

Efforts to promote investor empowerment were also evident outside the UK, as global policymakers equally pushed for investors to take on more responsibilities and embarked on financial literacy programmes to impress upon retail investors that they too 'have their share of responsibility',[9] hence reducing the need for regulatory intervention. The US Supreme Court, for example, observed that courts should not ascribe retail investors to 'child-like simplicity' and should not be 'misled by puffery'.[10] Similarly, at EU level, investor empowerment has been considered 'a key driver of innovation, competition and productivity',[11] as the retail market agenda of EU political and legal institutions places a recurring emphasis on the importance of the role that the 'informed investor' has in the market.[12] In practice, and despite various EU pronouncements hinting at a general safety net around retail investors,[13] the main thrust of the European Commission's policy has historically remained broadly based on the concepts of freedom of choice and investor empowerment, thereby encouraging retail investors to autonomously defend their own interests, assert their rights, exert discipline on the market and

[6] The Licensed Dealers (Conduct of Business) Rules 1960. These were substantially revised under The Licensed Dealers (Conduct of Business) Rules 1983.

[7] On the evolution of the UK investment services regime, see further Laurence CB Gower, *Review of Investor Protection: Part I* (Cmnd 9215, 1984); Andrew Large, *Financial Services Regulation: Making the two tier system work* (SIB 1993); Arthur Selman, 'Regulation of UK retail investment business' (1996) 3 *European Financial Services Law Journal* 331, 332; Howard Davies, 'Law and Regulation' (1999) 3 *Company Financial and Insolvency Law Review* 1, 5; Iain MacNeil, *An Introduction to the Law on Financial Investment*, 2nd edn (Sweet & Maxwell Ltd, 2012) ch 2.

[8] Dimity Kingsford Smith, 'Regulating investment risk: individuals and the global financial crisis' (2009) 32 *University of New South Wales Law Journal* 514, 514–15.

[9] BaFIN, 'We need even more transparency' Speech by Dr Elke König (Frankfurt am Main, 13 March 2013): www.bafin.de/SharedDocs/Veroeffentlichungen/EN/Fachartikel/2013/fa_bj_2013_03_interview_koenig_verbraucher_en.html, accessed 11 December 2014. On the need for investors to take on more responsibilities in other EU jurisdictions, see also Jaques Delmas-Marsalet, 'Report on the marketing of financial products' (2005) 42; AFM, 'Policy and Priorities for the 2007–2009 Period' (2007).

[10] Barbara Black, 'Behavioural Economics and Investor Protection: Reasonable Investors and Efficient Markets' (2013) 44 *Loyola University Chicago Law Journal* 1493, 1494.

[11] European Commission, 'Consumer Decision-Making in Retail Investment Services: A Behavioural Economics Perspective, Final Report' (2010) 3.

[12] Stephen Weatherill, 'The Role of the Informed Consumer in European Community Law and Policy' (1994) 2 *Consumer Law Journal* 49, 49.

[13] See eg European Commission, 'Financial Services Action Plan' (1999); European Commission, 'Initial Report of the Committee of Wise Men on the Regulation of European Securities Markets' (2000).

exercise informed choice.[14] This is further substantiated by the high threshold imposed by the CJEU in defining the 'average consumer', and is also reflected in the spirit of the original MiFID regime which hails disclosure as the 'dominant regulatory mechanism' and assumes that the investor is 'rational, competent, and capable of exercising informed choice'.[15] Even now, the EU's regulatory strategy still generally 'cling[s] to the rational actor model'[16] and presumes 'an informed retail community with high levels of competence in decoding information'.[17]

This regulatory commitment to markets which implicitly endorsed a form of *caveat emptor*, placed high expectations on the retail investor, entrusting him with the 'civic duty'[18] of making decisions in terms of 'risk-bearing and investment choice'.[19] In this sense, the retail investor was portrayed as a 'junior entrepreneur'[20] or an 'Olympian empowered investor'[21] as he becomes entrenched in the regulatory process and is expected to act as 'an agent of the government'[22] to fulfil the objective of creating a marketplace comprising financially capable and empowered retail investors. Consequently, such investors were expected to emerge as a 'knowledgeable, competent, confident, self-reliant and willing market participant[s]',[23] accountable for aspects of governance that would be typically expected from the regulator. This lax approach to regulation persisted until numerous crises

[14] Jacqueline Minor, 'Consumer protection in the EU: searching for the real consumer' (2012) 13 *European Business Organisation Law Review* 163, 166 (see also European Commission, 'Increasing Financial Capability' Speech by Charlie McCreevy (Increasing Financial Capability Conference Brussels, 28 March 2007): http://europa.eu/rapid/press-release_SPEECH-07-202_en.htm, accessed 9 December 2014).

[15] Niamh Moloney, 'Large-Scale Reform of Investor Protection Regulation: The European Union Experience' (2007) 4 *Macquarie Journal of Business Law* 147, 160 (see also European Commission, 'Financial Services Policy 2005–2010' COM (2005) 629 final 7; European Commission, 'Draft Commission Directive implementing Directive 2004/39/EC as regards organisational requirements and operating conditions' (2006) Background Note 15).

[16] Philipp Hacker, 'The Behavioral Divide: A Critique of the Differential Implementation of Behavioral Law and Economics in the US and the EU' (2015) 4 *European Review of Private Contract Law* 299, 299.

[17] Niamh Moloney, 'Large-Scale Reform of Investor Protection Regulation: The European Union Experience' (2007) 4 *Macquarie Journal of Business Law* 147, 171 (see also Anne-Lise Sibony, 'Can EU Consumer Law Benefit From Behavioural Insights? An Analysis of the Unfair Practices Directive' in Klaus Mathis (ed), *European Perspectives on Behavioural Law and Economics* (Springer International Publishing, 2015) 72–73).

[18] Niamh Moloney, 'Regulating the Retail Markets: Law, Policy and the Financial Crisis' in George Letsas and Colm O'Cinnéide (eds) *Current Legal Problems* (Oxford University Press, 2010) 392.

[19] ibid.

[20] Dimity Kingsford Smith, 'Regulating investment risk: individuals and the global financial crisis' (2009) 32 *University of New South Wales Law Journal* 514, 696.

[21] Niamh Moloney, 'Regulating the Retail Markets: Law, Policy and the Financial Crisis' in George Letsas and Colm O'Cinnéide (eds) *Current Legal Problems* (Oxford University Press, 2010) 391.

[22] ibid 392.

[23] Joanna Gray and Jenny Hamilton, *Implementing Financial Regulation: Theory and Practice* (John Wiley & Sons Ltd, 2006) 188 (see also Nikolas Rose, *Powers of Freedom: Reframing Political Thought* (Cambridge University Press, 1999) 144; Toni Williams, 'Empowerment of Whom and for What? Financial Literacy Education and the New Regulation of Consumer Financial Services' (2007) 29 *Law and Policy* 226, 231).

and scandals tested its appropriateness, leading policymakers to consider more intrusive regulatory oversight. In fact, when the global financial crisis struck and even more mis-selling scandals surfaced, the then FSA acknowledged that it had overestimated the industry's willingness to sacrifice corporate benefits in order to treat its customers fairly.[24] Most notably, the heavy reliance on non-binding guidance (such as that issued under its TCF initiative) failed to achieve what the then FSA had set out to accomplish in terms of embedding high standards of customer-oriented behaviours in the 'industry's DNA',[25] whilst also overlooking 'potential risks to the stability of the financial system'.[26]

Dependence on principles alone therefore enfeebled both the conduct and prudential objectives of regulation and ultimately amounted to 'a lack of regulation',[27] compelling the FSA to re-engage with a more rules-based regime supported by an aggressive enforcement strategy. Compounded by the findings and recommendations set out in the Turner Review,[28] the FSA was forced into 'product recall', insofar as principles were concerned, and re-launched itself under the 'new strapline of an "outcomes based regulator"'.[29] In so doing, it committed to heightened intervention in financial markets, placing significantly less reliance on market discipline, and having a more intrusive approach to supervision. This 'hybrid of high-level principles and detailed rules and guidance'[30] that also defines the FCA's regulatory approach today, is one that provides constrained discretion to the market and that enables the regulator to balance principles and rules, whilst also promoting the use of judgement on the part of both the regulator and the industry.[31] The resultant regulatory style thus retained elements of the principles-based approach but reinforced this with a greater focus on individual accountability and preventative enforcement. In embracing this approach, the regulator implicitly acknowledged that retail investors cannot always be expected to possess sufficient 'financial knowledge, information and understanding of complex products

[24] Eilís Ferran, 'Regulatory lessons from the payment protection insurance mis-selling scandal in the UK' (2012) 13 *European Business Organization Law Review* 247, 256–57, 259.

[25] Eilís Ferran, 'Regulatory lessons from the payment protection insurance mis-selling scandal in the UK' (2012) 13 *European Business Organization Law Review* 247, 259.

[26] Kern Alexander, 'Principles v rules in financial regulation: re-assessing the balance in the credit crisis' (2009) 10 *European Business Organization Law Review* 169, 173.

[27] Julia Black and Richard Nobles, 'Personal Pensions Misselling: The Causes and Lessons of Regulatory Failure' (1998) 61 *The Modern Law Review* 789, 819.

[28] 'Turner Review: A Regulatory Response to the Global Banking Crisis' (2009).

[29] Julia Black, 'The rise, fall and fate of principles-based regulation' in Kern Alexander and Niamh Moloney (eds), *Law Reform and Financial Markets* (Edward Elgar Publishing, 2011) 18 (see also FSA, 'Discussion Paper DP 09/2, A regulatory response to the global banking crisis' (2009) para 1.64).

[30] FSA, 'Better Regulation Action Plan: What we have done and what we are doing' (2005) 3.

[31] A nuanced application of rules and principles that does not necessarily favour one regulatory tool over another enjoys the support of various academics (see eg Colin Scott, 'Standard-Setting in Regulatory Regimes' in Robert Baldwin, Martin Cave, and Martin Lodge (eds), *The Oxford Handbook of Regulation* (Oxford University Press, 2010) 111; Robert Baldwin, 'Better Regulation: The Search and the Struggle' in Robert Baldwin, Martin Cave, and Martin Lodge (eds), *The Oxford Handbook of Regulation* (Oxford University Press, 2010) 267, 275).

and risks to decide what is best for them',[32] which accordingly places 'particular responsibility upon firms'.[33] The FCA has therefore found itself questioning whether it would be 'sensible'[34] to expect retail investors to take rational decisions in such a fluid and risky environment, which led it to shift to a relatively more paternalistic regulatory strategy that is influenced by behavioural law and economics theories.[35]

Other regulators have also accepted that retail investors 'do not always act rationally ... they occasionally act intuitively ... [and] often do not have the time or are afraid of how much it will cost to look into questions of investment'.[36] In fact, and in response to escalating mis-selling scandals, regulators globally have opted for more paternalistic measures, as well as further enhancing the visibility of their investor protection objective in deploying their regulatory strategies.[37]

Similarly, the European Commission acknowledged that consumers tend to depart from the behaviour predicted by the rational economic theory, displaying irrational behaviour as a result of behavioural biases, which may result in retail investor detriment and consequently requires adequate regulatory remedies

[32] FCA, 'The FCA's approach to advancing its objectives' (2013) 11.

[33] FSA, 'Feedback Statement FS11/3, Product Intervention: Feedback on DP11/1' (2011) para 2.66 (see also FCA, 'Structured Products: Thematic Review TR15/2, Product Development and Governance' (2015), and, more generally, the Responsibilities of Providers and Distributors for the Fair Treatment of Customers (RPPD) contained within the FCA Handbook).

[34] FCA, 'Making competition king – the rise of behavioural economics at the FCA' Speech by Martin Wheatley (Australian Securities and Investments Commission, Australia, 25 March 2014): www.fca.org.uk/news/making-competition-king, accessed 5 October 2015; see also FSA, 'My vision for the FCA' Speech by Martin Wheatley (British Bankers' Association, London, 25 January 2012): www.fsa.gov.uk/library/communication/speeches/2012/0125-mw.shtml, accessed 25 August 2015.

[35] See eg the FCA's submissions in *Green and Rowley v The Royal Bank of Scotland Plc* [2012] EWHC 3661 (QB), affd [2013] EWCA Civ 1197, [2014] Bus LR 168. This case dealt with the alleged mis-selling of complex IRHPs to corporate retail investors and will be discussed further alongside other similar cases in Part II of this book.

[36] BaFIN, 'Consumer protection and regulation – where we stand and what must still be done' Speech by Dr Elke König (BaFin Annual Press Conference, Frankfurt am Main, 20 May 2014): www.bafin.de/SharedDocs/Veroeffentlichungen/EN/Reden/re_140520_jahrespressekonferenz_p_en.html, accessed 11 November 2014; see also FINRA, 'Remarks from the Consumer Federation of America Consumer Assembly' Speech by Richard G Ketchum (Washington DC, 14 March 2013): www.finra.org/newsroom/speeches/031413-remarks-consumer-federation-america-consumer-assembly, accessed 13 June 2015.

[37] These include the recent German Retail Investors Protection Act, the establishment of the Consumer Financial Protection Bureau (CFPB) in the US in 2011 (see further www.consumerfinance.gov/, accessed 20 May 2016); the use of behavioural economic insights by the Australian Securities and Investments Commission (ASIC) in deploying its regulatory duties (see eg ASIC, 'Report 427, Investing in hybrid securities: Explanations based on behavioural economics' (2015) and ASIC, 'ASIC and behavioural economics: Regulating for real people' Speech by Peter Kell (The Impacts of Behavioural Economics on Financial Markets and Regulations Symposium, Brisbane, 18 October 2016): http://download.asic.gov.au/media/4051518/peter-kell-speech-qube-symposium-published-21-october-2016.pdf, accessed 24 May 2017); and other initiatives by other regulators and policymakers more broadly that are slowly pursuing the paths of nudging (see further BVA, 'French Government: Nudge Me Tender' (2014) and OECD, 'Behavioural economics and financial consumer protection' (2017)).

in response.[38] Enhancing investor protection in financial markets has thus become a 'key preoccupation of the European Parliament',[39] with the European Commission admitting that it was amiss in basing its regulatory framework on the assumption of market rationality and in adopting a 'laissez-faire' approach.[40] In the aftermath of the global financial crisis, the European Commission recognised that it was 'time to turn the telescope round' to look at financial services from the bottom-up, rather than from the top-down, thereby placing retail investors at the centre of regulatory policies.[41] Specifically in the context of the MiFID regime, a shift can also be perceived in the EU's approach from one which was focused on empowering retail investors (under MiFID I), to one which emphasised precautionary intervention (under MiFID II).[42]

It is common knowledge that the lax regulatory approach which was dependent on investor empowerment failed to engage in the 'the heavy lifting'[43] expected of it and lacked adequate mechanisms for the protection of retail investors.[44] Broadly speaking, therefore, there seems to be a general consensus among policymakers that stronger consumer protection mechanisms were necessary as 'an essential pillar of well-functioning financial markets'.[45] The investment services regulatory regime was said to be in need of a 're-think' as it relied excessively on the traditional advice and sales regulation, which had failed to prevent mis-selling scandals and financial crises from occurring.[46] As they re-examined the character of regulation, regulators across Europe have been described as 'practically falling over themselves to demonstrate their commitment to protecting the humble retail investor',[47] with this process being criticised for creating a 'siloed' approach

[38] European Commission, 'Staff Working Document on the follow up in retail financial services to the consumer markets scoreboard' SEC (2009) 1251 final (see also European Commission, 'Applying Behavioural Sciences to EU Policy-making' (2013) EUR 26033 EN).

[39] European Parliament, 'Consumer Protection Aspects of Financial Services' (2014) 96.

[40] European Commission, 'Forging a New Deal between Finance and Society: Restoring Trust in the Financial Sector' Speech by Michel Barnier (European Financial Services Conference, Brussels, 26 April 2010): http://europa.eu/rapid/press-release_SPEECH-10-178_en.htm?locale=en, accessed 4 January 2015.

[41] European Commission, 'Turning around the telescope – consumers at the centre of financial services policies' Speech by Jonathan Hill (Emerging Challenges in Retail Finance and Consumer Policy Conference, Brussels, 18 November 2014).

[42] Niamh Moloney, 'Conduct Rules and Investor Protection: The Evolution of the EU's Approach' in Matthias Casper and others (eds), *Festschrift für Johannes Köndgen* (RWS Vlg Kommunikationsforum, 2016) 407.

[43] Niamh Moloney, 'The Investor Model Underlying the EU's Investor Protection Regime: Consumers or Investors?' (2012) 13 *European Business Organization Law Review* 169, 177.

[44] See further FSUG, 'Making financial services work for financial users, Paper 1: New model financial regulation' (2012) 4; Niamh Moloney, 'Financial Market Governance and Consumer Protection in the EU' in Ester Faia and others (eds), *Financial Regulation: A Transatlantic Perspective* (Cambridge University Press, 2015) 222.

[45] European Parliament, 'Consumer Protection Aspects of Financial Services' (2014) 18.

[46] Niamh Moloney, 'Regulating the Retail Markets: Law, Policy and the Financial Crisis' in George Letsas and Colm O'Cinnéide (eds) *Current Legal Problems* (Oxford University Press, 2010) 343.

[47] Phil Davies, 'Protecting investors proves tricky' *Financial Times Fund Management* (London, 20 March 2011) 11. Further, Alexander and Moloney caution against an over-reaction in terms of

to investor protection which, in turn, causes duplication, divergent definitions, increased compliance costs, and a lack of clarity for the industry and investors.[48]

Although this exercise has forced regulators to become more appreciative of retail investors' vulnerabilities and their need for enhanced protection thereon, this awareness appears to be restricted to individual retail investors.[49] To this end, it is here argued that the reforms that have come into effect in recent years are primarily targeted at protecting individual retail investors, despite being indicative of a stronger pro-investor stance being adopted by regulators. Corporate retail investors, however, remain largely in the same disadvantaged position as they were prior to these reforms. To support this statement, the EU-wide amendments to the MiFID regime, the UK's deployment of the Retail Distribution Review (RDR), and the statutory amendments to the FCA's objectives, coupled with additional product intervention powers being vested in the FCA, are analysed hereunder.[50] Consistent with the decline of the 'financial citizen' concept discussed in this chapter, the stated aim of these measures was predominantly to secure a stronger retail investor protection regime as well as restrict the degree of investor autonomy typically associated with the empowerment model.[51]

A. The MiFID II Investor Protection Reforms

At inception, the MiFID regime was expressly designed to enhance retail investor protection through its pivotal conduct of business obligations, which have been described as 'one of the mainstays of investor protection',[52] whilst also seeking

regulatory reforms, when they describe policymakers as being 'gripped by the imperative to 'do something' in the wake of crisis' (Kern Alexander and Niamh Moloney (eds), *Law Reform and the Financial Markets* (Edward Elgar Publishing Ltd, 2011) ix).

[48] European Commission, 'Summary of contributions to the 'Call for Evidence': EU regulatory framework for financial services' (2016) 11.

[49] As discussed in ch 2, the FCA in particular fails to acknowledge that its concerns around retail investor autonomy are equally relevant to the circumstances of corporate retail investors.

[50] These measures are considered to be the most relevant in the context of the matters being considered by this book. Apart from the reforms discussed in this chapter, other developments (outside the scope of this book) include the establishment of ESMA, which has brought a new dynamic to retail market law and policy, the establishment of the European Commission's FSUG (which replaces the earlier Forum of User Experts in the Area of Financial Services, FIN-USE), enhanced disclosure under the Prospectus Directive (Directive 2010/73/EU), and the cross-sector PRIIPs reforms.

[51] See eg Niamh Moloney, 'Financial Market Governance and Consumer Protection in the EU' in Ester Faia and others (eds), *Financial Regulation: A Transatlantic Perspective* (Cambridge University Press, 2015); Niamh Moloney, *EU Securities and Financial Markets Regulation*, 3rd edn (Oxford University Press, 2014) 789; Olha O Cherednychenko, 'Freedom of Contract in the Post-Crisis Era: Quo Vadis?' (2014) 10 *European Review of Contract Law* 390.

[52] European Commission, 'Proposal for a Directive of the European Parliament and of the Council on Investment Services and Regulated Markets, and amending Council Directive 85/611/EEC, Council Directive 93/6/EEC and European Parliament and Council Directive 2000/12/EC' COM (2002) 625 final 21.

to address the failure of the precursor ISD[53] to secure a 'bedrock of harmonised investor protection'.[54] The global financial crisis, however, coupled with episodes of mis-selling, challenged the effectiveness of the MiFID I retail investor framework and its ambition to 'build a cohort of informed and competent retail investors'.[55] The incidence of the crisis was further exacerbated by a combination of scarce retail investor participation, an immature retail investment services market, lacking supervisory experience, and the heavy use of ex-post regulatory techniques. Consequently, the EU launched a consultation process for a review of MiFID I,[56] which eventually led to the adoption of the revised MiFID II and the introduction of MiFIR.

The definition of 'retail' investors in the revised MiFID II regime mirrors that contained in MiFID I, which definition does not distinguish between individual and corporate investors, thereby inferring that all investors falling within that 'retail' category are exposed to the same biases and vulnerabilities and, therefore, merit the same level of regulatory protection. From an investor protection perspective, the revised MiFID regime expects more refined levels of knowledge and competence from investment advisors across the EU.[57] Under MiFID II, investment firms must also issue a statement of suitability prior to advising on investment transactions or immediately after the retail investor becomes bound, specifying how the advice given meets the preferences, objectives, and other characteristics of the investor.[58] Such suitability reports must also be updated on a periodic basis where discretionary management services are being provided to retail clients or where the investment firm has informed a particular retail client that it will carry out a periodic suitability assessment.[59] Whilst the criteria for assessment of appropriateness and suitability have not been fundamentally altered,[60] the list of products to be considered de facto 'non-complex', and that hence can be sold to retail investors on an execution-only basis without the need to assess appropriateness, has been restricted.[61]

[53] Niamh Moloney, *EU Securities and Financial Markets Regulation* (3rd edn, Oxford University Press, 2014) 783.

[54] European Commission, 'Proposal for a Directive of the European Parliament and of the Council on Investment Services and Regulated Markets, and amending Council Directive 85/611/EEC, Council Directive 93/6/EEC and European Parliament and Council Directive 2000/12/EC' COM (2002) 625 final 23.

[55] Niamh Moloney, 'Large-Scale Reform of Investor Protection Regulation: The European Union Experience' (2007) 4 *Macquarie Journal of Business Law* 147, 156, 177.

[56] European Commission, 'Proposal for a Directive of the European Parliament and of the Council on Investment Services and Regulated Markets, and amending Council Directive 85/611/EEC, Council Directive 93/6/EEC and European Parliament and Council Directive 2000/12/EC' COM (2002) 625 final.

[57] MiFID II, Recital 79. Investment firms must be able to demonstrate that their knowledge and competence levels meet the minimum criteria to be prescribed by Member States (as required by MiFID II, Recital 82 and Art 25(1)).

[58] ibid Art 25(6).

[59] ibid.

[60] See Section 4.1.1 in relation to suitability and appropriateness assessments under MiFID.

[61] MiFID II, Art 25(4).

MiFID II further expands on the existing MiFID suitability provisions by, inter alia, adding the requirement to assess suitability of the overall package where advice is provided on a package of bundled products or services,[62] as well as providing for the investment firm to remain responsible for the suitability assessment where advice or discretionary management services are offered wholly or partly through an automated or part-automated system.[63] Other revisions centre on stricter governance and organisational requirements, including those relating to product design and distribution;[64] comprehensive presentation and disclosure requirements;[65] and new obligations relating to remuneration packages and sales targets to ensure that these do not create incentives for staff to recommend inappropriate financial instruments to retail investors.[66] MiFID II also introduces the notion of 'independent advice', requiring investment firms to inform investors in advance whether or not the advice is given on an independent basis; is based on a broad analysis of the market (as opposed to a more restricted one); and is limited to a range of financial instruments issued or provided by entities related to the investment firm.[67]

The application of certain MiFID II provisions, including conduct of business rules, has been expanded to also cover structured deposits,[68] which led EU legislators to acknowledge that insurance-based investment products (IBIPs) have similar characteristics to the other financial instruments subject to MiFID and hence investors transacting in IBIPs merit the same level of protection.[69] In order to address this, MiFID II-type restrictions around the marketing and sale of IBIPs, as well as supplementary conduct obligations pertaining to, inter alia, governance and remuneration structures as well as the undertaking of appropriateness and suitability assessments, have also been introduced pursuant to the Insurance Distribution Directive (IDD).[70]

Despite the MiFID II reforms having been described as promoting a 'fresh approach'[71] to retail market regulation, they generally seem to consolidate requirements that investment firms are familiar with through their obligations under the existing domestic investment services regime.[72] In particular, MiFID II reforms in

[62] ibid Art 25(2).

[63] MiFID II Delegated Regulation, Art 54(1).

[64] See eg MiFID II, Art 9(4) and Art 16(3).

[65] MiFID II, Art 24 and Art 27.

[66] ibid Art 24(10).

[67] Investment firms that provide advice on an independent basis must assess a sufficiently large number and diversity of financial instruments available on the market and should not limit the range to instruments issued by the investment firm or related entities (see further MiFID II, Recitals 72–73 and Arts 24(4) and 24(7)(a)).

[68] ibid Recital 39 and Art 1(4).

[69] ibid Recital 87.

[70] The IDD (Directive (EU) 2016/97) replaces the Insurance Mediation Directive (Directive 2002/92/EC, IMD).

[71] Niamh Moloney, *EU Securities and Financial Markets Regulation*, 3rd edn (Oxford University Press, 2014) 835.

[72] See eg FCA, 'Investor protection in the UK: New tools, new challenges' Speech by Maggie Craig (FCA MiFID II Conference, London, 18 September 2014): www.fca.org.uk/news/investor-protection-in-the-uk-new-tools-new-challenges, accessed 6 October 2014 (see also FCA, 'Investor protection

terms of product governance, incentives structures and sales standards, resonate with themes that the FCA had clearly identified pre-MiFID II through its supervisory work as well as through its experience in dealing with mis-selling scandals. Equally, curbs on inducements, provisions on independent advice, tougher product-banning powers, and requirements around product governance, should not feel entirely new to firms operating in the UK. In effect, MiFID II has been described as 'Europe's answer to the RDR'[73] since most of the amendments to the European investment protection regime contain elements of the additional requirements on investment advisers introduced through the RDR initiative, launched by the national regulators in the UK (to be discussed in Section IB below) and the Netherlands, and also considered by Switzerland and Spain.[74]

Notably, the reforms to the MiFID regime do not address the concerns stemming from the distinction between individual and corporate retail investors in common law and statute, the acutely vulnerable position of the latter category of investors when transacting in complex investment products on a non-advised basis, and the ambiguity surrounding the distinction between 'information' and 'investment advice' (discussed further in chapter four). Since MiFID II does not alter the scope of the appropriateness and suitability tests, and neither does it shed further light on the distinction between 'information' and 'investment advice', corporate retail investors remain exposed to mis-selling, particularly where the transaction is contractually classified as 'non-advised'. As a result, the rights of these investors, and consequently the responsibility of investment firms towards them, are restricted.

This suggests that retail investors suffering from over-confidence and over-optimism biases, for example, can still by-pass the protection afforded by the regime at various points. Non-advised services, for instance, enable these investors to access markets without obtaining prior investment advice even when transacting in complex investment products. In the same way as pre-contractual disclosures fail to rationalise investors' decision-making, risk warnings provided to investors that fail the appropriateness test in the context of non-advised sales are also likely to be ineffective. In particular, the standardised nature of the warning limits their effectiveness since it fails to take into account investors' biases, thereby suppressing the validity of any such warnings.[75]

under MiFID II' Speech by David Geale (FCA MiFID II Conference, London, 19 October 2015): www.fca.org.uk/news/investor-protection-under-mifid-ii, accessed 21 October 2015).

[73] Sam Shaw, 'Mifid II: Europe's answer to RDR' (*Money Marketing*, 19 June 2014): www.moneymarketing.co.uk/opinion/more-opinion/mifid-ii-europes-answer-to-rdr/2011229.article, accessed 8 January 2015.

[74] See eg Jennifer G Hill, 'Why did Australia fare so well in the global financial crisis?' in in Eilís Ferran and others (eds), *The Regulatory Aftermath of the Global Financial Crisis* (Cambridge University Press, 2012).

[75] See further ibid 446; Brigitte Haar, 'From public law to private law: market supervision and contract law standards' in Stefan Grundmann and Yeşim M Atamer (eds), *Financial Services, Financial Crisis and General European Contract Law – Failure and Challenges of Contracting* (Kluwer Law International BV, 2011) 267–68.

B. The Retail Distribution Review (RDR)

In 2006, the then FSA launched the RDR as part of its investor protection strategy and in response to persistent cycles of mis-selling and failures to comply with suitability rules. The RDR concerns the advice and distribution of retail investment products, including regulated and unregulated collective investment schemes, life assurance policies with an investment component, all investments in investment trusts schemes, certain types of pensions, and structured investment products. The scope of the RDR also extends to IRHPs since IRHPs fall within the definition of a 'retail investment product'.[76] The RDR applies to all regulated advice and any sales guidance concerning these and related products.

Admittedly, the RDR brought about a fundamental shake-up of the retail investment distribution market.[77] The stated aim of the RDR was that of establishing 'a resilient, effective and attractive retail investment market that consumers can have confidence in and trust at a time when they need more help and advice than ever with their retirement and investment planning'.[78] Seen as a 'once in a generation change to make retail investment markets work better for consumers',[79] the RDR initiative stemmed from regulatory concerns around the perception that there existed considerable confusion among retail investors over what the terms 'advice' and 'independent' actually meant in practice. This ambiguity was exacerbated by the perceived relatively low quality of financial advice and professional standards of those who distributed these products. Given that the solutions proposed by the RDR could result in an increase in the cost of full financial advice, the FSA at the time was also interested in exploring economical ways to deliver simple advice on simple products to a wider audience of retail investors.[80]

The regulatory changes stemming from the RDR focus on several key aspects of the advice and distribution process. In particular, the RDR forces a clear distinction between 'independent' and 'restricted' advice, whilst also raising the minimum qualification standards for advisers. Commission inducements were banned by the RDR and the concept of adviser and consultancy charges was introduced. Furthermore, the RDR seeks to promote the transparency of charges and efficiency in delivering wealth management services. Several RDR reforms are also

[76] The FCA Handbook defines 'retail investment product' as including 'any other designated investment which offers exposure to underlying financial assets, in a packaged form which modifies that exposure when compared with a direct holding in the financial asset'. This is in turn defined to include a contract for difference (CFD) under Art 85 of the Financial Services and Markets Act 2000 (Regulated Activities) Order (RAO), which includes IRHPs.

[77] See further FSA, 'Discussion Paper DP08/5, Consumer Responsibility' (2008); PFS and CII, 'The FSA's Retail Distribution Review: A Background' (2010); and more generally www.fsa.gov.uk/rdr, accessed 31 October 2014.

[78] FCA, 'Post-implementation review of the RDR – Phase 1' (2014) para 1.1.

[79] ibid.

[80] See further FSA, 'Discussion Paper DP08/5, Consumer Responsibility' (2008); PFS and CII, 'The FSA's Retail Distribution Review: A Background' (2010).

reflected in the MiFID II framework, such as those related to adviser charging as well as the requirement to classify advice as independent or otherwise.[81] Fears of a contraction in adviser capacity as a consequence of RDR-related measures have not completely materialised and the remaining advisers are now better-qualified, resulting in a lower level of complaints to the FOS.[82] The RDR is also said to have forced investment advisers 'to engage more intensively with customer-centred suitability, and not merely to treat suitability as a duty that can be discharged by adhering to policies and processes or box-ticking'.[83]

Yet, notwithstanding these positive outcomes, the scope of the RDR has been described as somewhat 'straight-jacketed' in that it 'does not deal with situations outside of the 'investment' context'.[84] Most notably, the RDR is aimed at mitigating conflicts of interest and does nothing to address substantive investor-facing duties in terms of suitability or appropriateness assessments. Further, although IRHPs fall within the scope of the RDR, the RDR does not capture investment services other than those of an advisory nature, and hence does not extend to those transactions that are contractually entered into on a non-advised basis. Accordingly, the RDR initiative does nothing to reduce the exposure of retail investors to the risk of mis-selling where these transact in complex products on a non-advised basis, and neither does it improve the chances of obtaining adequate compensation for financial detriment suffered as a result of such mis-selling. This indicates that comparable initiatives being deployed on a pan-European level, predominantly through the revised MiFID regime, are likely to be similarly limited in coverage and impact.

C. Changes to FCA Powers and Objectives

The FSA 2012 granted a considerable number of new powers to the FCA, enabling it to broaden its reach across the financial services industry as well as position itself on the forefront of early intervention. These powers have been subsumed in the revised FSMA regime and particularly relate to new powers around product intervention (FSMA, s 137D); powers to direct a firm to withdraw or amend misleading financial promotions with immediate effect and publish the fact that it has done so (FSMA, s 137S); and powers to make an early publication of disciplinary action

[81] The RDR rules went significantly further than MiFID I and have, to that extent, gold-plated it. In some areas, MiFID II provisions now go beyond those required under the RDR, eg in relation to the general ban on portfolio managers retaining commission from third parties (MiFID II, Art 24(8)), whilst in exceptional cases, MiFID II allows Member States to maintain additional rules on areas such as inducements and independence where certain criteria can be satisfied (MiFID II, Art 24(12)).

[82] Association of Professional Financial Advisers, 'The Advice Market Post RDR Review' (2014); Europe Economics, 'Retail Distribution Review: post-implementation review' (2014).

[83] Iris H-Y Chiu, 'Does the Retail Distribution Review protect consumers?' (2012) 33 *Company Lawyer* 225, 226.

[84] ibid. Here Chiu argues that the RDR would benefit from an extension in its scope to capture all financially-related advice.

(FSMA, s 391). The FCA also took over the regulation and supervision of consumer credit from the OFT,[85] and acquired new competition powers (FSMA, s 1E).

The change in the FCA's operational objectives following the FSMA reform through the FSA 2012, is equally indicative of a shift in the retail market strategy of the FCA, as it leans towards a more interventionist stance and is less geared towards retail investor empowerment. The former FSA operational objective of fostering public awareness[86] was seen as an attempt to 'recast citizens as proactive and risk-aware consumers of financial services and products', who are keen to participate on the marketplace and who 'accept responsibility' for their investment choices.[87] This was also used as a means of communicating expectations around the *caveat emptor* principle, which holds that consumers should take responsibility for their decisions. The removal of this objective from the FCA's portfolio[88] is indicative of a more focused remit for the FCA which is directed at retail investor protection regulation, without having to also drive initiatives that seek to foster financial capability amongst retail investors.

From a different angle, the recent changes in the SMCR[89] spearheaded by the FCA can likewise be envisaged as an attempt by the regulator to place additional responsibilities on the shoulders of firms, particularly members of senior management. These changes suggest that these individuals should be held accountable for the firms' actions, as well as providing an incentive to prevent mis-selling and enabling regulators to hold individuals to account in the event of mis-selling.[90] Equally, culture and internal governance are being placed under the spotlight, with firms being set to be held up against 'stricter ethical standards'.[91]

Perhaps one of the more significant additions to the FCA's suite of powers is that relating to the use of product intervention tools. One of the main criticisms

[85] This relates to consumer credit activities that were formerly licensable under the Consumer Credit Act 1974 (CCA 1974) and that are now regulated activities under FSMA and supervised by the FCA (since 1 April 2014).

[86] Former FSMA, s 4.

[87] Joanna Gray and Jenny Hamilton, *Implementing Financial Regulation: Theory and Practice* (John Wiley & Sons Ltd, 2006) 47.

[88] The Money Advice Service (MAS) was tasked to take over the public awareness objective from the FCA. The FCA has the statutory responsibility for overseeing the MAS and work closely with this organisation (FSMA, Sch 1A). In the 2016 Budget, the UK Government announced that, following the restructuring of the statutory financial guidance providers, the MAS will be abolished and replaced by a 'new, slimmed down money guidance body' (HM Treasury, 'Budget 2016' (HC 901, 2016) para 2.228).

[89] The SMCR is designed to encourage individual accountability for decision-making in regulated entities, and was implemented by the FCA to reflect the recommendations of the PCBS. The SMCR was introduced in banks in 2016 and is in the process of being rolled out to all FCA-regulated firms.

[90] The new SMCR regime represents a sea-change from the previous Approved Persons Regime (APER), particularly in the light of criminal offence for senior managers, punishable by up to seven years in prison (Financial Services (Banking Reform) Act 2013, s 36), for taking a decision which causes a financial institution to fail, as well as the reversed burden of proof (FSMA, s 66A, as introduced by the Financial Services (Banking Reform) Act 2013, s 66B).

[91] FCA, 'Ethics and Economics' Speech by Martin Wheatley (Worshipful Company of International Bankers, London, 4 March 2014): www.fca.org.uk/news/speeches/ethics-and-economics, accessed 25 February 2016.

of UK regulation has been its perceived 'lack of muscle and sinew',[92] such that it has been described as 'toothless',[93] accused of being based on 'backward-looking mechanistic rules',[94] and blamed for not having recognised that regulation of a more interventionist nature was required. The UK regulator was thus perceived as having misjudged the risks as well as having allowed mis-selling scandals to assume 'vast proportions',[95] as a consequence of slow and inadequate regulatory responses. Against this backdrop, the regulator was keen to revisit its suite of powers, as well as its willingness to use those powers, through a more pre-emptive, forward-looking approach to product regulation. Despite product regulation not being a dominant feature of investment services regulation historically, it now appears to represent 'the high watermark' of post-crisis and post-scandals regulatory resurgence in consumer protection, adopting a 'pre-emptive, paternalistic approach to consumer protection' by imposing 'top-down command and control powers upon the industry'.[96] In this sense, it is considered to have intensified the level of paternalism in regulatory design amidst the existing strong paternalistic elements that have characterised the post-crisis retail investment market.[97] Whilst the extent of intervention can range from softer 'nudges' to outright bans of certain categories of products, the common thread across any form of intervention is the claim that this protective approach improves investors' decision making by reducing errors attributable to cognitive biases and bounded rationality.[98]

A more intrusive style of regulation is thus being utilised by the UK regulator as a tool to direct investors towards products that may be different from the ones they would ordinarily choose if left to decide unaided. Investment firms, on the other hand, may potentially be forced to offer different products which may not necessarily maximise their profits.[99] In this context, product intervention is perceived as 'fundamental to shaping the regulatory philosophy' of the FCA,[100] as it has shown willingness to intervene directly in the market when it identifies situations where the potential for consumer harm is not sufficiently reduced.

[92] FCA, 'Building on experience' Speech by Martin Wheatley (The future of financial services conference, Lansons, London 17 April 2013): www.fca.org.uk/news/speeches/building-experience, accessed 5 May 2015.

[93] ibid.

[94] Joint Committee on the draft Financial Services Bill, *Draft Financial Services Bill* (HL 236 HC 1447, 2010–12) 6.

[95] PCBS, *Changing banking for good: Report of the Parliamentary Commission on Banking Standards, Volume I* (HL Paper 27-I, HC 175-I, 2013) 53.

[96] Mads Andenas and Iris H-Y Chiu, *The Foundations and Future of Financial Regulation: Governance for Responsibility* (Routledge, 2014) 253.

[97] Niamh Moloney, 'Regulating the Retail Markets' in Niamh Moloney, Eilís Ferran, and Jennifer Payne (eds), *The Oxford Handbook of Financial Regulation* (Oxford University Press, 2015) 763–64.

[98] Joshua D Wright and Douglas H Ginsburg, 'Behavioral law and economics: Its origins, fatal flaws, and implications for liberty' (2012) 106 *Northwestern University Law Review* 1033, 1055.

[99] David S Evans, 'Why Now Is Not the Right Time to Revamp Consumer Financial Protection' (2010) (A paper based on remarks made during Panel III at New York University-New York Federal Reserve Conference on Regulating Consumer Financial Products, 6 January 2010) 4.

[100] FSA, 'Discussion Paper DP11/1, Product Intervention' (2011) 3.

In fact, the FCA has begun to 'flex its muscles'[101] in pursuing its more paternalistic agenda through the use of its new powers, as evidenced by, for example, the restrictions issued on the retail distribution of contingent convertible instruments (CoCos);[102] the introduction of price caps on high-cost short-term credit;[103] the ban on opt-out selling across financial services;[104] restrictions imposed around retail binary options and other derivative products;[105] and a potential prohibition of the sale to retail consumers of derivatives referencing certain types of cryptoassets.[106] Notably, other European regulators have also shown interest in pursuing product intervention policies as part of their respective regulatory agendas,[107] and similar powers have likewise been endorsed at EU level.[108]

This form of product intervention has been condemned for potentially introducing 'important tradeoffs … between consumer protection and consumer

[101] Berwin Leighton Paisner LLP, 'Trends in the FCA's use of 'hard' and 'soft' powers' (2015).

[102] FCA, 'Temporary Product Intervention Rules – Restrictions in relation to the retail distribution of contingent convertible instruments' (2014); FCA, 'Consultation Paper CP14/23, Restrictions on the retail distribution of regulatory capital instruments' (2014).

[103] The FCA's duty to make rules restricting charges for high-cost short-term credit has been enacted under FSMA, s 137C, as amended by the Financial Services (Banking Reform) Act 2013, s 131.

[104] FCA, 'Policy Statement PS15/22: General Insurance Add-Ons Market Study – Remedies: banning opt-out selling across financial services and supporting informed decision-making for add-on buyers' (2015).

[105] FCA, 'Consultation Paper CP 16/40, Enhancing conduct of business rules for firms providing contract for difference products to retail clients' (2017) para 4.13; FCA. 'Consultation Paper CP18/37, Product intervention measures for retail binary options' (2018); FCA, 'Consultation Paper CP18/38, Restricting contract for difference products sold to retail clients and a discussion of other retail derivative products' (2018).

[106] FCA, 'Conclusions from the Cryptoassets Taskforce' Speech by Christopher Woolard (The Regulation of Cryptocurrencies event, London, 20 November 2018): www.fca.org.uk/news/speeches/conclusions-cryptoassets-taskforce, accessed 10 February 2019.

[107] See eg actions taken by the Dutch, Belgian, French, Portuguese, German, Irish and Italian regulators to this effect, respectively: AFM, 'Summary Annual Report for 2012' (2012) 4; AFM, 'Central Focus on Client Interests at banks and insurers' (2011); Financial Services and Markets Authority, 'Moratorium on the distribution of particularly complex structured products' (2011); Financial Services and Markets Authority, 'Communication for undertakings that distribute non-mainstream financial products (such as CFD's, binary options, etc.) online' (2014), and 'Regulation of the Financial Services and Markets Authority governing the distribution of certain derivative financial instruments to retail clients' (2016); AMF and ACP, 'Marketing of complex financial instruments' (2010) AMF position no 2010–05 and ACP recommendation no 2010-R-10; CMVM, 'Policy on complex financial products' (2012); BaFIN, 'Consumer protection and regulation – where we stand and what must still be done' Speech by Dr Elke König (BaFin Annual Press Conference, Frankfurt am Main, 20 May 2014): www.bafin.de/SharedDocs/Veroeffentlichungen/EN/Reden/re_140520_jahrespressekonferenz_p_en.html, accessed 11 November 2014; Central Bank of Ireland, 'Consultation on the Protection of Retail Investors in relation to the Distribution of CFDs: Consultation Paper 107' (2017); CONSOB, 'Communication on Distribution of Complex Financial Products to Retail Investors, Communication No 0097996' (2014).

[108] The European Commission first explored extended supervisory powers in its public consultation document on the Review of MiFID (European Commission, 'Public Consultation: Review of the Markets in Financial Instruments Directive (MiFID)' (2010)), wherein it had proposed the introduction of product intervention and product prohibition powers, including powers that would arm the European Commission with the possibility to ban certain investment services activities, products or practices. These proposals were eventually embedded in MiFIR, Arts 42 and 43 on product

choice, between effective regulation to prevent customer detriment and the costs that [it] will inevitably impose',[109] thereby leaving the industry to question the wide discretionary product intervention power afforded to the regulator. The industry has expressed reservations around the regulator's 'licence to intervene',[110] which can be used as a stepping-stone to full-blown product authorisation requirements and which may lead the FCA to regulate the actual design of the product. Equally, academics observed that the new interventionist regime 'carries some risks'[111] and leads one to question substantive issues such as those relating to the enforcement and supervision, resourcing pressures and the level of knowledge and expertise required at the level of national competent authorities (NCAs).

The FCA's powers, under FSMA, s 137E, to make temporary product intervention rules (TPIRs) were also frowned upon by the industry. The FCA is empowered to make TPIRs in order to address exceptional circumstances where urgent product-related issues arise that may cause substantial consumer detriment if not addressed in a timely manner.[112] Such authority has been envisaged to contribute to a blurring of the boundaries between 'soft' supervisory powers and 'hard' enforcement powers, whilst also risking to stifle innovation.[113] Further, it was argued that these powers may not be compatible with the intervention provisions stipulated under MiFID, which may limit swiftness in taking action.[114] In this context, soaring regulatory costs and limited product availability are seen as

intervention. Equally, the FSUG recommended that product regulation be envisaged as a 'principle of financial consumer protection' given that it can directly address and control the characteristics of the products being sold (FSUG, 'Making financial services work for financial users, Paper 1: New model financial regulation' (2012) 4).

[109] FSA, 'Discussion Paper DP11/1, Product Intervention' (2011) 4.

[110] Charlotte Hill and William Maycock, 'Temporary Product Intervention Rules: transient or intransigent?' (*Compliance Monitor*, 1 June 2012): www.compliancemonitor.com/uk-regulation/supervision/temporary-product-intervention-rules-transient-or-intransigent-56259.htm, accessed 1 February 2015.

[111] See eg Niamh Moloney, 'Conduct Rules and Investor Protection: The Evolution of the EU's Approach' in Matthias Casper and others (eds), *Festschrift für Johannes Köndgen* (RWS Vlg Kommunikationsforum, 2016) 409–10.

[112] Product intervention rules made without consultation under FSMA, s 138M are limited to a maximum duration of 12 months (see further FSA, 'Consultation Paper CP12/35, The FCA's use of temporary product intervention rules' (2012)).

[113] See eg Clifford Chance, 'Briefing Note: FSA's Discussion Paper on Product Intervention' (2011); Julian Harris, 'Will the FCA's product intervention strategy work?' (2011) 32 *Company Lawyer* 321; Herbert Smith Freehills LLP, 'Product Intervention: some thoughts on the FCA's interactions with Europe' (2012); Ernst & Young, 'Product Intervention – Consumer Agenda: Global regulatory reform' (2014).

[114] MiFIR, Arts 42 and 43 provide for product intervention powers of ESMA and the EBA in the case of structured deposits. The need to consult and notify ESMA and other NCAs in terms of MiFIR, Art 42(3) could limit rapid temporary product intervention and thus reduce the effectiveness of the exemption from the need to consult provided for under FSMA, s 138M. Hence, since ESMA will be able to take direct action in national markets, overriding any action (or inaction) by the local regulator, this could place investment firms in a difficult position if they are receiving conflicting directions from national and European regulators and may therefore be challenging to implement in practice.

the most significant repercussions brought about by the 'nanny state'[115] created through the use of intervention measures. It has also been observed that intensive intervention as a result of these 'increasingly broad and draconian'[116] powers may be adopted simply to create the impression that the regulator is more in control of the markets and, since product intervention is 'an unwieldy and untested tool', the use of such powers may have unexpected repercussions and may lead to an 'overly ambitious and heavy-handed approach'.[117] The NAO also expressed concern about the FCA still lacking the tools to systematically draw together the aims and success criteria for related interventions, and to evaluate how these fit together. This is perceived by the NAO as potentially giving rise to the risk that interventions are not successful or otherwise badly coordinated, particularly since the FCA measure cannot measure the cost-effectiveness of such measures.[118]

The FCA has attempted to alleviate these concerns by assuring the market that its product intervention tools will be applied 'in an appropriate and proportionate way, taking into account the nature of the investment product, the investment service, and the target market for the product'.[119] It has also announced its plan to introduce a new sourcebook for Product Governance and Product Intervention (PROD), which may, in future, incorporate or replace the existing guidance which is currently contained in the RPPD.[120] This notwithstanding, it is here argued that the FCA's product intervention regime, as applied at present, does not represent a radical shift in the general retail market regulatory design, but it can be described as an 'incremental step'[121] in the FCA's regulatory trajectory, which has recently been leaning towards greater regulatory retail market intervention. The FCA itself has acknowledged this by stating that its new approach to product intervention takes forward its existing approach and should be viewed as 'an evolution of existing standards', which is not likely to require significant change.[122] It is therefore contended here that more radical intervention aimed at tightening investment criteria for retail investors, as well as their eligibility to purchase complex investment products, is desirable.[123]

[115] Adam J Levitin, 'The Consumer Financial Protection Bureau: An Introduction' (2013) 32 *Review of Banking and Financial Law* 321, 336.

[116] Berwin Leighton Paisner LLP, 'Trends in the FCA's use of 'hard' and 'soft' powers' (2015).

[117] Niamh Moloney, 'The legacy effects of the financial crisis on regulatory design in the EU' in Eilís Ferran and others (eds), *The Regulatory Aftermath of the Global Financial Crisis* (Cambridge University Press, 2012) 143, 196.

[118] National Audit Office (NAO), 'Financial services mis-selling: regulation and redress' (HC 851, 2015–16) 6, 21-22. The FCA has welcomed this NAO report and accepted its findings (see further www.fca.org.uk/news/national-audit-office-misselling-report, accessed 2 April 2016).

[119] FCA, 'Consultation Paper CP 16/29, Markets in Financial Instruments Directive II Implementation – Consultation Paper III' (2016) para 13.18.

[120] ibid para 13.19.

[121] Niamh Moloney, 'Regulating the Retail Markets' in Niamh Moloney, Eilís Ferran, and Jennifer Payne (eds), *The Oxford Handbook of Financial Regulation* (Oxford University Press, 2015) 764.

[122] FCA, 'Consultation Paper CP 16/29, Markets in Financial Instruments Directive II Implementation – Consultation Paper III' (2016) para 13.18.

[123] See further ch 7 for recommendations to this effect.

II. The Limitations of the Redress Options Available to Corporate Retail Investors

Prima facie, it may appear that the legal mechanisms for rectifying retail financial damage (such as that brought about by the mis-selling of IRHPs) are wider in the regulatory state relative to conventional private law enforcement measures.[124] Indeed, corporate retail investors are generally perceived to have access to a number of viable routes in claiming compensation for damages suffered as a consequence of mis-selling. Yet, the mis-selling of IRHPs uncovers a 'complex web of interconnected sources'[125] through which corporate retail investors have attempted to obtain redress unsuccessfully. Consequently, once corporate retail investors fall victim to mis-selling, their chances of obtaining adequate redress are slim, irrespective of whether compensation is sought under the regulatory framework or in court.

A. Regulatory Review and Redress Schemes

FSMA, section 404 provides that the FCA may direct investment firms to establish and operate a 'consumer redress scheme', through which consumers are compensated for any damages suffered as a result of compliance failures by regulated entities. In practice, however, the regulator decides on its approach to redress 'on a case-by-case basis', typically by having regard to attributable regulatory failings and the estimated investor detriment.[126] In the case of IRHPs, for example, the then FSA did not opt for the FSMA, section 404 route, but chose to enter into a voluntary agreement with the investment firms involved, in terms of which the latter agreed to carry out a full review of IRHP sales to 'non-sophisticated' investors and award compensation where appropriate. This voluntary agreement was sought pursuant to a pilot review launched by the FSA during 2012 when claims alleging the mis-selling of IRHPs started to surface. This pilot review, which was intended to sample selected IRHP transactions, had uncovered 'serious failings' on the part of investment firms.[127] The structure and conclusions of the full review undertaken pursuant to this voluntary agreement were contested on

[124] Joanna Gray, 'The Legislative Basis of Systemic Review and Compensation for the Mis-Selling of Retail Financial Services and Products' (2004) 25 *Statute Law Review* 196, 198.

[125] Rodrigo Zepeda, 'Derivatives mis-selling by British banks and the failed legacy of the FSA' (2013) 28 *Journal of International Banking Law and Regulation* 209, 211.

[126] National Audit Office (NAO), 'Financial services mis-selling: regulation and redress' (HC 851, 2015–16) 38.

[127] The FSA's pilot review found that 90% of the sampled IRHP sales failed to meet regulatory requirements. Predominantly, these failings included inappropriate sales of the more complex IRHP varieties (such as structured collars) and generally poor sales practices (such as hard-selling and insistence that IRHPs were to be entered into as a condition precedent or subsequent to a loan agreement) (see further FSA, 'Interest Rate Hedging Products Pilot Findings' (2013)).

various counts, including the excessively-restrictive eligibility criteria and the review methodology.

The review was open to investors who, at the date of the IRHP transaction, were classified as either a 'private customer' (for trades on or before 31 October 2007) or a 'retail client' (for trades on or after 1 November 2007), however, these investors were also subjected to a further assessment, known as the 'sophistication test', in order to determine whether they were actually eligible for review or otherwise. This arbitrary sophistication test proved to be a major set-back for a number of corporate retail investors, not least because the criteria adopted by the FSA for the purposes of the sophistication test reflected the test used in section 382 of the Companies Act 2006 to determine whether a company can take advantage of the lighter reporting requirements, rather than the criteria used to distinguish between 'retail' and 'professional' clients under the MiFID regime or, prior to the MiFID regime coming into force, the conditions for classifying an investor as a 'private customer' under the COB. At the time, the FSA justified the use of the Companies Act thresholds by stating that investors who fell within these parameters were 'less likely to have staff or advisers with appropriate knowledge and skills',[128] however, this meant that fewer investors were classified as 'non-sophisticated' than would have been the case had the MiFID thresholds been adopted instead.

In addition, the selected methodology was disputed on the basis that it gave rise to conflicts of interest, particularly since the process was overseen by 'independent reviewers' – namely comprising 'Big Four' audit firms – which had close relationships with the investment firms implicated in the alleged mis-selling. It was also argued that the review process was shrouded in subjectivity as different reviewers adopted different metrics, which meant that the process lacked consistency and the outcome relied primarily on the reviewers' judgment, albeit these having been approved by the FSA.[129] On more than one occasion, corporate retail investors sought judicial review on various parts of the review process, including the said sophistication criteria as well as the decisions of independent reviewers, but were unsuccessful in their attempts. This was the case in a combined judicial

[128] ibid. The original sophistication test provided that the investor would have to pass a quantitative or qualitative test. The quantitative test provided that 'sophisticated' investors would at least meet two of the following criteria: (1) turnover of more than £6.5 million; (2) balance sheet total of more than £3.26 million; and (3) more than 50 employees. These criteria were later amended to suit different types of arrangements, including special purpose vehicles and groups of companies. For the purposes of the qualitative test, an investor could be deemed 'sophisticated' if the investment firm was able to demonstrate that, at the time of the IRHP transaction, and irrespective of the size of the business, the investor had the necessary experience and knowledge to understand the service and the type of product or transaction, including the complexity and risks involved.

[129] See eg Adam Samuel, 'Who is the sophisticated investor?' (*Compliance Monitor*, 10 December 2013): www.compliancemonitor.com/products-and-delivery/client-classification-and-suitability/who-is-the-sophisticated-investor-95038.htm, accessed 12 April 2015; Cat McLean and Neil Morrison, 'Hedges: a financial plague' (2014) 59 *The Journal of the Law Society of Scotland* 20, 21; Lloyd Maynard, 'Holmcroft Properties: will a contractual phoenix rise from its ashes?' (2016) 31 *Journal of International Banking and Financial Law* 356, 356.

review filed by a group of corporate retail investors which had failed to qualify as 'non-sophisticated' asking the court to order the regulator to widen in-scope investors by aligning the criteria underlying the sophistication test to MiFID rules. This review failed the 'sifting process' and, reportedly, claimants were not able to proceed due to lack of funding. Eventually, another judicial review relating to the review process was filed in *R (on the application of Holmcroft Properties Ltd) v KPMG LLP*.[130] The court initially granted permission to judicially review KPMG's assessment, but the application was subsequently dismissed in *R (on the application of Holmcroft Properties Ltd) v (1) KPMG LLP; (2) FCA; (3) Barclays Bank Plc*[131] after the court found that there was no unfairness by the investment firm and also found no basis on which KPMG was to be considered in breach of any regulatory duty. Holmcroft Properties was granted permission to appeal on 23 February 2017,[132] and the Court of Appeal confirmed the conclusions of the Divisional Court, meaning that the decision of the independent reviewer is not amenable to judicial review.[133]

Other claimants argued that investment firms owed them, as their customer, a duty of care in tort in respect of the review process. For example, initially, in *Suremime Ltd v Barclays Bank Plc*,[134] the court had allowed the claimant to amend its case to include new claims in tort in respect of the defendant's conduct of the IRHP review process. The existence of a private law remedy for breaches by the defendant during the review shall now be considered at trial. However, this precedent was not applied in *CGL Group Limited v The Royal Bank of Scotland Plc*[135] and *Elite Property Holdings Ltd and Another v Barclays Bank Plc*,[136] where, in both cases, the court held that no Suremime-type duty of care was owed directly to the investor in connection with past business review, and that any such common law duty would circumvent the existence of a statutory scheme.

More recently, in three conjoined cases on the matter,[137] the Court of Appeal refused permission to appeal to the claimants and decided, particularly on the basis of the tripartite test in *Caparo Industries Plc v Dickman*,[138] that the investment firms do not owe a duty of care to customers.

[130] [2015] EWHC 1888 (Admin).

[131] [2016] EWHC 323 (Admin), [2016] 2 BCLC 545.

[132] Case reference C1/2016/1159.

[133] Judgment reference [2018] EWCA Civ 2093.

[134] [2015] EWHC 2277 (QB).

[135] [2016] EWHC 281 (QB).

[136] [2016] EWHC 3294 (QB).

[137] *(1) CGL Group Limited; (2) Jacqueline Bartels and Adrian Bartels; (3) WW Property Investments Limited v (1) The Royal Bank of Scotland plc and National Westminster Bank plc; (2) Barclays Bank plc; (3) National Westminster Bank plc* [2017] EWCA Civ 1073.

[138] [1990] 2 AC 605 (HL). To determine whether a duty of care exists in relation to an economic loss, the court in *Caparo* set out a three-fold test: (i) the harm must be reasonably foreseeable as a result of the defendant's conduct; (ii) the parties must be in a relationship of proximity; and (iii) it must be fair, just and reasonable to impose liability.

In light of these concerns, and upon the recommendation of the Treasury Committee,[139] the FCA recognised 'the potential merit in conducting a review of how the redress scheme has been operating'[140] in order to restore confidence in the process. It stated that this review will take the form of a 'lessons learned exercise',[141] hence suggesting that it does not intend to re-open and re-adjudicate individual cases. The findings from this assessment are likely to underline the inconsistencies between the definition of 'sophistication' as adopted for the purpose of the review and that applicable under the COB/COBS regime (as defined by the criteria used for classifying investors as 'private' and 'retail' respectively), as well as highlight the lack of apparent logic in adopting the former test.[142] It is submitted here that, had the regulator adopted the COB/COBS criteria in determining the sophistication of IRHP investors, this would not only have helped to ensure consistency in the scope and application of the regulatory perimeter, but would also have avoided costly and futile litigation for most of these corporate retail investors.

The FCA's approach to the IRHP review and redress scheme portrays a somewhat detached approach, particularly when this is compared to its attitude to other mis-selling episodes, chief of which is the PPI scandal. Notwithstanding that the losses experienced by PPI mis-selling victims were far less serious that those attributable to IRHP claimants, the regulator adopted less of an active stance with the IRHP scandal than it did with the PPI debacle.[143] Notwithstanding that investment firms selling IRHPs were equally bound by the then FSA's high-level principles, including that of having due regard to the interests of customers and treating them fairly, the regulator, in the case of IRHPs, limited itself to entering into a voluntary review and redress agreement, and its public reprimands in connection with investment firms involved in IRHP mis-selling were far less heavy-handed than those issued in relation to the mis-selling of PPI. In this context, it is fair to note that PPI mis-selling affected a much larger cohort of individuals, with the risk of damaging public trust in financial institutions, and, hence the FCA must have bowed down to public pressure and put forward its best efforts to ensure that it

[139] Treasury Committee, *Conduct and competition in SME lending* (HC 204, 2015) Eleventh Report para 115.

[140] FCA, 'Response to the Eleventh Report of the Treasury Committee, 2014-15 Conduct and Competition in SME Lending' (2015) para 3.5.

[141] Treasury Committee, *Oral Evidence: Financial Conduct Authority* (HC 515, 2016) response of Tracy McDermott (in her capacity as FCA Acting Chief Executive) to Q338. The timing of this exercise shall depend on the closure of a small number of cases which are still outstanding.

[142] Had the FSA applied the latter test, this would have meant that all corporate investors classified as 'private' or 'retail' investors would have had their IRHP transactions eligible for redress consideration.

[143] By way of example, the measures taken by the FCA in response to the latter incident were increasingly draconian eg, in June 2015, the FCA issued its largest ever retail fine (of £117 million) to Lloyds Bank Plc, Royal Bank of Scotland Plc and Black Horse Ltd for failing to treat customers fairly when handling PPI complaints between March 2012 and May 2013, describing PPI complaint-handling as a 'high priority issue for the FCA' (FCA, 'Lloyds Banking Group fined £117m for failing to handle PPI complaints fairly' (2015): www.fca.org.uk/news/press-releases/lloyds-banking-group-fined-£117m-failing-handle-ppi-complaints-fairly, accessed 4 October 2016).

made it amply clear to service providers, and to society at large, that mis-selling is not acceptable. Further, it is also recognised that, since the mis-selling of IRHPs, the regulatory rulebook, as well as the regulatory approach to supervision and enforcement, have developed to become more interventionist, and, therefore, the regulator was careful not to act retrospectively when handling IRHP claims such that it would not be accused of hindsight bias.

Notwithstanding the above, it is however also true that victims of PPI mis-selling had recourse to other valid redress avenues (which were not available to investors in the case of IRHPs' mis-selling for the reasons explained in this Section) and the losses experienced by individual PPI victims were far less significant than those attributable to corporate retail investors which were mis-sold IRHPs, many of which were driven out of business and remain uncompensated. Indeed, now that the unsatisfactory outcome of IRHP claims has become clear, one notes that this mis-selling episode has equally had consequences for public confidence in investment firms, the regulator and the English courts,[144] and it would have hence merited higher priority from all parties concerned. More importantly, investment firms selling IRHPs were, at the time of sale, still bound to follow a robust regulatory framework, which the regulator failed to enforce in the same way that it did with PPI. This thus brings to the fore the practical distinction which the regulator makes between different categories of retail investors, suggesting that individual retail investors (including victims of PPI mis-selling) are more worthy of regulatory protection that their corporate counterparts (such as those investors which were mis-sold IRHPs).

B. The Financial Ombudsman Service (FOS)

The FOS was set up to resolve disputes between consumers and financial services providers,[145] after taking over from a number of pre-existing (mainly voluntary) schemes.[146]

Having been established as an informal alternative to the Civil Courts, the FOS takes a different approach to resolving disputes. Unlike the court system, it adopts an 'inquisitorial' approach which enables it to ask questions and obtain additional facts on a case as it deems relevant, rather than concentrating exclusively on matters presented to it, and need not determine a complaint in accordance with

[144] See further ch 5 for further discussion on the role of English courts in IRHP mis-selling as well as an assessment of case-law on IRHP mis-selling.

[145] FSMA, Part XVI provides for the setting up of an Ombudsman Scheme.

[146] These included The Banking Ombudsman, The Building Societies Ombudsman, The Insurance Ombudsman Scheme, The Personal Insurance Arbitration Services, the FSA's complaints handling services, The Personal Investment Authority Ombudsman, the SFA complaints and arbitration services, and The Investment Ombudsman (see further House of Commons, *Common Financial Services Questions* (2016) Briefing Paper No 07262, 14).

common law.[147] The FOS does not limit itself to considering merely the issues that the complainant would have highlighted in his complaint but seeks to supplement these statements by soliciting information from the parties in the course of the dispute where it considers it appropriate to do so. The decisions of the FOS are based on what it considers 'fair and reasonable in all the circumstances of the case',[148] taking also into account relevant laws and regulations; rules, guidance and standards promulgated by the regulator; codes of practice; and what the FOS considers to have been good industry practice at the time of the occurrence of the event being complained about.[149]

An award granted by the FOS under FSMA, section 229(2) is not linked to the amount of the respondent's liability to the complainant, but to an amount that the FOS considers as 'fair compensation for loss or damage'. The rules of the FOS may, inter alia, 'specify matters which are to be taken into account in determining whether an act or omission was fair and reasonable',[150] which 'matters' would not necessarily emulate those that are typically taken into account in determining liability for negligence or breach of contract or statutory duty under the common law. This approach is consistent with the expressed object of the statutory provisions establishing the FOS, which is to create 'a scheme under which certain disputes may be resolved quickly and with minimum formality by an independent person'.[151]

Given its expeditious and practical approach to adjudication, the FOS presents itself as a 'cheaper, less formal alternative to the courts'.[152] Its legitimacy has also been acknowledged by English courts, having described the FOS as a 'much more informal, and much more economical kind than pursuing, without the kind of resources which the banks have expensive proceedings in the High Court'.[153] Yet, recourse to the FOS has proven to be particularly restrictive in the context of IRHP mis-selling on two counts. First, until 31 March 2019, only individuals, 'micro-enterprises', and certain charities or trustees had the right to bring complaints to the FOS;[154] since 1 April 2019, access to the FOS has been extended

[147] In *R (on the application of Heather Moor & Edgecomb Limited v The Financial Ombudsman Service and Simond Lodge (Interested Party)* [2008] EWCA Civ 642, [2008] Bus LR 1486 [34]-[41], it was confirmed that the FOS is free to depart from common law rules relating to advice that is alleged to have been negligent or unsuitable.

[148] FSMA, s 228(2).

[149] DISP 3.6.4.

[150] FSMA, Sch 17 para 14(2)(a).

[151] FSMA, s 225(1).

[152] FCA, 'Discussion Paper DP15/7, Our approach to SMEs as users of financial services' (2015) para 1.14.

[153] *Templars Estates Ltd and Others v National Westminster Bank and The Royal Bank of Scotland Plc* [2016] EWHC 2020 (Comm) [8].

[154] At the time of the IRHP mis-selling scandals, in terms of the then DISP 2.7.3, only private individuals, 'micro-enterprises' (entities having an annual turnover of less than €2 million and fewer than 10 employees), a charity with an annual income of less than £1 million at the time the complainant refers the complaint to the respondent, and a trustee of a trust with a net asset value of less than £1 million at the time the complainant refers the complaint to the respondent, could bring complaints to the FOS.

to 'small businesses', defined as those enterprises having an annual turnover below £6.5 million and fewer than 50 employees or an annual balance sheet below £5 million.[155] Secondly, the maximum monetary compensation that the FOS could award to a claimant at the time of the IRHP mis-selling scandals was capped at £150,000 (£100,000 for complaints received before 1 January 2012) in terms of the then DISP 3.7.4. The compensation limits have also been revisited upwards such that for complaints referred to the FOS on or after 1 April 2019, the maximum amount of compensation that the FOS can require investment firms to pay out has increased from £150,000 to £350,000.[156] The limitations around access to the FOS, even following the confirmed and proposed amendments to the FOS' jurisdiction, mean that a number of corporate retail investors are either precluded from raising complaints to the FOS because they do not meet the eligibility criteria[157] or otherwise will not be able to claim the full extent of their loss since the damage suffered exceeds the said maximum pay-out.[158]

C. The Private Right of Action Under FSMA, Section 138D

Aggrieved corporate retail investors also attempted to enforce the statutory right of action set out under FSMA, section 138D (formerly FSMA, s 150) in an effort to recover losses sustained as a consequence of having been mis-sold an IRHP.

FSMA, section 138D(2) provides that:

> A contravention by an authorised person of a rule made by the FCA is actionable at the suit of a private person who suffers loss as a result of the contravention, subject to the defences and other incidents applying to actions for breach of statutory duty.

The provisions giving rise to such actionability are determined both by statute and by the regulator.[159]

[155] FCA, 'Policy Statement PS18/21, SME access to the Financial Ombudsman Service – near-final rules' (2018); FCA, 'Policy Statement PS19/8, Increasing the award limit for the Financial Ombudsman Service' (2019) (see also amended DISP 2.7.3).

[156] FCA, 'Consultation Paper CP18/31, Increasing the award limit for the Financial Ombudsman Service' (2018); FCA, 'Policy Statement PS19/8, Increasing the award limit for the Financial Ombudsman Service' (2019) (see also amended DISP 3.7.4).

[157] Indeed, the revised eligibility criteria which took effect from 1 April 2019 are still far more restrictive than the SME definition adopted by the EU and the thresholds applied by the MiFID regime to distinguish between professional and retail investors.

[158] Claimants' individual losses linked to IRHP transactions typically ranged between £181,000 and £921,000. This notwithstanding, it is acknowledged that, should the claimant be entitled to claim in the first place, the higher pay-out which has become possible from 1 April 2019 would have at least resulted in the claimant being potentially entitled to a redress equivalent to a significant portion of the losses suffered.

[159] FSMA, s 138D ss (2) and (3) provide that FCA rules are actionable unless the FCA determines otherwise and Sch 5 to the COBS sets out which rules give rise to actionability. The court in *R (British Bankers' Association) v (1) Financial Services Authority and (2) The Financial Ombudsman Service; (3) Nemo Personal Finance Ltd (Interested Party)* [2011] EWHC 999 (Admin), [2011] Bus LR 1531 confirmed that the FCA has the discretion to decide whether breach of a particular rule is actionable

In principle, and in order to establish a contravention, the following criteria must be satisfied: (1) the nature and extent of the duty need to be determined by interpreting the relevant regulatory rule; (2) the claimant must meet the definition of 'private person' (as defined below); and (3) the rule, as a matter of interpretation, must seek to protect this 'private person'.

A 'private person' is defined under Regulation 3 of the Financial Services and Markets Act 2000 (Rights of Action) Regulations 2001 (Rights of Action Regulations) as: 'any individual, unless he suffers the loss in question in the course of carrying on any regulated activity or any activity which would be a regulated activity',[160] as well as 'any person who is not an individual, unless he suffers the loss in question in the course of carrying on business of any kind', to the exclusion of governments, local authorities (in the UK or elsewhere) and international organisations. FSMA, section 138D(4) further provides that a contravention of a rule which would be actionable at the suit of a private person is also actionable at the suit of a person who is not a private person where any of the criteria set out in Regulation 6(3) of the Rights of Action Regulations apply. These criteria comprise the following:

a) the rule that has been contravened prohibits an authorised person from seeking to make provisions excluding or restricting any duty or liability;
b) the rule that has been contravened is directed at ensuring that transactions in any security or contractually based investment (within the meaning of the RAO) are not effected with the benefit of unpublished information that, if made public, would be likely to affect the price of that security or investment;
c) the action would be brought at the suit of a person (who is not a private person) acting in a fiduciary or representative capacity on behalf of a private person and any remedy would be exclusively for the benefit of that private person and could not be effected through an action brought otherwise than at the suit of the fiduciary or representative.

In attempting to pursue a right of action under FSMA, section 138D corporate retail investors claimed that they fell within the scope of the definition of a 'private person' in terms of Regulation 3 of the Rights of Action Regulations by virtue of the fact that investing was not part of their day-to-day business activities, and that they only invested on a sporadic and ad hoc basis. This line of argumentation was considered by the High Court alongside the Rights of Action Regulations in the landmark case of *Titan Steel Wheels Ltd v The Royal Bank of Scotland Plc*.[161] In providing its interpretation of the phrase 'in the course of carrying on business of any kind', the court distinguished the purpose of the Rights of Action Regulations

or not. The statute itself (FSMA, s 138D(5)) explicitly excludes certain rules from the actionability provision.

[160] The definition omits any exclusion made by RAO, Art 72 (overseas persons).

[161] [2010] EWHC 211 (Comm), [2010] 2 Lloyd's Rep 92. In *Titan* the claimant alleged that it had suffered damages as a result of the mis-selling of two currency swap products by the defendant.

from other contexts wherein the courts may consider a diverse range of factors to determine whether the activity can be considered as part of the claimant's business or otherwise.[162] In so doing, it observed that the wording of the Rights of Action Regulations specifically included the words 'of any kind', as opposed to merely stopping at 'in the course of business',[163] which meant that the exclusion was to be interpreted broadly to include any corporate entity who may have sustained losses as a result of purchasing investment products, provided that it is in a business of some kind.[164] As a consequence, any such entity would fall outside the definition of private person and would therefore not be entitled to pursue a private action under FSMA, section 138D. The determination of the court in *Titan* set a precedent that was followed by the courts in similar mis-selling cases.[165]

The scope of the Rights of Action Regulations was also challenged from a different perspective to that of *Titan*. In *Bailey*, for example, the claimant referred to Regulation 6(3)(a) of the Rights of Action Regulations to argue that the defendant sought to limit or exclude its duties under the regulatory system by including non-reliance provisions in the standard terms of business, thus breaching COBS 2.1.2(R) (exclusion of liability)[166] and the related guidance under COBS 2.1.3(G).[167] Whilst noting that the claimant's case on breach of COBS 2.1.2(R) was 'obscure',[168] the court found that the terms themselves did not purport to exclude liability under the regulatory system and the court was not persuaded that there was any 'reasonably arguable'[169] allegation of breach of the rules contained in the COBS,

[162] These factors may include the regularity of trades, whether the trades were an integral part of the company's business, and, where there was only one trade, whether the trade was a one-off trade with a view to profit, which would suggest it was carrying out business (see eg *Davies v Sumner* [1984] 1 WLR 1301 (HL); *R&B Customs Brokers v United Dominion Trust* [1988] 1 WLR 321 (CA, Civ Div); *Pensher Security Door Company Limited v Sunderland City Council* [2000] RPC 249 (CA, Civ Div)).

[163] eg, as specified in the former Trade Descriptions Act 1968, s 1(1)(a) and the Unfair Contract Terms Act 1977 (UCTA), s 12(1).

[164] Steel J, in *Titan* [70], contrasted these entities with charities and similar bodies, describing the latter as 'more obvious exceptions' and which would therefore fall within the definition of 'private person'.

[165] See eg *JP Morgan Chase Bank and Others v Springwell* [2008] EWHC 1186 (Comm), affd [2010] EWCA Civ 1221, [2010] 2 CLC 705; *Camerata Property Inc v Credit Suisse Securities (Europe) Ltd* [2011] EWHC 479 (Comm), [2011] 2 BCLC 54; *Grant Estates Ltd and Others v The Royal Bank of Scotland Plc and Others* [2012] CSOH 133, 2012 GWD 29-588; *Green and Rowley*; *Nextia Properties Limited v (1) The Royal Bank of Scotland Plc; (2) National Westminster Bank Plc* [2013] EWHC 3167 (QB); *(1) Mark Thomas Raymond Bailey; (2) MTR Bailey Trading Limited v Barclays Bank Plc* [2014] EWHC 2882 (QB); *Crestsign Ltd v (1) National Westminster Bank Plc; (2) The Royal Bank of Scotland Plc* [2014] EWHC 3034 (Ch), [2015] 2 All ER (Comm) 133; *Thornbridge Ltd v Barclays Bank Plc* [2015] EWHC 3430 (QB); *Suresh Sivagnanam v Barclays Bank Plc* [2015] EWHC 3985 (Comm).

[166] COBS 2.1.2(R) states that: 'A firm must not, in any communication relating to designated investment business, seek to: (1) exclude or restrict; or (2) rely on any exclusion or restriction of; any duty or liability it may have to a client under the regulatory system'.

[167] COBS 2.1.3(G)(1) states that: 'In order to comply with the client's best interests rule, a firm should not, in any communication to a retail client relating to designated investment business: (a) seek to exclude or restrict; or (b) rely on any exclusion or restriction of; any duty or liability it may have to a client other than under the regulatory system, unless it is honest, fair and professional for it to do so.'

[168] *Bailey* [46].

[169] ibid [49].

rendering the issue irrelevant. The claimant company applied for permission to appeal, and permission was granted for the Court of Appeal to consider the restriction on companies generally in bringing a right of action for damages under FSMA, section 138D within the context of this case. An appeal hearing was listed to commence in early July 2016, but the case was settled shortly before then, in what can be seen as an effort by investment firms to preserve the *Titan* precedent.

The current position at law (as also supported by relevant court judgments) is, therefore, that corporate retail investors engaged in any kind of business are excluded from the definition of 'private person' and any attempt by an individual, who had chosen to invest through a corporate vehicle, 'to pierce the veil of his own company'[170] is not acceptable. The corporate entity is ultimately deemed to be the investor and not the individuals it is fronting. The circumstances set out Regulation 6(3) of the Rights of Action Regulations are equally of limited relevance to corporate retail investors since the matters contemplated therein would have either been exhausted in court,[171] are irrelevant in the context of mis-selling cases,[172] or are otherwise intrinsically linked to natural persons.[173] Collectively, therefore, the restrictions contained in this statutory right and the English courts' interpretation of its scope, are likewise unhelpful to corporate retail investors as a means of securing financial redress.

D. English Courts' Reverence to the Rule of Law: The Principles of 'Freedom to Contract' and 'Legal Certainty'

When engaging in investment transactions, retail investors are often faced with what is defined as a 'standard form contract' (or 'adhesion contract')[174], the terms of which investors have to either accept as presented without any prospect of negotiation, or otherwise opt not to enter into the contractual relationship (although in most cases this is not always a feasible alternative). Through these types of contracts, which have become commonplace and which were also used with IRHPs, investment firms attempt to hedge their risks and responsibilities by using excessive 'small print' exclusion clauses and qualifications. By consenting

[170] *Diamantis Diamantides v JP Morgan Chase Bank and Others* [2005] EWHC 263 (Comm), affd [2005] EWCA Civ 1612 [28]. The 'piercing the corporate veil' doctrine was re-assessed by the Supreme Court in *Prest v Petrodel Resources Ltd* [2013] UKSC 34, [2013] 2 AC 415, wherein it undertook a review of the principles of English law which determine in what circumstances, if any, a court may set aside the separate legal personality of a company from its members and attribute to its members the legal consequences of the company's acts. The Supreme Court's conclusions in the *Prest* case do not, however, cast doubt on the validity of the court's conclusions in the *Diamantides* case insofar as they relate to matters discussed in the context of this book.

[171] Rights of Action Regulations, Reg 6(3)(a).

[172] ibid Reg 6(3)(b).

[173] ibid Reg 6(3)(c).

[174] Anthony T Kronman, 'Paternalism and the Law of Contracts' (1983) 92 *The Yale Law Journal* 763, 770–71.

to these terms, the adhering party normally confirms that it has not relied on any representations save for those expressly set out in the contract and accepts that the drafter limits potential liability for pre-contractual representations.[175] Underpinning the judicial support for such clauses are the traditional foundations of English contract law, primarily revolving around the notions of contractual freedom and legal certainty, as discussed in turn hereunder.

Whilst still seeking to protect investors from any unfair business practices, English contract law largely follows the guiding principle of contractual freedom, which enables contracting parties to agree on any arrangement which best fits their needs. In this spirit, English law adopts a literal interpretation to the construction of contracts, setting clear limits on 'commercial common sense', which 'should not be invoked to undervalue the importance of the language of the provision which is to be construed'.[176] More specifically, the basic aim of contractual interpretation under the English common law system is objectively to determine the intention of the parties by reference to 'what a reasonable person having all the background knowledge which would have been available to the parties would have understood them to be using the language in the contract to mean',[177] hence deriving all consequences of the contract from the will and intentions of the contracting parties as evidenced by the terms of the contract. By contrast, civil law jurisdictions often have recourse to rules and, rather than enquiring on the terms agreed to by the parties, as would be the case in a common law jurisdictions, civil law regimes will primarily query the type of contract entered into by the parties.[178] In particular, certainty and fairness tend to be treated significantly differently, as common law jurisdictions traditionally promote 'certainty over flexibility … and individualism over community',[179] whilst their civil law counterparts place a stronger emphasis on fairness. Contractarians thus advocate that the common law principles should remain *jus dispositivum*, in that legislation should be delegated to contracting parties and its concepts applied in line with the intentions of those parties.[180]

[175] Nelson Goh, 'Non-reliance clauses and contractual estoppel: corporately sensible or anomalous?' (2015) 7 *Journal of Business Law* 511, 511.

[176] *Arnold v Britton and Others* [2015] UKSC 36, [2015] AC 1619 [17].

[177] *Chartbrook Ltd v Persimmon Homes Ltd* [2009] UKHL 38, [2009] 1 AC 1101 [14].

[178] See further Barry Nicholas, 'Rules and Terms – Civil Law and Common Law' (1973–1974) 48 *Tulane Law Review* 946; Sir George Leggatt, 'Making sense of contracts: the rational choice theory' (2015) 131 *Law Quarterly Review* 454. See also relevant case law, eg, *Davis Contractors Ltd v Fareham Urban District Council* [1956] UKHL 3, [1956] AC 696; *Investors Compensation Scheme Ltd v West Bromwich Building Society* [1999] Lloyd's Rep PN 496 (Ch); *Bank of Credit and Commerce International SA (in Compulsory Liquidation) v Munawar Ali and Others* [2001] UKHL 8, [2002] 1 AC 251; *Napier Park European Credit Opportunities Fund Ltd v Harbourmaster Pro-Rata CLO 2 BV* [2014] EWCA Civ 984.

[179] Elaine A Welle, 'Freedom of Contract and the Securities Laws: Opting Out of Securities Regulation by Private Agreement' (1999) 56 *Washington and Lee Law Review* 519, 521 (see also Jeremy Bentham, *The Works of Jeremy Bentham* published under the Superintendence of his Executor, John Bowring (William Tait 1838–1843) iii, 33).

[180] Friedrich Kessler, 'Contracts of Adhesion – Some Thoughts About Freedom of Contract' (1943) 43 *Columbia Law Review* 629, 629.

Hence, the contract is envisaged as a 'private affair',[181] and not a 'social institution',[182] which is to be 'held sacred'[183] and enforced accordingly by the courts.

Commercial parties in particular (including corporate retail investors) are viewed by the English legal system as 'creatures of contract',[184] which can freely shape their own contractual terms without interference. Regulation purporting to restrict the contractual freedom of parties is thus perceived as the 'born enem[y]'[185] of common law systems founded on party autonomy. Consequently, investor protection regulation is considered to be 'mostly superfluous'[186] and indeed 'generally counter-productive',[187] as well as being an undesirable departure from the 'time-honoured'[188] principle of caveat emptor. Investors are seen to be adequately protected through the operation of the market and any intervention is believed to distort the ability of the market to self-regulate. In this sense, the process of private contracting becomes a form of 'self-regulation',[189] as contracting parties act as the source of rules, monitor each other's compliance, and self-enforce the terms contained therewith. Contractual freedom is also believed to promote 'the underlying ethic of self-interest and self-reliance',[190] suggesting that the maximisation of one's own interests fosters freedom amongst investment firms to achieve their business goals, while investors are left to rely on disclosures, as well as their own judgement, in making complex investment decisions.

It follows, therefore, that, barring limited exceptions such as fraudulent activity,[191] the position prevailing under common law holds that a party to an executed contract is bound by such contract, whether he has read and understood it before signing or otherwise. Under this 'arm's-length narrative'[192] freedom of

[181] ibid 630.

[182] ibid.

[183] ibid 631.

[184] Elaine A Welle, 'Freedom of Contract and the Securities Laws: Opting Out of Securities Regulation by Private Agreement' (1999) 56 *Washington and Lee Law Review* 519, 526.

[185] Johannes Köndgen, 'Policy responses to credit crisis: does the law of contract provide the answer' in Stefan Grundmann and Yeşim M Atamer (eds), *Financial Services, Financial Crisis and General European Contract Law – Failure and Challenges of Contracting* (Kluwer Law International BV, 2011) 38.

[186] Colin Scott and Julia Black, *Cranston's Consumers and the Law*, 3rd edn (Butterworths, 2000) 26.

[187] Joanna Benjamin, 'The Narratives of Financial Law' (2010) 30 *Oxford Journal of Legal Studies* 787, 793.

[188] HMSO, *Financial Services in the UK: A New Framework for Investor Protection* (Cmnd 9432, 1985) para 3.4.

[189] Hugh Collins, *Regulating Contracts* (Oxford University Press Inc, 1999) 63, 66–67.

[190] Chris Willett, 'General clauses and the competing ethics of European consumer law in the UK' (2012) 71 *Cambridge Law Journal* 412, 415.

[191] Where fraudulent misrepresentation can be shown, very different principles would apply and the courts would not allow a party who has committed fraud to escape liability by reliance on contractual terms (see eg *UBS AG (London Branch) and Another v Kommunale Wasserwerke Leipzig GmbH* [2014] EWHC 3615 (Comm)).

[192] Joanna Benjamin, 'The Narratives of Financial Law' (2010) 30 *Oxford Journal of Legal Studies* 787, 792–97.

contract therefore maintains a 'privileged position'[193] such that risk-takers who are unsuccessful in their business dealings are generally held responsible for their losses, however ruinous and unfair the agreement might have been in the first place – in other words, 'they should have known better'.[194] To this end, English courts have typically sought to facilitate private contracting and promote economic efficiency by adopting 'a more conservative, classical, conceptualist approach that emphasizes freedom of contract and marketplace economies'.[195] Most notably, English courts have not shown any particular interest for softer nuances underlying the transaction (such as verbal communications between the parties), but have 'knelt down and worshipped … the idol, "freedom of contract"'.[196]

The notion of contractual freedom is supported by another key element of English contract law – legal certainty – which is considered to facilitate business activity and to ensure that contracts are enforced by the court so as to 'prevent disappointment of well-founded expectations'.[197] Since predictability is critical to any legal system, the courts rely on contractual terms to eliminate, or at least reduce, uncertainty, as well as to allocate the respective risks and responsibilities between parties. In other words, the courts draw upon the legal certainty 'that results from being able to consult the black and white terms of properly executed legal documentation'.[198] When a written agreement is validly entered into, this would generally enhance certainty if the legal system pursued a literal interpretation of the wording and prevented the parties from relying on rights and obligations not set out in the written contract.[199] It follows, therefore, that the notions of legal certainty and predictability suggest that it is not the role of the law to specify in detail, or otherwise guide, the parties' corporate behaviour but, rather, the law

[193] Aurelia Colombi Ciacchi, 'Freedom of contract as freedom from unconscionable contracts' in Mel Kenny, James Devenney, and Lorna Fox O'Mahony (eds), *Unconscionability in European Private Financial Transactions: Protecting the Vulnerable* (Cambridge University Press, 2010) 8.

[194] Joanna Benjamin, 'The Narratives of Financial Law' (2010) 30 *Oxford Journal of Legal Studies* 787, 793.

[195] Elaine A Welle, 'Freedom of Contract and the Securities Laws: Opting Out of Securities Regulation by Private Agreement' (1999) 56 *Washington and Lee Law Review* 519, 524.

[196] *George Mitchell (Chesterhall) Ltd v Finney Lock Seeds Ltd* [1983] QB 284, 297.

[197] Thomas E Holland, *Elements of Jurisprudence*, 12th edn (Oxford University Press, 1917) 262. In a similar vein, Goodhart speaks about the 'moral basis of contract', whereby 'the promisor has by his promise created a reasonable expectation that it will be kept' (AL Goodhart, *Hamlyn Lectures: English Law and the Moral Law* (Stevens & Sons Ltd, 1953) 10). See also Iain MacNeil, 'Uncertainty in commercial law' (2009) 13 *Edinburgh Law Review* 68, 69.

[198] Stevie Loughrey and Charles Enderby Smith, 'Banking litigation: a changing landscape?' (2015) 9 *Journal of International Banking and Financial Law* 563, 565.

[199] In *Arnold* [108], eg, the Supreme Court observed that the approach to the interpretation of contracts should not be one that creates tension between the words chosen by parties to express their bargain and the court's view of the underlying corporate objective. The judgment emphasised that the interpretation should focus on the former. In *Wood v Capita Insurance Services Ltd* [2017] UKSC 24 [11]–[12], which is the latest determination of the Supreme Court on contractual interpretation, the court did not seek to drastically depart from its conclusions in *Arnold*, but emphasised that both the factual background and implications of rival constructions (namely business common sense) should be closely examined to balance the indications given by each.

should limit itself to creating 'an outer limit on what will not be tolerated'.[200] To this effect, any attempt to use the legal system to reallocate market losses or undo the contractual loss allocation agreed upon *a priori* between commercial parties, will not be accepted lightly by the courts.[201]

The quest for legal certainty also means that the concept of 'equity' has no place in commercial transactions. English contract law demonstrates 'hostility to equity',[202] and equity principles are resisted on the basis that their influence would prejudice legal certainty together with the security of commercial transactions.[203] English courts, particularly in contractual commercial transactions, look towards certain and fixed principles of law, rather than being dependent upon rules and constructions of equity. The latter tend to be regarded as 'arbitrary and uncertain', and largely dependent 'upon the will and caprice of the judge'.[204]

The principles of legal certainty and contractual freedom underpinning the English common law system have proven to be an insuperable obstacle for corporate retail investors pursuing their case through civil litigation. By invoking the notions of legal certainty and contractual freedom, English courts have adhered strictly to the terms contained in standard form contracts and consequently concluded that, based on the non-reliance clauses contained therein, investment firms had not assumed any responsibility towards investors. To this end, the 'signature rule'[205] is enforced to ensure that, once the terms are signed, the parties are bound by the terms of the contract, clearly indicating that the role of the courts is limited to interpreting contracts but not making them.[206] The interplay of these

[200] Hugh Beale, 'The Impact of the Decisions of the European Courts on English Contract Law: The Limits of Voluntary Harmonization' (2010) 18 *European Review of Private Law* 501, 521 (see also Joanne Scott and Susan Strum, 'Courts as Catalysts: Re-Thinking the Judicial Role in New Governance' (2006) 13 *Columbia Journal of European Law* 565).

[201] Joanna Gray, 'Legal Commentary: *Titan Steel Wheels Ltd v Royal Bank of Scotland Plc*' (2010) *18 Journal of Financial Regulation and Compliance* 293, 300 (see also *Arnold* and *Wood*).

[202] Patrick S Atiyah, *The Rise and Fall of Freedom of Contract* (Clarendon Press, 1979) 398.

[203] Peter Millett, 'Equity's Place in the Law of Commerce' (1998) 114 *Law Quarterly Review* 214, 214.

[204] John J Powell, *Essay upon the Law of Contracts and Agreements* (J Johnson and T Whieldon, 1790) x.

[205] The roots of the 'signature rule' can be traced back to sixteenth century litigation in *Browning v Beston* [1555] 75 ER 202 (KB) and *L'Estrange v Graucob* [1934] 2 KB 394, 403, where Scrutton LJ stated that when a contract is signed, and in the absence of fraud or misrepresentation, 'the party signing the contract is bound and it is wholly immaterial whether he has read the document or not'. Since then, English courts have confirmed its validity in a number of more recent mis-selling-related judgments.

[206] Exceptions to the general principle that a party is bound by their signature arise where the party is found to have a lack of understanding due to 'defective education, illness, or innate incapacity' (see eg *Saunders (Executrix of the Will of Rose Maud Gallie, Decd) v Anglia Building Society* [1970] UKHL 5, [1971] AC 1004, 1); where the party is induced to sign the document as a result of misrepresentation (see eg *Curtis v Chemical Cleaning & Dyeing Co Ltd* [1951] 1 KB 805); where the document was not intended to have contractual effects (see eg *Grogan v Robin Meredith Plant Hire* [1996] CLC 1127 (CA, Civ Div)); where there exist collateral contracts made between the parties which can override or change certain clauses in the main contract (see eg *City and Westminster Properties (1934) Ltd v Mudd* [1959] Ch 129); and where the court concludes that an overriding oral warranty was made which prevails over the written document (see eg *J Evans & Sons (Portsmouth) Ltd v Andrea Merzario Ltd* [1976] 1 WLR 1078 (CA, Civ Div)).

elements places corporate retail investors at a disadvantage and further restricts their chances of successfully arguing their case in court. In fact, IRHP mis-selling case law has brought to the fore the extent to which common law judicial reasoning is influenced by strong individualistic values,[207] which has meant that corporate retail investors were left at the mercy of the 'chill winds of the common law',[208] as the free will of the more powerful contracting parties was vindicated in the pursuit of 'freedom, fairness and equity'[209] and all the consequences emanating from the contract were attributed 'to the will of those who made it'.[210] In its pure form, English contract law is therefore 'blind to details of subject matter and person',[211] completely uninterested in substantive justice or fairness.[212] In this sense, freedom of contract is seen as a counterparty of free enterprise,[213] and operates to the detriment of corporate retail investors.

English courts' interest in promoting contractual freedom and legal certainty can be traced back to a history of cases predominantly concerning commercial transactions characterised by high value contracts between sophisticated and well-advised parties.[214] Yet, whereas the traditional notions of freedom to contract, sanctity of contract, and self-reliance might be seen as plausible in the presence of these elements, the nature of the cases brought before the courts in recent years, chief amongst which those dealing with the alleged mis-selling of complex investment products such as IRHPs, is clearly distinct. Increasingly, unsophisticated and vulnerable counterparties are pursuing transactions that are too complex for them to comprehend due to their restricted knowledge, experience and risk tolerance, whilst also being 'compelled to accept disadvantageous terms dictated by businesses'[215] without having the time and resources to read and understand the terms, and without being given the opportunity question or negotiate the contents.

[207] Chris Willett, 'General clauses and the competing ethics of European consumer law in the UK' (2012) 71 *Cambridge Law Journal* 412, 431.

[208] Ewan McKendrick, *Contract Law*, 3rd edn (Oxford University Press, 2007) 789.

[209] Vera Bolgár, The Contract of Adhesion – A Comprehension of Theory and Practice' (1972) 20 *The American Journal of Comparative Law* 53, 78.

[210] Patrick S Atiyah, *The Rise and Fall of Freedom of Contract* (Clarendon Press, 1979) 405.

[211] Lawrence M Friedman, *Contract Law in America* (University of Wisconsin Press, 1965) 20.

[212] Patrick S Atiyah, *The Rise and Fall of Freedom of Contract* (Clarendon Press, 1979) 402. In this context, the application of the parol evidence rule has been said to promote certainty 'sometimes even at the expense of justice' (Sir Guenter Treitel, *The Law of Contract*, 11th edn (Sweet & Maxwell Ltd, 2003) 194).

[213] See eg Patrick S Atiyah, *The Rise and Fall of Freedom of Contract* (Clarendon Press, 1979) 112–38, 226–31, 398–405.

[214] Hugh Beale, 'The Impact of the Decisions of the European Courts on English Contract Law: The Limits of Voluntary Harmonization' (2010) 18 *European Review of Private Law* 501, 520. By the same token, Parry identifies a 'corporate or economic' rationale behind the sanctity of contracts in English law (David H Parry, *The Sanctity of Contracts in English Law* (Stevens & Sons London, 1959) 4).

[215] Colin Scott and Julia Black, *Cranston's Consumers and the Law*, 3rd edn (Butterworths, 2000) 77. The authors observe that this compulsion operates on two levels – in the first instance, investors have no option but to enter certain contracts if they are to act as ordinary members of society; secondly, adverse terms are forced upon investors and may subtract from the rights which the law would otherwise give them or which are reasonable for them to expect.

Consequently, standard terms are often one-sided to favour the investment firm, written in small print and couched in legal jargon that is difficult for retail investors to understand.[216] In addition, complex IRHP transactions were set as a pre-condition for corporate retail investors to be granted the financing that they desperately needed to secure the continuation of their business operation and which they were thus pressured into accepting.

Although the courts have recognised difficulties in a relationship portraying 'a classic instance of superior bargaining power',[217] their ability to limit the enforcement of certain terms is restricted due to the operation of the common law principles. The courts therefore continue to hold corporate retail investors, in particular, 'to a high standard of rationality that may not comport with observed reality'.[218] In these circumstances, freedom of contract lacks 'substance'[219] and becomes 'more myth than reality'.[220] Corporate retail investors' negotiating power is inexistent when presented with standard form contracts, and the small print intrinsic to these contracts is 'in no real sense freely agreed with consumers',[221] such that, upon realising that they have little or no power to separately negotiate new terms, these investors often fail to read the forms that they sign. The vast majority of corporate retail investors transacting in complex products would not be represented by legal advisers, which further demonstrates that these investors cannot appreciate the complexities and risks attached to complex products and the potential implications that investments of this nature can have on their business. Contractual freedom cannot therefore be used as an excuse to justify standard terms withdrawing the protection investors would otherwise enjoy.

[216] Lee C Mason, 'Consumers and Unfair Contract Terms: Inadequate Legal Protection and Suggestions for Reform' (2014) 44 *Hong Kong Law Journal* Part 1, 83.

[217] *A Schroeder Music Publishing Co Ltd v Macaulay (Formerly Instone)* [1974] 1 WLR 1308 (HL) 1316. This was also recognised at EU level, when AG Trstenjak observed that 'an imbalance of economic power' is created through the use of standard-form contracts, which are 'imposed unilaterally on the consumer' (Case C-484/08 *Caja de Ahorros y Monte de Piedad de Madrid v Asociación de Usuarios de Servicios Bancarios (Ausbanc)* [2010] ECR I-04785, Opinion of AG Trstenjak, para 39, and confirmed by judgment of the court (First Chamber) of 3 June 2010).

[218] Barbara Black, 'Behavioural Economics and Investor Protection: Reasonable Investors and Efficient Markets' (2013) 44 *Loyola University Chicago Law Journal* 1493, 1495.

[219] J A Jolowicz, 'The protection of the consumer and purchaser of goods under English Law' (1969) 32 *The Modern Law Review* 1, 8.

[220] Elaine A Welle, 'Freedom of Contract and the Securities Laws: Opting Out of Securities Regulation by Private Agreement' (1999) 56 *Washington and Lee Law Review* 519, 578 (see also Philip Rawlings, Andromachi Georgosouli, and Costanza Russo, 'Regulation of financial services: Aims and methods' (2014) *Queen Mary (Centre for Corporate Law Studies)* 29).

[221] OFT, 'Unfair contract terms guidance: Guidance for the Unfair Terms in Consumer Contracts Regulations 1999' (2008) 10. The *caveat emptor* principle has been rejected even in the context of transactions in tangible property, where the emptor can at least physically see and touch the property on offer. On this basis, it seems even more inappropriate that this notion be applied where the investor is being offered a piece of paper (being the contract) representing 'an intangible and complicated bundle of rights' (Laurence CB Gower, *Review of Investor Protection: A Discussion Document* (Cmnd 9125, 1982) para 7.01(b)). See also Steven Friel and Michael Williams, 'New Targets for Litigation?' (2009) 159 *New Law Journal* 444.

Whilst the 'reflexive character'[222] of private law finds its best fit where parties are free to negotiate the terms of the contract, the imposition of standard form contracts upon corporate retail investors is likely to advance exclusively the interests of the party drafting the terms. Despite standard terms being highly adaptable to the investment firm's interests, they fail to accommodate the investor's concerns and expectations, making standard form contracts naturally inclined to 'over-protect the drafting party'.[223] In addition, contractual freedom in its purest form (without any form of regulatory intervention) is said to give rise to the phenomenon of 'market for lemons',[224] where investors accept standard contract terms without reading them as they consider that the time spent going through the agreement, searching for better terms, and negotiating more favourable terms is likely to be futile and, therefore, not worth the effort.[225] As a consequence, investment firms will be tempted to offer lower-quality terms to consumers by shifting additional risks onto such consumers.[226] This accumulation of 'seller-protective'[227] clauses harnesses potential for retail investor detriment in the event of a dispute and 'trenches on the freedom on the adhering party',[228] whereby the use of a lethal combination of exclusion clauses and restrictions on possible avenues for obtaining legal redress arms the drafter with stronger bargaining power even in post-breach negotiations.[229] This adverse selection is likely to result in a 'race to the bottom'[230] where the most detrimental contract terms for retail investors are ultimately expected to prevail as these investors are not able to distinguish between

[222] Hugh Collins, *Regulating Contracts* (Oxford University Press Inc, 1999) 67.

[223] Todd D Rakoff, 'Contracts of Adhesion: An Essay in Reconstruction' (1983) 96 *Harvard Law Review* 1173, 1242 (see also Hugh Collins, 'Regulating Contract Law' in Christine Parker and others (eds), *Regulating Law* (Oxford University Press Inc, 2004) 25).

[224] George Akerlof, 'The Market for "Lemons": Quality Uncertainty and the Market Mechanism' (1970) 84 *The Quarterly Journal of Economics* 488.

[225] On the basis of the 'market for lemons' rationale, investors are presumed to accept standard contract terms because they do not see any added value in making the effort to read the 'small print' and attempt to negotiate changes, or alternatively seek competitive offers from other suppliers. Even if they had to read carefully the contents of the contract, there is nothing retail investors can do to alter the content of clauses which are not in their favour (see eg Oren Gazal-Ayal, 'Economic analysis of standard form contracts: the monopoly case' (2007) 24 *European Journal of Law and Economics* 119; Michael Schillig, 'Legislative Comment: Directive 93/13 and the "price term exemption": a comparative analysis in the light of the "market for lemons" rationale' (2011) 60 *International and Comparative Law Quarterly* 933, 941).

[226] Michael Schillig, 'Legislative Comment: Directive 93/13 and the "price term exemption": a comparative analysis in the light of the "market for lemons" rationale' (2011) 60 *International and Comparative Law Quarterly* 933, 936.

[227] Karl N Llewellyn, 'What Price Contract? An Essay in Perspective' (1931) 40 *The Yale Law Journal* 704, 734.

[228] Todd D Rakoff, 'Contracts of Adhesion: An Essay in Reconstruction' (1983) 96 *Harvard Law Review* 1173, 1236.

[229] Hugh Collins, *Regulating Contracts* (Oxford University Press Inc, 1999) 229. In a post-breach scenario, investment firms can resort to their impenetrable and one-sided terms to point to clauses disclaiming, or otherwise significantly diminishing, their responsibility and consequent duty of care towards the investor, which may also discourage the investor from pursuing legal action at the outset.

[230] ibid 280.

investments which are suitable for them and those which are likely to cause them financial detriment.[231]

E. The Statutory Framework Surrounding Standard Form Contracts

In response to the English contract law regime's 'general predisposition in favour of freedom of contract',[232] policymakers introduced a series of statutory measures to protect consumers against unfair terms or contracts. In particular, these included the establishment of the UK's UCTA,[233] followed by the EU's UTCCD[234] (implemented in the UK by the Unfair Terms in Consumer Contracts Regulations, UTCCR)[235] as well as the UCPD[236] (implemented in the UK by the CPUTR)[237]. More recently, the Consumer Rights Act 2015 (CRA 2015), which implements in part the CRD,[238] came into force to cover the use of unfair terms in consumer contracts.[239] Taken together, these regimes cut across all sectors and are aimed at preventing or limiting stronger contracting parties from exploiting weaker counterparties.

While the UCTA and the CRA 2015 purport to void clauses that exclude or restrict liability in respect of a breach of any obligation,[240] the respective protection they provide is vastly dependent on whether the courts construe a term as forming part of the 'basis' clauses of a contract, or otherwise deem this term to constitute an 'exclusion' clause. The courts have ruled that carefully drafted disclaimers contained in standard form contracts fall outside the scope of the UCTA since these were regarded as basis clauses (as opposed to exclusion clauses) that seek to define and constrain the scope of the obligations undertaken by the investment

[231] In the IRHP mis-selling scenario, investment firms offered the same unfavourable standard terms to corporate retail investors (including non-reliance clauses and other contractual terms disclaiming responsibility for advice). This gave rise to a 'market for lemons' environment in respect of which the risks and adverse consequences only become apparent upon the occurrence of a trigger event (eg the sustained decrease in interest rates in case of IRHPs).

[232] Lord Morris of Borth-y-Gest, Unfair Contract Terms Act Deb 23 May 1977, vol 383 col 1100.

[233] The UCTA originated from the Second Report of the Law Commission on Exemption Clauses (Law Com No 69, 1975) and was designed to assist persons dealing as consumers, as well as other parties lacking bargaining power and who could not therefore effectively negotiate standard terms of contracts.

[234] Directive 93/13/EEC (Unfair Terms in Consumer Contracts Directive, UTCCD).

[235] UTCCR 1994 (SI 1994/3159) and UTCCR 1999 (SI 1999/2083).

[236] Directive 2005/29/EC (Unfair Corporate Practices Directive, UCPD).

[237] Consumer Protection from Unfair Trading Regulations 2008 (SI 2008/1277).

[238] Directive 2011/83/EU (Consumer Rights Directive, CRD).

[239] The CRA 2015 replaced the UTCCR as well as the rules on unfair exclusions in consumer-to-consumer contracts previously governed by the UCTA and the Misrepresentation Act 1967. The UCTA and the Misrepresentation Act 1967 were amended to deal only with business-to-business contracts. The CPUTR will remain in force.

[240] UCTA, s 3(2); CRA 2015, s 31, s 47, s 57.

firm, thereby forming the 'basis' of contracting. The courts' interpretation has thus restricted the scope of the UCTA and the CRA 2015 accordingly.[241]

On a different level, it is to be observed that the 'consumer' envisaged by the above-mentioned consumer-centric EU directives is more narrowly-construed when compared to the 'retail investor' in terms of MiFID. In this respect, it is here suggested that these inconsistencies can be considered to stem from two underlying reasons: in the first instance, these directives are owned by different Commission Directorates within the EU, having different agendas and objectives thereon;[242] secondly, the MiFID regime is designed to specifically contemplate the protection of persons dealing in investment products, thereby having to cater for a complex blend of investment risks that cannot be dealt with by the more overarching consumer-related directives applicable to a wide variety of goods and services.

A confined view of the 'consumer' hence underlines another key limitation of the CRA 2015 in that it only applies to natural persons 'acting for purposes that are wholly or mainly outside that individual's trade, business, craft or profession'.[243] To that end, the consumer protection measures it purports to introduce have a limited coverage, which excludes those categories of retail investors that do not fall within the definition of natural persons or that are acting in the course of business. The same restriction is found in the CPUTR, which also define a 'consumer' as 'any individual who in relation to a corporate practice is acting for purposes which are outside his business'.[244] Consequently, corporate retail investors do not have recourse to these statutes given that they do not fall within the respective definitions of 'consumer'. Ironically, while corporate retail investors are excluded, high-net-worth individuals who may well be categorised as 'professional' investors under MiFID[245] (and in respect of which investment firms are not required to apply certain conduct of business obligations since these investors are considered to be less in need of protection) may still satisfy the definition of 'consumer' and hence be eligible for the safeguards afforded by these frameworks.

These themes have been contemplated by the UK Government in the past, when it consulted on a hypothetical extension to the definition of 'consumer' in the UTCCR to include small businesses whose bargaining power in a contract

[241] English courts have not yet ruled on the application of the CRA 2015 in this respect, however, the CRA 2015 similarly covers exclusion clauses and hence it can be inferred that any disclaimers considered by the court to constitute basis clauses will be equally excluded from the scope of the CRA 2015.

[242] The CRD, eg, falls within the portfolio of the European Commissioner for Justice, Consumers and Gender Equality, whilst ownership of the MiFID regime rests with the European Commissioner for Financial Stability, Financial Services and Capital Markets Union.

[243] CRA 2015, s 2(3). Here, therefore, a sole-trader signing investment-related documents concerning his business and containing unfair terms, for example, is still not protected under this regime, even though, as a retail investor, he may not possess the necessary knowledge and experience to distinguish between fair and unfair terms and his weaker position may thus be exploited by the drafter of the standard form contract.

[244] CPUTR, Reg 2(1).

[245] eg, individuals who have a sizeable financial instrument portfolio, carry out frequent transactions, and work in the financial sector.

is as weak as that of an individual, but in respect of which little protection is available.[246] This proposed extension was not implemented notwithstanding the agreement of a number of key bodies and industry players[247] and notwithstanding that the UTCCD specifically allows for such an extension – in fact, several other Member States (including Italy, Germany, Austria, France and Sweden) have availed themselves of this extension.[248] Similarly, the government did not extend the CRA 2015 to corporate entities even though the CRD affords this discretion,[249] and notwithstanding that the concept of extending protection to corporate retail investors is not a novel situation insofar as the UK regulatory regime is concerned, as the UK consumer credit regime recognises (since the CCA 1974) that certain persons, other than natural persons, acting in a business context need protection and hence statutory protection was extended accordingly beyond the minimum levels envisaged by the Consumer Credit Directive (CCD).[250]

The above-mentioned statutes have been enacted to 'protec[t] consumers against one-sided agreements'[251] and to 'preven[t] the exploitation of consumers'[252] that are particularly vulnerable to unfair commercial practices. Yet, the restrictions discussed in this Section demonstrate that UK policymakers presume that corporate retail investors have a greater degree of sophistication as well as wider access to financial and other professional advice when compared to individual retail investors, and should therefore not qualify for protection under these statutory instruments. Consequently, the legislative framework fails to

[246] See further Department for Business, Enterprise, and Regulatory Reform, 'Consumer Law Review: Call for Evidence' (2008).

[247] See further Department for Business, Innovation and Skills, 'Consumer Law Review: Call for Evidence: Summary of Responses' (2009).

[248] Department for Business, Innovation and Skills, 'Enhancing Consumer Confidence by Clarifying Consumer Law: Consultation on the Supply of Goods, Services and Digital Content' (2012) 27 (see also European Commission, 'Report from the Commission to the European Parliament, the Council and the European Economic and Social Committee: First Report on the application of Directive 2005/29/EC of the European Parliament and of the Council of 11 May 2005 concerning unfair business-to-consumer corporate practices in the internal market and amending Council Directive 84/450/EEC, Directives 97/7/EC, 98/27/EC and 2002/65/EC of the European Parliament and of the Council and Regulation (EC) No 2006/2004 of the European Parliament and of the Council' (2013).

[249] CRD, para 13.

[250] In a regulated consumer credit agreement, CCA 1974, s 189(1) (as amended by Consumer Credit Act 2006, CCA 2006) defines a 'debtor' as also including: 'a partnership consisting of two or three persons not all of whom are bodies corporate; and … an unincorporated body of persons which does not consist entirely of bodies corporate and is not a partnership'. This definition is broader than that contained in Art 3(a) of the CCD (Directive 2008/48/EC), which defines a 'consumer' in the context of consumer credit agreements as 'a natural person who … is acting for purposes which are outside his trade, business or profession'. However, it is noted that the protection afforded to 'business' debtors is still more limited than that extended to non-business debtors. In fact, consumer credit/hire agreements in excess of £25,000 and which are 'entered into by the debtor or hirer wholly or predominantly for the purposes of a business carried on, or intended to be carried on, by him' are not regulated under the CCA 2006 (see further RAO, Art 60C(3)–(7)).

[251] OFT, 'Unfair contract terms guidance: Guidance for the Unfair Terms in Consumer Contracts Regulations 1999' (2008) para 19.2.

[252] UCPD, Recital 18.

acknowledge that the elements contributing to this vulnerability, including, inter alia, investors' 'necessity, indigence, lack of experience, unfamiliarity with the subject matter of the contract, [and] weak bargaining position',[253] relate to factors which are common to all retail investors, irrespective of whether they are individuals or corporate entities. It is therefore argued here that this approach prejudices the position of corporate retail investors and further restricts their chances of securing adequate redress in a mis-selling scenario.

III. Concluding Remarks

The investor's 'God-given right to make a fool of himself',[254] coupled with the reminiscence of caveat emptor, have traditionally informed the drafting of the securities regulation in general. Early pre-crisis references to regulatory intervention struggled to obtain political buy-in, as it was feared to inhibit innovation and competitiveness. Further, policymakers were predisposed to 'trust people to behave themselves',[255] which made the retail investor a 'participant in the machinery of the market'[256] and resulted in an 'extreme … form of confidence in markets and confidence in the ideas that markets were self-correcting'.[257] However, this 'watchful consumer paradigm'[258] failed to protect retail investors from mis-selling, as the dramatic effects of crises and mis-selling scandals appeared to 'shake the status quo'.[259] Consequently, regulators loosened their expectations of retail investors and worked towards the re-engineering of the regulatory framework. The influence of the traditional *caveat emptor* principle in dictating the regulatory strategy is now heavily diluted, as regulators have come to appreciate the inequality in bargaining power between investment firms and retail investors.[260] Further, the regulators' increasingly interventionist strategy is indicative of a shift in the

[253] *Director-General of Fair Trading v First National Bank Plc* [2001] UKHL 52, [2002] 1 AC 481 (HL) 494, a case applying the UTCCR.

[254] Louis Loss, 'The Protection of Investors: The Role of Government' (1963) 80 *South African Law Journal* 53, 60.

[255] Laurence CB Gower, *Review of Investor Protection: A Discussion Document* (Cmnd 9125, 1982) para 6.84.

[256] Dimity Kingsford Smith, 'Regulating investment risk: individuals and the global financial crisis' (2009) 32 *University of New South Wales Law Journal* 514, 701.

[257] Treasury Select Committee, *Banking Crisis – FSA and FSCS: Minutes of Evidence* (25 February 2009) response of Lord Turner of Ecchinswell (in his capacity as Chairman of the FSA) to Q2156.

[258] Toni Williams, 'Who wants to watch? A comment on the new international paradigm of financial consumer market regulation' (2013) 36 *Seattle University Law Review* 1217, 1241.

[259] Eilís Ferran, 'Crisis-driven regulatory reform: where in the world is the EU going?' in Eilís Ferran and others (eds), *The Regulatory Aftermath of the Global Financial Crisis* (Cambridge University Press, 2012) 1.

[260] Legal Services Consumer Panel 'Risk and responsibility: Implications for regulating legal services' (2013) para 2.5.

'political licence'[261] of regulators, as regulation is 'back in fashion'[262] to 'reassert'[263] regulatory power.

Yet, regulatory measures to date, including those discussed in this chapter, have been described as the end product of a 'spaghetti approach' under which policymakers resorted to a strategy of randomly 'throwing ideas against the wall to see what sticks'.[264] As a result, it is claimed that, notwithstanding actions taken by regulators, 'there remain substantial risks of further mis-selling'.[265] Apart from not deriving any direct benefit from the reforms in the investment services regime,[266] it is apparent that corporate retail investors still face an uphill struggle in pursuing mis-selling claims, also because the principal protections under the general UK consumer law regime only cover non-business individual investors and exclude corporate retail investors.[267]

Equally, the courts' reverence to the principles of contractual freedom and legal certainty in a commercial context is unhelpful to the case of corporate retail investors, and English courts have repeatedly cautioned against attempts to over-define the situations when equity will intervene to displace a deal that has been done. Even where there is an actual or apparent inequality between an investor and the investment firm in terms of their respective knowledge and understanding of particular products, this will not necessarily suffice for a court to find that it would be unfair to hold the investor to the terms of the agreement.[268]

In order for corporate retail investors to benefit from adequate regulatory protection mechanisms, more intense reforms targeted at 'debiasing through law'[269]

[261] Julia Black, 'The Role of Risk in Regulatory Processes' in Robert Baldwin, Martin Cave, and Martin Lodge (eds), *The Oxford Handbook of Regulation* (Oxford University Press, 2010) 329.

[262] David Moss and John Cisternino (eds), *New Perspectives on Regulation* (The Tobin Project, 2009) 7.

[263] Mads Andenas and Iris H-Y Chiu, *The Foundations and Future of Financial Regulation: Governance for Responsibility* (Routledge, 2014) 273.

[264] Martin Wheatley, 'Rethinking investor protection' (2011) 2 *JASSA The Finsia Journal of Applied Finance* 6, 8.

[265] House of Commons, Committee of Public Accounts, *Forty-First Report: Financial services mis-selling: regulation and redress* (HC 847, 2016) 3.

[266] In this sense, Moloney observes that the crisis-era reforms to conduct of business regulations have been 'less dramatic' in that conduct regulation has not, over time, experienced the major re-designs and disruptions to which prudential regulation has long been subject. This, she explains, arises as a result of retail regulation being associated more with domestic markets and domestic risks rather than the widespread financial risks that trigger major cycles of regulatory redesign in the prudential context (Niamh Moloney, 'Conduct Rules and Investor Protection: The Evolution of the EU's Approach' in Matthias Casper and others (eds), *Festschrift für Johannes Köndgen* (RWS Vlg Kommunikationsforum, 2016) 400).

[267] See further Centre for Competition Policy and Federation of Small Businesses, 'Small Businesses As Consumers: Are They Sufficiently Well Protected?' (2014) para 3.9.

[268] On undue influence and unconscionable bargain, see eg *Allcard v Skinner* (1887) 36 Ch D 145; *The Royal Bank of Scotland Plc v Etridge (AP)* [2001] UKHL 44, [2002] 2 AC 773; *The Libyan Investment Authority v Goldman Sachs International* [2016] EWHC 2530 (Ch). These cases emphasise that, as a starting point, the courts will still seek to uphold the notions of freedom of contract and commercial certainty unless the facts of the case clearly demonstrate that it would not be fair to do so.

[269] Christine Jolls, 'Behavioral Law and Economics' (2007) National Bureau of Economic Research Working Paper No 12879, 34.

are required to curb mis-selling. The use of more targeted remedies that deal directly with behavioural biases by seeking to correct them or by finding ways of working with investors' biases is thought to deliver a better course of action. When regulation serves a 'debiasing role', the liberal paternalist slant is directed towards educating investors without eliminating choice and without affecting the decisions of the more sophisticated and less behaviourally-challenged players.[270]

[270] See eg Colin Camerer and others, 'Regulation for Conservatives: Behavioral Economics and the Case for "Asymmetric Paternalism"' (2003) 151 *University of Pennsylvania Law Review* 1211; Iain Ramsay and Toni Williams, 'The crash that launched a thousand fixes: Regulation of consumer credit after the lending revolution and the credit crunch' in Kern Alexander and Niamh Moloney (eds), *Law Reform and the Financial Markets* (Edward Elgar Publishing Ltd, 2011) 229.

PART II

The Regulatory and Legal Interpretation of 'Information' and 'Investment Advice'

The difference between 'information' and 'investment advice' is the element of opinion or judgment on the part of the adviser.[1]

[1] FCA, 'Finalised Guidance FG15/1, Retail Investment Advice' (2015) para 3.11.

4

Distinguishing between 'Information' and 'Investment Advice'

I. 'Information' v 'Investment Advice' – A Regulatory Perspective

The delineation between 'information' and 'investment advice' is an important aspect of the domestic and EU investment services regime since the nature of the service being provided dictates the responsibilities of the provider, as well as the level of regulatory protection that the retail investor is entitled to. Further, the redress mechanisms available to corporate retail investors are also dependent on this distinction – where 'investment advice' is deemed to have been provided, the mis-selling claims of corporate retail investors have a higher probability of success.

Yet, the conceptual difference drawn in investment services regulation between these two notions remains unclear and retail investors seem to struggle with distinguishing between decisions made on the basis of neutral information, which would be indicative of a non-advisory service, and decisions made pursuant to a particular product being recommended to them as suitable for their investment needs and personal circumstances, and thus indicative of 'investment advice'. This uncertainty is caused, in part, by a lack of knowledge attributable to retail investors, but also arises as a result of the behaviour of investment firms, which may mimic 'investment advice' by promoting an investment product as particularly well-suited for the retail investor and therefore casually recommending the transaction on a non-contractual basis to the investor, without having to accept the legal and regulatory burden attached to the investment advice regime.[2] In practice, therefore, the ambiguities that arise in distinguishing between promotion, guidance, and advice, mean the burden of proof becomes problematic for these investors when seeking to offer evidence that the investment firm was not distributing products on an 'information' basis only but was also providing 'investment advice' outside a contractually-regulated framework.[3]

[2] Paolo Giudici, 'Independent Financial Advice' in in Danny Busch and Guido Ferrarini (eds), *Regulation of the EU Financial Markets: MiFID II and MiFIR* (Oxford University Press, 2017) 153.

[3] ibid 154.

A. The Distinction between 'Information' and 'Investment Advice' Under the MiFID Regime

Conduct regulation first featured on the EU agenda in 1977 as part of a 'soft' law code of conduct,[4] eventually taking shape as a harmonised regime under the 1993 Investment Services Directive (ISD).[5] The ISD introduced a 'rather elementary scheme'[6] which made no distinction between types of investment services, particularly because it was intended as a minimum harmonisation regime and hence Member States retained the discretion to implement their own conduct rules for investment firms at a national level.[7] The ISD framework was thus characterised by 'overly generic principles'[8] that were not supported by operational guidance. Consequently, this gave rise to wide divergences between different Member States, and was singled out in the Financial Services Action Plan[9] as potentially creating a barrier to achieving one of the EU's priorities, being that of 'facilitating the successful participation of all investors in an integrated market'.[10] Moreover, the investor protection regime under the ISD was considered to be 'inflexible and out-of-date'.[11]

The effect of these shortcomings was exacerbated by the investment services market being in a constant state of flux, as it responded to emerging new types of investment products and novel technologies.[12] This prompted the EU to introduce a more detailed, stringent conduct of business regime in the form of the MiFID framework, which was envisaged as a 'far-reaching modernisation and

[4] European Commission Recommendation 77/534/EEC concerning a European code of conduct relating to transactions in transferable securities [1977] OJ L212/37.

[5] Directive 93/22/EEC.

[6] Danny Busch and Guido Ferrarini, 'Who's Afraid of MiFID II?' in Danny Busch and Guido Ferrarini (eds), *Regulation of the EU Financial Markets: MiFID II and MiFIR* (Oxford University Press, 2017) 5.

[7] The provisions contained in the ISD, Art 11(1) on the assessment of appropriateness and suitability were limited to prescribing that an investment firm should seek information from investors on 'their financial situation, investment experience and objectives as regards the services provided'. ISD, Art 11(3) hinted at investor categorisation by providing that 'the professional nature of the client must be taken into account when executing orders'.

[8] European Commission, 'Proposal for a Directive of the European Parliament and of the Council on Investment Services and Regulated Markets, and amending Council Directive 85/611/EEC, Council Directive 93/6/EEC and European Parliament and Council Directive 2000/12/EC' COM (2002) 625 final19.

[9] European Commission, 'Communication in Implementing the Framework for Financial Markets Action Plan' (Communication) COM (1999) 232.

[10] European Commission, 'The application of conduct of business rules under Art 11 of the Investment Services Directive (93/22/EEC)' (Communication) COM (2000) 722 final 2.

[11] European Commission, 'Proposal for a Directive of the European Parliament and of the Council on Investment Services and Regulated Markets, and amending Council Directive 85/611/EEC, Council Directive 93/6/EEC and European Parliament and Council Directive 2000/12/EC' COM (2002) 625 final 4.

[12] European Commission, 'The application of conduct of business rules under Art 11 of the Investment Services Directive (93/22/EEC)' (Communication) COM (2000) 722 final 2.

reinforcement of the obligations of investment firms'.[13] Most notably, through the MiFID I regime, the EU sought to create different levels of obligations depending on the investment service being provided (for example, 'advised' sales as opposed to 'non-advised' sales), whilst also pursuing a more streamlined regime across Member States. Still, in the aftermath of the global financial crisis, as well as the mis-selling scandals that occurred in a number of Member States, the effectiveness of MiFID I came under scrutiny, such that the European Commission launched a consultation process to reform this framework,[14] which eventually resulted in the adoption of the revised MiFID regime.

Collectively, MiFID I, MiFID II and the related guidance, exhibit the conceptual distinction between 'information' and 'investment advice'. Under both MiFID I and MiFID II, providers of 'investment advice' must comply with more onerous requirements than those that would otherwise apply when providing 'information'. These notably include the requirement to ensure that any 'personal recommendation' made to investors as part of the investment advice, is suitable.[15] To this end, a clear delineation between 'information' and 'investment advice' becomes critical as it informs the extent of due diligence that the investment firm is obliged to undertake on the retail investor.

i. Defining 'Information'

Whilst 'information' is not specifically defined by MiFID, pronouncements from CESR (now ESMA)[16] provide guidance to suggest that the provision of information under MiFID is limited to 'statements of fact and figures', and that the simple provision of objective information 'without making any comment or value judgment on its relevance to the decisions which an investor may make', is not equivalent to a 'personal recommendation' (which constitutes an integral part of the MiFID definition of 'investment advice' as shall be explained hereunder).[17]

[13] European Commission, 'Proposal for a Directive of the European Parliament and of the Council on Investment Services and Regulated Markets, and amending Council Directive 85/611/EEC, Council Directive 93/6/EEC and European Parliament and Council Directive 2000/12/EC' COM (2002) 625 final 20.

[14] European Commission, 'Public Consultation: Review of the Markets in Financial Instruments Directive (MiFID)' (2010).

[15] MiFID II, Art 25(2).

[16] The Committee of European Securities Regulators (CESR) was an independent committee of European securities regulators established by the European Commission on 6 June 2001. Its role was to improve the coordination among securities regulators, act as an advisory group to assist the European Commission, and work on the implementation of community legislation. On 1 January 2011, CESR was replaced by ESMA, which is similarly tasked with developing guidelines and recommendations with a view to establishing consistent, efficient and effective supervisory practices, and ensure the common, uniform and consistent application of EU law. Whilst these pronouncements are not legally binding, NCAs must make every effort to comply or otherwise explain why they do not intend to comply. Financial market participants can also be required to report publicly whether they comply (see further www.esma.europa.eu/page/esma-short, accessed 12 February 2015).

[17] CESR, 'Questions and Answers: Understanding the definition of advice under MiFID' (2010) 7.

Hence, if it is apparent that judgement on the part of the investment firm is absent from the process, such that the investment firm's input is limited to assisting an investor in making his own choice of product, this service is not likely to involve 'investment advice'.

ii. Defining 'Investment Advice'

In terms of MiFID II, Article 4(1)(4), 'investment advice' is defined as 'the provision of personal recommendations to a client, either upon his request or at the initiative of the investment firm, in respect of one or more transactions relating to financial instruments'. This replicates the definition of 'investment advice' contained in MiFID I, Article 4(1)(4). For the purposes of the MiFID definition of 'investment advice', the recommendation must be presented as suitable for that person or must be based on a consideration of the circumstances of that person.[18]

MiFID therefore emphasises the 'personal recommendation' element of the communication to determine whether the service in question should be classified as 'investment advice' or otherwise. In this context, 'investment advice' must include 'a recommendation as to a course of action, which may be presented to be in the interest of the investor', and hence 'requires an element of opinion on the part of the adviser'.[19] On this basis, one can distinguish 'information' from 'investment advice' in that the former would not result in a personal recommendation, but would be limited to objective information including, for example, listing of share and unit prices; company news or announcements; an explanation of the terms and conditions of an investment; a comparison of the benefits and risks of one investment as compared to another; league tables showing the performance of investments of a particular kind against set published objective criteria; alerts about the happening of certain events (for example, certain shares reaching a certain price); and details of directors' dealings in the shares of their own companies.[20] Through the provision of 'investment advice', therefore, the investment firm seeks to transform the standardised and generic information available on the market into a recommendation which is tailored to a retail investor's needs and which does not cover the functioning of the market at large.

It is to be emphasised that the recommendation made to the investor need not be *actually* suitable for the investor, but one must consider whether it is implicitly or

[18] This was also confirmed by the CJEU in Case C-604/11 *Genil 48 SL, Comercial Hostelera de Grandes Vinos SL v Bankinter SA, Banco Bilbao Vizcaya Argentaria SA* [2013] ECR, a case concerning the interpretation of MiFID I, Arts 4(1)(4) and 19(4), (5) and (9) in relation to the definition of 'investment advice' and the related conduct of business obligations when providing investment services to clients.

[19] CESR, 'Questions and Answers: Understanding the definition of advice under MiFID' (2010) 7.

[20] ibid.

explicitly *presented* as suitable.[21] Hence, if a recommendation is portrayed in such a way that a reasonable observer would view it as being based on a consideration of an investor's circumstances or presented as suitable, this would amount to investment advice, subject to the other aforementioned conditions being met.[22] It is thus possible for information to be regarded as a recommendation if the circumstances in which it is provided 'give it the force of a recommendation'.[23] This may occur when the information provided becomes of a subjective and persuasive nature, such that it influences the investor's decision and leads the investor to select particular products over others.[24] More importantly, whilst acknowledging that an investment firm may use disclaimers to confirm the nature of the service being provided when it presents the information, regulators have also stated that 'even if a clear, prominent and understandable disclaimer is provided stating that no advice or recommendation is being given, a firm could still be viewed as having presented a recommendation as suitable for the client'.[25] The investment firm does not need to explicitly notify the investor that a recommendation is being given, nor does the investor have to act upon a recommendation, for it to be regarded as a recommendation.[26]

In the context of online services using, for example, decision trees as an intricate part of their processes, the fundamental considerations are similar and relate to: (1) whether or not the decision tree process is limited to assisting an investor to make his own choice of product; and (2) whether or not the decision tree process is likely to be perceived by the investor as assisting them to make their own choice of product, taking into account the features that the investor regards as important. For a decision tree not to constitute a personal recommendation, it should avoid making any judgement or assessment that would result in products, being identified as suitable for the investor, whether as a result of the information provided by the investor or otherwise. To the contrary, it is reasonable for a decision tree to provide a range of options for the investor to consider, insofar as these options are not presented as suitable for the investor.[27]

[21] See eg FSA, 'FSA advises industry on definition of "mis-selling"' (2003): www.fsa.gov.uk/library/communication/pr/2003/052.shtml, accessed 1 December 2014. This was confirmed by English courts in *Stafford v Conti Commodity Services Ltd* [1981] 1 All ER 691 (QB), a case concerning the duties of a commodity broker in giving advice.

[22] FCA, 'Consultation Paper CP17/28, Financial Advice Market Review (FAMR): implementation Part II and insistent clients' (2017) para 4.10.

[23] CESR, 'Questions and Answers: Understanding the definition of advice under MiFID' (2010) 7.

[24] ibid.

[25] ibid 12 (see also FCA, 'Finalised Guidance FG15/1, Retail Investment Advice' (2015)). This contrasts with the views expressed by English courts, which, to date, have based their judgments on contractual agreements between investment firms and investors, as shall be discussed further in ch 5.

[26] CESR, 'Questions and Answers: Understanding the definition of advice under MiFID' (2010) 7.

[27] ibid 8; FCA, 'Finalised Guidance FG15/1, Retail Investment Advice' (2015) para 3.8–3.10. ESMA has also released guidelines on the use of robo-advice, particularly in relation to disclosures to investors and reliability of information relating to the suitability assessment (see further ESMA, 'Final Report: Guidelines on certain aspects of the MiFID suitability requirements' ESMA35-43-869 (2018)).

iii. Assessing Suitability and Appropriateness Under the MiFID Regime

Once the nature of the investment service to be provided is determined on the basis of the foregoing analysis, MiFID II, Article 25 becomes relevant in that it outlines the type of assessments to be conducted by the investment firm depending on whether the transaction is of an advisory nature or of a non-advised nature.

MiFID II, Article 25(2) discusses the key elements of the suitability test, which test must be undertaken by the investment firm when it provides 'investment advice' to investors.[28] In these instances, the investment firm must solicit from the investor information regarding the investor's knowledge and experience in the investment field relevant to the specific type of product,[29] his financial situation,[30] and his investment objectives.[31] On the basis of this information, the investment firm should be able to recommend instruments that are suitable for the investor.[32]

MiFID II, Article 25(3) provides for the appropriateness test, which is to be undertaken when providing non-advised investment services to retail investors. In this respect, the investor should be requested to provide only a sub-set of the information requested for the purpose of the suitability test, limited to information concerning that investor's knowledge and experience in the investment field which is relevant to the specific type of product or service offered or demanded. This should enable the investment firm to assess the appropriateness of the investment service or product. Where, in the light of the information provided, the investment firm does not consider the product or service to be appropriate for the investor, it is bound to warn the investor. Likewise, a warning is warranted where insufficient or incomplete information is provided, such that the investment firm cannot determine whether the product or service in question is appropriate in the investor's circumstances.

[28] In terms of MiFID II, Art 25(2), the provision of portfolio management services is subject to the same requirements as investment advice. Portfolio management services are however outside the scope of this book and shall therefore not be considered further.

[29] Here the investment firm is to request information on the types of services, transactions and financial instruments the investor is familiar with; the nature, volume and frequency of the investor's transactions in financial instruments; the period over which these transactions were carried out; the investor's level of education; and the profession or relevant former profession of the investor (see eg FSA, 'Finalised Guidance FG11/05, Assessing suitability: Establishing the risk a customer is willing and able to take and making a suitable investment decision' (2011)).

[30] This would include the ability to bear losses determined by the source and extent of regular income, information about investment, real property and other assets, and regular financial commitments (see further FSA (ibid); MiFID II Delegated Regulation, Art 54(4)).

[31] Here the investment firm must determine risk tolerance by reference to the information on the length of time for which the investor wishes to hold the investment, his preferences regarding risk-taking, his risk profile, and the purpose of that investment (see further MiFID II Delegated Regulation, Art 54(5)).

[32] As part of the process, ESMA is expected to propose a number of additional requirements in relation to the suitability assessment. Most notably, ESMA is suggesting that further requirements should be imposed to ensure that suitability reports are personalised and that investors are alerted if a periodic review is needed. These additional provisions are not expected to bring about radical changes, but should merely constitute a refinement to the MiFID regime (see further ESMA, 'Consultation Paper MiFID II/MiFIR' ESMA/2014/549 (2014)).

MiFID II, Article 25(4) caters for situations where certain investment services may be provided without the application of the appropriateness test, and therefore without the need to obtain information about the knowledge and experience of the investor. This is only possible where the investment services being provided consist exclusively of execution or reception and transmission of client orders, excluding the granting of credits or loans, and where the product in question falls to be categorised as a 'non-complex' instrument in terms of MiFID II, Article 25(4).

iv. Non-advisory Services – A 'Light-touch' Approach to Retail Investor Protection

In discussions preceding the introduction of MiFID I, and more recently MiFID II, debates at EU level contemplated whether to retain the option of a non-advised service, or to abolish this service altogether, or to otherwise impose supplementary obligations upon investment firms to ascertain retail investor suitability. In the MiFID I original proposal, the European Commission recommended the imposition of basic suitability requirements on non-advisory services but the European Parliament opposed this suggestion, arguing that the investor should be free to use his own judgement whilst relying on safeguards in the form of conduct of business rules and product standards. It was also noted that the imposition of suitability tests on non-advisory services would drive up the costs of these services, possibly rendering them 'uneconomic' and 'severely limiting investor choice', whilst also 'discouraging saving'.[33]

In a later report,[34] the European Parliament reiterated its support for a 'low-cost … no-frills service' and emphasised that 'fast, low cost and value for money' services should be made available to investors, such that they should not be 'compelled to pay for advice which they neither need nor want'.[35] In essence, the abolition of non-advisory services was envisaged as deterring saving and imposing 'an unreasonable restriction on investor choice'.[36] Non-advised services were also regarded as being already 'sufficiently regulated'[37] through contract law, conduct

[33] Committee on Economic and Monetary Affairs (ECON), 'On the proposal for a European Parliament and Council directive on investment services and regulated market, and amending Council Directives 85/611/EEC, Council Directive 93/6/EEC and European Parliament and Council 2000/12/EC (COM (2002) 625-C5-0586/2002-2002/0269 (COD))' Rapporteur Theresa Villiers, A5-0287/2003 (2003) 11, 92.

[34] ECON, 'Recommendation for Second Reading on the Council common position for adopting a European Parliament and Council directive on markets in financial instruments, amending Council Directives 85/611/EEC and 93/6/EEC and Directive 2000/12/EC of the European Parliament and of the Council and repealing Council Directive 93/22/EEC (13421/3/2003-C5-0015/2004-2002/0269(COD))' Rapporteur Theresa Villiers, A5-0114/2004 (2004).

[35] ibid 42.

[36] ibid.

[37] ECON, 'On the proposal for a European Parliament and Council directive on investment services and regulated market, and amending Council Directives 85/611/EEC, Council Directive 93/6/EEC and European Parliament and Council 2000/12/EC (COM (2002) 625-C5-0586/2002-2002/0269 (COD))' Rapporteur Theresa Villiers, A5-0287/2003 (2003) 92.

of business rules, product regulation, and other regulation relating to the distribution of promotional and explanatory material. As a result, suitability requirements were confined to services where advice is given and not imposed on non-advisory services. This form of 'light-touch', non-advisory regime, also received strong support from investment firms.[38]

The public consultation launched by the European Commission in anticipation of MiFID II,[39] led to similar debates. With respect to non-advised sales, the consultation document had proposed two alternative options: (1) expanding the scope of the appropriateness test by increasing the list of products to be classified as 'complex' by default; or (2) completely abolishing the non-advisory regime on the basis that retail investors should always expect a higher standard of service. The impact assessment report that followed the consultation process,[40] highlighted the uncertainty surrounding non-advisory services and concerns about the quality of investment advice as areas in which investor protection had revealed deficiencies, but still concurred with the conclusions reached prior to the introduction of MiFID I and recommended that the non-advisory regime be retained to preserve the freedom of investors. It was hence agreed that the option of narrowing the list of products that can be treated as 'non-complex', would achieve the objectives of higher investor protection and a better assessment of investors' profile.[41]

By default, therefore, EU law presumes that there is always a need to 'inform' (without necessarily going to the extent of advising), particularly where the investment product in question is a complex product, such that a vulnerable contracting party has an opportunity to understand and assess his rights and duties before entering into a contract and exercising those rights if required. In fact, the inclusion of certain information in a contract, including the extent and content of product and risk disclosures, has been a primary focus of EU law given the peculiarities of investment services products as 'abstract legal products'.[42] Owing to the distinctiveness of investment services products, EU law aims at ensuring that investors receive sufficient information to arrive at their own investment decisions. The duty to inform in terms of EU law, by providing impersonal and generic information, can be conceptualised as the default rule that lays down the foundation for an investment services contract between a retail investor and an investment firm. Any advisory role taken on by the latter is then regarded as an 'add-on' to the basic

[38] Niamh Moloney, 'Building a retail investment culture through law: the 2004 Markets in Financial Instruments Directive' (2005) 6 *European Business Organization Law Review* 341, 397.

[39] European Commission, 'Public Consultation: Review of the Markets in Financial Instruments Directive (MiFID)' (2010).

[40] European Commission, 'Impact Assessment accompanying the document: Proposal for a Directive of the European Parliament and of the Council on Markets in Financial Instruments [Recast] and the Proposal for a Regulation of the European Parliament and of the Council on Markets in Financial Instruments (COM (2011) 656 final) and (SEC (2011) 1227 final)' SEC (2011) 1226 final.

[41] ibid 54.

[42] Martin Ebers, 'Information and Advising Requirements in the Financial Services Sector: Principles and Peculiarities in EC Law' (2004) 8.2 *Electronic Journal of Comparative Law* 1, 4.

information duty. In practice, however, investment firms are taking advantage of this flexibility and are using standard form contracts to narrow the scope of services to the exclusion of advisory mandates, thereby creating an expectation gap in connection with the balance of responsibilities of the retail investor vis-à-vis the investment firm, as well as poking holes in the safety net that the MiFID framework has sought to establish around retail investors.

B. The UK Position

i. The Regulated Activity of 'Advising on Investments'

Under English law, 'advising on investments' became a regulated activity under the FSA 1986, where it was defined as:[43]

> Giving, or offering or agreeing to give, to persons in their capacity as investors or potential investors advice on the merits of their purchasing, selling, subscribing for or underwriting an investment, or exercising any right conferred by an investment to acquire, dispose of, underwrite or convert an investment.

The original FSMA regime, which replaced the FSA 1986, set out a very similar definition when it defined 'investment advice' as:[44]

> Giving or offering or agreeing to give advice to persons on –
>
> a) buying, selling, subscribing for or underwriting an investment; or
> b) exercising any right conferred by an investment to acquire, dispose of, underwrite or convert an investment.

The current version of FSMA still applies this same definition.[45]

The FSMA definition cannot be assessed in isolation but should be read alongside the definition prescribed by the Financial Services and Markets Act 2000 (Regulated Activities) Order 2001,[46] which, under Article 53, defines the regulated activity of 'advising on investments' as follows:

> Advising a person is a specified kind of activity if the advice is –
>
> a) given to the person in his capacity as an investor or potential investor, or in his capacity as agent for an investor or a potential investor; and
> b) advice on the merits of his doing any of the following (whether as principal or agent):
>   i. buying, selling, subscribing for or underwriting a particular investment which is a security or a contractually based investment, or
>   ii. exercising any right conferred by such an investment to buy, sell, subscribe for or underwrite such an investment.

[43] FSA 1986, Sch 1, Pt II, para 15.
[44] FSMA (original version), Sch 2, Pt I, para 7.
[45] FSMA (current version), Sch 2, Pt I, para 7.
[46] SI 2001/554.

The above definition is broader than the MiFID definition of 'investment advice', the latter being based on there being a 'personal recommendation', which is not a pre-requisite under Article 53. The discrepancy between the two definitions was also considered by the Financial Advice Market Review (FAMR),[47] which found that the MiFID definition was not only clearer for investment firms and investors but was also easier for investment firms to incorporate in their compliance processes. It was therefore recommended that the government should consult on amending the definition under Article 53 to bring it in line with the MiFID definition of 'investment advice', such that only advice which involves a personal recommendation would be regulated. Subsequently, the government issued a consultation paper proposing to amend the wording in Article 53 by reflecting the text set out in MiFID.[48] In its response to the consultation,[49] the government agreed that a new definition for 'investment advice' would be beneficial and, on 28 March 2017, the Financial Services and Markets Act 2000 (Regulated Activities) (Amendment) Order 2017[50] was published. The Order became effective on 3 January 2018 and, inter alia, transposes the MiFID II definition of 'investment advice' without change. As a result of these amendments, regulated firms with permission to conduct activities other than Article 53 advice only fall within Article 53 advice if they provide a personal recommendation, whereas other firms and individuals continue to be subject to the current broader definition of advice in Article 53 and are not able to provide investment advice even where this does not involve a personal recommendation.[51]

In addition to the foregoing, there also exists other UK-specific regulatory guidance which merits further consideration in the following paragraphs. Notwithstanding that it draws heavily upon the EU framework discussed in Section IA, this guidance still useful in discerning the difference between 'information' and 'investment advice'.

ii. Perimeter Guidance Manual

The FCA's Perimeter Guidance Manual (PERG)[52] provides examples of recommendations that would constitute 'investment advice' depending on whether they

[47] HM Treasury and FCA, 'Financial Advice Market Review: Final report' (2016) 31.

[48] HM Treasury, 'Amending the definition of financial advice: consultation' (2016).

[49] HM Treasury, 'Amending the definition of financial advice: consultation response' (2017).

[50] SI 2017/488.

[51] Due to concerns about unregulated firms escaping regulation by providing guidance on risky products, the government decided to change the definition of 'investment advice' for regulated firms only.

[52] The PERG is issued under FSMA, s 139A (power of the FCA to give guidance). Notwithstanding that it represents the regulator's view and is, therefore, non-binding, its persuasive value cannot be discounted. In fact, the court, in *Helden v Strathmore Ltd* [2011] EWCA Civ 542, [2011] Bus LR 1592 [83], recognised that although the PERG 'merely represents the FSA's views and does not bind the Courts', comments made in the PERG 'are still of interest'. This observation was also upheld by the courts in a number of other cases, including: *R (on the application of Chancery (UK) LLP) v Financial Ombudsman Service Ltd* [2015] EWHC 407 (Admin), [2015] BTC 13; *Newmafruit Farms Ltd and*

involve the provision of 'advice on the merits' of buying or selling investments or not.[53] On the basis of these examples, it is observed that the distinction between an action being deemed to constitute regulated advice or otherwise is primarily centred on whether the investment firm is steering the investor in the direction of a particular product or whether the investor takes the relevant decisions on his own accord.[54] PERG 8.28.2G further observes that the provision of neutral information should be free from 'any comment or value judgment on its relevance to decisions which an investor may make' for it not to venture into the advisory sphere, given that, in terms of PERG 8.28.1G, 'advice requires an element of opinion on the part of the adviser … it is a recommendation as to a course of action. Information, on the other hand, involves statements of facts or figures'.

PERG 2.7.15G goes on to say that giving generic advice (for example, to invest in instruments linked to one particular jurisdiction rather than another) is not a regulated activity nor is the provision of neutral information without advice (for example, listings or company news). However, PERG 8.28.4G emphasises that 'information may take on the nature of advice if the circumstances in which it is provided give it the force of a recommendation'. This implies that the context in which something is communicated may affect its character – for example, if an investment firm gives information on share price and, when it does so, it also indicates that this would be a good time for the investor to buy or sell, then this would be considered to constitute 'advising on investments'.

Moreover, the PERG provides additional guidance to the market when deciding whether what was said by an adviser in a particular situation does or does not amount to 'investment advice'. To this end, one should look at the query to which the adviser was responding – if an investor asks for a recommendation, any response is likely to be regarded as advice; if, however, a customer makes a purely factual inquiry, it may be the case that a reply which simply provides the relevant factual information is no more than that.[55]

iii. The FCA Rulebook

Once authorised, investment firms are subject to the FCA's rulebook, in particular the COBS. The COBS already adopts the MiFID definition of 'investment advice', by requiring that the advice be tailored, through the communication of a 'personal recommendation' to the investor. A 'personal recommendation' is defined in the FCA Handbook Glossary as 'a recommendation that is advice on investments … and is presented as suitable for the person to whom it is made, or is based on a consideration of the circumstances of that person', thereby mirroring the MiFID

Others v Alan Pither and Others [2016] EWHC 2205 (QB); *Personal Touch Financial Services Ltd v SimplySure Ltd* [2016] EWCA Civ 461, [2016] Bus LR 1049.

[53] See PERG 8.29.

[54] See examples set out under PERG 8.29.7G.

[55] PERG 8.28.7G and 8.28.8G.

equivalent. Where an investment firm makes a personal recommendation, then the requirements under COBS 9A (regulating advised sales) are to be complied with, whilst, in the absence of a personal recommendation, COBS 10A (regulating non-advised sales) becomes applicable. It is therefore the 'personal recommendation' element that drives the application of the suitability rules set out in COBS 9A as opposed to the lighter set of rules set out under COBS 10A, in line with MiFID obligations.

It is also to be noted that the definition of 'investment advice' under the COBS evolved from a rather skeletal definition which historically defined investment advice as 'a recommendation given to a specific person', and later made more specific to read 'a recommendation which is advice on investments given to a specific person'. With effect from 1 November 2007, the present COBS definition was implemented to align itself to the MiFID regime, thereby embracing the concept of a 'personal recommendation'.

iv. A Spectrum of Investment Services – From 'Information' to 'Full Advice'

Over the years, the UK regulator recognised that retail investors struggle to understand the distinguishing features that set apart 'information' from 'investment advice'. To this end, the regulator released guidance through which it also sought to address the expectation gap that exists between investment firms and investors when it comes to the provision of advised and non-advised services.[56] Further, this guidance helped clarify that there exist other services between pure 'information' and fully-fledged 'investment advice', which comprise elements of both. Depending on how acute the 'personal recommendation' factor is in the service being provided, this will determine whether the service in question sits closer to the 'information' end of the spectrum or whether it leans more towards the opposing 'investment advice' end. In its 2005/2006 Business Plan, the then FSA first hinted at the creation of a 'depolarised advice system', through a 'menu' designed to explain to investors the cost of advice.[57] It then proposed a spectrum of services in its Discussion Paper on the RDR,[58] attaching varying degrees of advice-related obligations, which have, since then, evolved as explained hereunder.

At the advisory end of the spectrum, one finds the 'full advice' service, which requires investment firms to undertake a detailed assessment of the investor's complete range of needs and circumstances. This includes 'independent advice', which is defined in the updated FCA Handbook Glossary as 'a personal recommendation

[56] See eg FSA, 'Discussion Paper DP07/01, A Review of Retail Distribution' (2007); FSA, 'Finalised Guidance FG12/15, Retail Distribution Review: Independent and Restricted Advice' (2012); FSA, 'Finalised Guidance FG12/10, Simplified Advice' (2012); FCA, 'Finalised Guidance FG15/1, Retail Investment Advice' (2015).

[57] FSA, '2005/2006 Business Plan' (2005) 11.

[58] FSA, 'Discussion Paper DP07/01, A Review of Retail Distribution' (2007).

to a client where the personal recommendation provided meets the requirements of the rule on independent advice'.[59] Where independent investment advice is being provided, the investment firm must assess a sufficient range of relevant products available on the market which must be sufficiently diverse with regard to their type and issuers or product providers, and which must not be limited to products issued or provided by the investment firm itself or entities having close links with the investment firm. An investment firm that holds itself out as providing independent advice may provide broad and general advice or specialist and specific advice. In the latter case, the investment firm shall market itself in a way that is intended only to attract clients with a preference for those categories of financial instruments and shall also require clients to indicate that they are only interested in investing in the specified category of instruments.[60]

'Restricted advice' (or 'streamlined' advice) is a second service of an advisory nature where the advice provided has a narrower scope in that it may be focused, at the request of the client, on the provision of personal recommendations relating to a specific need, designated investment and/or particular assets ('focused advice'), or otherwise simplified by the investment firm itself through the setting of boundaries that limit the personal recommendation to one or more of an investor's specific needs and therefore does not involve analysis of the investor's circumstances that are not directly relevant to those needs ('simplified advice'). Restricted advice must meet the same suitability, inducement, adviser charging, and professionalism standards as independent advice.[61]

The foregoing options sit on the 'investment advice' end of the spectrum, and thus attract more onerous requirements on the part of the investment firm. As one moves away from a personal recommendation towards the other end of the continuum, one finds a range of non-advisory services. 'Generic advice'[62] or 'guidance' is one such service that does not relate to a particular investment and that therefore does not constitute regulated 'investment advice'.[63] Whilst it may include, for example, advice on the merits of investing in one geographical zone rather than another or advice on the merits of investing in certain asset classes when compared to others, generic advice is typically intended for the general public, and is hence not based on an evaluation of the personal circumstances of a particular investor, nor does it appear to be presented as suitable for that investor.[64] Hence, whereas

[59] The concept of 'independent advice' is contemplated by both the FCA Handbook (COBS 6.2B.11R) as well as the MiFID II framework.

[60] See COBS 6.2B.14(G) to COBS 6.2B.15(EU).

[61] See further FCA, 'Policy Statement PS17/14, Markets in Financial Instruments Directive II Implementation – Policy Statement II' (2017).

[62] Following the Thoresen Review, 'generic advice' falls under the remit of MAS (see further HM Treasury, 'Thoresen Review of Generic Financial Advice: Final Report' (2008)). Note that, following the restructuring of the statutory financial guidance providers, the MAS will be abolished and replaced by another money guidance body (see further n 88 in ch 3).

[63] Although the provision of purely factual information or generic advice is not generally 'investment advice', if the information or generic advice is given in the course of providing 'investment advice' it can form part of that regulated activity (MiFID II Delegated Regulation, Recitals 15 and 16).

[64] CESR, 'Questions and Answers: Understanding the definition of advice under MiFID' (2010) 10.

generic advice may involve discussions with an investor around the asset class that would best suit his needs, any indication by the investment firm as to a particular instrument within that asset class would then represent 'investment advice'. What distinguishes unregulated generic advice from regulated investment advice is, therefore, that the former does not result in a specific product recommendation, whereas the latter does.[65] The final service relates to non-advised transactions where investors choose a particular product without being specifically advised to do so, thereby basing their decision on factual 'information' provided to them by the investment firm. Since the 'personal recommendation' factor is completely absent from the latter two services, the requirements attached to 'investment advice' do not apply in relation to these services.

The FCA has stated that its guidance on retail investment advice[66] should be considered as the 'definitive source of information on the FCA's view on the boundaries of advice for retail investment products', and should therefore 'take precedence over any previous non-handbook guidance which deals with the same material other than the Perimeter Guidance Manual'.[67] Notwithstanding the objective of this guidance to serve as 'definitive' guidance, however, the FCA still makes use of terms such as 'likely' and 'not likely' in describing whether or not a particular action or service constitutes a personal recommendation or regulated advice, which does not, therefore, address the subjectivity inherent in categorising a service as 'advisory' or 'non-advisory'. In its communications on the concept of 'investment advice', the FCA appears to acknowledge this by emphasising the importance of the context and the circumstances in which information is provided, which can tip the balance either way. Furthermore, it suggests that, should information be provided on a selected, rather than a balanced, basis in such a way that it influences or persuades the investor, this may still amount to 'investment advice'.[68]

Although a tiered system of different degrees of investment advice allows investors to select the most appropriate form of regulated advice to fit their needs, considerable design challenges emerge. This differentiated system may also lead to industry risks where the applicability of suitability requirements is unclear,

[65] HM Treasury, 'Thoresen Review on Generic Financial Advice: Interim Report, Annex 4 – Paper on regulatory boundary of generic financial advice' (2007) (see also HM Treasury, 'Financial Capability: the Government's long-term approach' (2007) para 4.40). Earlier drafts of MiFID I included generic advice on financial planning and asset allocation, which was not linked to specific investment recommendations, within the definition of 'investment advice'. This approach was designed to reflect the reality that inexperienced investors are likely to rely on general investment advice, particularly in light of their limited levels of financial acumen. However, this broad definition provoked hostile market reactions primarily due to the costs involved in imposing suitability and information-gathering requirements at an early stage of the firm/investor relationship. As a result, the definition of 'investment advice' was scaled back to the present one (see further European Commission, 'Draft Commission Directive implementing Directive 2004/39/EC as regards organisational requirements and operating conditions' (2006) Background Note 31).

[66] FCA, 'Finalised Guidance FG15/1, Retail Investment Advice' (2015).

[67] ibid para 2.5.

[68] FCA, 'Finalised Guidance FG15/1, Retail Investment Advice' (2015) para 3.12.

particularly given the limited ability of retail investors to choose between, and monitor, different advice services.[69] On this point, the FAMR observed that forms of simpler advisory services 'have been slow to develop'[70] and that the number of terms describing advisory services can be 'confusing for firms and consumers'.[71] Nevertheless, the FAMR acknowledged that streamlined advisory models have a number of benefits and it therefore recommended that a clear framework is developed to equip investment firms with the confidence to 'provide streamlined advice on simple consumer needs in a proportionate way'.[72]

The FCA addressed these calls for action by issuing Guidance Consultation GC17/4 on, inter alia, the provision of streamlined advice.[73] By means of this publication, the FCA clarified that, although streamlined advice services may be designed to deal with more limited client needs and may not, therefore, involve an analysis of all the client's circumstances, any personal recommendation which is given to a client through a streamlined advice service must still be suitable, thereby emphasising that: '[o]ffering a streamlined advice service, with a narrower scope, does not allow a firm to lower the level of protection due to clients'.[74] In these instances, the investment firm must also disclose information about the nature of the service being provided, which is likely to involve an explanation of the differences between the scope of its streamlined advisory service and other types of advice available,[75] and which, therefore, should make it easier for the retail investor to discern the difference between one advisory service and another.

v. UK Retail Investors' Perceptions of Advised and Non-advised Sales

Research commissioned by the FCA revealed a noticeable growth in the number of complex investment products purchased by retail investors on a non-advised basis,[76] leading the FCA to commission a further study into the market for non-advised sales.[77] This study revealed that, in general, when using most online services without regulated advice, investors are clear that the transaction is undertaken on a non-advised basis. The provision of information or product guidance in face-to-face settings where there is human interaction, however, tends to be

[69] See further Niamh Moloney, *How to Protect Investors: Lessons from the EC and the UK* (Cambridge University Press, 2010) 278–79.

[70] HM Treasury and FCA, 'Financial Advice Market Review: Final report' (2016) 33.

[71] ibid 34.

[72] ibid 35.

[73] FCA, 'Guidance Consultation GC17/4: Financial Advice Market Review (FAMR): Implementation part 1' (2017).

[74] ibid para 2.3.

[75] ibid para 2.19–2.20.

[76] NMG Consulting, 'Impact of the Retail Distribution Review on consumer interaction with the retail investments market: A quantitative research report' (2014) 9.

[77] NMG Consulting, 'The motivations, needs and drivers of non-advised investments: A qualitative research report' (2014).

misinterpreted as 'investment advice', such that investors emerge from these meetings feeling that a product had been recommended and that the investment firm selected the product which was most suited to their needs, even though such exchanges would relate to non-advised transactions.

Apart from the 'personal' element in face-to-face interaction, which may be the primary driver of this confusion, the research also refers to the expectation gap between retail investors and investment firms and suggests that this misconception is 'compounded by the fact that what "advice" means to a consumer can be very different to what "advice" means within the industry'.[78] Retail investors thus tend to interpret the term 'investment advice' in a much broader way than the parameters within which regulation defines it. As a result, they will commonly perceive services such as assisted non-advised sales as being 'investment advice', which risks creating an expectation on their part that they can rely on a suitability assessment carried out by the investment firm.[79] Misconceptions around 'investment advice' also occur where the process does not involve an actual product purchase. To this effect, retail investors appear to draw assumptions around the point at which they are receiving advice, including, for example, that advice always relates to the purchase of a product.[80] More recent research undertaken by the Financial Advice Working Group arrived at similar conclusions, which indicate that retail investors have conflicting views on what constitutes 'advice' and 'guidance'.[81]

Whether or not an investor feels that he is receiving a personal recommendation will not in itself determine whether 'investment advice' is actually being provided or otherwise. Hence, while the investor's own perception of the service received is considered important, it might well be that the investor is not always correct in his understanding. Still, as mentioned earlier in this chapter, if a recommendation is presented in such a way that a reasonable observer would view it as being based on a consideration of the investor's circumstances or put forward as being suitable, then this is likely to amount to a personal recommendation.[82]

[78] ibid 44–45.

[79] FSCP, 'Advice Gap Research' (2012) 18. The FSCP observed that investors tend to use the term 'advice' more broadly to also encompass help, information, guidance and regulated advice (FSCP, 'Position Paper on Advice' (2012) para 3.4).

[80] It has been suggested that regular signposting throughout the process to indicate whether the investor is being advised or is otherwise not receiving advice would help to ensure that investors are clear on the service being provided (see further NMG Consulting, 'Impact of the Retail Distribution Review on consumer interaction with the retail investments market: A quantitative research report' (2014) 41).

[81] As a result of this finding, the Financial Advice Working Group recommended that the market should adopt (subject to the FCA's required process of analysis, appropriate public consultation and cost/benefit analysis) a single consistent set of consumer-friendly explanations for 'advice' and 'guidance' in a form which is substantially similar to those proposed in by the Financial Advice Working Group itself (see: Financial Advice Working Group. 'Consumer explanations of "advice" and "guidance"' (2017) 4).

[82] FCA, 'Finalised Guidance FG15/1, Retail Investment Advice' (2015) para 4.13–4.16; CESR, 'Questions and Answers: Understanding the definition of advice under MiFID' (2010) 4; PERG 8.28.5G.

II. Views from the Academic Universe and Consumer Bodies

'Investment advice' has been described as a 'key perimeter for the regulatory regime',[83] in that whether or not a service amounts to 'investment advice' determines the applicability of suitability requirements. The distinction between advised and non-advised sales has been portrayed as a 'blur'[84] or 'illusion',[85] which can tempt retail investors to 'view information as communication'[86] and consequently as personalised advice. 'Information' and 'investment advice' are thus conceptualised as merging into one another, such that any distinction between the two concepts is 'too subtle'[87] for retail investors to detect.

The academic world has sought to contribute towards the distinguishing features of 'information' and 'investment advice'. 'Information' has been defined as the 'mere transfer of facts and prognosis',[88] which is 'acontextual, non-reflexive and impersonal',[89] and thus viewed as being based on objective, neutral facts without the involvement of any personal consultation whatsoever. In a non-advised sale, the investor is expected to take away the information, supplement this with own research if necessary, evaluate it independently, and exercise his own opinion in arriving at the final investment decision. To the contrary, where 'investment advice' is provided, the onus is on the adviser to procure the necessary information about the investor and provide a 'professional assessment and recommendation taking into consideration the customer's life circumstances and interests'.[90] 'Investment advice' is therefore seen and bridging the gap between 'information and knowledge and understanding',[91] in that the investor is no longer left to his own devices to shape the information to fit his situation. Where 'investment advice' is given, the adviser is tasked with creating a 'bridge' through which information is filtered and tailored to the investor's circumstances and investment objectives in the form of a personal recommendation.

[83] Niamh Moloney, *How to Protect Investors: Lessons from the EC and the UK* (Cambridge University Press, 2010) 203.

[84] ibid 261.

[85] Paul Marshall, 'Interest rate swaps and the sale of the unknown: blind alleys, an enfeebled equity and the triumph of certainty over fairness' (2014) 29 *Journal of International Banking and Financial Law* 9, 14.

[86] Joanna Gray and Jenny Hamilton, *Implementing Financial Regulation: Theory and Practice* (John Wiley & Sons Ltd, 2006) 223.

[87] Gerard McMeel and John Virgo (eds), *McMeel and Virgo on Financial Advice and Financial Products: Law and Liability* (Oxford University Press, 2001) para 1.59.

[88] Martin Ebers, 'Information and Advising Requirements in the Financial Services Sector: Principles and Peculiarities in EC Law' (2004) 8.2 *Electronic Journal of Comparative Law* 1, 3–4.

[89] Joanna Gray and Jenny Hamilton, *Implementing Financial Regulation: Theory and Practice* (John Wiley & Sons Ltd, 2006) 223.

[90] See n 88.

[91] See n 89.

Consumer bodies have similarly expressed their concern about the distorted interpretation of neutral 'information' as opposed to recommendations and related 'investment advice'. The FSCP, for instance, observed that there still exists a 'significant mismatch'[92] between retail investors' expectation of the role of investment firms, and the investment firms' actual understanding of the extent of their role, particularly in the context of non-advised transactions. Once again a common concern re-surfaces around the expectation gap, in that retail investors might perceive a personal recommendation in a communication that was intended merely as objective information from the investment firm's perspective. Equally, the obscure divide between 'information' and 'investment advice' also weighs heavily on investor groups which have described the enforcement of the MiFID investor protection regime as '*weak*', and highlighted that, in practice, 'advice is often couched as plain information'.[93]

Based on the interplay between regulatory pronouncements and academic inferences, it can be concluded that the main factors distinguishing 'information' from 'investment advice' are two-fold, and relate to: (1) the role embodied by the investment firm; and (2) the extent of responsibility which the investor is expected to take on. In the first instance, when the service being provided is limited to 'information', the investment firm has the passive role of merely relaying on to the investor neutral and objective information. In contrast, when acting in an advisory capacity, the investment firm takes on a more active stance, whereby he is required to solicit sufficient information from the investor so as to formulate an understanding of the suitability of the product for the investor, which will in turn form the basis of the personal recommendation and 'investment advice' given to the investor. It follows, therefore, that the investor is expected to take on a greater degree of responsibility when the service he receives is limited to factual information ('investor-led'[94]). To the contrary, in an advised sale environment, reliance is placed on the investment firm to recommend the investment which is most suitable for the investor ('adviser-led'[95]). This balance of responsibilities is also pertinent in light of the manner in which the regulator applies the 'investor responsibility' principle to corporate retail investors, as well as in analysing the conclusions reached by English courts in the context of IRHP mis-selling, in order to provide a practical dimension to the interpretation of the theoretical concepts of 'information' and 'investment advice'.

[92] FSCP, 'Response to DP 08/5: Consumer Responsibility' (2009) 17.

[93] Guillaume Prache, Managing Director of EuroInvestors, a Brussels-based organisation representing a number of investor organisations and individual investors, as quoted in Phil Davies, 'Protecting investors proves tricky' *Financial Times Fund Management* (London, 21 March 2011) 11.

[94] Niamh Moloney, *How to Protect Investors: Lessons from the EC and the UK* (Cambridge University Press, 2010) 239.

[95] ibid.

III. A Fair and Reasonable Perspective – The View of the Financial Ombudsman Service

The distinction the FOS makes between 'information' and 'investment advice' comes appears to be largely dependent on the manner in which information is presented (selectively as opposed to comprehensively), as well as the role taken on by the investment firm (a passive role limited to the provision of factual information as opposed to a more active role leading to a personal recommendation being put forward to the investor). Where an investment firm opts for selective communication when presenting information to investors, by focusing on explaining a particular product over others, the FOS is thus likely to conclude that this amounts to 'investment advice', given that the investor will probably interpret it as a personal recommendation.[96] This approach appears to provide a plausible interpretation of the facts and circumstances of the case, consistent with the 'fair and reasonable' guiding principle of the FOS itself. Regrettably, in view of the FOS' limited jurisdiction, not many aggrieved investors can benefit from such a practical and sensible approach, which, in the right circumstances might actually lead to adequate compensation for mis-selling victims.

IV. The English Courts' Interpretation of the Notions of 'Information' and 'Advice'

In a court of law, pinning down the difference between 'information' and 'investment advice' is crucial since the court's conclusion as to the nature of the service being provided determines the extent of common law duties, if any, owed to the investor by the investment firm. The centrality of this distinction is highlighted through a number of cases decided by the English courts primarily around allegations concerning mis-selling and the carrying out of unauthorised business, which are discussed below.

English courts have recognised that the analysis of the nature of the relationship between a bank and its customer in the context of investment services is 'one of some delicacy',[97] given that the circumstances that courts have been asked to examine go beyond the conventional banker-customer relationship and extend to settings where a bank, acting in its capacity as an investment firm, markets novel and complex derivative products, possibly of its own devising, to retail investors. Against this backdrop, the courts have acknowledged that 'the line that separates

[96] This approach emphasises the importance of considering the 'context' in which any communication on investment decision-making takes place, as also set out in PERG 8.28.4G and as highlighted by the then CESR (CESR, 'Questions and Answers: Understanding the definition of advice under MiFID' (2010) 4, 7) and FCA, 'Finalised Guidance FG15/1, Retail Investment Advice' (2015).

[97] *Bankers Trust International Plc v PT Dharmala Sakti Sejahtera* [1996] CLC 518 (Comm) 530.

provision of information from giving advice may be a fine one',[98] particularly due to the fact that 'investment advice' may be conveyed by presenting 'information' selectively. The separation point on this continuum is typically fact-dependent and there may be disagreement about whether the line has been crossed or otherwise. In attempting to find an objective measure to conclude whether 'investment advice' had been provided or otherwise, the courts' interpretation of the definition of 'investment advice' appears to hinge on whether the investment firm formally assumed responsibility for the provision of 'investment advice' during the course of the relationship and, if so, whether or not this assumption of responsibility was reflected in the written contractual agreement between the parties.

In this context, the *SAAMCO*[99] case provides the authoritative interpretation of the House of Lords (as it then was) on the distinction between 'information' and 'advice' in the context of surveyors' negligence.[100] Of particular relevance is the distinction that Lord Hoffmann makes when explaining that the scope of the duty of care differs depending on whether the service being provided is restricted to 'information' or otherwise constitutes 'advice'. In this respect, Lord Hoffmann notes that a duty to provide information for the purpose of enabling someone else to decide upon a course of action should be set apart from a duty to advise someone as to what action he should take, and proceeds to state that:

> If the duty is to advise whether or not a course of action should be taken, the adviser must take reasonable care to consider all potential consequences of that course of action. If he is negligent, he will therefore be responsible for all the foreseeable loss which is a consequence of that course of action having been taken. If his duty is only to supply information, he must take reasonable care to ensure that the information is correct and, if he is negligent, will be responsible for all the foreseeable consequences of the information being wrong.[101]

The quoted statement underlines the importance of clearly distinguishing 'information' from 'advice' given that different degrees of duty of care are attached to the respective services, which will in turn dictate the ensuing consequences. This point was more recently emphasised in Manchester Building Society v Grant Thornton UK LLP,[102] wherein the Court of Appeal clarified that a case is to be

[98] *Crestsign* [115].

[99] *South Australian Asset Management Corporation v York Montague Ltd; United Bank of Kuwait Plc v Prudential Property Services Ltd; Nykredit Mortgage Bank Plc v Edward Erdman Group Ltd (Formerly Edward Erdman, an Unlimited Company) (SAAMCO)* [1997] AC 191 (HL).

[100] The defendants, as valuers, were asked by the plaintiffs to value properties on the security of which they were considering advancing money on mortgage. In each case, the defendants considerably overvalued the property. Loans were made following the valuations, which loans would not have been granted had the plaintiffs known the true property values. The borrowers subsequently defaulted and, in the meantime, the property value had fallen substantially, thereby significantly increasing the losses eventually suffered by the plaintiffs. The plaintiffs brought actions against the defendants claiming damages for negligence and breach of contract.

[101] *SAAMCO* [24]. The incidence of fraud constitutes an exception to this limitation (see eg *Doyle v Olby (Ironmongers) Limited* [1969] 2 QB 158, [1969] 2 WLR 673).

[102] [2019] EWCA Civ 40.

considered as an 'advice case' if the adviser is responsible for considering what matters should be taken into account in deciding whether to enter into a particular transaction, and for guiding the whole decision-making process. Otherwise, it will be an 'information case', and the adviser will be responsible only for the foreseeable consequences of the information being wrong rather than being held liable for all the foreseeable financial consequences of the transaction. In demonstrating the counter-factual, namely that loss would not have been suffered if the advice had been correct, the burden of proof rests on the claimant and, in practice, applying the relevant counter-factual scenario so as to determine which, if any, losses are recoverable remains a complex exercise.

In the context of investment mis-selling case law, the decisions reached by English courts in interpreting the definition of 'investment advice' as a regulated activity (that is whether the defendant should have obtained regulatory authorisation prior to providing the services in question) are instrumental in shedding light on the distinction between 'information' and 'investment advice'. Some of these cases have occurred under a different regulatory regime governed by the FSA 1986 and against a background of self-regulatory organisations (SROs),[103] where the definition of 'investment advice' had not as yet evolved to include reference to the present notion of a 'personal recommendation'.[104] Even then, however, the courts conceptually appear to have paid due regard to the presence of a 'personal recommendation', coupled with consideration of the investor's specific circumstances, which go beyond highlighting the advantages and disadvantages of a particular product.

In concluding whether communications between an investment firm and an investor constituted the regulated activity of 'investment advice' and whether the rules in the COB that were in force at the time were applicable, the courts assessed the extent to which communication between the parties was limited to the provision of factual and neutral information, as opposed to tailored 'investment advice' aimed at addressing the investor's circumstances and objectives, and influencing his decision. Hence, 'advice on the merits' of purchasing a particular investment arises where the investment firm provides 'guidance as to the course of action which the user should take in relation to buying or selling of the investments'.[105]

[103] See eg *Re Market Wizard Systems (UK) Ltd* [1998] EWHC 1209 (Comm); *Michael Martin and Another v Britannia Life Limited* [2000] Lloyd's Rep 412 (Ch); *Michael David Walker v (1) Inter-Alliance Group Plc (In Administration); (2) Scottish Equitable Plc* [2007] EWHC 1858 (Ch), [2007] Pens LR 347.

[104] The notion of 'personal recommendation' appeared in the COBS as a result of the domestic transposition of MiFID I (which became applicable as from 1 November 2007). Whilst the regulatory regime as its stands is no longer governed by the FSA 1986 and rules set by the respective SROs, the principles are nevertheless relevant since the FSA 1986 definition of 'investment advice' is still valid today. To this effect, the interpretation of the term 'advising on the merits' is significant in concluding whether the communication in question is based on purely factual information or otherwise whether it seeks to influence the investor's decision.

[105] *Re Market Wizard* [34]. In this case the defendant firm was in the business of marketing and selling a computer package known as the 'Market Wizard Equity Options Trading System'. Purchasers of this system would be provided with daily information and the system generated buy, sell or hold signals in respect of options in each of the twelve traded stocks. The investment firm was not authorised under the FSA 1986, yet its advertising material claimed that purchasers of the system could make substantial profits on their investment.

When considering what constitutes 'advice on the merits' of buying a particular investment product, English courts did not limit their interpretation to a discussion around the advantages and disadvantages of the investment product, but, rather, they focused on whether a personal recommendation had been made by the defendant to the claimant. On this basis, English courts generally emphasised that 'advice on the merits' of buying or surrendering an investment cannot be 'confined to a consideration of the advantages or disadvantages of a particular 'investment' as a product',[106] thereby implying that, in rendering 'investment advice', the investment firm would need to draw upon the wider financial context such that the advice is based on 'as full an examination of the client's personal circumstances as the client is prepared to allow'.[107] The court observed that: 'the provision of purely factual information does not become objectionable merely because it feeds into the client's own decision-making process and is taken into account by him'.[108] However, it went on to say that: 'any element of comparison or evaluation or persuasion is likely to cross the dividing line'.[109] This underlines the importance of finding that a tailored recommendation, targeted at influencing the investor's decision, had been communicated to the investor in order to ascertain that 'investment advice' has been provided.

In the absence of a personal recommendation, a generic discussion which may have hinted at the benefits and drawbacks of the particular investment product, was not sufficient for the courts to conclude that the defendant firm had in effect provided 'investment advice'. Hence, whilst the provision of generic market

[106] *Martin* [5.2.5]. In this case, the claimant claimed damages against the defendant, an insurance group, on grounds that he received negligent advice resulting in financial losses. He contended that the defendant had failed to exercise due care and skill in giving proper advice on the nature and degree of the risks, alleging a contravention of the Code of Conduct under the LAUTRO Rules 1998, and consequently claiming damages under the private right of action conferred pursuant to FSA 1986, s 62. By way of background, Sch 2 to the LAUTRO Rules 1988 set out the Code of Conduct, which provided that, *inter alia*, prior to advising an investor on the surrender or cancellation of an investment, the investment firm must assess the financial needs of that investor, disclose all the relevant consequences of that decision, and recommend actions suited to the investor. In terms of r 3.4(4) of the LAUTRO Rules 1988, all members were explicitly obliged to ensure that their representatives comply with this Code.

[107] *Martin* [5.2.5]. This resonates with what was concluded in *Green and Rowley*, where the court held that a discussion about the advantages and disadvantages of a particular investment product is not, in itself, indicative that the defendant crossed the line separating the activity of providing 'information' from the activity of giving 'investment advice', hence implying that the broader context must be considered. On limited occasions, however, English courts concluded otherwise. For example, in *Zaki and Others v Credit Suisse (UK) Limited* [2011] EWHC 2422 (Comm), [2011] 2 CLC 523, affd [2013] EWCA Civ 14, [2013] 2 All ER (Comm) 1159 [83], Teare J stated that 'advice on the merits' refers to 'the advantages and disadvantages of purchasing the product', which, he added, must be presented as suitable for the investor.

[108] *Walker* [30].

[109] ibid. This claim was brought under the former regulatory regime of the FSA 1986 and the Personal Investment Authority (PIA) Rules. The claimant contended that the defendant, in breach of the principle of polarisation as enunciated in the PIA Rules, r.1.2.2(5)(a), r.4.2.1 and r.4.2.4, as well as the defendant's own compliance manual, had given investment advice to him on which he had acted to his detriment. PIA Rule, r.1.2.2(5)(a) prevented the second defendant from engaging in any investment business activity that its category did not allow, including offering investment advice.

information, for example, may contain traces of advice and recommendations, these inferences are likely to be regarded as 'incidental'[110] to the relationship between the parties and do not go beyond the daily interactions of a sales force with a purchaser.[111] As such the courts did not consider these to constitute 'advice on the merits' of a particular transaction and presumed that such advice, when given as part of the sales process, does not generally give rise to a duty of care.

The courts have also sought to apply a practical approach to the distinction between 'information' and 'investment advice', suggesting that it is 'corporately unreal'[112] to expect an investment firm to control communications with investors at all times in such a way that its representatives rigorously categorise whatever they say as 'information', 'opinion', 'advice', 'recommendations', and the like. In the court's view, this would make 'no corporate sense' and the regulatory regime would be 'impossible' to implement and comply with.[113] Insofar as the communication can be described as 'exchanging information ... bouncing ideas off each other ... [and] swapping hunches about the market' in a spontaneous manner, such discussions are thus not likely to amount to 'investment advice'.[114] Against this backdrop, and in line with PERG 8.28.4G as well as guidance issued in relation to the MiFID definition of 'investment advice', the courts have observed that the concept of 'investment advice' is to be construed broadly to capture:

> any communication with the client which, in the particular context in which it is given, goes beyond the mere provision of information and is objectively likely to influence the client's decision whether or not to undertake the transaction in question.[115]

The conclusions reached by English courts indicate that for a recommendation to constitute 'investment advice', this has to be adapted to the investor's personal needs, circumstances, and investment profile. Further, where an investment firm procures, or endeavours to procure, investors to enter into investment arrangements, English courts suggested that this activity would imply that the investment firm is advising the investor that it would be appropriate for the latter to purchase a product, and would thus extend beyond simply accentuating the advantages and

[110] *Michael Duthie Wilson, PS Trustees Limited v (1) MF Global UK Limited; (2) GNI Limited (in Members' Voluntary Liquidation)* [2011] EWHC 138 (QB) [80]. In this case, the court found that it was 'fundamentally important' that the parties had entered into an 'execution only' arrangement (see also *Wachner* [196]–[197], wherein it was stated that 'trading room opinions' could only give rise to a 'low level duty of care' and not the sort of duty or breach that was contended).

[111] *Thornbridge* [70].

[112] *Titan* [91].

[113] *Diamantides* [28].

[114] In *Wilson* [96], the claimants sought to recover trading losses caused by alleged breaches of duties said to be imposed by FSMA and contractual terms by the defendant financial investment brokers. The court held that the adoption of a rigid approach that analyses in detail each and every term used by the broker would make it close to impossible for brokers to entertain discussions with investors, such that communication exchanges would be 'drastically curtailed'. Similar conclusions were reached in *City Index Limited (t/a FinSpreads) v Romeo Balducci* [2011] EWHC 2562 (Ch), [2012] 1 BCLC 317 and *Wachner*.

[115] *Walker* [97] (see also, *Zaki*).

disadvantages of a particular product.[116] Even though the user is free to follow or otherwise disregard the advice, this is not relevant to the decision as to whether the activity being considered amounts to 'investment advice' or otherwise.[117]

The regulatory pronouncements taken into consideration by the courts in the cases being discussed, contained similar references to the notion of 'personal recommendation', indicating that 'investment advice' arises where communications made by the investment firm are aimed at 'influencing investment decisions of investors'.[118] To this end, where investment firms engage in 'interpretative functions' which go beyond the provision of 'purely factual information' such that they give users 'recommendations directly or indirectly', 'investment advice' is deemed to have been provided.[119] In this respect, the courts' conceptual interpretation appears to come close to the approach adopted by the FOS, particularly since it envisages that, in an advised sale, the investment firm takes on a more active role in which it attempts to match available products with the personal needs and circumstances of the investor, thereby giving a personal recommendation to the investor, which consequently amounts to 'investment advice'. Yet, where the relationship between the parties is governed by a contractual agreement which disclaims responsibility for, inter alia, investment advice, the provisions contained in this agreement would take precedence over any other non-contractual verbal communications that may have passed between the investment firm and the investor, even though these informal discussions may potentially contradict the formal contractual clauses.

V. Concluding Remarks

Despite the extensive pronouncements attempting to clarify the point at which neutral 'information' becomes 'investment advice', this chapter has demonstrated that investors have different tolerance levels for information. Further, other subtle elements, such as the body language of investment firms, may also come into play, purposely or otherwise, to suggest that a particular investment product should be favoured over another, such that the service being provided becomes of an advisory nature. Collectively, these factors contribute to the ambiguity which clouds

[116] *Martin* [5.2.5].

[117] *Re Market Wizard* [34] (see also CESR, 'Questions and Answers: Understanding the definition of advice under MiFID' (2010) 7).

[118] ASIC, 'Policy Statement 118 on Investment advisory services: media, computer software and Internet advice' (1997) para 118.22. As *Re Market Wizard* proceedings were underway in English courts, the sale of similar systems was also being investigated by ASIC. Amidst concerns relating to the significant role played by these computerised systems, ASIC issued this Policy Statement to disseminate guidance on such software.

[119] ASIC, 'Policy Statement 118 on Investment advisory services: media, computer software and Internet advice' (1997) para 118.31 (see also SIB, 'Chief Executive Annual Report for 1996/1997' (1997); draft letter from the SIB used to respond to enquiries from people offering 'technical analysis' – as referred to by Carnwath J in *Re Market Wizard* [30]).

the distinction between 'information' and 'investment advice' and which has led the regulator to acknowledge that 'the regulatory distinction between information and advice might not be readily understood by consumers'.[120]

Recent findings from an ESMA assessment concluded that the work done by NCAs to verify whether or not clients in practice are receiving (or have the perception that they receive) investment advice leaves much to be desired.[121] Further, the MiFID II reforms discussed in Section IA of chapter three have not sought to address this uncertainty and, as a result, it is still possible for investment firms to easily provide personal recommendations in a non-advised context and then defend themselves against allegations of regulatory breaches by contractually asserting that they were not advising on the transaction.[122] Guidance aimed at spelling out the distinguishing features of the two services has been, and is likely to remain, to a large extent futile and more stringent regulatory measures are therefore warranted. To this end, it is argued here that regulators should adopt a more paternalistic approach in securing a higher degree of protection to corporate retail investors in particular, given the restricted redress measures currently available to these investors as well as the unwillingness on the part of English courts and the regulator to acknowledge their limitations in terms of behavioural biases and lack of experience, knowledge and access to professional and financial resources.

As explored further in the next chapter, the shift from non-advised to advised services is extremely difficult to prove for an investor in the absence of a contractual undertaking explicitly assuming responsibility for the provision of 'investment advice'. English courts' emphasis on written contracts has meant that, although the investment firm may have crossed the information-only boundary by verbally advising the retail investor on a particular product, this does not necessarily imply that, in so doing, the former has assumed a legal responsibility to take reasonable care in connection with that advice. It is in this context that objective evidence, predominantly in the form of a formal assumption of responsibility embedded in the contractual terms of business becomes pivotal, thereby leading to the reforms being proposed in chapter seven.

[120] FSA, 'Regulation of Stakeholder Pensions – Feedback on CP61' (2001) para 3.8.

[121] ESMA, 'MiFID Suitability Requirements Peer Review Report' ESMA/2016/584 (2016) 4.

[122] Paolo Giudici, 'Independent Financial Advice' in in Danny Busch and Guido Ferrarini (eds), *Regulation of the EU Financial Markets: MiFID II and MiFIR* (Oxford University Press, 2017) 162–63.

5

Championing the Written Contract as the Decisive Tool for Managing Expectations: A Focus on the Mis-selling of IRHPs to Corporate Retail Investors

Part I of this book established that corporate retail investors lack the resources (predominantly in terms of experience, knowledge and financial support) to plough their way through endless standard terms of business and risk disclosures prior to making complex investment decisions. In so doing, it has challenged the presumption that this category of retail investors is less in need of regulatory protection measures in comparison to individual retail investors. The limitations of corporate retail investors become even more evident in this chapter which discusses the English courts' treatment of 'the ultimate tool for managing expectations'[1] in the context of an investment transaction, that is, the written contract.

English contract law has been developed 'with the aim of being consistent with the reasonable expectations of commercial parties',[2] and the current judicial approach is still 'stubbornly clinging'[3] to elements of the caveat emptor principle. More specifically, the analysis of English courts' decisions in the IRHP mis-selling cases set out in this chapter reveals an 'institutional pragmatic preference for the expedient of legal certainty',[4] which arguably results in 'manifestly unfair outcomes'[5] for corporate retail investors in particular. In fact, the judgments considered here suggest that 'a degree of self-seeking and ruthless behaviour is expected and accepted to a degree',[6] which goes against the spirit of the conduct of

[1] Adam Samuel, 'Contract Certainty – the new regulatory battlefield' (*Compliance Monitor*, 1 June 2005) 1: www.compliancemonitor.com/products-and-delivery/insurance/contract-certainty--the-new-regulatory-battlefield-40968.htm?origin=internalSearch, accessed 11 November 2014.

[2] Lloyd Maynard, 'Holmcroft Properties: will a contractual phoenix rise from its ashes?' (2016) 31 *Journal of International Banking and Financial Law* 356, 356.

[3] Friedrich Kessler, 'The Protection of the Consumer Under Modern Sales Law' (1964) 74 *Yale Law Journal* 262, 266.

[4] Paul Marshall, 'Novating mis-sold swaps: the poverty of narrowly contractual analysis' (2015) 30 *Journal of International Banking and Financial Law* 11, 11.

[5] ibid.

[6] *Vercoe and Others v Rutland Fund Management Ltd and Others* [2010] EWHC 424 (Ch), [2010] Bus LR D141 [343]. This message is also reiterated by the Courts in the IRHP mis-selling judgments considered in this chapter.

business framework contained in the MiFID regime[7] and the FCA's TCF initiative. The outcome of these cases revolves around the use of non-reliance standard form clauses, which are now commonplace in commercial contracts and through which investors confirm that they have not relied on any representations save for those expressly set out in the contract. Through these disclaimers, investment firms classify the investment service being provided to the retail investor as a non-advisory service, thereby limiting potential liability for pre-contractual representations and other common law duties that would arise had the same service been classified as 'investment advice'.

Underpinning the judicial support for such clauses are the traditional foundations of English contract law, primarily revolving around the notions of contractual freedom and legal certainty introduced in Section IID of chapter three, on the basis of which English courts appear to 'express great confidence in the reasonable investor's cognitive abilities'.[8] This approach runs counter to the behavioural law and economics school of thought presented in chapter two and, most notably, operates to the detriment of corporate retail investors, while also emerging as largely exceptional when compared to the judicial thinking in other jurisdictions displaying a pro-investor bias.

I. The Irrelevance of Investor Protection Objectives in Private Law

Historically, consumers' legal rights were derived primarily from the ordinary common law of contract, where a contractual relationship was described as 'the creation of the parties, who give it life … and subordinate to their will',[9] and where predictability, stability and free choice comprised the crucial elements underlying contract law principles to be found 'in every corner of contract law'.[10] The traditional focus of contract law on crude legal principles means that economic, social and behavioural concerns are typically addressed by other disciplines.[11] This however often renders private law an inadequate tool for investor protection, given

[7] eg, MiFID II, Art 24(1) imposes a general duty on an investment firm to 'act honestly, fairly and professionally in accordance with the best interests of its clients'.

[8] Barbara Black, 'Behavioural Economics and Investor Protection: Reasonable Investors and Efficient Markets' (2013) 44 *Loyola University Chicago Law Journal* 1493, 1493.

[9] Patrick S Atiyah, *The Rise and Fall of Freedom of Contract* (Clarendon Press, 1979) 36.

[10] ibid 95, 114, 399–400, 408. Robert J Pothier, in his book *A Treatise on the Law of Obligations, or Contracts* (A Strahan 1806) is the person who first gave expression to the notion that a contract is primarily an agreement based on the intention of the parties, and that it is their will which creates the legal obligation. Today, this remains the theory of contractual liability on which the English legal system is based.

[11] Karl Riesenhuber, 'Policy responses to credit crisis: does the law of contract provide the answer' in Stefan Grundmann and Yeşim M Atamer (eds), *Financial Services, Financial Crisis and General European Contract Law – Failure and Challenges of Contracting* (Kluwer Law International BV, 2011) 62–63.

that private law is not concerned with fairness or justice, and tends to 'run counter to equality and democracy'.[12]

In the context of standard form contracts, the judiciary acknowledged, on more than one occasion, that contract law principles tend to favour the party with the stronger bargaining power. On a European level, the CJEU admitted that the consumer is in a weaker position when compared to the supplier 'as regards both his bargaining power and his level of knowledge', which leads the former to agree to terms drawn up in advance by the latter without being able to exert any influence whatsoever.[13] This echoed what had already been observed by the UK House of Lords (as it then was) in *Suisse Atlantique Société d'Armement Maritime SA v NV Rotterdamsche Kolen Centrale*,[14] where the Court noted that:

> In the ordinary way the customer has no time to read them, and if he did read them he would probably not understand them. And if he did understand and object to any of them, he would generally be told he could take it or leave it. And if he then went to another supplier the result would be the same.[15]

Notwithstanding the above, and other cases where the courts have stressed the detrimental effect which the 'small print' buried in standard contracts is likely to have on consumers,[16] English Courts seem unlikely to 'sacrifice … [the] sacred cows of the law'[17] – namely contractual freedom and legal certainty – particularly in the context of commercial transactions. In the context of investment services, this has led to 'highly disproportionate'[18] agreements between investment firms holding superior bargaining power and corporate retail investors being in a much weaker negotiating position, and has been shown to hinder vulnerable corporate retail investors from obtaining adequate redress, especially due to the extensive disclaimers inserted by investment firms to limit their risks and responsibilities.

This is particularly evident from the conclusions reached by English courts in cases concerning the mis-selling of IRHPs, which clearly bring to the fore a judicial approach that favours defendant firms and penalises corporate retail investors despite their vulnerable position.[19] Whilst the underlying facts may differ, one

[12] Anthony Ogus, *Regulation: Legal Form and Economic Theory* (Oxford University Press, 1994) 26 (see also Joanna Benjamin, 'The Narratives of Financial Law' (2010) 30 *Oxford Journal of Legal Studies* 787, 795).

[13] Case C-240/98 *Océano Grupo Editorial SA v Murciano Quintero, Salvat Editores SA v Sánchez Alcón Prades* [2000] ECR I-4963, para 25. In the context of these joint cases, the CJEU was called to consider the jurisdictional clause with respect to Directive 93/13/EEC on unfair terms in consumer contracts, particularly the power of the national Court to examine of its own motion whether that clause is unfair.

[14] [1967] 1 AC 361 (HL), a landmark English contract law case, concerning the notion of a fundamental breach of contract relating to the chartering of a ship.

[15] ibid 406 (see also *Thornton v Shoe Lane Parking Ltd* [1970] EWCA Civ 2; *Schroeder*; *George Mitchell*).

[16] See eg *Abbey National Plc*.

[17] JA Jolowicz, 'The protection of the consumer and purchaser of goods under English Law' (1969) 32 *The Modern Law Review* 1, 18.

[18] Arthur A Leff, 'Contract as thing' (1970) 19 *The American University Law Review* 131, 141.

[19] See Section III of ch 1 for further detail on the IRHP mis-selling scandal.

can identify a discernible pattern in the principles adopted by English courts in addressing IRHP mis-selling claims – the investor, by having signed the standard terms of business, is deemed to have acknowledged the implied risks together with any limitations in the role and responsibilities of the investment firm as specified in the agreement, including reference to the nature of the service provided being exclusively non-advisory. In turn, those terms operate as a 'contractual estoppel' as a result of which the investor cannot subsequently maintain that he relied upon the advice provided by the defendant. In practice, this means that the bar for successfully alleging mis-selling of complex investments remains high for aggrieved corporate retail investors. Since English courts attribute a high degree of sophistication to corporate retail investors, contractual private agreements were fundamental in determining the underlying responsibilities of both parties to the IRHP contract, whilst also dictating the extent to which one party can be deemed to owe a duty of care towards the other and representing the exclusive source of the parties' voluntarily-assumed rights and obligations.

In establishing the extent of responsibilities that can be attributed to investment firms in the context of mis-selling allegations, two principal issues arise for the courts to consider.[20] In the first instance, the courts assess the applicability of any statute-based or other regulatory regime, and its impact on the regulatory classification of the claimant and the defendant, together with the nature of the service being provided and the relevant contractual arrangements. The court here considers the duties and liabilities that may arise out of the said regulatory regime and the extent to which this may modify what would otherwise be the common law position.[21] Secondly, the courts also consider other potential causes of action, which may comprise claims in relation to common law duties, including those founded on contract law, tort law and fiduciary duties. The discussion and observations being made hereunder are concerned with the latter set of issues, centring on the typical terms of business governing the relationship between the corporate retail investor and the investment firm.

A. Contractual Duty of Care in Advised and Non-advised Investment Transactions

At common law, a contract to provide advice gives rise to contractual and tortious duties on the part of the adviser to apply reasonable care and skill in providing that advice. This includes a duty to explain, which, in the context of investment advice,

[20] Rupert M Jackson, Roger Stewart and John Powell, *Jackson & Powell on Professional Liability*, 7th edn (Sweet & Maxwell Ltd, 2012) para 15-012.

[21] As further discussed in ch 6, considerations of this nature were not directly applicable to IRHP mis-selling cases given that corporate retail investors did not have recourse to a private right of action under FSMA, s 138D for breach of regulatory rules. Moreover, the courts failed to find a co-extensive relationship between private law and regulation insofar as IRHP-related claims were concerned.

translates into 'proper dialogue and communication between adviser and client … to ensure the client understands the advice and the risks attendant on a recommended investment'.[22] If this duty is breached, the adviser is liable in damages for the loss caused to the investor. Yet the duty of care may in some circumstances be restricted, or excluded altogether, by appropriate contractual drafting in relation to, for example, the nature of the service being provided, such that, where the service being contracted for is described as a 'non-advisory' one, the standard of care expected of an investment firm is much lower. The specific categorisation of the service being provided has proved to be pivotal in the context of the mis-selling of IRHPs to corporate retail investors. More specifically, as concluded in the seminal case of *Springwell*, in the absence of an advisory mandate, no contractual duty of care arises on the part of the defendant towards the claimant to advise him on the suitability of the investments.[23]

By adopting this position and relying heavily on contractual documentation, the courts were keen to keep alive the notion of contractual freedom. It is evident from their conclusions, that English courts believe that commercial parties merit utmost liberty when contracting. To this end, parties should have unfettered discretion to allocate risk in a way that 'preclude[s] any wider obligation arising from a common law duty of care'.[24] The lack of a clear advisory mandate is thus seen as an 'insurmountable obstacle'[25] to the imposition of an advisory duty of care as well as 'a strong indicator against the existence of any contractual or tortious duty of care'.[26]

The English courts' approach in this regard is also faithful to the parol evidence rule,[27] in that, notwithstanding other indicators pointing towards the existence

[22] *O'Hare* [204]. The extent of such a duty is governed by *Montgomery v Lanarkshire Health Board* [2015] UKSC 11, [2015] AC 1430, a case on patient consent, where the Supreme Court held that the medical adviser must 'take reasonable care to ensure that the patient is aware of any material risks involved in any recommended treatment, and of any reasonable alternative or variant treatments' [87]. The test of materiality in this context is 'whether, in the circumstances of the particular case, a reasonable person in the patient's position would be likely to attach significance to the risk, or the doctor is or should be aware that the particular patient would be likely to attach significance to it' [87].

[23] In so concluding, Gloster J, in *Springwell* singled out the following factors as being significant to the absence of a duty of care: 1. Springwell was considered to be a sophisticated investor since it had engaged in other similar transactions in the past with other financial institutions; 2. there was no advisory agreement between the parties and no further document evidencing an advisory relationship between them; and 3. if any advice was provided, this was in the form of recommendations, options and exchange of views, which communications were limited to information incidental to the non-advisory service being provided.

[24] *Titan* [89] (see also *Henderson and Others v Merrett Syndicates and Others* [1995] 2 AC 145 (HL); *Springwell*).

[25] *Wachner* [189] (see also *Green and Rowley*).

[26] *Springwell* (first instance) [130].

[27] Where the contract constitutes the entire agreement between the parties, the parol evidence rule disallows evidence to be admitted to contradict, vary, add to or subtract from the terms of a written contract or part thereof. The rule is intended preserve the integrity of a written agreement and allows it to be interpreted using well-established principles of contractual construction, which purport to promote certainty in resolution of legal disputes. A party may hence be refused evidence extrinsic to the contract, as the 'written instrument', that could potentially contradict its contents and hence its

of an advisory duty of care, as for example may have transpired from verbal discussions between the parties, the written contractual terms of agreement are held supreme and regarded as the 'acid test' in determining the existence of such contractual duty of care.[28] In effect, English courts have recognised that the terms of business might not have formed an accurate representation of the actual relationship between the parties, suggesting that relationship managers were 'indeed giving advice'[29] and providing 'a personal recommendation about the merits of the various products that he was offering …'[30] (at least in verbal discussions with the investor). The courts admitted that in such circumstances a relationship manager would act as a 'salesman to his bones',[31] taking advantage of the fact that the claimant knew next to nothing as to how the IRHP mechanism worked and thus 'fail[ing] to grasp [IRHPs] intellectually or appreciate their implications'.[32] Yet, this acknowledgement only symbolised a 'Pyrrhic victory'[33] for claimants, as investment firms were still deemed not to have assumed any contractual obligation to advise the claimant about the suitability of the investments, based on the 'general absence of any indicia'[34] in the standard terms that could give rise to any such duty. This reaffirms the legal significance of appropriate and well-drafted agreements, as well as the English Courts' view that conclusions should be based on 'inferences drawn from the documentary evidence and known probable facts',[35] as opposed to witness recollections or other verbal conversations.

The fact that contractual disclaimers take precedence over any verbal communications between the parties has been challenged in regulatory pronouncements issued by CESR (as it then was) and the FCA.[36] These two regulatory bodies observed that, even if disclaimers stating that no advice or recommendation is being provided are presented in a clear, prominent and understandable manner, this does not necessarily change the basic nature of a communication and it may still constitute a personal recommendation and henceforth investment advice.[37]

validity (see eg *Roe v R A Naylor Ltd* [1917] 1 KB 712; *Jacobs v Batavia and General Plantations Ltd* [1924] 1 Ch 287; *Turner v Forwood* [1951] 1 All ER 746 (CA); Law Commission, *The Parol Evidence Rule* (HMSO Working Paper No 70, 1976); Law Commission, *Law of contract: the parol evidence rule* (HMSO Cmnd 9700, 1986)).

[28] See eg *Springwell* (first instance).

[29] ibid [107].

[30] ibid.

[31] *Crestsign* [31].

[32] ibid [38].

[33] Gregory Mitchell, 'To advise or not to advise?' (2014) 29 *Journal of International Banking and Financial Law* 686, 689.

[34] *Springwell* (first instance) [441] (see also *Thornbridge*).

[35] *Gestmin SGPS SA v (1) Credit Suisse (UK) Limited; (2) Credit Suisse Securities (Europe) Limited* [2013] EWHC 3560 (Comm) [22], where the claimant alleged that investment advice given by the defendant was negligent and asked the Court to award damages for loss it suffered as a result of making the investment.

[36] CESR 'Questions and Answers: Understanding the definition of advice under MiFID' (2010) 12; FCA, 'Finalised Guidance FG15/1, Retail Investment Advice' (2015) para 3.53.

[37] See eg OFT, 'Unfair contract terms guidance: Guidance for the Unfair Terms in Consumer Contracts Regulations 1999' (2008) paras 18.5.5–18.5.7; FCA, 'Business Plan 2014/2015' (2014) 37.

Similarly, in the context of the pensions mis-selling scandal in the UK, the then SIB and PIA carried out a review into the pensions selling practices and found that some investment firms operated a deliberate policy to only formally offer non-advisory services to clients, thereby avoiding having to comply with the duties of best advice and suitability applicable at the time to advisory services and also disclaiming the respective liability as a consequence. To this end, the SIB and PIA concluded that, in the absence of convincing evidence (which had to go beyond a customer's signature on a standard document attesting that no advice was given), these cases were not to be treated as non-advised services and the duties of best advice and suitability had to be satisfied.[38]

Despite the relationship between the claimant and the defendant in IRHP-related cases potentially extending into the 'advice' territory, however, English courts considered this to be irrelevant in a situation where the claimant consented to the non-reliance statements embedded in the contract. By signing the agreements, the corporate retail investor was thus considered to have accepted a particular state of affairs which might have been different from the actual reality.[39] In this sense, non-reliance clauses serve an important purpose in the eyes of English courts, in that they bring greater certainty by maintaining the integrity of the written agreement. Clauses of this nature are perceived by the courts as being designed to protect one contracting party from the other party 'threshing through the undergrowth'[40] in the hope of unearthing a chance remark or representation, made during pre-contractual negotiations, which turned out to be false, and on which to base a claim for rescission of the agreement despite the parties having agreed that any such representations have not been made or are otherwise not to be relied upon. Equally, English courts dismissed any internal documentation referring to the investment firm as 'advising' the investor as merely 'internal and informal documents'[41] which do not constitute objective evidence and which do not support the existence of an obligation on the part of the investment firm to take reasonable care or otherwise give advice on the transactions.[42]

[38] PIA, 'Pension Transfer and Opt Outs: Review of Past Business' (1995) paras 23–24 (see also SIB, 'Pension Transfers and Opt Outs: Further Safeguards for Future Business' (1994) paras 41–48; Julia Black and Richard Nobles, 'Personal Pensions Misselling: The Causes and Lessons of Regulatory Failure' (1998) 61 *The Modern Law Review* 789, 804).

[39] *Standard Chartered Bank v Ceylon Petroleum Corporation* [2011] EWHC 1785 (Comm), affd [2012] EWCA Civ 1049 [544]. In this case, Hamblen J accepted that the relationship manager would seek to come up with products suiting the investor's requirements, possibly putting a positive spin on certain choices, yet still ruled in favour of the investment firm.

[40] *Inntrepreneur Pub Co v East Crown Ltd* [2000] 2 Lloyd's Rep 611 Ch D 614. In so stating, Lightman J was referring to 'entire agreement clauses', which, in their extended form, can also include non-reliance clauses and other disclaimers of a similar nature.

[41] *Ceylon Petroleum Corporation* (first instance) [495].

[42] See eg *Springwell* (first instance) [380], where Gloster J contended that the meaning of phrases such as 'trusted financial adviser' found in internal documents or in correspondence between the parties, should be considered in their relevant context and may well be 'a mere "slogan" or buzzword … intended to encourage relationship managers to maintain close relationships with their customers and to understand their business as a whole.'

In essence, therefore, the contractual agreement between the parties is deemed by the courts to have 'broader evidential significance'[43] in negating the existence of a general advisory duty of care than any peripheral factors that may suggest otherwise. This allows the court to safeguard its role as an 'impartial and reasonable observer',[44] where what matters are the disclaimers contained in the agreement that 'prevent a representation from having been made, or … exclude liability for making it'.[45] By so doing, however, the courts fail to consider whether the investment firm has correctly categorised the service as 'non-advisory' or otherwise as required by the applicable regulatory framework. This has also meant that the courts have dismissed IRHP mis-selling cases as 'case[s] based on hindsight',[46] rather than clear mis-selling cases where corporate retail investors had been advised to enter into an investment in unsuitable circumstances. On this basis, it can be concluded that, indirectly, the courts have enabled investment firms to circumvent the additional regulatory obligations incumbent upon them (as a result of the advice which was effectively provided) by contractually defining the service being provided as a non-advised service rather than an advised service.

This position is to be distinguished from similar cases of alleged mis-selling where the relationship between parties was governed by a different form of contractual agreement containing less restrictive disclaimers.[47] In these circumstances, the court cannot immediately conclude that the investment firm was not willing to assume responsibility for the provision of advice and hence must also weigh other indicators (including informal discussions and internal documentation). As a result, the court cannot limit its analysis to the wording of the contractual agreement in deciding whether or not the defendant had 'crossed the line' to provide 'advice on the merits' of a particular investment transaction and whether it had breached its common law duty of care or otherwise.[48] In the absence of a contractual delineation of responsibility, the court is more at liberty to consider other factors outside the terms of the contract to decide on the nature of the relationship and whether this gives rise to an advisory duty of care or otherwise.[49] In this context, the court looks at whether an 'impartial observer',[50] having due regard to

[43] ibid [478].

[44] *Crestsign* [112].

[45] ibid.

[46] *Thornbridge* [226].

[47] See eg *Riyad Bank and Others v Ahli United Bank (UK) Plc* [2006] EWCA Civ 780, [2006] 1 CLC 1007; *Zaki*; *David Anderson v Openwork Ltd* [2015] EW Misc B14 (18 June 2015); *Philip Thomas and Another v Triodos Bank NV* [2017] EWHC 314 (QB). It is to be noted that repeated transactions in the context of an ongoing relationship between a retail investor and an investment firm tend to be governed by detailed contractual agreements containing a series of disclaimers. On the other hand, one-off transactions are typically not subject to a formal contract defining the scope of the obligations and hence it is easier for claimants to successfully argue that advice was indeed provided.

[48] See eg *David Anderson*.

[49] *Grant* [75].

[50] *Rubenstein v HSBC Bank Plc* [2011] EWHC 2304 (QB), [2011] 2 CLC 459, revd [2012] EWCA Civ 1184, [2013] 1 All ER (Comm) 915 [83].

the regulatory regime and relevant guidance, as well as all the communications between the parties, would conclude that advice had been given or otherwise. In these circumstances, the regulatory regime and the obligations it imposes on investment firms have a significant bearing, which is not the case where there is a clear non-advisory mandate.

i. The Approach of Overseas Judiciary

Courts in overseas jurisdictions have repeatedly considered claims relating to classification of investment services as 'advisory' and 'non-advisory', as well as the extent to which advisory relationships can be excluded by reference to the contractual undertakings between the parties. Generally speaking, the foreign judicial authorities examined by this book have tended towards a pro-investor bias when enforcing standard form contracts in the context of mis-sold complex investment products (including IRHPs and other products of a similar nature) by, inter alia, acknowledging the superiority of the drafter's bargaining power and attaching due weight to verbal exchanges between parties.[51]

This pro-investor bias is particularly acute in civil law jurisdictions, which not only are notoriously less reliant on paper-based evidence, but actually classify MiFID conduct of business rules as norms with a dual legal nature, with the effect that these rules also qualify as private law norms apart from being regulatory rules.[52] In such countries, regulatory rules help to define the pre-contractual and contractual duty of care of investment firms under private law,[53] such that the courts in these jurisdictions interpret the conduct of business obligations of investment firms under the regulatory regime in a manner which tips the balance of responsibility for investment decisions towards investment firms.[54] On this

[51] Predominantly, this approach has informed the judgments handed by the courts in Germany, the Netherlands, Spain, Belgium, Holland, and Italy, as shall be referred to in this Section (see further Arthur S Hartkamp, Marianne M Tillema and Annemarie EB ter Heide, *Contract Law in the Netherlands*, 2nd edn (Kluwer Law International, 2011); Fernando Zunzunegui, 'Mis-selling of preferred shares to Spanish retail clients' (2014) 29 *Journal of International Banking Law and Regulation* 174).

[52] Danny Busch, 'The private law effect of MiFID: the Genil case and beyond' (2017) 13 *European Review of Contract Law* 70, 70–71.

[53] ibid 72.

[54] See eg German cases: *Haftung der Bank für unzureichende Anlageberatung – Bond-Anleihe* (BGH 6 July 1993, BGHZ 123, 126), and *Ille Papier Service GmbH v Deutsche Bank AG* (XI ZR 33/10) (unreported, 22 March 2011) BGH (Ger); and Dutch cases Ermes/Haviltex, *NJ* 1981, 635 (a case establishing what is known as the 'Haviltex formula'), Lundiform/Mexx, 5 April 2013, *LJN* BY8101, and *Burgo v Rabobank*, 29 February 2012, FR 2012/48; *De T v Dexia Bank Nederland NV, Levob Bank NV v B* and *GBD and Strichting Gedupeerden Spaarconstructie v Aegon Bank NV*, 5 June 2009, *RvdW* 2009, which followed the Opinion of the Advocate General of 13 February 2009. See also Olha O Cherednychenko, 'Full Harmonization of Retail Financial Services Contract Law in Europe: A Success or a Failure?' in Stefan Grundmann and Yeşim M Atamer (eds), *Financial Services, Financial Crisis and General European Contract Law – Failure and Challenges of Contracting* (Kluwer Law International BV, 2011) 253; Paul Marshall, 'Fault lines in English financial law: Thornbridge v Barclays Bank' (2016) 31 *Journal of International Banking and Financial Law* 266, 266.

basis, it can be concluded that the equivalent of the 'signature rule' and the 'parol evidence rule' (both considered sacrosanct by English courts) are, by comparison, less central to the considerations of the courts in these other jurisdictions, as the latter are more willing to scrutinise and challenge commercial contracts on the basis of an imbalance in the parties' bargaining position as well as in light of the holistic exchanges between the parties starting from the inception of the parties' relationship. Indeed, civil courts in these jurisdictions would have little hesitation in giving precedence to financial supervision law over the contractual terms of business. A clause stipulating that an investment firm does not provide advice is thus likely to be set aside on the basis of a reasonable interpretation of the contract as well as following consideration of any ancillary discussions between the parties. More importantly, such a limitation may also be seen as being unreasonably onerous when applied to corporate retail investors.[55]

The methodology adopted by foreign judiciary in considering the knowledge and experience of retail investors also departs from the English courts' approach. In determining the nature of the relationship and the duties attached thereto, continental courts have also considered the knowledge and experience of the investor with reference to regulatory rules, apart from the contractual undertakings governing the relationship. More specifically, the courts in these jurisdictions have held that, although the claimant may have already entered into other complex interest swap agreements prior to concluding the transaction in question, this does not affect the defendant's duty to explore the risk profile of the investor, as the nature of the risks and complexities attached to the respective transactions may not be directly comparable.[56] Further, just because one is knowledgeable about a particular product, one is not assumed to be necessarily willing to take on risks and, therefore, such prior knowledge of a product does not in any way limit the investment firm's duty to explore the investment objectives of the investor.[57]

English courts' conclusions in relation to IRHP judgments do not appear to have been based on any such detailed assessments into the respective knowledge and experience of claimants. English courts did not consider the specific complexities and risk factors pertaining to individual products that may require additional knowledge and experience on the part of the retail investor. In this sense, English courts appear to consider *any* past experience in *any* complex investment as a prima facie indication of experience, thereby treating the investor as sophisticated

[55] Danny Busch, 'Agency and Principal Dealing under MiFID I and MiFID II' in Danny Busch and Guido Ferrarini (eds), *Regulation of the EU Financial Markets: MiFID II and MiFIR* (Oxford University Press, 2017) 242.

[56] *Ille Papier.*

[57] See eg the German case of *Ille Papier* and the Spanish case of Provincial Court of Alava, 27 March 2009 (80/2009). See also European Commission, 'Study on the application of Directive 2005/29/EC on Unfair Corporate Practices in the EU, Part 2 – Country Reports' Conducted by Civic Consulting (2011) para 9.2.13, which notes that an assessment of the specific knowledge of the particular investor, or prospective investor, is crucial for evaluating the appropriateness of the information provided.

and practically at par with the investment firm.[58] This is not only hardly ever the case in practice but also overlooks the fact that, in relation to past investments, the investor may have entered into these earlier transactions unwisely, or may otherwise have similarly fallen victim to mis-selling in the past.[59] Most notably, English courts made no distinction between claimants that had been classified as 'private' or 'retail' investors, and those which belonged to the professional categories, in terms of the applicable conduct of business regulatory regime which acknowledges that the former categories of investors are entitled to a higher level of protection.

The literal enforcement of the 'duty to read' principle, the signature rule and the parol evidence rule that have inspired common law jurisprudence in the UK as confirmation and protection of the freedom of contract and legal certainty principles, has therefore been met with scepticism in civil legal systems that tend to consider other broader circumstances and that claim that freedom of contract can be realised only if both parties can exercise it by giving their assent about content that they actually understand and accept.[60] Overall, continental courts tend to adopt a more interventionist approach in the context of investment services, suggesting that, everything else being equal, UK claimants may be at a disadvantage when compared to their counterparts in other EU jurisdictions.[61]

Contrary to the judicial stance of the aforementioned civil law jurisdictions, the approach of courts in certain common law countries, namely Hong Kong, has been remarkably similar to that of the UK. The Hong Kong judicial position echoes that of English courts in relation to, inter alia, its adherence to the parol and signature rules as well as, the importance it attributes to clear and express contractual terms that disclaim responsibility for the provision of advisory services and the duty of care attached thereto.[62] Where the contractual agreements between the parties have not been specific in outlining the nature of the investment services being provided, the Hong Kong judiciary's approach can also be compared to that of English courts. In these instances, the wider factual matrix underpinning the relationship is considered, which would include marketing materials contained

[58] With reference to the UK cases discussed in this chapter, the courts' conclusion that the claimants, being corporate retail investors, are to be treated as 'sophisticated' counterparties was not backed by any technical analysis of claimants' previous investments suggesting that such investments had comparable risk profiles and on which, therefore, the defendant could rely to assume knowledge and experience on the part of the claimant.

[59] Marc Kruithof, 'Policy responses to credit crisis: does the law of contract provide the answer' in Stefan Grundmann and Yeşim M Atamer (eds), *Financial Services, Financial Crisis and General European Contract Law – Failure and Challenges of Contracting* (Kluwer Law International BV, 2011) 157–58.

[60] Elena D'Agostino, *Contracts of Adhesion Between Law and Economics: Rethinking the Unconscionability Doctrine* (Springer International Publishing, 2015) 4.

[61] See eg Jacob Bonavita, 'Case comment: The regulation of 'speculative interest-rate bets' by the German Federal Court of Justice – new dimensions of market intervention hidden behind the old information model' (2012) 13 *European Business Organization Law Review* 271, 271.

[62] See eg, Hong Kong cases: *Kwok Wai Hing Selina v HSBC Private Bank (Suisse) SA* HCCL 7/2010; *DBS Bank (Hong Kong Limited) v San-Hot HK Industrial Company Limited and Hao Ting* [2013]

in brochures, the degree of investors' experience, the reason for investing (for example preservation of capital as opposed to speculative trading), as well as other verbal and written communications exchanged between the parties.[63]

B. The Principle of 'Assumption of Responsibility'

Prior to the authoritative decision of the House of Lords (as it then was) in *Hedley Byrne & Co Ltd v Heller & Partners Ltd*,[64] the notion that a party may owe another a duty of care in respect of statements on which the other may reasonably rely had been rejected, with the only remedy for such losses being in contract law. In *Hedley Byrne*,[65] however, the then House of Lords overruled this previous position in recognising liability for mis-statement causing pure economic loss not arising from a contractual relationship. This introduced the concept of 'assumption of responsibility' where the relationship between the parties is sufficiently 'proximate' as to create a duty of care and can, therefore, create relationships 'equivalent to contract',[66] such that a party can be found liable in tort for his actions. This was subsequently confirmed by the House of Lords (as it then was) in *Henderson*[67] and *Commissioners of Customs & Excise v Barclays Bank*,[68] suggesting that, notwithstanding the need to take into account all the relevant facts of the case in the overall determination,[69] an assumption of responsibility on the part of the defendant towards the claimant emerges as 'a core area of liability for economic loss'[70] and is therefore 'necessary to establish a cause of action'.[71] This is evident from a number of other landmark judgments which indicate that in cases where the loss has been caused by the claimant's reliance on communications made by the defendant, the decision to be made is whether the defendant assumed responsibility for such communications towards the claimant or otherwise.[72]

HKEC 352; *DBS Bank (Hong Kong) Limited v Sit Pan Jit* [2015] HKEC 548, affd [2017] HKEC 298, FAMV 45/2016.

[63] See eg *Chang Pui Yin and Others v Bank of Singapore Limited* [2016] HECK 1721; *Li Kwok Heem John v Standard Chartered International (USA) Limited (formerly known as American Express Bank Limited)* [2016] 1 HKC 535.

[64] [1964] AC 465 (HL).

[65] ibid.

[66] ibid 30. In using this term, Lord Devlin borrowed the words of Lord Shaw in *Nocton v Ashburton* [1914] AC 932 (HL) 972, a case concerning a solicitor who had allegedly persuaded his client to release a charge thus advancing the solicitor's own subsequent charge on the same property.

[67] *Henderson*.

[68] [2006] UKHL 28, [2007] 1 AC 181.

[69] Lord Hoffmann, in *Commissioners of Customs & Excise* (ibid) [35], stated that the court should consider 'what would reasonably be inferred from [the defendant's] conduct against the background of all circumstances of the case'.

[70] ibid [83].

[71] *Henderson* 180.

[72] See eg *Hedley Byrne*; *Caparo*; *Smith v Eric S Bush* (A Firm) [1990] UKHL 1, [1990] 1 AC 831 (HL); *Williams v Natural Life Health Foods Ltd* [1998] 1 WLR 830 (HL).

Notwithstanding the above, in the IRHP-related mis-selling claims considered by this book, the courts were not prepared to find a party liable where, in the contractual agreement between the parties, the investment firm disclaimed responsibility for the provision of advisory services and the duty of care attaching thereto. Thus, where parties contractually define the terms upon which they will conduct business, including by means of clauses rejecting responsibility for the provision of investment advice, this would typically constitute 'a clear and often determinative indication as to the non-existence of any wider tortious duty',[73] and would prevail over any peripheral exchanges which the parties might have had. Hence, whilst the existence of an underlying contract does not automatically exclude the general duty of care which the law imposes, the nature and terms of the contractual agreement between the parties 'will be determinative of the scope of the responsibility assumed' and may also 'exclude any assumption of legal responsibility' or otherwise 'modify and shape the tortious duties which, in the absence of a contract, would be applicable'.[74] Posited differently, an assumption of responsibility will be subject to any term of the contract which may exclude or restrict liability and may therefore 'be negatived by an appropriate disclaimer'.[75]

To this end, the Court in *Green and Rowley*[76] found that: '[t]he duty to take care not to mis-state is much narrower than the advisory duty where one would expect that relevant professional standards would form part of the assessment as to whether it had been broken'. Thus, if the contractual terms limit the scope of the investment firm's duties under the agreement, the investment firm's tortious duty of care shall also be limited to the same extent.[77] This reflects the observations made by Lord Scarman in *Tai Hing Cotton Mill Ltd v Liu Chong Hing Bank Ltd and Others*,[78] when he noted that tortious duties should not generally be allowed to extend the content of contractual obligations subsisting between contracting parties, and also resonates with the Court's decision in *Finch and Another v Lloyds TSB Bank Plc and Others*,[79] where the allegation that the defendant had voluntarily assumed a tortious duty to advise was rejected. Similarly, the three Court of Appeal judges in *Wellesley Partners LLP v Withers LLP*[80] unanimously agreed that, in cases of concurrent liability, the test of remoteness should be the contractual

[73] *Springwell* (first instance) [475].

[74] *Henderson* 206.

[75] ibid 181E. See also *White and Another v Jones and Another* [1995] UKHL 5, [1995] 2 AC 207, 268.

[76] *Green and Rowley* (first instance) [82].

[77] Rupert M Jackson, Roger Stewart and John Powell, *Jackson & Powell on Professional Liability*, 7th edn (Sweet & Maxwell Ltd, 2012) para 15-034.

[78] [1986] AC 80 (PC) 107, a case concerning a claim by a company seeking to recover sums of money from three banks, where money was allegedly wrongfully debited from the claimant's current account.

[79] [2016] EWHC 1236 (QB), [2017] BCLC 34, a case which contemplates a lending transaction. In this instance, the court also observed that the close working relationship which arose between the bank and the borrowers did not override the fact that the corporate interests of the two organisations were 'diametrically opposed' [51]–[54].

[80] [2015] EWCA Civ 1146, [2016] 2 WLR 1351 [60]–[80] (Floyd LJ), [145]–[163] (Roth LJ); [181]–[188] (Longmore LJ). This case concerns a professional negligence claim against the defendant for the negligent drafting of a partnership agreement between the claimant and its new investor.

one and that this should exhaustively govern the relationship, whilst noting that since the tortious liability of a professional normally arose from an assumption of responsibility, it was only logical to apply to it the rules of assumed, rather than imposed, liability.

In the context of IRHP cases, investment firms hence 'went out of their way'[81] to ensure that standard terms excluded the possibility of a duty of care arising – both as a result of poor advice being provided and of this advice potentially giving rise to economic loss. This is to be contrasted with a situation where contractual terms specifically provide for an advisory duty, which constitute a clear assumption of responsibility on the part of the investment firm and establish a higher degree of proximity between the parties. Where the terms of business are silent, in that there are no provisions seeking to exclude a duty of care and there are no clauses making direct reference to an advised transaction, the court would also be free to refer to the broader circumstantial evidence, which may indicate that proximity and consequent assumption of responsibility would apply. In these instances, the court may find the investment firm negligent in recommending a product that was unsuitable for the investor, whilst also concluding that the former did not use reasonable care in providing its advice.[82]

Against this backdrop, therefore, it is here noted that English courts have established that there is 'a clear distinction between giving advice and assuming legal responsibility for that advice',[83] and, in the court's view, where the investment firm is subject to a regulatory regime by law, rather than by agreement, the case for inferring that it assumed responsibility to the investor for compliance with the regime becomes less strong because the investment firm has no option but to comply with such regulatory regime.[84] English courts have made it clear that only expressed undertakings are to be considered as forming part of the terms of business, noting that if the investment firm had assumed responsibility for the provision of investment advice, then the court would have expected that the scope of such duties would have at least been defined in a written document, particularly in view of the complexity of the transactions in question and the substantial amounts of money linked thereto.[85] Implications are therefore not to be read into the contract and the courts do not see it as part of their role to inquire whether one party *had* in fact relied upon the other, but, rather, their focus is on determining whether that party *ought* to have done so in terms of the contract. Similarly, the

[81] *Crestsign* [111].

[82] In *Crestsign* [130], eg, Kerr J noted that, but for his conclusion on contractual estoppel, he '... would find a clear breach of the [Hedley Byrne] duty in recommending [the investment] as suitable products'. He also observed that the disparity in knowledge, expertise, and roles embodied by the representatives of the investment firm, were such that it was to be reasonably expected that the claimant would rely of the relationship manager's skill and judgement, and, aside from the terms of agreement, it would be reasonable for him to do so.

[83] *Ceylon Petroleum Corporation* (first instance) [508].

[84] See further *Thomas* [80].

[85] See eg *Springwell* (first instance) [435].

courts have no interest in what the claimant might have acquired as a result of the transaction in question, but what matters to the judiciary is what he was *entitled* to acquire, such that any 'unbargained-for reliance' is not legally justifiable and neither is it legally protected.[86]

All in all, it is noted that English courts have steered clear of interpreting contracts by invoking commercial common sense 'retrospectively'[87] in a way that creates a deal that the parties might have reached had they anticipated the events. To a great extent, however, investment firms appear to be exploiting this fundamental contractual principle in their dealings with weaker parties, including corporate retail investors, to the detriment of the latter.

C. Misrepresentation Act 1967 and Unfair Contract Terms Act 1977 – The English Courts' Emphasis on Legal Certainty

Aggrieved claimants in IRHP mis-selling cases have invoked two main provisions of the Misrepresentation Act 1967 to support their claim. First, they sought rescission of the contract under section 2 of the Misrepresentation Act 1967, and requested that they be placed in the same position that they would have been had they never entered into the contract in question. Secondly, they invoked section 3 of the Misrepresentation Act 1967 since it operates to prevent a person from excluding or restricting liability for misrepresentation, or any remedy available for misrepresentation, by a contractual term, unless it satisfies the requirement of reasonableness as set out in section 11 of the UCTA. In parallel, their claim was also made pursuant to sections 2 and 3 of the UCTA, which respectively provide that a person cannot exclude or restrict liability for negligence or for a breach of the terms of agreement by a contractual term or notice unless it satisfies the requirement of reasonableness.[88] In the context of IRHP litigation, non-reliance provisions and the related disclaimers embedded in standard form contracts have prevented claims in misrepresentation from being upheld as they have operated to successfully limit the liability of the investment firm, notwithstanding that the claimants were relatively small and inexperienced corporate retail investors.

The case of *Peekay Intermark Ltd v Australia and New Zealand Banking Group Ltd*[89] can be considered as the landmark IRHP judgment on misrepresentation

[86] Atiyah Patrick S Atiyah, *The Rise and Fall of Freedom of Contract* (Clarendon Press, 1979) 467.

[87] *Arnold* [19]. In *Arnold*, the Supreme Court reiterated the importance of upholding the letter of the contract over 'corporate common sense'. In *Wood* the Supreme Court promoted a more balanced view by suggesting that both elements be considered.

[88] Claimants in alleged financial mis-selling cases have drawn upon these provisions to argue that contractual clauses excluding representation and reliance should be seen as attempts to exclude liability for misrepresentation to which s 3 of the Misrepresentation Act 1967 and ss 2 and 3 of the UCTA should apply.

[89] [2005] EWHC 830 (Comm), [2005] 2 CLC 111, revd [2006] EWCA Civ 386, [2006] 1 CLC 582.

claims. In the first instance, the trial judge held that the nature of the product had indeed been misrepresented to Mr Pawani, acting on behalf of the claimant company, Peekay.[90] The Court of Appeal, however, reversed the decision upon considering that Mr Pawani himself was at fault for not having read the contract in enough detail to notice that the nature of the product had changed. Consequently, the Court of Appeal did not uphold the action for misrepresentation against the investment firm. Equally, challenges in English courts via recourse to the UCTA have been largely unsuccessful as a result of the courts' interpretation of the nature of the contested clauses. The question of whether a clause properly describes the future relationship between the parties (a 'basis' clause not subject to the UCTA) or whether it seeks to exclude liability on the part of the investment firm (an 'exclusion' clause subject to the UCTA) has been considered by the courts in IRHP mis-selling cases,[91] with the courts generally favouring the former, which significantly weakens the protection measures afforded by the UCTA.

In the case of IRHP mis-selling allegations, contractual agreements do not go as far as excluding the duty once it has arisen and hence were considered as defining the scope of the duty undertaken, which consequently falls outside the scope of the UCTA.[92] Consequently, English courts concluded that the numerous disclaimers and non-reliance clauses set out in the IRHP-type standard contracts should not be 'characterised in substance as a notice excluding or restricting a liability for negligence',[93] but, rather, are to be regarded as basis clauses defining the relationship between the parties to the contract wherein 'X agrees with Y that Y is not acting as an adviser or assuming any responsibility'.[94] To this effect, any such wording was described by the court as: 'defin[ing] the basis of [the parties'] trading or banking relationship and allocat[ing] risk in a way which negates any possibility of

[90] The nature of the product that was sold was considered materially different from the product described originally by the account manager, which led the court to conclude at first instance that the claimant was entitled to damages equal to the difference between the actual return on the product and the original investment.

[91] A 'basis' clause may have similar effects to an 'exclusion' clause that is subject to statutory control under the UCTA, but the former is significantly more effective because it precludes the antecedent relevant duties from arising in the first place, and therefore falls outside the scope of statutory control and protection, whilst also giving rise to 'contractual estoppel'.

[92] Even so, the respective terms of agreement in most of the cases hereby considered would have satisfied the test of reasonableness of the UCTA since claimants were considered as 'sophisticated' by the courts. It is to be noted that the claimant in *Crestsign* was granted permission to appeal on, inter alia, whether the relevant clause contained in the defendant's standard terms actually prevented the claimant's cause of action against the defendant for negligent advice (a basis clause) or whether it was in fact an exclusion clause which must be subject to the UCTA reasonableness test. The appeal hearing was due to take place in the Spring of 2016, but, on 19 February 2016, the parties reached a confidential settlement whereby Crestsign agreed to withdraw its appeal and pursue no other claims in respect of the IRHPs.

[93] *IFE Fund SA v Goldman Sachs International* [2006] EWHC 2887 (Comm), [2006] 2 CLC 1043, 1060, affd [2007] EWCA Civ 811.

[94] *Raiffeisen Zentralbank Österreich AG v The Royal Bank of Scotland Plc* [2010] EWHC 1392 (Comm), [2011] 1 Lloyd's Rep 123 [304].

a general or specific advisory duty coming into existence',[95] thereby consequently refuting any assumption of responsibility on the part of the defendant. As a result of the English courts' 'undesirability of intervening in commercial transactions',[96] and because the courts are reluctant to cast doubt on the enforceability of standard form contracts in such a way that would generate uncertainty, the Misrepresentation Act 1967 and the UCTA become 'of very limited application in the case of commercial contracts between commercial counterparties'.[97]

Corporate retail investors thus face significant obstacles in bringing claims for negligent misrepresentation where the documentation negates any advisory duty. Unsurprisingly, these investors are more likely to be successful in their claims under the Misrepresentation Act 1967 and the UCTA where the relationship between the parties is governed by a clear contractual undertaking to provide advice. This is because once an investment firm recommends a particular investment as suitable for a client or prospective client, this recommendation embeds implicit representations stating that the investment firm has carefully assessed the nature of the investment in light of the investor's knowledge, experience, financial situation and investment objectives, and that the investment firm assumes responsibility for that assessment.[98]

In the context of misrepresentation claims, corporate retail investors have also been assessing the possible impact, on their IRHP claims, of the LIBOR rigging allegations on their IRHP mis-selling claims, specifically regarding alleged misrepresentations made by investment firms relating to the LIBOR. Still, whilst the court ruled that a LIBOR fixing claim was a triable issue in one instance,[99] and ordering, in a separate case, that investment firms make available LIBOR-related documentation for inspection as these were considered relevant to the mis-sale of an IRHP,[100] there is, at the time of writing, no definite case law on the matter as these disputes were either settled out of court ahead of the trial taking place or are currently still at trial stage. If investment firms were to lose on LIBOR matters, and especially if rescission of the contract is granted by the court, an avalanche of LIBOR-related claims can be expected to follow, with the respective probability of success in each turning on the facts of the respective case.

[95] *Grant* [73] (see also *Springwell*; *Titan*; *Avrora Fine Arts Investment Ltd v Christie, Manson & Woods Ltd* [2012] EWHC 2198 (Ch), [2012] PNLR 35; *Deutsche Bank AG v Unitech Global Ltd* [2013] EWHC 2793 (Comm), [2014] 2 All ER (Comm) 268; *Thornbridge*).

[96] *Ceylon Petroleum Corporation* (first instance) [571].

[97] *Springwell* (first instance) [630].

[98] Rupert M Jackson, Roger Stewart and John Powell, *Jackson & Powell on Professional Liability*, 7th edn (Sweet & Maxwell Ltd, 2012) para 15-015.

[99] *Graiseley Properties Ltd and Others v Barclays Bank Plc* [2013] EWHC 67 (Comm).

[100] *Property Alliance Group Ltd v The Royal Bank of Scotland Plc* [2016] EWHC 3342 (Ch). The claimant subsequently sought permission to appeal from the Court of Appeal (following the High Court's dismissal of its application to appeal) and, on 22 May 2017, the application was allowed (case reference: A3/2017/0482). The appeal was subsequently dismissed, affirming in full the judgment in first instance (judgment reference [2018] EWCA Civ 355).

The stand taken by English courts on misrepresentation claims is comparable to that of the Hong Kong judiciary where such claims in respect of relationships considered to be of a non-advisory nature were rejected by Hong Kong courts on the basis of defences comparable to those adopted by defendants in the UK. Even so, however, and in response to the pro-bank approach taken by Hong Kong courts, the Hong Kong regulator took on a more active stance in securing redress to investors through other channels, when compared to the measures taken by the UK regulator that were discussed in Section IIA of chapter three.[101] In addition, stricter investor protection measures have been introduced recently in an attempt to counteract this rigid judicial thinking.

Specifically, the HKSFC introduced new provisions to enhance the enforcement of the 'Suitability Requirement' set out in the Code of Conduct for Persons Licensed by or Registered with the Securities and Futures Commission.[102] On its own, the Suitability Requirement empowered the HKSFC to take disciplinary action against an investment firm that breaches this clause, but did not give aggrieved investors a contractual right to seek compensation against the investment firm in court, as express terms contained in the contract generally prevailed over the requirements set forth in the Code of Conduct. The HKSFC sought to address this by introducing a requirement for a new provision which must be incorporated into client agreements as a contractual term, stating the following:

> If we [the investment firm] solicit the sale of or recommend any financial product to you [the client], the financial product must be reasonably suitable for you having regard to your financial situation, investment experience and investment objectives. No other provision of this agreement or any other document we may ask you to sign and no statement we may ask you to make derogates from this clause.[103]

This new requirement is intended to arm aggrieved investors with a contractual right to claim damages, thereby also addressing the judiciary's inclination to rely on contractual terms to uphold disclaimers. This non-derogation clause, coupled

[101] In the case of the settlement of the structured notes saga, for example, banks in Hong Kong were encouraged to conduct internal investigations and settle with customers directly if appropriate. The Hong Kong Securities and Futures Commission (HKSFC) facilitated banks' willingness to settle voluntarily with implicit disciplinary action against banks after conducting an investigation, and also entered into a collective agreement with banks under which banks agreed to repurchase the notes from investors (see press releases by the HKSFC at: www.sfc.hk/sfcPressRelease/EN/sfcOpenDocServlet?docno=08PR171 and www.sfc.hk/sfcPressRelease/EN/sfcOpenDocServlet?docno=09PR100, accessed 15 March 2015, and see also Christopher Chen Chao-hung, 'The resolution of the structured notes fiasco in Hong Kong, Singapore and Taiwan' (2013) 34 *Company Lawyer* 119).

[102] Paragraph 5.2 of the Code of Conduct for Persons Licensed by or Registered with the Securities and Futures Commission states the following: 'Having regard to information about the client of which the licensed or registered person is or should be aware through the exercise of due diligence, the licensed or registered person should, when making a recommendation or solicitation, ensure the suitability of the recommendation or solicitation for that client is reasonable in all the circumstances.'

[103] Paragraph 6.2(i) of the Code of Conduct for Persons Licensed by or Registered with the Securities and Futures Commission. This new clause came into effect in June 2017 (see further Mayer Brown JSM, 'Suitability Requirement – Now a Contractual Obligation on Licensed and Registered Persons' (2016)).

with the requirement that investment firms are obliged not to 'mis-describe [the] actual services',[104] together render non-reliance provisions ineffective, such that investment firms can no longer defend mis-selling claims by relying on contractual estoppel and aggrieved investors can seek contractual remedy under the client agreements. These revisions to the Hong Kong regulatory framework are considered as positive investor protection measures which will most likely dampen the pro-business mind-set that the Hong Kong judiciary has been adopting.

D. Fiduciary Duties and the Establishment of a Fiduciary Relationship in the Context of Non-advised Sales

Banks' traditional activities of deposit-taking and lending are not typically considered to give rise to fiduciary duties. Yet, as banks diversify their activities and move towards providing more advisory-based investment services, it has been suggested that this new role may give rise to fiduciary relationships between banks (acting as investment firms) and retail investors.[105] This has led the Australian judiciary to establish that 'contractual and fiduciary relationships may co-exist between the same parties' such that 'the existence of a basic contractual relationship has in many situations provided a foundation for the erection of a fiduciary relationship'.[106]

In the UK, however, the definition and scope of fiduciary duties have been construed narrowly by English courts, particularly in commercial contracts, such that the courts have been reluctant to impose fiduciary duties in ordinary commercial relationships,[107] as demonstrated by IRHP case law. In this sense, English courts established that the mere fact that one party to a relationship trusts the other party is not sufficient to establish a fiduciary relationship, hence observing that trust alone is not sufficient to create a legitimate expectation that the investment firm would subordinate its own interests to those of the claimant in the ambit of their commercial relationship, unless one party is 'entitled to expect' that the other will act in his interests in, and for the purpose of, the relationship.[108] By cherishing the notions of freedom of contract and legal certainty, the courts

[104] Paragraph 6.5 of the Code of Conduct for Persons Licensed by or Registered with the Securities and Futures Commission.

[105] Alastair Hudson, *The Law of Finance*, 2nd edn (Sweet & Maxwell Ltd, 2013) para 5–17.

[106] *Hospital Products Ltd v United States Surgical Corporation* [1984] HCA 64 [70], a case concerning the distribution of surgical products and the fiduciary duties arising therefrom. In English courts, a comprehensive definition of 'a fiduciary' was given in *Bristol and West Building Society v Mothew (t/a Stapley & Co)* [1998] Ch 1 at 18, where it was expressed *as 'single-minded loyalty'* (see also *(1) Shelley Barnes; (2) Darren Barnes v Black Horse Ltd* [2011] EWHC 1416 (QB), [2011] 2 All ER (Comm) 1130 [17]).

[107] Law Commission, 'Fiduciary Duties of Investment Intermediaries' (Law Com No 350, 2014) para 10.78.

[108] See eg *Lloyds Bank v Bundy* [1975] QB 326; *Re Goldcorp Exchange Ltd (In Receivership)* [1994] UKPC 3, [1995] 1 AC 74; *Arklow Investments Ltd and Another v Ian Duart Maclean and Others* [2000] 1 WLR 594 (PC) 599; *Springwell* (first instance) [574]; James J Edelman, 'When Do Fiduciary Duties

have upheld limitation clauses and concluded that, although the existence of an underlying contract does not automatically exclude the co-existence of concurrent fiduciary duties, the contract 'can and does modify the extent and nature of the general duty that would otherwise arise'.[109] This suggests, therefore, that any application of a fiduciary duty in the context of non-advisory agreements would impose non-contractual duties on contractual relationships where the parties would not have bargained for such duties.[110]

English law draws heavily on contract and tort law to provide relief, if at all, against a perceived wrong suffered in commercial relationships. Under the English legal system, certainty has been seen to 'triumph over fairness'[111] and it is widely assumed that 'commercial parties could and should look after their own interests and should bear the risk of their failure to do so'.[112] Fundamentally, the courts have accepted that: '[i]n a commercial context … a degree of self-seeking and ruthless behaviour is expected and accepted to a degree'.[113] In IRHP cases, English courts have therefore steered away from creating an analogy between fiduciary duties on the one hand and tort and contract law principles on the other, predominantly because the latter set of principles considers parties as independent and equal actors who maximise their own self-interest and hence the courts' main concern here is the preservation of the parties' contractual freedom. By contrast, the essence of a fiduciary relationship is that one party has pledged to act in the best interests of the other and hence the freedom of the fiduciary is reduced by the nature of the obligation it has undertaken.[114] To the extent that 'the recognition of fiduciary responsibility is grounded on consent',[115] parties to commercial transactions are thus expected to 'be the authors of their own rights and obligations',[116] and the imposition of any fiduciary obligations on parties to a commercial arrangement is envisaged to do 'more harm than good'.[117] Where the courts attempt to

Arise?' (2010) 126 *Law Quarterly Review* 302, 317–18; Julia Smith, 'Out with 'TCF' and in with 'fiduciary'?' (2012) 27 *Journal of International Banking and Financial Law* 343, 344.

[109] *Henderson* 206.

[110] Jerry W Markham, 'Protecting the Institutional Investor – Jungle Predator or Shorn Lamb' (1995) 12 *Yale Journal on Regulation* 345, 375.

[111] Paul Finn, 'Common Law Divergences' (2013) 37 *Melbourne University Law Review* 511, 520.

[112] ibid 515–16.

[113] *Vercoe* [343].

[114] Unlike in the context of a commercial contractual arrangement, the fiduciary relationship is envisaged as having trust, not self-interest, at its core, with the irreducible core of fiduciary duty being the duty of undivided loyalty (see eg *Bristol* wherein it was held that a breach of contract or tort should not become a breach of fiduciary duty).

[115] Gerard McMeel and John Virgo (eds), *McMeel and Virgo on Financial Advice and Financial Products: Law and Liability* (Oxford University Press, 2001) para 11.02.

[116] Law Commission, 'Fiduciary Duties of Investment Intermediaries' (Law Com No 350, 2014) para 10.44.

[117] Peter Millett, 'Equity's Place in the Law of Commerce' (1998) 114 *Law Quarterly Review* 214, 217. Markham similarly argues that fiduciary duties seem 'particularly inappropriate' where two commercial parties are dealing with each other in an arm's length relationship (Jerry W Markham, 'Protecting the Institutional Investor – Jungle Predator or Shorn Lamb' (1995) 12 *Yale Journal on Regulation* 345, 375).

extend certain equitable doctrines, inter alia fiduciary duties, to a commercial relationship, they are therefore seen as 'doing infinite mischief',[118] as this could 'paralyse the trade of the country and fundamentally affect the security of business transactions'.[119]

It follows, therefore, that where there is no explicit requirement for the investment firm to advise a customer on a particular matter, or there is otherwise a specific contractual delineation of the scope of the content of fiduciary duties such that responsibility in connection with these duties is fully disclaimed, the investment firm will not be deemed to owe fiduciary duties towards the investor.[120] To this end, English courts have observed that:

> there is no general doctrine of good faith in English contract law and such a term is unlikely to arise by way of necessary implication in a contract between two sophisticated commercial parties negotiating at arms' length.[121]

Further, even if there was an implied term of good faith, 'it would not and could not circumscribe or restrict what the parties had expressly agreed …'[122] It follows, therefore, that implying duties of a fiduciary nature into a contract would go against the spirit of the express terms of the agreement excluding equitable or fiduciary duties.[123]

This means that the English legal system is less influenced by equity jurisprudence when compared to other common law jurisdictions, such as Australia and Canada.[124] More specifically, these jurisdictions tend to make concessions for the possibility of a retail investor being especially vulnerable to exploitation by larger, well-resourced investment firms, due to the former's lack of power and urgent need for access to funding,[125] as in the case of corporate retail investors that were

[118] *Manchester Trust v Furness* [1895] 2 QB 539.

[119] Sir Anthony Mason, 'The Place of Equity and Equitable Remedies in the Contemporary Common Law World' (1994) 110 *Law Quarterly Review* 238, 245, citing *Manchester Trust* and *In Re Wait* [1927] 1 Ch 606 CA.

[120] Apart from the IRHP cases being discussed, see also *Horace Brenton Kelly v Margot Cooper and Another* [1993] AC 205 (PC); *Clark Boyce v Mouat* [1994] 1 AC 428 (PC); *Australian Securities and Investment Commission v Citigroup Global Markets Australia Pty Ltd* [2007] FCA 963.

[121] *Greenclose v National Westminster Bank* [2014] EWHC 1156 (Ch), [2014] 1 CLC 562 [150].

[122] *TSG Building Services Plc v South Anglia Housing Limited* [2013] EWHC 1151 (TCC), [2013] BLR 484 [51].

[123] *Property Alliance* [250].

[124] Australia and Canada draw heavily upon equitable doctrines to promote flexibility in awarding appropriate remedies as well as encouraging discretion, appropriateness and practical justice Notably, in these jurisdictions, the equitable doctrine is reinforced by significant statutory provisions (see further Paul Finn, 'Common Law Divergences' (2013) 37 *Melbourne University Law Review* 511, 535). On Australian law, see further *Australian Consumer Law* (Schedule 2 of the Competition and Consumer Act 2010) part 2-2 on unconscionable conduct, and on Canadian law, see generally Gerald H L Fridman, *The Law of Contract in Canada*, 5th edn (Carswell, 2006) ch 9.

[125] See eg *McBean v Bank of Nova Scotia* (1981) 15 BLR 296, affd (1982) 17 ACWS (2d) 154 and *Hayward v Bank of Nova Scotia* (1984) 45 OR (2d) 542, affd (1985) 51 OR (2d) 193, two Canadian cases concerning investment services provided by banks in which the fiduciary duty was assimilated to the doctrine of undue influence and unequal bargaining power.

mis-sold IRHPs. This is an allowance that the English courts are not prepared to make, as their quest to preserve contractual freedom and legal certainty overrides any potential of equity principles to control the abuse of power in commercial relationships and promote fair dealing.[126]

English courts' conclusions in connection with fiduciary responsibilities demonstrate that the chances of proving that a non-advisory relationship gives rise to fiduciary obligations are generally non-existent. Where the investor is deemed to have exercised independent judgement and the investment firm is merely seen as executing the investor's instructions or simply commenting on factual matters relating to the current state of the market, the role of investment firms is seen as being limited to providing information and hence fiduciary duties do not arise. In other words, the duties of the investment firm are deemed to end with the duty to execute the investor's instructions and, therefore, a relationship of a fiduciary nature 'cannot be superimposed upon the contract in such a way as to alter the operation which the contract was intended to have according to its true construction',[127] or to otherwise 'improve the nature or extent of the remedy'.[128] On the other hand, where an adviser undertakes to advise another as to its financial affairs, the courts are likely to find that 'the adviser has placed himself under fiduciary obligations to that other'.[129]

On this basis, the prospect of fiduciary duties arising or otherwise can be envisaged as residing on a 'sliding scale'[130] such that fiduciary duties are more likely to arise as the investment firm exercises greater control over the investor's activities. In this manner, a fiduciary relationship is created by virtue of a 'factual matrix which can justify both entitlement to expect that the adviser is acting, and the consequential obligation that he must act, in the other's interest in the giving of advice, information, etc'.[131] In the context of investment services, a fiduciary relationship originates where the relationship between the investment firm and the corporate retail investor is of an advised nature, and where the investment firm contractually assumes responsibility for that advice thereby acting in an advisory capacity, as opposed to its role merely being that of an 'order-taker'.[132]

II. Invoking the Doctrine of 'Contractual Estoppel'

The notion of contractual estoppel operates on the principle that where parties express an agreement in a contract, they cannot subsequently deny the existence

[126] Paul Finn, 'Common Law Divergences' (2013) 37 *Melbourne University Law Review* 511, 536.
[127] *Hospital Products* [70].
[128] *Nornberg v Wynrib* [1992] 2 SCR 226 [272].
[129] *Investors Compensation Scheme* 509.
[130] Jerry W Markham, 'Protecting the Institutional Investor – Jungle Predator or Shorn Lamb' (1995) 12 *Yale Journal on Regulation* 345, 375.
[131] Paul Finn, 'Fiduciary Law and the Modern Corporate World' in Ewan McKendrick (ed), *Corporate Aspects of Trusts and Fiduciary Obligations* (Clarendon Press, 1992) 10.
[132] *Kent v May* (2001) 298 AR 71, affd (2002) 317 AR 381 (CA) 51–53.

of the facts and matters upon which they have agreed and towards which the contract was directed. In other words, where parties have entered into a binding contract by virtue of which they acknowledge a certain state of affairs, the doctrine of contractual estoppel will prevent the party attesting to that statement from asserting in litigation that the opposite was true. The principle of party autonomy, which underlies the common law of contract, thus 'lies at the heart of contractual estoppel',[133] such that a party can seek to rely on 'contractual estoppel' regardless of whether the contractual terms give a truthful account of the state of affairs or otherwise.[134]

The modern foundation of contractual estoppel is *Peekay*,[135] where the Court of Appeal concluded that by signing the terms of the agreement, which included a description of his investment and an acknowledgement that the terms and conditions had been read and understood, the corporate retail investor was precluded from arguing that he had been induced into the agreement by a misrepresentation of the nature of the investment. To this end, the Court of Appeal held that there was 'no reason in principle why parties to a contract should not agree that a certain state of affairs should form the basis for the transaction, whether it be the case or not',[136] whilst also endorsing the signature rule as 'an important principle of English law which underpins the whole of commercial life'.[137] Hence, where parties 'express an agreement … in a contractual document', then 'neither of the parties can subsequently deny the existence of the facts and matters upon which they have agreed … [since] … the contract itself gives rise to an estoppel'.[138]

The doctrine of contractual estoppel was consolidated in *Springwell*[139] and has had 'corporate utility'[140] ever since, operating as a precedent in IRHP cases and considered as one of the main reasons why claimants have been unsuccessful in their claims against investment firms. English courts have recognised contractual estoppel as a confirmation that, as a matter of freedom of contract, parties should be able to agree that they are contracting on the basis of a certain state of

[133] Richard Hooley, 'Contractual estoppel and the Misrepresentation Act 1967' (2016) University of Cambridge Legal Studies Research Paper No 57/2016, 17 (see also *Prime Sight Ltd v Lavarello* [2013] UKPC 22, [2014] AC 436 [46]–[47]).

[134] Once it can be proven (generally from the clauses within the agreement itself) that the parties have agreed that a certain state of affairs will form the basis of their transactions (eg, a non-advisory relationship under which the investment firm disclaimed responsibility for investment advice) the other party (being the investor in this context) is estopped from asserting that the true facts were different.

[135] *Peekay*. The roots of the broader concept of contractual estoppel can be traced to more historical origins which are not related to the provision of investment services (see eg *Lowe v Lombank* [1960] 1 WLR 196 (CA); *Alman and Benson v Associated Newspapers Group Ltd* (unreported, 20 June 1980); *Colchester Borough Council v Smith* [1991] Ch 448, affd [1992] Ch 421 (Civ Div); *E A Grimstead & Son Ltd v Francis Patrick McGarrigan* [1999] EWCA Civ 3029).

[136] *Peekay* (appeal) [56].

[137] ibid [43].

[138] ibid. In making this observation, Moore-Bick LJ relied upon the decision of the court in *Colchester Borough Council*.

[139] *Springwell* (appeal) [143].

[140] Jo Braithwaite, 'The origins and implications of contractual estoppel' (2016) 132 *Law Quarterly Review* 120, 132.

affairs, which also fosters commercial certainty.[141] Notwithstanding criticisms of the application of the doctrine of contractual estoppel by the courts,[142] the discussions on contractual estoppel in IRHP-related cases have been rooted in freedom of contract, thereby positioning the doctrine 'within one of the most pervasive and powerful traditions in English corporate law'.[143]

The fact that claimants in IRHP mis-selling cases were retail investors and not large sophisticated commercial parties did little to assist their plea, as the doctrine of contractual estoppel 'bluntly fails to distinguish between parties of equal bargaining power and one-sided contracts', such that it has had 'a profound and unintended consequence of limiting the weak from overcoming a standard clause'.[144] The contractual estoppel arising from boilerplate language may therefore mean that the desire for commercial legal certainty is taken to an 'unnecessary and potentially unjust'[145] extreme, particularly because non-reliance clauses in standard form contracts are constituted in favour of the more powerful party and generally serve to insulate this party against legitimate claims raised by the weaker counter-party.[146] Notably, the operation of contractual estoppel in IRHP-related litigation allowed defendants to 'contract out' of the regulatory system, such that the court was 'unable to resist the conclusion that the banks successfully disclaimed responsibility for any advice', even though the court acknowledged that such advice had indeed been provided verbally.[147]

Although it has been argued that other species of estoppel, namely estoppel by convention, may operate to limit the effectiveness of contractual estoppel,[148] this is unlikely to be the case in the context of the mis-selling claims being discussed

[141] ibid 120.

[142] See eg Gerard McMeel, 'Documentary Fundamentalism in the Senior Courts: The myth of contractual estoppel' (2011) *Lloyd's Maritime and Corporate Law Quarterly* 185, 206; Sean Wilken and Karim Ghaly, *The law of waiver, variation and estoppel*, 3rd edn (Oxford University Press, 2012) paras 13.22–13.24; Jo Braithwaite, 'The origins and implications of contractual estoppel' (2016) 132 *Law Quarterly Review* 120, 121; Shantanu Majumdar, 'Entire agreement, non-reliance clauses and contractual estoppel – what do they prevent and how?' Radcliffe Chambers (undated).

[143] Jo Braithwaite, 'The origins and implications of contractual estoppel' (2016) 132 *Law Quarterly Review* 120, 131.

[144] Nelson Goh, 'Non-reliance clauses and contractual estoppel: corporately sensible or anomalous?' (2015) 7 *Journal of Business Law* 511, 526.

[145] Gerard McMeel, 'Documentary Fundamentalism in the Senior Courts: The myth of contractual estoppel' (2011) *Lloyd's Maritime and Corporate Law Quarterly* 185, 207.

[146] This aspect was also considered by Lord Denning in *Chesterhall* [297], when, in referring to the superior party, he observed that 'freedom was all on the side of the big concern … without regard to the little man'.

[147] *Crestsign* [114] (see also *Thornbridge*).

[148] Nicholas Elliott, Charles Hewetson and David Warne (eds), *Banking Litigation*, 3rd edn (Sweet & Maxwell Ltd 2011) para 11-081. The doctrine of estoppel by convention provides that if an investment firm deals with an investor in a manner that, contrary to the contractual disclaimers, encourages the investor to rely on the former's expertise or representations and knows that the investor does in fact place reliance on same, the effect might be that the investment firm is estopped by convention from asserting that those terms formed part of the true agreement if that would lead to consequences that may be considered unjust or unconscionable.

in this chapter. In particular, this is because a key element of an effective estoppel by convention is 'unconscionability or unjustness on the part of the person said to be estopped to assert the true legal or factual position'.[149] Since English courts have treated corporate retail investors as sophisticated counterparties, this would strongly suggest that the court is unlikely to conclude that corporate retail investors are subject to unconscionability or unjustness which leads to detrimental reliance in the context of a commercial transaction. Consequently, estoppel by convention would not operate in a manner which would override the contractual terms. This has already been tested in *Springwell* where the Court of Appeal rejected the argument that there is no juristic concept of contractual estoppel which is distinct from the doctrine of estoppel by convention and concluded that contractual estoppel is a 'separate doctrine'[150] to other estoppel doctrines, including estoppel by convention and estoppel by representations. In so stating, the Court of Appeal noted that the reason why, in the case of estoppel by convention, the party that wishes to rely on this estoppel must demonstrate that it would be unconscionable for the other party to resile from the conventional state of affairs that the parties have assumed, 'is precisely because there is no contract between the parties', and hence 'some other mechanism' must come into play to make the non-contractual convention enforceable.[151]

Outside the investment services space, two Court of Appeal cases in particular have recently considered the legal effect of clauses stipulating that a contract can only be varied in writing with appropriate consent. Most standard form IRHP contracts contained similar anti-oral variation clauses to prevent the investor from later arguing that key contractual terms (such as non-reliance provisions or non-advisory disclaimers) have been varied orally or by course of conduct. In both *Globe Motors Inc and Others v TRW Lucas Varity Electric Steering Ltd and Others*[152] and *MWB Business Exchange Centres Ltd v Rock Advertising Ltd*,[153] the Court of Appeal unanimously expressed the view that, in principle, a contract containing such a clause may still be varied informally. Although there were policy considerations in favour of anti-oral variation clauses being effective (including to promote certainty and avoid false or frivolous claims of an oral agreement), the Court of Appeal did not find any principled reason as to why an oral variation or agreement by conduct could not be formed, provided that the party arguing for a variation of

[149] *Mears Ltd v Shoreline Housing Partnership Ltd* [2015] EWHC 1396 (TCC), 160 Con LR 157 [49].
[150] ibid (appeal) [177].
[151] ibid (see also Jo Braithwaite, 'The origins and implications of contractual estoppel' (2016) 132 *Law Quarterly Review* 120, 123).
[152] [2016] EWCA Civ 396, [2017] 1 All ER (Comm) 601, a case concerning a long-term contract for supply of certain products to the automotive industry.
[153] [2016] EWCA Civ 553, [2016] 3 WLR 1519, a case concerning a claim for arrears of licence fees and other charges. It is noted that MWB was granted permission to appeal to the Supreme Court on 31 January 2017 (case reference: UKSC 2016/0152) and the appeal was subsequently allowed ([2018] UKSC 24).

the contract shows the same elements that go to form a contract in the first place, namely offer, acceptance, consideration and intention to create legal relations.

Prima facie, this line of argumentation may prove helpful to corporate retail investors in situations where, although the contract formally provided for non-advisory services, the relationship evolved such that investment firms provided information, analysis, and other related services which might ordinarily be equated to investment advice. Yet, these conclusions are unlikely to have a broad, all-encompassing application. In particular, the Court of Appeal in *Globe Motors*[154] was unanimous in noting that anti-oral variation clauses still have practical significance because they raise the bar in terms of showing that the oral discussion was intended to constitute a variation and, therefore, parties may face greater difficulty in demonstrating mutual unwritten intention to reach an agreement by conduct affecting their written obligations where they have agreed to a provision requiring formal variation.[155] Indeed, whilst an informal variation is legally possible, the court is likely to require 'a powerful reason'[156] before finding that there has been an oral variation of a contract, and, in any event, the validity of clauses of this nature would typically be fact-dependent.[157]

It is important to note that these arguments remain untested in the field of investment services, and, especially given the binding precedent set by past IRHP-related litigation and the clear messages communicated by English courts so far, it is here submitted that non-advisory disclaimers and anti-oral variation clauses will continue to offer a strong contractual safeguard for investment firms, such that the hurdle of contractual estoppel remains an extremely high one for any corporate retail investor to surmount.

III. The Relevance of Alternative Doctrines

Retail investors outside the UK have resorted to a number of legal doctrines in an attempt to prove their mis-selling claim in court. These doctrines, the equivalent of which are not found in the English legal system or are generally not otherwise applied by English courts in a commercial context, have generally proved to be an effective compensatory mechanism for these investors by contributing to the success of their claim. Specifically, elements of the Portuguese and Italian regimes that have come to the rescue of corporate retail investors in IRHP-type cases are discussed hereunder.

In the context of IRHP-related mis-selling claims raised by Portuguese corporate retail investors, the Supreme Court of Portugal drew upon the doctrine of

[154] *Globe Motors*.

[155] ibid [117].

[156] *MWB* [34].

[157] In *Globe Motors* [64], eg, the Court of Appeal attached considerable weight to the agreement being of a long-term nature and which therefore ought to be interpreted with a certain degree of flexibility.

alteração das circunstâncias ('change of circumstances')[158] to declare the termination of a swap IRHP contract with retroactive effect, when as a consequence of the 2008 financial crisis, the interest rate suddenly dropped below the floor agreed to in the contract. The effects of the change of circumstances, according to the court, were not covered by the contractual distribution of risks. Under the new circumstances, the court concluded that the performance of the obligations, as originally agreed to, could not be requested of the affected party, because a significant decrease in the interest rate was beyond the risk that could be considered reasonable or foreseeable in the economic context existing at the time of the conclusion of the contract.[159]

Whilst comparable doctrines exist elsewhere, claims for a change in circumstances were met with limited success in certain other overseas jurisdictions.[160] The aleatory nature of the swap means that it may be reasonable to assert that in a swap the parties have assumed the risks inherent to the contract, being those related to the variation of the interest rate, and, therefore, this seems to be the main impediment for the adoption of this doctrine.[161] This notwithstanding, the conclusions reached by the Portuguese court on the basis of this doctrine encourage other courts to 'explore beyond the risks associated to the contract'[162] and identify additional grounds on which the validity of an IRHP can be successfully disputed, including the complexity of the product, the lack of knowledge, experience and sophistication on the part of the investor, and other similar factors. Although elements of the doctrine of unforeseen circumstances, or the doctrine of

[158] Article 437 of the Portuguese Civil Code, as referred to by Momberg (Rodrigo Momberg, 'Beyond the Risk: Swaps, Financial Crisis and Change of Circumstances; Comparative Case Note: Supreme Court of Portugal – 10.10.2013' (2015) 23 *European Review of Private Law* 81, 81).

[159] See further decision of the 10 October 2013 of the Supreme Court of Portugal as summarised by Momberg (ibid); Juan Carlos M Dastis, 'Change of Circumstances (Section 313 BGB) Trigger for the Next Financial Crisis?' (2015) 23 *European Review of Private Law* 85.

[160] The parallel doctrine of *imprévision* also exists in the Belgian and French legal discourse. It is also recognised in national civil systems, including the Italian Civil Code (referred to as the concept of 'excessive onerousness') and the German Bürgerliches Gesetzbuch. The Spanish *clausula rebus sic stantibus* is yet another parallel concept. In all these jurisdictions, the respective courts have rejected, or are said to be likely to reject, the application of the doctrine (see further Denis Philippe, 'Unforeseen Circumstances in Belgian Law' (2015) 1 *European Review of Private Law* 101; Rossella Esther Cerchia, 'Interest Rate Swaps' Contract and "Excessive Onerousness": An Italian Viewpoint' (2015) 23 *European Private Law Review* 121; Rodrigo Momberg, 'Beyond the Risk: Swaps, Financial Crisis and Change of Circumstances; Comparative Case Note: Supreme Court of Portugal – 10.10.2013' (2015) 23 *European Review of Private Law* 81, Juan Pablo Murga Fernández, 'Interest Rate Swap and Rebus sic Stantibus Clause' (2015) 23 *European Private Law Review* 133).

[161] Rodrigo Momberg, 'Beyond the Risk: Swaps, Financial Crisis and Change of Circumstances; Comparative Case Note: Supreme Court of Portugal – 10.10.2013' (2015) 23 *European Review of Private Law* 81, 151; Denis Philippe, 'Unforeseen Circumstances in Belgian Law' (2015) 1 *European Review of Private Law* 101, 106.

[162] Rodrigo Momberg, 'Beyond the Risk: Swaps, Financial Crisis and Change of Circumstances; Comparative Case Note: Supreme Court of Portugal – 10.10.2013' (2015) 23 *European Review of Private Law* 81, 151.

frustration, also exist under English law,[163] the application of these concepts in a commercial context is exceptional, given that their very essence appears to conflict directly with the default principle that contracts should be upheld and enforced according to the terms agreed between the parties.[164]

Another alternative argument is that raised successfully by claimants in Italy in the context of IRHP-related litigation, which is tied to the doctrine of '*causa concreta*'.[165] By basing their conclusions on a lack of '*causa concreta*', the Italian judiciary declared IRHP-type contracts null and void on a number of occasions for three main reasons: (i) a lack of hedging purpose for which IRHPs had been originally entered into;[166] (ii) the IRHP being unsuitable to achieve the purpose for which it had been entered into;[167] and (iii) the obligations arising out of the contractual framework being considered unequal from the onset.[168] Most notably, Italian Courts have described complex investment contracts, such as those concerning IRHP transactions, as 'a bet placed by both parties',[169] noting that the bet would only be legitimate at law if both parties are fully informed of the nature and the scope of the risks associated with the transaction, which is not necessarily the case in IRHP-related transactions.

[163] See eg Ewan McKendrick, *Contract Law: Text, Cases and Materials* (Oxford University Press, 2004) 849; Hugh Beale (ed), *Chitty on Contracts*, 32nd edn (Sweet & Maxwell Ltd, 2015).

[164] Charles Proctor, 'The euro – fragmentation and the financial markets' (2011) 6 *Capital Markets Law Journal* 5, 12; Richard A Lloyd, *Williston on Contracts*, 4th edn (Lawyers Cooperative Publishing, 2012) § 77:95.

[165] Under Italian Civil law, the existence of a valid and legitimate 'causa' is necessary for the agreement to be binding. Art 1418 of the Italian Civil Code, which sets forth general principles of Italian contract law, provides for the nullity of the contract in the case, of, inter alia, a lack of '*causa*'. The concept of '*causa*' has been interpreted by Italian courts as referring to the typical social and economic function of the contract, giving the court extensive control over private agreements (see further Alberto Monti, 'Formation of Contracts' in Luisa Antoniolli and Anna Veneziano (eds), *Principles of European Contract Law and Italian Law: A Commentary* (Kluwer Law International, 2005) 91).

[166] Vestini makes reference to a decision of the Court of Lucera (dated 26 April 2012), which emphasises the interplay between the credit agreement and the derivative contract and which concludes that, since the borrower never received the financing that was agreed with the investment firm, the swap lacked the hedging purpose (the '*causa*') for which it was created. Vestini also notes that a similar conclusion was reached by the Court of Florence (decision dated 5 June 2012) (see further Luca Vestini, 'Recent decisions of Italian Courts on Interest Rate Swaps' (2013) 3 *Bankpedia* 7, 8).

[167] Vestini (ibid 9) refers to a decision by the Court of Monza (dated 17 July 2012), which found that the swap proved to be totally inapt to achieve its functions as, over the years, it resulted in the borrower having to pay a negative difference in addition to the mark-to-market amount charged by the investment firm for early termination. The court also found that the investment firm had failed to provide an accurate assessment relating to the foreseeable fluctuation of interest rates even though it had a duty to do so pursuant to communications from CONSOB, the Italian regulator. As a result, it declared that the contract was null and void because it was unsuitable to provide the protection for which it was designed (thus a lack of '*causa*'). On a related matter, the Trento Tribunal arrived at the same conclusion (Trib. Trento 46/2012).

[168] The Court of Orvieto (decision dated 12 April 2012) concluded that IRHPs are affected by a sort of 'genetic deficiency' brought about by the disparity in the position of the parties, which makes them null and void (ibid 10).

[169] C.App Milan 3459/2013.

Certain key civil law concepts, such as that of '*causa concreta*', that operate to protect the weaker party, have no role in the formation and validity of contracts in English common law.[170] This, coupled with the unwillingness of English courts to apply certain other doctrines in a commercial context (such as the 'doctrine of frustration'), precludes the courts from considering a range of relevant factors from which investors could benefit, including, for example, whether there has been any abnormal alteration of the circumstances on which the parties had based their decision to enter into the contract, or whether the actual purpose of the investment was achieved or otherwise. Consequently, corporate retail investors in the UK bore financial detriment as a result of transactions in IRHPs which they did not even request at own initiative but which they were coerced to accept by investment firms holding superior bargaining power.

IV. Concluding Remarks

Bad investor deals, often structured using 'complicated and nasty terms buried in long forms',[171] are a long-standing problem that the law has had to grapple with. Even though contractual formalism and legal certainty have arguably led to unfair outcomes, they have become deeply ingrained in English legal culture. This has contributed to a 'lack of judicial sympathy'[172] in respect of mis-selling claims brought by corporate retail investors, and has illustrated that the common law is unable to provide the necessary protection to these investors.

The romantic ideology promoting contractual freedom and legal certainty is however based on the unrealistic assumption that all commercial transactions are negotiated by sophisticated, fully-informed parties of equal bargaining power and that are capable of protecting their own self-interests in such a way that they arrive at a mutually-beneficial agreement.[173] In practice, however,

[170] The notion of '*causa*' is at times associated to the common law doctrine of consideration. The latter, however, has a much narrower application than the former, since 'consideration' consists of some benefit to the promisor or a detriment to the promisee, whereas '*causa*' is the essential reason for the contract (see further Dimitar Stoyanov, 'Causa and Consideration – A Comparative Overview' (Challenges of the Knowledge Society conference, Bucharest, May 2016); Hugh Beale and Ole Lando (eds), *Principles of European Contract Law: Parts I and II* (Kluwer Law International, 2000) 140–42).

[171] Jean Braucher, 'Form and Substance in Consumer Financial Protection' (2013) 7 *Brooklyn Journal of Corporate, Financial and Commercial Law* 107, 107.

[172] Paul Marshall, 'Novating mis-sold swaps: the poverty of narrowly contractual analysis' (2015) 30 *Journal of International Banking and Financial Law* 11, 12 (see also Charlotte Thomas, 'What role should substantive fairness have in the English law of contract? An overview of the law' (2010) 6 *Cambridge Student Law Review* 177, 191; Paul Marshall, 'Humpty Dumpty is broken: 'unsuitable' and 'inappropriate' swaps transactions' (2014) 29 *Journal of International Banking and Financial Law* 679, 679).

[173] Elaine A Welle, 'Freedom of Contract and the Securities Laws: Opting Out of Securities Regulation by Private Agreement' (1999) 56 *Washington and Lee Law Review* 519, 576. It has been observed that contracting parties must occupy positions of broad equality in order for them to be confident that their

'serious inequality'[174] in bargaining strength exists between investment firms and corporate retail investors, which arises from factors such as the parties' financial resources, knowledge, experience, access to information and advice, as well as information asymmetry,[175] and which reveals that the agreement 'might not be genuinely consensual and voluntary'.[176] In fact, as illustrated by IRHP case law and as also discussed in Section IID of chapter three, a corporate retail investor cannot be portrayed as a free, willing buyer because, in truth, this investor would have been 'bullied' into the agreement by the more dominant investment firm. In other words, the roots of the problem lie in the very 'stripped-down, biased or skewed, but dominant',[177] conception of the investor whose exercise of freedom is being valued, who is also 'self-sufficient, self-knowing, rationally self-interested' and 'super-detached'.[178] The draconian strictness used in enforcing the principle of contractual estoppel is seen to provide 'obvious corporate benefit'[179] to the investment firm, whilst, however, ignoring the vulnerabilities and behavioural biases that corporate retail investors suffer from and which make them a significantly less sophisticated counterparty. The interplay of these elements is neatly summarised by Beale when he observes that: 'English contract law is not for everyone: not for all courts, nor for all parties. It is in effect designed for big businesses. Small and medium-sized enterprises may have different needs'.[180]

The inherent limitations of private law and its underlying principles mean that it cannot provide an adequate foundation for retail investor protection.[181] This has also been dealt with in IRHP case law, when Kerr J, in *Crestsign*,[182] acknowledged that the common law does not provide any remedy to claimants where the investment firm has successfully disclaimed responsibility for the advice it gave

agreement 'is truly consensual' (see further Karen Yeung, 'Better Regulation, Administrative Sanctions and Constitutional Values' (2013) 33 *Legal Studies* 312, 329–30).

[174] Karen Yeung, 'Better Regulation, Administrative Sanctions and Constitutional Values' (2013) 33 *Legal Studies* 312, 330.

[175] Charles YC Chew, 'Statutory aspects of unjust banking contracts: a legal analysis' (2014) 29 *Journal of International Banking Law and Regulation* 312, 314.

[176] Karen Yeung, 'Better Regulation, Administrative Sanctions and Constitutional Values' (2013) 33 *Legal Studies* 312, 300.

[177] Mindy Chen-Wishart, 'Undue Influence: Vindicating Relationships of Influence' (2006) 59 *Current Legal Problems* 231, 240.

[178] ibid 240–41.

[179] Sean Wilken and Karim Ghaly, *The law of waiver, variation and estoppel*, 3rd edn (Oxford University Press, 2012) para 13.21.

[180] Hugh Beale, 'The Impact of the Decisions of the European Courts on English Contract Law: The Limits of Voluntary Harmonization' (2010) 18 *European Review of Private Law* 501, 525.

[181] In support of this view, see eg Donald L Horowitz, *The Courts and Social Policy* (Brookings Institution Press, 1977) 34–56; Peter Cartwright, *Consumer Protection in Financial Services* (Kluwer Law International Ltd, 1999) 8–9; Katharina Pistor and Chenggang Xu, 'Incomplete Law – A Conceptual and Analytical Framework and its Application to the Evolution of Financial Market Regulation' (2003) 35 *Journal of International Law and Politics* 931; Nicola Gennaioli, 'Contracting in the Shadow of the Law' (2006) Institute for International Economic Studies, Stockholm University; Richard A Posner, *How Judges Think* (Harvard University Press, 2008).

[182] *Crestsign* [114].

in relation to the suitability of a particular investment, which was negligent but not actionable. It is evident from the conclusions reached by English courts in the IRHP cases discussed in this chapter that there is an 'unsatisfactory interface'[183] between investment services regulation and private law arrangements, particularly because common law principles do not address the investor detriment caused by investment firms that take advantage of investors' vulnerability.

Especially where the interests of retail investors are most deeply at stake, 'there is a prima facie case for regulatory intervention in the public interest'[184] and regulation is thus called upon to protect investors against unscrupulous contractual terms of business and further repression,[185] as demonstrated by, for example, the measures implemented by the Hong Kong regulator. It is in this spirit that the recommendations set out in chapter seven have been devised.

[183] Paul Marshall, 'Interest rate swaps and the sale of the unknown: blind alleys, an enfeebled equity and the triumph of certainty over fairness' (2014) 29 *Journal of International Banking and Financial Law* 9, 9.

[184] Anthony Ogus, *Regulation: Legal Form and Economic Theory* (Oxford University Press, 1994) 18–22 (see also JA Jolowicz, 'The protection of the consumer and purchaser of goods under English Law' (1969) 32 *The Modern Law Review* 1, 8).

[185] Molony Committee, *Final Report of the Committee on Consumer Protection* (Cmnd 1781, 1962) para 46.

PART III

Concluding Remarks and Recommendations

The fact is that both regulation and civil law have a role to play in protecting economic interests, and neither is sufficiently effective that it leaves no room for the other … regulation and [private] law are complementary rather than alternative to one another.[1]

1 Peter Cane, *Tort Law and Economic Interests* (Clarendon Press, 1996).

6

Exploring the Co-extensive Relationship between Private Law and Regulation

The landscape of legal obligations imposed on providers of investment services comprises regulatory duties as well as duties arising under the common law framework. In principle, EU law is blind to the distinction between private law and regulatory law when it comes to implementing rules of EU law, and it therefore follows that insofar as investment services activities are concerned, the maximum harmonisation standard set by the MiFID regime should also apply to the courts.[2] Yet, the English courts' conclusions in IRHP mis-selling cases show that the courts impose a stricter benchmark for corporate retail investors than that required by the applicable regulatory framework.

This chapter draws upon these and other cases to explore the 'radiating effect'[3] that the common law and regulatory standards have had on each other's development, whilst also identifying conflicting duties in certain areas relevant to corporate retail investors. In light of the latter divergences, the investment services framework for corporate retail investors emerges as lacking a 'unifying regime',[4] as it struggles to achieve the twin aims of effective regulatory supervision and private law implementation.

I. A Conceptual Approach to Co-extensiveness

The FSA 1986 introduced a fresh dimension to financial services regulation which required consideration of, inter alia, corporate governance, internal controls and the manner in which investment firms managed their relationships with customers, thereby moving away from a historically reactive regulatory approach.[5] Existing

[2] See eg Case C-51/13 *Nationale-Nederlanden Levensverzekering Mij NV v Hubertus Wilhelmus van Leeuwen* [2015] ECR (para 28), a case concerning direct life assurance legislation, specifically the information to be provided to the policyholder and the obligation for the insurer to provide further information on costs and premiums under the general unwritten rules of Dutch national law.

[3] Olha O Cherednychenko, 'European Securities Regulation, Private Law and the Investment Firm-Client Relationship' (2009) 17 *European Review of Private Law*, 925, 937.

[4] Iris H-Y Chiu, 'The nature of a financial investment intermediary's duty to his client' (2008) 28 *Legal Studies* 254, 255.

[5] Jenny Hamilton, 'Negligence in the corridor? The interaction between "separate rooms" of regulation and the common law in financial services' (2007) 23 *Professional Negligence* 134, 137.

common law principles had significant influence over the development of this regulatory rulebook, such that most of the conduct of business rules governing the provision of investment services are rooted in common law, particularly those relating to duties of care in the wider sphere of professional negligence. Further, where commercial parties are involved, regulatory rules typically adhere to the long-standing principle of freedom of contract.[6]

This influence has been mutual – whilst common law principles were instrumental in assisting the regulator to determine in what circumstances regulatory intervention is warranted, the evolving investment services regulation is likewise perceived to have helped 'shape the common law'.[7] Over the years, the traditional sources of the duties and obligations of professionals were informed and supplemented by regulation and other published professional standards.[8] Case law on investment services historically offered little guidance as to what measures investment firms should take in the course of providing investment services, so the advancement of regulatory conduct of business rules was helpful in that it elaborated on the 'know your customer', 'appropriateness' and 'suitability' duties, as well as distinguishing between the various categories of investors and investment services in respect of which these duties arise. In this sense, the statutory rules on conduct drawn up by Member States in the transposition of the ISD and MiFID in particular, are envisaged to broaden liability for breach of statutory duties, as well as shape the courts' determination of what constitutes a breach of the common law duty of care in certain circumstances.

Despite these close links, however, the process through which the duties of care at common law are formed differs from the one shaping comparable duties arising from the regulatory framework. Their primary objectives are also distinct. The former places significant weight on judicial interpretation, where the courts, in establishing liability and in awarding compensation, apply common law principles based on the facts of the respective cases, whilst also having regard to the doctrine of precedent. On the other hand, the duty of care imposed on professionals through regulation is detailed in the regulatory rulebook and supplemented by other general principles (such as those contained in the FCA's Principles for Business, the desired outcomes promulgated by the TCF initiative, or the proposed additional Prescribed Responsibility under the SMCR), the purpose of which is to raise the standard across the industry, foster the smooth running of the financial system and secure effective supervision over the compliance of investment firms.[9]

[6] FCA, 'Discussion Paper DP15/7, Our approach to SMEs as users of financial services' (2015) para 4.13.

[7] FSA, 'Discussion Paper DP08/5, Consumer Responsibility' (2008) para 3.4.

[8] Rupert M Jackson, Roger Stewart and John Powell, *Jackson & Powell on Professional Liability*, 7th edn (Sweet & Maxwell Ltd, 2012) para 2–007.

[9] See further Jenny Hamilton, 'Negligence in the corridor? The interaction between "separate rooms" of regulation and the common law in financial services' (2007) 23 *Professional Negligence* 134, 134; Olha O Cherednychenko, 'European Securities Regulation, Private Law and the Investment Firm-Client Relationship' (2009) 17 *European Review of Private Law* 925, 930–31; Alastair Hudson, *The Law of Finance*, 2nd edn (Sweet & Maxwell Ltd, 2013) para 3–02.

This basic distinction between common law and regulation is also evident in the process of allocating risks between contracting parties. In this respect, the regulatory conduct of business regime attempts to redress the ordinary common law position of *caveat emptor* as the investment firm is required to assess the appropriateness or suitability of the retail investor as applicable, thereby shielding the investor from his own lack of expertise.

To the contrary, the common law is reliant on what parties agree to in their private contractual arrangement, such that these terms dictate the respective rights and obligations of each of the parties and any limitations attached thereto. As a result, no positive obligations to act are ordinarily imposed on a person under the common law system unless he has voluntary accepted them, which can be contrasted with conduct of business regulation where there is a positive regulation to act, for example, in the client's best interests as well as to generally act honestly and fairly.[10] To a great extent, therefore, private law and regulatory standards develop in 'separate rooms', whilst still being forced to remain in an 'uneasy co-existence' as they negotiate their relationship around one another.[11] This also contributes to the tension between the two regimes, which has proven to be particularly acute in cases concerning the mis-selling of IRHPs.

II. English Courts' Approach to Co-extensiveness

Because of discrepancies in the private law regimes of different jurisdictions, the relationship between regulation and private law in the investment services sphere emerges as an uncomfortable one and one which is potentially at odds with the principle of maximum harmonisation promoted by the MiFID framework. As discussed in chapter five, there is significant variation in the extent to which different jurisdictions rely on their regulatory regimes and, consequently, the degree of influence that this has on the litigation process. As a result, different models of the relationship between the regulatory duties and traditional private law duties of investment firms emerge.[12] In a number of European jurisdictions, including Germany, Netherlands and Spain, regulation and private law have mutually

[10] See eg MiFID II, Arts 24 and 27, and the corresponding rules in the COBS 11.2A.

[11] Julia Black. 'Law and Regulation: The Case of Finance' in Christine Parker and others (eds), *Regulating Law* (Oxford University Press Inc, 2004) 42, 45.

[12] Differences primarily arise from diverging legal traditions and legal cultures of common law and civil law jurisdictions. In relative terms, the former tend to rely on private agreements and the courts, whilst the latter appear to draw more heavily on regulation. Cherednychenko discusses three models in this context, which she describes as the 'complementarity', 'integration' and 'separation' models (see further Olha O Cherednychenko, 'Contract Governance in the EU: Conceptualising the Relationship between Investor Protection Regulation and Private Law' (2015) 21 *European Law Journal* 500, 511–18).

influenced each other's development, whereas the position of English courts on the matter has instead turned on the facts of the particular case. To this end, subject to the conditions discussed under Section IIA being met, the English judiciary has been willing to 'accommodate'[13] regulatory standards into the common law, but, where these conditions are not present, the courts have insisted on separating regulatory conduct of business rules from traditional private law duties, maintaining that these should operate in parallel to each other, as demonstrated by the discussion in Section IIB.

Notably, the courts' consideration revolves around whether the claimant, who must have suffered a loss as a result of a possible breach of advisory duty of care by the investment firm, has a right of action under FSMA, s 138D. Once this right is established, the duty breached would be actionable and the court may not even need to consider whether or not the investment firm is liable at common law in negligence, as the claim for breach of statutory duty would typically provide an adequate remedy. In these circumstances, the regulatory rulebook would inform the courts' assessment of damages. If, on the other hand, the breach relates to a non-actionable rule or the claimant is not entitled to a right of action under statute, then the courts would tend to rely exclusively on the contractual terms between the parties. Hence, where the courts have been called upon to decide on claims lodged by corporate retail investors (not having a right of action under FSMA, s 138D) in respect of matters excluded by contract (for example the provision of advice), the contractual terms of business have reigned supreme over the regulatory standards that may have significantly impinged on the relationship between the parties. The regulatory rules and definitions governing the classification of the service being provided as well as the distinction between retail and professional investors drawn by regulation which, of itself, affords increased protection to the former cohort of investors which may include corporate entities, have therefore been entirely disregarded.

The English courts' conclusions on co-extensiveness are particularly relevant to this book because they accentuate the impact on corporate retail investors arising as a consequence of categorising an investment service as 'advised' or 'non-advised'. In effect, the courts' determinations suggest that, in an advised sale context, a common law duty of care arises by reference to the relevant regulatory standards. In these circumstances, the suitability criteria prescribed by the regulatory rulebook are regarded by the court as 'basic duties which common sense dictates should be applied to any financial advisory situation' and, hence, it would be 'a strange toothless duty of care if advice was given, yet these obligations excluded'.[14] In non-advised sales, however, the existence of a duty of care rests

[13] Eva Z Lomnicka, 'The Impact of Rule-Making by Financial Services Regulators on the Common Law: The Lessons on PPI' in Louise Gullifer and Stefan Vogenauer (eds), *English and European Perspectives on Contract and Corporate Law: Essays in Honour of Hugh Beale* (Hart Publishing Ltd, 2014) 51.

[14] *David Anderson* [23].

exclusively on the written terms of the contractual agreement between the parties and the disclaimers contained therein, and the courts do not question whether the regulatory obligations in relation to the classification of the service and the obligations attached thereto had been fulfilled by the investment firm or otherwise. Consequently, the existence of a common law duty depends on the relationship between the parties being one which gives rise to such duty.

A. Merging Common Law Duties with Regulatory Standards

Conduct of business obligations have been, in certain instances, highly influential in shaping common law standards of care and the courts' perception of what constitutes proper behaviour in financial markets, even by non-regulated persons. In the cases that follow, English courts have interpreted common law duties of care as being aligned to regulatory standards, thereby acknowledging that duties at common law are substantially informed by the regulatory framework. This is not because the regulatory rules themselves represent private law obligations but because compliance with the relevant regulatory rules is ordinarily expected of the service provider.[15] English courts have thus invoked regulatory rules and standards to assist them in determining whether or not an obligation under the common law exists in the first place and, if so, whether this has been breached or otherwise, thereby suggesting that compliance with the rules of the regulatory regime should be the starting point for determining the standard of duty,[16] and accepting that:

> whilst the ambit of the duty of care owed by a financial adviser at common law is not necessarily co-extensive with the duties owed by that adviser under the applicable regulatory regime, the regulations afford strong evidence as to what is expected of a competent adviser in most situations.[17]

Similarly, in finding a duty of care following negligent investment advice, the courts have held that 'the skill and care to be expected of a financial adviser would ordinarily include compliance with the rules of the relevant regulator',[18] such that the reasonable steps required under the regulatory rulebook 'correlate with the exercise of reasonable care required in contract and tort to achieve the same ends',[19] and breach of the rules contained in the COBS 'will ordinarily also amount to a

[15] Paul Marshall, 'Fault lines in English financial law: Thornbridge v Barclays Bank' (2016) 31 *Journal of International Banking and Financial Law* 266, 268 (see also Law Commission, 'Fiduciary Duties of Investment Intermediaries' (Law Com No 350, 2014) para 10.59).

[16] See eg, *Clifford Shore v (1) Sedgwick Financial Services Ltd; (2) Barclays Financial Planning Limited* [2007] EWHC 3054 (QB), affd [2008] EWCA Civ 863, [2009] Bus LR 42.

[17] *Seymour v Caroline Ockwell & Co* [2005] EWHC 1137 (QB), [2005] PNLR 39 [77]. In support of this proposition, the Judge cites *Lloyd Cheyham & Co Ltd v Littlejohn* [1987] BCLC 303 (QB).

[18] *Loosemore v Financial Concepts* [2001] Lloyd's Rep PN 235 (QB) 241 (see also *Rubenstein* (first instance); *Green and Rowley* (appeal); *O'Hare*).

[19] *Basma Al Sulaiman v (1) Credit Suisse Securities (Europe) Limited; (2) Plurimi Capital LLP* [2013] EWHC 400 (Comm), [2013] 1 All ER (Comm) 1105 [18].

breach of … [the] common law duty'.[20] Indeed, English courts have concluded that it would be 'difficult to see how reasonable skill and care could be taken in giving advice about a financial product without the essence of those [regulatory] rules being satisfied',[21] to the extent that the courts have also made reference to guidance and other publications issued by regulatory bodies to support their conclusions.[22] In the context of a duty to explain investment risks, the court's decision in *O'Hare* to adopt the *Montgomery* test over the *Bolam* test[23] was also supported by reference to the regulatory regime, which was considered to provide 'strong evidence of what the common law requires',[24] particularly because the COBS includes a duty to explain in similar terms to *Montgomery* which, unlike *Bolam*, does not depend on the opinion of a reasonable body within the profession.

Further, there have been isolated cases in which the courts have concluded that even if the parties had not expressly incorporated certain regulatory rules into the contractual terms, these rules would still have been incorporated as an implied term where, for example, the client agreement stated that the transaction in question would be governed by the regulatory rulebook. This actually gives regulation the status of contract terms so that contravention of the rules becomes actionable at common law as a breach of contract, and hence the courts are not willing to apply this broadly.[25]

In other circumstances not strictly concerning the provision of investment services, the courts have equally sought guidance from regulatory standards and industry practices. By way of example, the provisions of the City Code on Takeovers and Mergers influenced the outcome of civil litigation between parties, when the court considered these provisions to have been 'laid down by responsible and experienced persons' and representative of the 'fair and reasonable conduct'[26]

[20] *O'Hare* [208].

[21] *David Anderson* [24], quoting the District Judge.

[22] In *Andrew Harrison and Elaine Harrison v Black Horse Limited* [2011] EWCA Civ 1128, [2012] ECC 7 [60]–[62], the court made reference to publications by the then FSA, including a policy statement and a report on the PPI mis-selling scandal. The court considered these publications to have 'fortified' its conclusions.

[23] *Bolam v Friern Hospital Management Committee* [1957] 1 WLR 582 (QB). The *Bolam* test asks whether the defendant was acting 'in accordance with a practice accepted as proper by a responsible body of … men skilled in that particular art'. This test was overturned in a medical context (so far as the duty to explain is concerned), in favour of a duty to take reasonable steps to ensure the patient is aware of any material risks.

[24] *O'Hare* [207].

[25] In *Larussa-Chigi v CS First Boston Ltd* [1998] CLC 277 (QB), the Court observed that the London Code of Conduct would be impliedly incorporated. This must however be contrasted with the court's determination in, eg, *Clarion Ltd v National Provident Institution* [2000] 1 WLR 1888, where the court concluded that the SIB Principles were not implied into the contract in question. Similarly, in *Bear Stearns Bank Plc v Forum Global Equity Ltd* [2007] EWHC 1576, the court ruled that the rules of the Loan Market Association rules were not implied, and, in *Flex-E-Vouchers Ltd v The Royal Bank of Scotland Plc* [2016] EWHC 2604 (QB), the court concluded that rules contained in the COB were also not implied.

[26] *Re St Piran* [1981] 1 WLR 1300 (Ch) 1307 D–G.

expected of service providers.[27] The courts have also considered normally accepted behaviours, practices and standards in other professions, such as accounting standards[28] and the Law Society professional standards,[29] as being highly relevant. More recently, the High Court, in *Thomas*,[30] took into consideration the fact that the defendant bank had subscribed to the Business Banking Code (a voluntary code of practice),[31] thereby demonstrating the court's recourse to documents other than the contractual agreement in assessing whether the service provider had breached its duty not to misrepresent as well as its information duty to explain.

Whilst it is a breach of a common law duty of care, rather than a regulatory duty, that gives rise to a claim, the courts have considered the regulatory framework as setting the standards of care attached to such common law duties. It follows, therefore, that it would be possible for the common law standard to impose more onerous obligations on investment firms. In this sense, the English judiciary observed that, whilst the courts 'can be expected to attach considerable weight to the content of [regulatory] codes', they are still 'not excluded from making their own assessment of a situation', also emphasising that silence of the regulatory framework on a particular issue does not exclude the power of the court to consider whether a duty of care exists or otherwise.[32] Similarly, the courts drew upon the higher standards set by common law to rule against an investment firm which had breached its duty of care towards its client, despite acknowledging that a reasonable body of financial practitioners would have provided advice of a standard similar (or even inferior) to that of the investment firm.[33]

The conclusions of the courts in these instances suggest that standards and norms from the regulatory context can be absorbed into common law, potentially extending the circumstances in which investment firms will owe a duty of care,[34] thus creating an overlap between common law duties and regulatory duties, such that the skill and care to be expected of a reasonably competent investment firm would typically include compliance with relevant regulatory standards. This hybrid approach enables the courts to give recognition to regulatory standards while

[27] For other cases drawing on the provisions of the City Code on Takeovers, see also *Crabtree v Hinchcliffe (Inspector of Taxes)* [1972] AC 707 (HL); *Dunford & Elliott Ltd v Johnson and Firth Brown Ltd* [1977] 1 Lloyd's Rep 505 (CA, Civ Div); *Dawson International Plc v Coats Paton Plc* 1989 SLT 655 (IH).

[28] See eg *Lloyd Cheyham*; *Revenue and Customs Commissioners v William Grant & Sons Distillers Ltd* [2007] UKHL 15, [2007] 1 WLR 1448.

[29] See eg *Charis Manolakaki v John Constantinides and Others* [2004] EWHC 749 (Ch).

[30] *Thomas*. The claim concerned an alleged breach of duty by the defendant bank to explain to the claimants the financial implications of fixing the interest rate on the claimants' loan.

[31] The Business Banking Code referred to in *Thomas* had been replaced by the Lending Code and, on 1 July 2017, this Lending Code has also been superseded by the Standards of Lending Practice.

[32] *Gorham and Others v British Telecommunications Plc and Others* [2000] 4 All ER 867 (CA, Civ Div), 878.

[33] See eg *Loosemore*. It is noted that instances where the common law is applied more widely are infrequent.

[34] *Commissioners of Customs & Excise* [36].

managing the application of the common law and allowing the latter to develop in parallel with the regulatory system, rather than in a revolutionary way.[35]

Insofar as the cases discussed in this Section are concerned, English courts were prepared to find a co-extensive relationship between private law and regulatory standards because the services being provided were such that they gave rise to an advisory duty of care at common law, and because claimants fell within the definition of 'private person' for the purposes of FSMA, section 138D (formerly section 150). In effect, recourse to the right of action under FSMA, section 138D allows the court to engage with common law duties insofar as those classes of investors which Parliament intended to protect are concerned. In these instances, the courts established that the imposition of the common law duty of care should not overlook the obligations incumbent upon investment firms as a result of the regulatory regime within which they operate.[36]

B. Setting Apart Common Law Duties from Regulatory Standards

The fact-specific nature of the cases discussed in Section IIA means that the conclusions reached by the courts in these cases cannot be readily applied to other financial mis-selling claims. Indeed, where the facts of the cases differ from those discussed in Section IIA,[37] English courts have excluded the existence of a co-extensive relationship between the two frameworks. Notably, the courts observed that the existence or otherwise of a common law duty 'has to be determined in accordance with established legal principles', which principles 'are not altered' by the engagement of the regulatory regime.[38] Therefore, although the regulatory regime 'may provide relevant background for the application of those principles',[39] the court has no reason to draw upon regulatory principles in instances where the

[35] See further Jack Beaston, 'The relationship between regulations governing the financial services industry and fiduciary duties under the general law' in Ewan McKendrick (ed), *Corporate aspects of trusts and fiduciary obligations* (Clarendon Press, 1992) 60–61, 67. For additional case law supporting this approach, see eg *Investors Compensation Scheme*; *Brandeis (Brokers) Limited v Herbert Black, American Iron and Metal Company Incorporated, Lito Trade Incorporated* [2001] 2 All ER (Comm) 980, [2001] 2 Lloyd's Rep 359; *Alan John Patrick Beary v Pall Mall Investments (a firm)* [2004] EWHC 1608 (Ch), affd [2005] EWCA Civ 415, [2005] PNLR 35.

[36] Paul Marshall, 'Interest rate swaps and the sale of the unknown: blind alleys, an enfeebled equity and the triumph of certainty over fairness' (2014) 29 *Journal of International Banking and Financial Law* 9, 11–12.

[37] eg, the terms of the agreement include disclaimers that would be inconsistent with the exercise of an advisory duty of care, and provide that the claimant falls outside the scope of FSMA, s 138D (similar to the terms included in IRHP agreements).

[38] *Andrew Brown and Others v InnovatorOne Plc and Others* [2012] EWHC 1321 (Comm) [653], [1031] (see also Alex Fox and Clare Arthurs, 'Negligence: Don't bank on it: borrowers, lenders and the duty of care' (2013) 52 *Corporate Litigation Journal* 4, 6).

[39] *Andrew Brown* [653].

common law does not provide for a duty of care in non-advisory relationships. As extensively demonstrated by the discussion of mis-selling case law in chapter five, an advisory duty of care at common law can only arise by contract, or upon responsibility being assumed, none of which are present in the context of a non-advisory relationship. In this spirit, the Court of Appeal in *Green and Rowley*[40] rejected the argument that the mere existence of the regulatory framework gives rise to a co-extensive duty of care at common law incorporating regulatory terms. In so doing, it stated that using the co-extensiveness argument to widen the protections provided for in the statute would violate the access to statutory claims which had been carefully demarcated in FSMA, section 138D and would hence be akin to 'driv[ing] a coach and horses through the intention of Parliament'.

This was recently confirmed by the Court of Appeal in *CGL and Others*,[41] which noted that financial services providers operate in a highly regulated environment where Parliament has set out circumstances in which specified individuals could institute proceedings and take other action within a framework which grants wide powers to the FCA. In the Court of Appeal's view, the overall regulatory regime 'is a clear pointer against the imposition of a duty of care' and the recognition of a free-standing duty of care would therefore undermine the regulatory regime, as well as circumvent the intention of Parliament.[42]

The stark difference between the courts' treatment of the cases discussed in Section IIA and those cases considered in this Section IIB which relate to non-advised sales without recourse to FSMA, section 138D, is clearly demonstrated by an in-depth analysis of two particular IRHP mis-selling cases – *Thornbridge* and *Crestsign*. This assessment is helpful in that it not only supplements the extensive case law analysis in chapter five but also brings to the fore the courts' indifference towards regulatory requirements insofar as corporate retail investors (which are not entitled to a right of action under FSMA, section 138D) engaging in non-advised investment transactions are concerned. There are two issues in particular which merit further discussion in the context of these two cases and the wider arguments being made in this book, which relate to the classification of the investment service and the categorisation of the investor.

i. Classification of the Investment Service

It is to be noted that in both *Thornbridge* and *Crestsign*, the respective courts concluded that the service that had been provided was of a non-advisory nature. It is argued here that, in so concluding, the courts limited themselves to a superficial

[40] *Green and Rowley* (appeal) [23], [30]. This statement was made by the Court of Appeal in its assessment of the scope of the private right of action under the then FSMA, s 150. The issue was whether to extend a claim for breach of the regulatory duty to a person not covered by this provision. This was rejected by the Court of Appeal as the right of action provision was considered as being 'fit for purpose'.

[41] *CGL and Others* [84]–[87].

[42] ibid [87].

assessment of the regulatory framework applicable thereto, which led them to dismiss key communications between the parties as mere exchanges of information. These communications centred on a particular transaction in a specified financial instrument towards which the corporate retail investor was directed as a pre-condition of its lending arrangement with the bank, which, in this context, was also acting as an investment service provider. The latter entertained value judgements on the particular IRHP and compared different types of IRHPs on a selective, rather than balanced, basis thereby presenting IRHPs as being suitable to the claimant's circumstances and arguably influencing the ultimate decision taken by the claimant.[43] These behaviours are indicative of the investment firm crossing the line that divides the mere provision of factual 'information' from the more loaded 'investment advice' and the additional duties attached thereto.[44]

More importantly, it should be noted that it was a condition of the loan stated in the offer letter that, before the loan was drawn down, the claimant should either execute an interest rate hedge acceptable to the defendant or otherwise the interest was to be on a fixed basis. Investment firms actively encouraged corporate retail investors to go for the former. This, of itself, is in breach of MiFID provisions in that the claimant, a corporate retail investor, was specifically directed to the purchase of an IRHP as a complex investment product, without any suitability assessment being carried out by the defendant. In this respect, one notes the pronouncements made by the European Commission stating that a recommendation which is given to an investor with no consideration of its suitability would be forbidden 'in the light of the fiduciary obligations firms are subject to'.[45] This highlights the role of the *quasi*-fiduciary duty of the investment firm to act in the investor's best interest as a potential gap-filler and which is intended to prevent circumvention of the suitability test.[46] Further, the disclaimers contained in the marketing material relating to the IRHP expressly stated that such communication was being made available to persons who are 'investment professionals', when, as acknowledged by the court and as discussed throughout this book, IRHP claimants were generally retail, not professional, investors.

The respective courts did not rule out the provision of advice. In *Thornbridge* although the court concluded that the defendant did not recommend the IRHP, it still acknowledged the possibility of advice having been given in informal communications between the parties, to which, however, it did not attribute any importance since the defendant had not contractually assumed an advisory duty. More specifically, the court held that the pivotal factor is not whether advice was

[43] PERG 8.28.4(G) states that, under these circumstances, information may take on the nature of advice.

[44] See eg *Walker* and *Zaki*.

[45] European Commission, 'Your Questions on MiFID' (2008) Question 158.

[46] See further Luca Enriques and Matteo Gargantini, 'The Overarching Duty to Act in the Best Interests of the Client in MiFID II' in Danny Busch and Guido Ferrarini (eds), *Regulation of the EU Financial Markets: MiFID II and MiFIR* (Oxford University Press, 2017) 98–100.

given or otherwise but whether or not the relationship was contractually agreed as being of an advisory nature.[47] In *Crestsign*, the court was more forthcoming in admitting that the relationship between the parties was, in substance, an advisory one, as well as admitting that the investment firm was not concerned with ensuring that the claimant understood the products sufficiently to enable it to judge whether they were objectively suitable, or which was the most suitable.[48] Yet, notwithstanding this being in flagrant breach of COBS 9 (now COBS 9A), the court discounted these observations by stating that:

> the line that separates provision of information from giving advice may be a fine one … it is not always easy for a salesman … to know where one ends and the other begins. Reasonable people could disagree about whether the line is crossed in a particular case.[49]

In both of the cases being examined here, the courts relied on precedent cases, predominantly *Springwell*, to dismiss these exchanges as merely incidental to the wider relationship between the parties, thereby justifying the conclusion that the defendant had not assumed an advisory relationship resulting in a duty of care towards the claimant on the non-reliance provisions contained in the contract. The approach taken by the respective courts in these instances also echoes the position in *Grant*,[50] whereby, notwithstanding the terms of business stating that the applicable regulations shall prevail in the event that these are in conflict to the terms of business, the Scottish court still concluded that any advice that had been given in practice was immaterial due to the clear non-advisory disclaimers contained in the contractual terms. According to Lord Hodge, the aim of this provision was not to incorporate the rules contained in the COBS into the contract as this would have meant that the classification as advice under regulatory law would also apply for civil purposes and that an infringement of regulatory rules on advice would then automatically constitute a breach of contract. The court was therefore not willing to equate the rules contained in the COBS to the contractual rights.[51]

As clearly emerges from the foregoing discussion, there have been instances in which investment firms were found by the courts to have crossed the line between 'information' and 'investment advice', but still categorised the service as a non-advisory one, hence failing to undertake suitability assessments as required by MiFID II, Article 25(2) and COBS 9.2A. Notwithstanding these breaches, however, the disclaimers that had been embedded in the terms of business led English courts to uphold the contracts as valid, without the courts having regard

[47] *Thornbridge* [70], [96].

[48] *Crestsign* [39].

[49] ibid [115].

[50] *Grant* [63]–[67].

[51] ibid. See also Danny Busch, 'Agency and Principal Dealing under MiFID I and MiFID II' in Danny Busch and Guido Ferrarini (eds), *Regulation of the EU Financial Markets: MiFID II and MiFIR* (Oxford University Press 2017) 241.

to the regulatory requirements thereon.[52] It is also noted that, following the implementation of MiFID I, investment firms were precluded from selling complex products (including IRHPs) on an execution-only basis, such that any sale of a complex product must first pass the appropriateness test. To this effect, even if one had to consider the transaction in *Thornbridge* and *Crestsign* to be non-advisory in nature, investment firms were still in breach of COBS 10 (now COBS 10A) since the IRHP terms of business provided for the transaction in IRHPs being executed on an execution-only basis. Apart from discounting the obligations incumbent upon investment firms in terms of the aforementioned client classification and suitability rules, the courts equally overlooked the extent to which the behaviour of the investment firms complied with their obligation to ensure that all communications with the investor are fair, clear and not misleading,[53] as well as complying with the clients' best interests rule,[54] and ensuring best execution of any transaction for an investor.[55]

ii. Categorisation of the Investor

The courts' categorisation of the claimant also had a significant bearing on the courts' conclusions. The court in *Thornbridge* accepted that the claimant 'was a retail customer and not a professional investor and lacked experience in derivatives',[56] however, the court resolved that the claimant was being run by 'shrewd business people with considerable experience in dealing with banks',[57] who should have known that the investment firm was not assuming responsibility for an advisory relationship. This latter consideration took precedence over the regulatory categorisation in informing the court's conclusions. Similarly, the court in *Crestsign* accepted that the claimant was 'a retail client of the banks without … any realistic prospect of timely access to adequate expert advice',[58] yet, this did not stop Kerr J from finding in favour of the investment firm on the basis of the provisions contained in the contractual agreement between the parties.

The approach taken by the Courts in *Thornbridge, Crestsign*, and other cases discussed in chapter five, in terms of attributing a higher degree of knowledge and experience to corporate retail investors, is clearly indicative of the judiciary disregarding the regulatory rules in connection with the protection of retail investors. The court disregarded the definitions adopted by the MiFID regime, and consequently the COBS, in distinguishing between professional and retail investors,

[52] FSMA, s. 138E(2) provides that a breach of rules is not an offence, and that it does not render a transaction or a contract unenforceable or void.

[53] MiFID II, Art 24(3); COBS 4.2.1(R).

[54] MiFID II, Art 24(1); COBS 2.1.1(R).

[55] MiFID II, Art 27; COBS 11.2A.

[56] *Thornbridge* [95].

[57] ibid [115].

[58] *Crestsign* [151].

and the intention of that regime to establish an enhanced layer of protection for the latter category of investors. Notably, the judgments are heavily focused on analysing and framing the duties of the investment firm on the basis of the contractual terms of business rather than the obligations incumbent upon the investment firm as a result of the regulatory rulebook, and hardly refer to the regulatory regime, if at all.

Notwithstanding the view expressed by the Court in *O'Hare*[59] that compliance with the COBS was 'ordinarily enough to comply with a common law duty … while breach of them will ordinarily also amount to a breach of that common law duty', *Thornbridge* and *Crestsign* are two of many other cases discussed in chapter five that illustrate the English courts' tendency to regard the regulatory rulebook as not co-extensive with common law principles, particularly where corporate retail investors are concerned, since they lack recourse to the private right of action under FSMA, section 138D. Consequently, '… the statutory purpose of the COB regime pursuant to FSMA is to afford a measure of carefully balanced consumer protection to the "private person"',[60] therefore to the exclusion of other retail investors (namely corporate entities) that do not fall within the definition of 'private person' for the purpose of FSMA, section 138D. The courts' conclusions in this respect are clearly indicative of a lack of judicial sympathy towards corporate retail investors, which is also driven by unwillingness to extend the common law liability to parties which Parliament has excluded from the scope of the breach of statutory duty claim.

It is reiterated here that the courts' superficial assessment of the nature of the investment service and, consequently, whether the investment firms were correct in classifying this as non-advisory or otherwise, was predominantly driven by the perceived acumen of the claimants in complex investment products simply because they were corporate entities rather than individuals. In other words, the courts' findings in this respect were not informed by the regulatory rulebook or other detailed guidance promulgated by regulators over the years, as the 'retail' classification of these corporate entities was largely ignored. The courts' strict adherence to the terms of business, and the disclaimers contained therein, prevented the courts from engaging with the regulatory regime to consider the impact of issues of this nature on their conclusions.

In this context, it is also worth drawing an analogy between the duties incumbent upon investment firms and those applicable to the medical profession. Although, as recognised in *O'Hare*,[61] there is little consensus in the financial services industry about how investment risks should be managed by an investment firm, it is hereby submitted that, in an investment services context, the *Montgomery* test is also relevant because it emphasises the need for proper dialogue and

[59] *O'Hare* [208].
[60] *Rubenstein* (appeal) [115].
[61] *O'Hare* [206].

conversation between the investment firm and the investor, which communication is fact-sensitive and dependent on the investor's understanding of the risk, as well as his knowledge, experience and other similar factors which may impinge upon the decision as to whether he should engage in the transaction or otherwise. This does not emerge clearly from the application of the *Bolam* test.[62] The conclusions of the Court in *Montgomery*[63] relating to disengaged patients are also relevant to certain aspects of the relationship between an investment firm and a retail investor – because retail investors trust investment firms to make them aware of all material risks to a transaction, these investors typically choose to ignore the risk disclosures in information documents, prospectuses, terms of business, offering memoranda, and other similar materials, and, reliance is placed on investment firms to assess how best to explain the risks to these disengaged investors in an effective manner. Hence, the investment firm's duty to inform should not be considered to have been fulfilled by bombarding the retail investor with technical information which he cannot reasonably be expected to grasp, or by demanding signature on the terms of business as an acquiescence that the retail investor has 'read and understood' those terms (particularly in light of the investor's 'retail' – as opposed to 'professional' – status).[64]

III. Concluding Remarks

This chapter has concluded that there seems to be a consensus amongst English courts that once a duty of care is established (where investment advice is considered to be provided) and any breach of that duty is actionable under statute, the courts' assessment of damages would be determined by the regulatory framework. In this sense, the interaction between common law and investment services regulation continues to play a significant role in mis-selling claims, as the presumption is that 'the standard of the duty of care in negligence is likely to be largely co-extensive with that imposed by the regulatory rules'.[65] In this context, a contravention of an actionable rule laid out in the regulatory rulebook gives rise to concurrent civil liability in tort or contract and a failure by a regulated firm to comply with its regulatory obligations under the COBS would be equivalent to a breach of its common law duty of care.

[62] The *Montgomery* test has also been upheld in the context of a solicitor-client relationship, whereby the Court of Appeal in Northern Ireland concluded that: 'as in the medical context, the advisory role of the solicitor must involve proper communication and dialogue with the client' (see further *Baird v Stephen W R Hastings (Practising As Hastings & Company, Solicitors)* [2015] NICA 22 [34]).

[63] *Montgomery* [85].

[64] ibid [90].

[65] Rupert M Jackson, Roger Stewart and John Powell, *Jackson & Powell on Professional Liability*, 7th edn (Sweet & Maxwell Ltd, 2012) para 14-072.

Where, on the other hand, a relationship is governed by a non-advisory contractual arrangement, and the claimant is not entitled to a statutory right of action, English courts have not assessed the nature of the service being provided against regulatory benchmarks but, rather, they have based their conclusions on the disclaimers contained in the standard terms of business. The rationale suggested by the courts in this regard is that, if the common law was to imply a duty co-extensive with the rules contained in the COBS in circumstances where the retail investor is not a private person, this would circumvent the statutory distinction between those persons who can enforce the regulatory regime as a statutory duty under FSMA, section 138D and those who cannot.[66] Moreover, irrespective of how strong the argument on the facts that an advisory relationship has been entered into, the operation of contractual estoppel has meant that any advisory duty of care was excluded from arising where the contractual documentation disclaimed any responsibility on the part of the investment firm for the provision of investment advice. Clauses of this nature are therefore likely to jeopardise the investor protection aims of the MiFID regime, whilst also being detrimental to the level playing field that this regime seeks to establish.

Pursuant to the above, it becomes amply clear that the common law duty to advise the investor and warn him of the risks inherent in the transaction will not be implied by virtue of the regulatory standards governing other parts of the relationship where an investment service is contractually undertaken on a non-advisory basis. Similarly, the regulatory categorisation of claimants as 'retail' (or 'private' under the former pre-MiFID regime) has a very limited bearing, if any at all, on the court's assessment where corporate entities are involved. It is submitted here that by discounting this regulatory dimension, the courts may fail to correctly appreciate the retail investor's knowledge, expertise and experience in the investment field as well as the degree to which such investor is exposed to the risks presented by complex investment products in particular. Needless to say, the position of corporate retail investors is even more precarious due to these investors being excluded from the scope of FSMA, section 138D.

It is acknowledged here that the introduction of the general statutory duty of care discussed in Section III of chapter two could assist in fostering a co-extensive relationship between regulatory duties and common law duties, whilst also addressing the imbalance of information between retail investors and investment firms and the risks attached thereto for such investors. Yet, a blanket statutory duty of care may also have adverse repercussions on the industry, particularly if it is introduced as a general standard which does not distinguish between retail and professional clients and between complex and non-complex investment products.

This notwithstanding, the absence of a mechanism that connects private law to investor protection regulation in these circumstances thus poses a real risk that the former fails to adequately assess the interests of the parties, particularly those in

[66] See further *Thomas* [78].

need of the highest protection, including corporate retail investors. Hence, whilst the introduction of the statutory duty of care remains subject to ongoing debate, the solution proposed by this book in chapter seven is one which calls for regulatory intervention, with this being supported by an extension to the statutory right of action under FSMA, section 138D. This reform is aimed at counteracting the imbalances that exist in the treatment of corporate retail investors by the respective regimes.

7

Regulating to Prevent Mis-selling: Proposals for Reform

By focusing on corporate retail investors, this book has sought to demonstrate that dependence on inadequate reactive safeguards has led to an aura of 'regulatory indifference'[1] that has paved the way for the dissemination of complex, high-risk products amongst vulnerable corporate retail investors and which has meant that the regulator was largely unperturbed by the substantial financial detriment caused to such investors.[2] The analyses and discussions set out in previous chapters indicate that investment services regulation 'has not asked enough 'what if' questions' because it has been overly reliant on 'convenient or habitual assumptions'.[3]

The general perceptions of the retail investor have shifted over time, 'sitting on a spectrum between vulnerable consumer and empowered and engaged investor',[4] which led policymakers to modify their regulatory response accordingly. This constant flux in the regulatory strategy resulted in a myriad of regulatory reforms, the effectiveness of which has been challenged by this book, predominantly by drawing upon IRHP case law to illustrate the vulnerable position of corporate retail investors. As demonstrated by this book, these investors are prone to a series of behavioural biases and resource constraints that heighten their risk of falling victim to mis-selling. Furthermore, corporate retail investors have encountered significant hurdles when attempting to claim redress, not least by facing a less than sympathetic judiciary when litigating their case in court. Collectively, these factors demonstrate the continuing need for effective conduct regulation which captures corporate retail investors within its scope and which is 'more robust, sceptical, early interventionist, and precautionary'.[5]

[1] Eduardo Reyes, 'Roundtable: Financial Mis-selling: Costly business' (2013) *Law Society Gazette* 25, 1.

[2] This can be contrasted with the active and vocal position taken by the FCA in the wake of other scandals whose victims were individual (rather than corporate) retail investors.

[3] Donald C Langevoort, *Selling Hope, Selling Risk: Corporations, Wall Street, and the Dilemmas of Investor Protection* (Oxford University Press, 2016) 10.

[4] Niamh Moloney, 'Regulating the Retail Markets' in Niamh Moloney, Eilís Ferran, and Jennifer Payne (eds), *The Oxford Handbook of Financial Regulation* (Oxford University Press, 2015) 764.

[5] FSUG, 'Making financial services work for financial users, Paper 1: New model financial regulation' (2012) 7.

I. The Case for 'Libertarian Paternalism'

It is particularly challenging for any single regime to reconcile the needs of the more powerful party whilst also extending an adequate level of protection to the weaker one. The development of the law by the courts is 'reactive'[6] in nature in that the courts must wait for a dispute to arise and then respond in a fire-fighting manner; moreover, the courts' veneration towards standard form contracts accentuates the 'comparatively static machinery of the law',[7] which provides the basis for the justification of regulatory intervention.

This book underlines the English courts' 'strong respect for the written word',[8] which aims to identify 'the natural and ordinary meaning of the words which the draftsman has used'.[9] The doctrine of contractual estoppel emerges as a well-established concept and acts as a shield for investment firms when these are faced with claims for misrepresentation or inadequate advice in the context of relationships formally entered into on a 'non-advisory' basis. Where the terms provide that the parties expressly exclude any reliance on any advice or representations, those terms are equally effective against all retail investors but particularly damaging for corporate retail investors, since these investors have limited redress options, if any at all. In addition, and despite certain restrictions on the conduct of a professional person imposed by developments in the law of contract and tort,[10] investment firms appear to enjoy a privileged position since they do not typically guarantee the products they market or sell.[11] In essence, therefore, one can draw a direct link between the mis-selling scandals and the restricted liability for pure economic loss in negligence, which is also eased by the ability of investment firms to contract out of tortious and fiduciary duties in transactions that are contractually entered into on a 'non-advised' basis.

The operation of the foundations of the English legal system in this way is intensified through the use of standard form contracts. Notwithstanding certain

[6] Lord Chief Justice Thomas of Cwmgiedd, 'Corporate Justice in the Global Village: The Role of the Corporate Courts' (DIFC Academy of Law Lecture, Dubai, 1 February 2016) 6: www.judiciary.gov.uk/wp-content/uploads/2016/02/LCJ-commerical-justice-in-the-global-village-DIFC-Academy-of-Law-Lecture-February-2016.pdf, accessed 16 March 2016. This notwithstanding, it is recognised that the introduction of the new Financial List (Civil Procedure Rules, Part 63A) is an important addition to the UK's judicial process, aimed at ensuring that cases which raise issues of general importance to the financial markets are dealt with by judges with suitable expertise and experience in these markets (see further HM Courts and Tribunals Service, 'Guide to the Financial List' (2015)).

[7] David H Parry, *The Sanctity of Contracts in English Law* (Stevens & Sons London, 1959) 71.

[8] Hugh Beale, 'The Impact of the Decisions of the European Courts on English Contract Law: The Limits of Voluntary Harmonization' (2010) 18 *European Review of Private Law* 501, 524.

[9] *Breadner and Others v Granville-Grossman and Others* [2001] Ch 523, [2001] WLR 593, 535.

[10] These restrictions relate to fiduciary obligations, undue influence and confidentiality, which are of limited relevance in the context of non-advised sales.

[11] See further Rupert M Jackson, Roger Stewart and John Powell, *Jackson & Powell on Professional Liability*, 7th edn (Sweet & Maxwell Ltd, 2012) paras 2-004–2-006.

practical benefits being associated with the use of such contracts,[12] agreements of this nature caused financial detriment to corporate retail investors, particularly due to the complexity of the terms contained therein and the potential inherent risks to which the investor is exposed as a result, as well as the risk that widespread usage of the same terms 'can amplify any mistake that a court makes in deciding the proper meaning of such terms'.[13]

The limitations of the common law framework indicate that regulatory law should be at the forefront of issues that 'really matte[r] to society collectively'.[14] Indeed, the lethal combination of standard form contracts, information asymmetry and limited consumer competence, suggests that a degree of intervention in the contractual bargaining process may be justified.[15] In this sense, regulation emerges as a kind of 'preventive medicine',[16] taking on the leading role in creating reasonable boundaries to contractual freedom and addressing the lacunae that exist in the present framework.[17] Despite private law preserving its autonomy from regulatory law and retaining its role in ultimately dictating the relationship between private commercial parties, the interplay between private and regulatory law in this way means that contractual transactions become subject to a 'novel, 'hybrid' body of law' that can be described as 'regulatory contract law'.[18]

As the boundary between economic freedom and social legitimacy remains a fine one, it is here submitted that regulatory problem-solving should involve a combination of command-and-control regulation (predominantly via ex-post enforcement measures) as well as 'soft' regulatory measures which present themselves through 'behaviourally informed interventions'[19] that 'nudge' retail investors towards transacting in those products that are more aligned to their needs and

[12] Standard form contracts allow the drafter to reduce the costs of contracting and minimise uncertainty and liability. The use of standard terms across similar transactions also reduces bureaucracy and enables consistency (see further Elaine A Welle, 'Freedom of Contract and the Securities Laws: Opting Out of Securities Regulation by Private Agreement' (1999) 56 *Washington and Lee Law Review* 519, 577; Peter Van Wijck, 'Protection against Unfair Contracts: An Economic Analysis of European Regulation' (2000) 9 *European Journal of Law and Economics* 73; Randy E Barnett, 'Consenting to Form Contracts' (2002) 71 *Fordham Law Review* 627, 630–31; Dan Awrey, 'The Limits of Private Ordering Within Modern Financial Markets' (2014) 34 *Review of Banking and Financial Law* 183, 186).

[13] Jeffrey B Golden, 'The courts, the financial crisis and systemic risk' (2009) 4 *Capital Markets Law Journal* 141, 144.

[14] Mike Feintuck, 'Regulatory Rationales Beyond the Economic: In Search of the Public Interest' in Robert Baldwin, Martin Cave, and Martin Lodge (eds), *The Oxford Handbook of Regulation* (Oxford University Press, 2010) 56.

[15] Niamh Moloney, *How to Protect Investors: Lessons from the EC and the UK* (Cambridge University Press, 2010) 248.

[16] Jeffrey B Golden, 'The courts, the financial crisis and systemic risk' (2009) 4 *Capital Markets Law Journal* 141, 141.

[17] The underlying premise of the FSMA regulatory regime was precisely that general law is not capable of delivering an adequate degree of investor protection (see further Iain MacNeil, 'Rethinking conduct regulation' (2015) 30 *Journal of International Banking and Financial Law* 413, 414).

[18] Johannes Köndgen, 'Policy responses to credit crisis: does the law of contract provide the answer' in Stefan Grundmann and Yeşim M Atamer (eds), *Financial Services, Financial Crisis and General European Contract Law – Failure and Challenges of Contracting* (Kluwer Law International BV, 2011) 40.

[19] FCA 'Business Plan 2013/2014' (2013) 17.

risk preferences. The recommended reforms that are being put across by this book focus on the latter softer approach and are primarily targeted at supporting corporate retail investors, without directly interfering with the market for investment products.

II. Recommendations

By drawing upon the IRHP mis-selling case study, this book has explored the particular vulnerabilities of corporate retail investors that expose them to the risk of mis-selling, whilst considering the underlying circumstances which trigger this risk in the first place. Further to this assessment, it has concluded that, in substance, regulatory measures aimed at curbing mis-selling have turned out to be what can be described as 'more of the same'. Corporate retail investors continue to be exposed to the risk of mis-selling, and their chances of obtaining adequate redress for the financial detriment they may suffer as a direct consequence of mis-selling remain remote. The proposals set out in this Section therefore seek to address these lacunae from different perspectives that are as yet unexplored or which have otherwise been discounted.

It has been observed that the success or failure of a regulatory regime 'will depend on the quality of its remedies', and whether the regulator will 'make society better-off or worse-off'.[20] Indeed, the quest for the establishment of adequate redress mechanisms for retail investors is enshrined in the MiFID II regime, namely Article 69(2), which explicitly states that:

> [...] Member States shall ensure that mechanisms are in place to ensure that compensation may be paid or other remedial action be taken in accordance with national law for any financial loss or damage suffered as a result of an infringement of this Directive or of [MiFIR].[21]

[20] Tony Curzon Price and Peter Andrews, 'The game of caps and nudges' (Insight: Opinion and Analysis from the FCA, 27 July 2017): www.fca.org.uk/insight/game-caps-and-nudges, accessed 30 July 2017.

[21] No equivalent provision exists under MiFID I. In fact, in the *Bankinter* case (para 57), the CJEU held that MiFID I lays down administrative sanctions for investment firms' breach of national provisions transposing the same MiFID I but it does not require Member States to provide for contractual consequences. Therefore, it is up to the Member States themselves to determine the contractual consequences of non-compliance with MiFID obligations, as long as they observe the principles of equivalence and effectiveness as established under EU law by Art 47 of the Charter of Fundamental Rights and Art 19 of the Treaty on European Union. The conclusions in *Bankinter* follow those reached by the CJEU in Case C-591/10 *Littlewoods Retail Ltd and Others v Her Majesty's Commissioners of Revenue and Customs* [2012] ECR (para 27), Case C-147/01 *Weber's Wine World Handels-GmbH and Others v Abgabenberufungskommission Wien* [2003] ECR I-11365 (para 103) and Case C-291/03 *MyTravel v Commissioners of Customs & Excise* [2005] ECR I-8477 (para 17), all of which dealt with indirect taxation matters.

So far, the litigious efforts of corporate retail investors in the mis-selling of IRHPs have not been successful. Although the English courts have typically tended towards an approach which is less strict than the MiFID regime, a complete disregard of this Article would further jeopardise the retail investor protection aims of the MiFID framework as well as detract from the level playing field envisaged by the same regime. Whilst welcoming certain positive developments, including the extension of the jurisdiction of the FOS and the increase in the maximum compensation that can be awarded by the FOS, the following measures are being recommended. Collectively, these proposed measures seek to create a more robust investor protection framework for retail investors and secure adequate redress mechanisms for all retail investors.

A. Compulsory Investment Advice for Retail Investors Transacting in Complex Investment Products

It is typical for investment firms to engage in discussions with retail investors to make them aware of potential investments, inform them about the risks and rewards attached to each investment, and take the initiative for the execution of transactions with, or on behalf of, these investors. Whilst this exchange does not presume that the transactions would have been regarded as suitable to the investors to which they were addressed or that they would have otherwise been recommended as such, this book has demonstrated that communications of this nature are very likely to slip into concealed personal recommendations, and thus investment advice without the appropriate legal and regulatory safeguards being in place. In fact, investment advice provided in these circumstances is likely to occur without proper assessment of suitability, thereby exposing investors to the risk of mis-selling and, consequently, financial damage, especially where remedies at law are not sufficiently robust for these investors to claim adequate redress, as is evident in the case of corporate retail investors.

The endemic mis-selling that caused financial detriment to retail investors over the years, calls into question the ease with which retail investors can access complex products and whether or not this should be curtailed. The extensive literature referred to in chapter two in particular, supports the claim that traditional investor protection tools, such as risk disclosures and efforts to boost financial literacy, are not failsafe in protecting retail investors against 'mis-buying' or 'mis-selling', and that this may therefore justify regulatory intervention of a more radical nature. It has become 'unacceptable'[22] that the advisory duty of care is 'so commonly and easily avoided'[23] and, therefore, the imposition of paternalistic constraints, including limits on choice, is encouraged. Such measures should still allow investors

[22] Molony Committee, *Final Report of the Committee on Consumer Protection* (Cmnd 1781, 1962) para 397.

[23] ibid.

to retain their basic right to freedom to contract and the related liberty to invest in financial instruments of their choice, whilst establishing robust measures to 'nudge' these investors towards more suitable investment options.

The manner in which products are distributed and sold impacts the extent to which the risks associated with complex products are reduced or, alternatively, exacerbated. For instance, if products are marketed directly to investors or sold through non-advised channels, rather than on the recommendation of an adviser, this could significantly increase the risk that an investor may misunderstand the features and risks of the product, and may consequently lead investors to select products that are not aligned with their investment objectives, risks and requirements. On the other hand, in circumstances where the investor obtains advice from an adviser who understands the relevant product, is in a position to actively explain to the investor the key risks and features of the product, and conducts a suitability assessment, the investor is less likely to face a poor outcome than if he were to transact in the same product on a non-advisory basis. In the context of an advised sale, therefore, investment firms are responsible for ensuring that the advised products are selected based on the investors' needs – only if that advice is considered to be suitable must the investor be prepared to accept responsibility for his own investment decisions.[24] However, when investment products are sold on a non-advised basis, there is minimal accountability incumbent upon investment firms for sales to retail investors of an investment product which is not suitable for their needs and circumstances. Further, compliance with the general principle to act in the investor's best interest[25] is challenging when providing non-advisory services. This is because the exemption from undertaking suitability assessments in the context of non-advisory services means that investment firms are not compelled to collect information on certain investors' features (which information they would need to collect and consider when providing investment advice). This information is crucial for investment firms to act in the best interest of investors, and, therefore, investment firms cannot pursue their clients' best interest to the same extent as when providing investment advice.[26]

i. The Suitability Assessment Process as a Tool for Retail Investor Protection

The FCA has recently acknowledged that investors' responsibilities for their own financial choices are not only 'growing' but these choices are also becoming 'more complex', and has therefore urged service provides to address this by guiding retail

[24] See further *O'Hare* [201], quoting Roth J in *Barker v Baxendale Walker Solicitors (a firm)* [2016] EWHC 664 (Ch), [2016] STI 1266.

[25] As prescribed by MiFID II, Art 24(1) and COBS 2.1.1(R).

[26] Luca Enriques and Matteo Gargantini, 'The Overarching Duty to Act in the Best Interests of the Client in MiFID II' in Danny Busch and Guido Ferrarini (eds), *Regulation of the EU Financial Markets: MiFID II and MiFIR* (Oxford University Press, 2017) 122.

investors towards making suitable investment decisions.[27] The suitability assessment process is thus a central pillar of the investor protection regime as well as being an essential element of the regulatory distribution toolkit.[28] The validity of the suitability assessment is also grounded in behavioural law and economics, which recognises retail investor behaviour as 'an important challenge in financial services',[29] and which indicates, therefore, that the regulatory framework around the provision of advice should be a chief concern for regulators. In fact, research has convincingly shown that retail investors who neither seek financial advice nor are financially literate are those who lose out the most in financial markets, suggesting that regulators should take measures to improve retail investors' financial acumen and encourage these investors to seek investment advice.[30] Whilst efforts to improve financial literacy and advice should complement, rather than substitute, each other, the success of policy measures which aim at improving financial literacy may only become evident in the longer-term, if at all. Hence, promoting, and facilitating access to, investment advice should take centre stage in improving the performance of retail investors' portfolios.

Fiduciary-style duties, such as those transcended by suitability rules, are a well-grounded regulatory tool to reduce the risk of opportunistic behaviour, whilst also mitigating the limitations of the more traditional investor protection mechanisms and guarding against any loopholes in the conduct of business rules that investment firms may exploit to the detriment of retail investors. Suitability rules are seen to intervene more paternalistically to provide a higher degree of protection to the retail investor by obliging the adviser to carry out 'know your client' procedures and make a recommendation which is personalised to the investor's needs and risk profile. This is because, as the retail investor opts for advice, he cedes greater control over the investment decision such that more onerous obligations are imposed on the investment firm; by contrast, non-advised services leave the investor exposed and reliant on disclosure more generally.[31] Whilst an advisory mandate allows these investors to rely on the recommendations and statements made by their adviser, in the absence of such mandate, corporate retail investors

[27] FCA, 'Business Plan 2017/18' (2017) 8.

[28] See eg SIB, 'Review Committee Report' (1990) para 3.3; European Commission, 'Proposal for a Directive of the European Parliament and of the Council on markets in financial instruments repealing Directive 2004/39/EC of the European Parliament and of the Council (Recast)' COM (2011) 656 final 27; ESMA, 'Final Report: Technical Advice to the Commission on MiFID II and MiFIR' ESMA/2014/1569 (2014) 149; Niamh Moloney, *EU Securities and Financial Markets Regulation*, 3rd edn (Oxford University Press, 2014) 807.

[29] HM Treasury, *Treasury Minutes – Government responses on the Thirty Fourth to the Thirty Sixth; the Thirty Eight; and the Fortieth to the Forty Second reports from the Committee of Public Accounts: Session 2015–2016* (Cm 9323, 2016) para 4.2.

[30] See eg HM von Gaudecker, 'How Does Household Portfolio Diversification Vary with Financial Literacy and Financial Advice?' (2015) 70 *The Journal of Finance* 489; Paolo Giudici, 'Independent Financial Advice' in in Danny Busch and Guido Ferrarini (eds), *Regulation of the EU Financial Markets: MiFID II and MiFIR* (Oxford University Press, 2017).

[31] Niamh Moloney, 'Large-Scale Reform of Investor Protection Regulation: The European Union Experience' (2007) 4 *Macquarie Journal of Business Law* 147, 172.

have seen these communications being regarded as mere opinions incidental to a non-advised sale, falling prey to standard form contracts which limit the service to a non-advisory one and restrict the extent to which an investor can use the reliance argument in court to prove that the investment firm had a duty of care towards him when advising him on the most suitable investments.

Complex products, in particular, are made up of 'many different moving parts'[32] and are therefore likely to be too complicated for retail investors to understand given their limited knowledge and experience in transacting in products of this nature. To this end, the FCA recognised that the appropriate degree of protection for investors will depend to a large extent on 'the capability of the consumer and the complexity of the product or service',[33] whilst admitting that investment firms are expected to take on 'additional responsibilities'[34] when transacting in complex products. From a pan-European perspective, ESMA also noted that the degree of complexity of the financial instrument in question, should be considered when assessing whether there is a 'significant investor protection concern or a threat to the orderly functioning and integrity of financial markets or commodity markets and to the stability of the whole or part of the financial system of the Union',[35] hence seemingly justifying a more interventionist approach where products are complex and were retail investors are involved. It follows, therefore, that the protection of retail investors (be they corporate entities or individuals) transacting in complex products, should top the regulator's agenda.

ii. Proposal for a Change in the Regulatory Framework

In the wake of persistent mis-selling cases in the UK, both the NAO and the Public Accounts Committee recommended that the FCA implements additional measures to ensure that investment firms take sufficient measures to ensure that retail investors fully understand the products they invest in.[36] This book proposes to address this by drawing upon the interplay between suitability rules and behavioural theories, particularly because suitability rules are associated with minimising the behavioural weaknesses that can disable optimal investor decision-making.[37] The recommendation being made here is for an adjustment to be made to the rules

[32] FCA, 'Building on experience' Speech by Martin Wheatley (The future of financial services conference, Lansons, London 17 April 2013): www.fca.org.uk/news/speeches/building-experience, accessed 5 May 2015.

[33] FCA, 'Our Future Mission' (2016) 5.

[34] FSA, 'Discussion Paper DP 05/3, Wider Range Retail Investment Products: Consumer Protection in a Rapidly Changing World' (2005) para 4.28 (see also FSCP, 'Annual Report 2005/2006' (2006)).

[35] MiFIR, Arts 40(8) and 42(7); ESMA, 'Final Report: Technical Advice to the Commission on MiFID II and MiFIR' ESMA/2014/1569 (2014) 191–192.

[36] See eg National Audit Office (NAO), 'Financial services mis-selling: regulation and redress' (HC 851, 2015–16) 9; Committee of Public Accounts, *Forty-First Report: Financial services mis-selling: regulation and redress* (HC 847, 2016) 11.

[37] See eg Lawrence A Cunningham, 'A Prescription to Retire the Rhetoric of "Principles-Based Systems" in Corporate Law, Securities Regulation and Accounting' (2007) 60 *Vanderbilt Law Review* 1411.

contained in the COBS, which would require that complex investment products are sold to retail investors exclusively on an advisory basis.[38] As a consequence, this would ensure that investment firms can no longer disclaim responsibility for advice when selling complex products to individual and corporate retail investors, hence minimising the risk of investment firms mis-characterising the service being provided, whilst also drastically improving the chances of obtaining adequate redress for corporate retail investors. Further, it would ascertain that a suitability assessment is conducted for each and every transaction made by a retail investor in a complex product, thereby mitigating the risk of mis-selling at the outset, prior to the transaction being made.

Amidst the major difficulties in relying on 'judge-made' law to control complex and fast-moving financial markets,[39] this recommended extension in the scope of advisory services, and the consequent broader application of the suitability assessment, becomes even more sustainable, whilst also being consistent with the message delivered by the courts, which indicates that where an investor does not understand a product, proper advice should be obtained.[40] Due to the limitations of corporate retail investors and the circumstances in which the sale of complex products is typically undertaken (which is on the basis of non-negotiable standard terms), it is reasonable to conclude that corporate retail investors cannot be expected to understand comprehensively the implications and risks of complex products and that, therefore, investment firms should be prohibited from selling complex investment products to these vulnerable investors unless this is covered by an advisory mandate and the duty of care attached thereto. Most notably, it compels the court to look beyond the perception that corporate retail investors are 'sophisticated' parties purely because they are legal persons, and should therefore lead the court to question the validity of any recommendation made by the investment firm and the extent of the duties attached thereto, rather than merely stopping at a literal reading of the contractual terms.

Retail investors may not be prepared to pay for investment advice, which they somehow tend to consider an 'accessory' of the provision of investment services.[41] It is therefore acknowledged that the reform being proposed here may potentially create a financial barrier for corporate retail investors because of the higher costs incurred for the provision of advisory services as well as inhibit investment firms from providing these services because they are concerned about potential liability

[38] A restriction on the marketing, distribution and sale of certain financial instruments due to significant investor protection concerns is permitted by MiFIR, Art 42(2). Prior to making any such rules, the FCA is required, by FSMA, s 138I(1), to consult with the PRA and, after doing so, publish a draft of the proposed rules for public consultation containing, inter alia, the information prescribed by FSMA, s 138I(2) (see also Section IC of ch 3 on the FCA's product intervention powers).

[39] Law Commission, 'Fiduciary Duties of Investment Intermediaries' (Law Com No 350, 2014) para 11.5.

[40] Philip R Wood, *Regulation of International Finance* (Sweet & Maxwell Ltd, 2007) Volume 7, para 14-016. In the context of these observations, Wood draws upon the conclusions reached by English Courts in *Bankers Trust* and *Peekay* (appeal).

[41] Paolo Giudici, 'Independent Financial Advice' in in Danny Busch and Guido Ferrarini (eds), *Regulation of the EU Financial Markets: MiFID II and MiFIR* (Oxford University Press, 2017) 151.

and regulatory uncertainty.[42] From an investor's perspective, the potentially higher costs attached to advisory services can be contained by opting for a more streamlined advisory model which is not necessary 'full' or 'independent' advice. The use of alternative distribution models around 'restricted' advice, was looked into by the FCA with a view to making advisory services more accessible and affordable for investors, whilst still providing an adequate level of protection given that there will remain a duty of care incumbent on the investment firm. In this respect, the FCA observed that investment firms offering a streamlined advice service may collect only the information that is necessary to provide a suitable recommendation, which would also facilitate the process for investment firms. The offering of streamlined advice services is also consistent with the principle of proportionality entrenched in MiFID regime, which allows firms to collect the level of information proportionate to the products and services they offer, or on which the investor requests specific investment advice, whilst making sure that the overall level of protection due to client is maintained.[43]

Further, it is here contended that opting for a non-advisory regime that 'trumps the more interventionist, paternalistic response'[44] of the advisory framework purely on the basis of monetary considerations, is not conducive towards the establishment of a robust retail investor protection framework. Hence, even though non-advisory services may be regarded as a quicker and more flexible means for acquiring investments, the execution-only route is 'an inherently riskier service for retail clients … [since] [t]hey will not be protected from their own, potentially faulty, decision-making',[45] and should thus be limited as far as reasonably practicable. A shift from a non-advisory regime to an advisory spectrum is also encouraged by behavioural law and economics theories, which suggest that incentives encouraging reliance on investment firms reduce irrationality on the part of retail investors. Further, UK policymakers acknowledge that 'there is real value in giving people a strong nudge to seek financial advice',[46] and studies have also shown that the existence of default rules (in this case requiring transactions in complex products by retail investors to be undertaken solely on an advised basis) also impacts retail investors' behaviour.[47] Indeed, default rules have been

[42] See eg HM Treasury and FCA, 'Financial Advice Market Review: Final report' (2016) 19, 27–41.

[43] See further FCA, 'Guidance Consultation GC17/4: Financial Advice Market Review (FAMR): Implementation part 1' (2017) paras 2.28–2.29.

[44] Niamh Moloney, 'Building a retail investment culture through law: the 2004 Markets in Financial Instruments Directive' (2005) 6 *European Business Organization Law Review* 341, 398.

[45] ibid.

[46] HM Treasury and FCA, 'Financial Advice Market Review: Final report' (2016) 45 (see also Gregory La Blanc and Jeffrey J Rachlinski, 'In Praise of Investor Irrationality' (2005) Cornell Law School Research Paper No 05-006).

[47] Humans are generally hesitant to depart from the 'status quo' without valid reasons and are also likely to opt for the default option without giving it too much consideration, since it saves then the time and effort in hesitating between different alternatives (see further Lars Klohn, 'Preventing excessive retail investor trading under MiFID: a behavioural law and economics perspective' (2009) 10 *European Business Organization Law Review* 437, 452; European Commission, 'Emerging challenges in retail finance and consumer policy' Steering Notes: Session II – Behavioural economics and financial services (2014)).

described as harnessing the potential for being 'the most effective nudges'.[48] As 'prime nudges' default rules are conceived as interventions which maintain freedom of choice without imposing mandates or bans, but nonetheless inclining choices in a particular direction.[49] Relatedly, research reveals that the ideal time for a 'nudge' is at a 'frictionless moment',[50] which is defined as the point in time when a retail investor is on the cusp of making a financial decision, and which, in the context of this book, can be interpreted as the stage during which the investor decides whether to seek advice or otherwise.

This proposal, therefore, not only highlights the centrality of the 'protective ethic'[51] of regulation, but also ensures that the positive changes flowing from the RDR as well as the revised MiFID regime, are beneficial to all retail investors, including corporate retail investors.[52] It also helps ensure that investment firms are not allowed to contract out of their advisory duties towards the investor given that they must clearly state, in the contractual agreement with the investor, that it is the investment firm's responsibility to conduct the suitability assessment and provide the advice – no disclaimer (or any other similar type of statement) can in any way limit their responsibility.[53] Further, this recommendation not only secures the same level of protection to all UK retail investors, including corporate retail investors, but also addresses the pro-investment firm approach taken by the English courts which is drastically at odds with that taken by the courts in other EU jurisdictions. In this regard, it is noted that, although the UK regulator has historically resisted a categorical ban on non-advised sales on the basis that this would be too onerous and that the associated costs would outweigh the benefits, it has nonetheless considered restricting the marketing and sale of certain products to certain categories of investors, which indicates that the FCA is open to embracing a more interventionist stance.[54]

[48] Cass Sunstein, 'Nudging: A Very Short Guide' (2014) 37 *Journal of Consumer Policy* 583, 585.

[49] Cass Sunstein, 'Deciding by Default' (2013) 162 *University of Pennsylvania Law Review* 1, 5 (see also Cass Sunstein, 'The Ethics of Nudging' (2015) 32 *Yale Journal on Regulation* 413).

[50] Financial Advice Working Group, 'Rules of Thumb and Nudges: Improving the financial well-being of UK consumers' (2017) 8.

[51] Chris Willett, 'General clauses and the competing ethics of European consumer law in the UK' (2012) 71 *Cambridge Law Journal* 412, 415.

[52] Such positive measures relate to tighter requirements around assessment of suitability, including better-qualified, professional advisers, more objective advice that is not influenced or prejudiced by the remuneration of such advisers, the requirements around the provision of suitability reports (which could potentially bear a lot of weight in court or in the hands of a regulatory authority, should a claim be brought by the retail investor against the investment firm), and other similar measures discussed in Sections IA and IB of ch 3 on MiFID II reforms and the RDR respectively.

[53] Disclaimers of responsibility were common in IRHP transactions, as discussed in ch 5 of this book.

[54] The FSA had floated the idea that the sale of complex products would be restricted only to professional clients (see further FSA, 'Discussion Paper DP11/1, Product Intervention' (2011) paras 6.58–6.59). The FCA also hinted at the possibility of introducing a requirement for complex products 'to only be promoted with advice', which resonates with the recommendation put forward in this Section (see further FCA, 'Occasional Paper No 1: Applying behavioural economics at the Financial Conduct Authority' (2013) 43). Whilst the FCA already has a right to prevent non-advised sales as part of its more radical product intervention toolkit, under MiFIR any restriction to product access will need to be preceded by a formal notification to ESMA and other competent authorities (MiFIR, Art 42(3)) and shall be subject to ESMA's approval (MiFIR, Art 43(1) and Art 43(2)).

iii. Application to Professional Investors

Pro-investor default rules, such as the one recommended in this Section, should be designed to protect less sophisticated investors, whilst having a negligible impact on more sophisticated investors. Consequently, in order to make the most efficient use of scarce supervisory resources, investor protection mechanisms should be targeted at those investor categories that can most benefit from them, being all retail investors.[55] Less protection is required for professional investors who are presumed to have sufficient familiarity with the market to look after their own interests.[56] This mechanism is reflected in the recommendation put forward by this book which suggests that professional investors should still be excluded from a full-scope suitability assessment.[57] The fact that this recommendation is only targeted at retail investors, which comprise the more inexperienced and less knowledgeable category of investors, also embodies elements of softer, 'light-touch' paternalism, given that this form of intervention is set to create benefits for those who are most behaviourally-challenged and prone to making the most errors, while imposing less restrictions on those investors who have the necessary knowledge and experience.[58] More importantly, it supports the argument being made here that even corporate retail investors need to be captured in the regulatory safety net given that they are as vulnerable as individual retail investors.

iv. Risk Warnings

In practice, there may be situations where the investment firm is confronted with retail investors who insist in adopting a course of action that the investment firm would have assessed as being unsuitable for those retail investors, thereby acting against the investment firm's advice. The recommendation being made in this Section is not meant

[55] The Better Regulation Commission similarly acknowledged that regulation should be targeted on those who are most at risk (Better Regulation Commission, *Risk, Responsibility, Regulation: Whose Risk is it Anyway?* (Cabinet Office 2006) 38) (see also Alastair Hudson, *The Law of Finance*, 2nd edn (Sweet & Maxwell Ltd, 2013) paras 46–61, 46–62).

[56] It has long been recognised that retail investors need more protection than professional investors. Hence, extending the application of conduct of business rules to professional investors would increase costs and limit their use of innovative products, given that these rules have been designed with the retail investor in mind (see eg DTI, *Financial Services in the UK: A New Framework for Investor Protection* (HMSO, Cmnd 9432, 1985) paras 4.21–4.22; European Commission, 'The application of conduct of business rules under Article 11 of the Investment Services Directive (93/22/EEC)' COM (2000) 722 final 11–12).

[57] Under the MiFID II regime, and for the purpose of undertaking a suitability assessment, investment firms are entitled to assume that all professional clients possess the required knowledge and experience in connection with all investment products. Clients' financial situation must be assessed only in the case of elective professional clients and retail clients, such that investment firms are entitled to assume that this requirement is satisfied if dealing with per se professional clients. The investment objectives of clients must be taken into account for all investors, irrespective of whether they are professional or retail clients.

[58] Camerer and others title this form of paternalistic intervention as 'asymmetric paternalism' (Colin Camerer and others, 'Regulation for Conservatives: Behavioral Economics and the Case for "Asymmetric Paternalism"' (2003) 151 *University of Pennsylvania Law Review* 1211).

to encourage 'overbroad protectionism'[59] and, therefore, situations in which investment firms encounter such insistent retail investors must also be catered for. To this effect, this book believes that retail investors wanting to proceed with a transaction in a complex product, even if the advice provided by the investment firm is that the particular complex product is not suitable, should still be free to do so, provided that the investment firm issues a risk warning to the investor which prominently features as part of the suitability report and which clearly informs the investor of the fact that the investment product in question is not suitable for him, by, inter alia, explaining the risks he would expose himself to by proceeding with that specific course of action.[60] In other words, an investment firm can execute a transaction in a complex product on a non-advisory basis upon the insistence of a retail investor only when the proposed transaction is supported by a suitability report containing such a documented risk warning and after having received written instructions from the investor. In order to ensure compliance with the MiFID framework, the investment firm must establish robust arrangements that allow it to trace and keep records of the steps of its interaction with the retail investor, and enable it to demonstrate whether or not the transaction executed was indeed originated on the investor's insistence. At the very least, these records should include copies of suitability reports, the risk warnings contained therein, the written instructions provided by the retail investor, as well as ancillary correspondence with the retail investors and minutes of any meetings or telephonic discussions that were held. Retention of records to this effect should also serve as evidence that the investment firm has, inter alia, adhered to the client's best interest rule, whilst also fulfilling any obligation it may have under the applicable rules relating to appropriateness when providing the different service.

It is acknowledged here that allowing risk warnings in the context of advised sales may present an opportunity for investment firms to avoid liability and responsibility, or otherwise shift responsibility onto the retail investor, by issuing risk warnings even when these are not required. It is however being argued that this risk can be mitigated if regulators dictate the content of these warnings and the level of detail expected. By way of example, such warnings should not be standardised, as is currently permitted,[61] but, rather, should be tailored to the circumstances of the investor. Further, it is also suggested here that the content of the risk warning should be targeted at countering the typical biases that impair retail investors' decision-making, as well as setting out clearly the results of the

[59] Donald C Langevoort, 'Selling Hope, Selling Risk: Some Lessons for Law from Behavioural Economics about Stockbrokers and Sophisticated Customers' (1996) 84 *California Law Review* 627, 632.

[60] Recital 87 of the MiFID II Delegated Regulation specifically clarifies that investment firms 'should undertake a suitability assessment not only in relation to recommendations to buy a financial instrument … but for all decisions whether to trade including whether or not to buy, hold or sell an investment'. The FCA has set out its expectations when investment firms facilitate a request that conflicts with the personal recommendation they would have given (see FCA, 'Insistent clients: good and poor practice' (2016)) and is also proposing the introduction of an instrument – Conduct of Business Sourcebook (Insistent Clients) Instrument 2017 – in order to introduce rules and guidance on situations involving insistent clients in the COBS.

[61] MiFID II, Art 25(3) states that the risk warning 'may be provided in a standardised format'.

suitability assessment and the recommendation being made thereto. In addition, investment firms should be alerted that recurring switches from investment advice to execution services at the investor's initiative, or changes of investor's profiles near the closing date of any transaction that are not supported by a real modification of the investor's situation that would justify such a change, will not be viewed favourably by regulators and may therefore be challenged.

Whilst the issuance of a risk warning is possible, it is here being contended that the risk attached to this derogation is even lower since few retail clients, if any, will insist on proceeding with the transaction after being served with such a risk warning and after having been explicitly advised against the complex investment and its associated risks, especially if the adviser would have also recommended more suitable options to better suit the investors' circumstances and risk preferences. Due to their limited knowledge and experience in complex products, retail investors tend to trust their advisers and rely on the recommendation provided, and, therefore, any 'nudging' on the part of the advisers towards suitable products is therefore likely to be considered favourably by retail investors and accepted accordingly.

B. Assessment of Product Complexity

The sheer impact of product complexity on retail investors' decisions brings to the fore the imminent need for tighter rules in this area. MiFID has listed a number of investment products as de facto non-complex,[62] yet there is no complete and finite definition of 'complex', and a determination of complexity is based on a list of characteristics that can be deduced by consulting various sources.[63]

Pursuant to the recommendation made in Section IIA, complexity is set to play a pivotal role in determining whether a transaction for a retail investor can be serviced by a non-advisory mandate or otherwise, and the 'artificial line'[64] that separates 'complex' and 'non-complex' products may need to be explained through more formal and defined structures. To this end, it is suggested that the FCA be tasked with the responsibility of issuing a final determination on the complexity of a product. It is proposed that, as part of the product approval process,[65] the investment firm would be required to perform an in-house analysis of complexity for submission to the FCA, indicating whether it believes that the product in question should be treated as 'complex' or 'non-complex'. The FCA would then analyse this recommendation in

[62] MIFID II, Art 25(4)(a).

[63] See eg CESR, 'Questions and Answers: MiFID complex and non-complex financial instruments for the purpose of the Directive's appropriateness requirements' CESR/09-559 (2009); Investment Management Association, Panel Discussion, Speech by Guy Sears (FCA MiFID II Conference, London, 18 September 2014): http://play.buto.tv/fwKpd, accessed 5 December 2014; ESMA, 'Consultation Paper MiFID II/MiFIR' ESMA/2014/549 (2014); SMSG, 'Advice to ESMA: Investor Protection Aspects of the Consultation Paper on MiFID II and MiFIR' ESMA/2014/SMSG/035 (2014) paras 109–10).

[64] FSCP, Panel Discussion, Speech by Sue Lewis, (FCA MiFID II Conference, London, 18 September 2014): http://play.buto.tv/fwKpd, accessed 5 December 2014.

[65] MiFID II, Art 16(3).

light of the product's characteristics to arrive at a complexity determination. It would also be beneficial if the FCA were to publish on its website a list of all investment products that are considered to be complex, together with the main factors leading to the product being categorised as such. This, apart from ensuring a high degree of transparency, should assist investment firms in conducting their assessment of products to be launched in the future as well as focusing the attention of retail investors on the features that typically contribute to the complexity of a product.[66]

The recommendation for an assessment and attestation by the FCA on the degree of complexity in relation to a particular product should dovetail with the recent regulatory trajectory pointing towards an intensification of the degree of intervention through which the FCA is adopting a more cautious approach to risk-taking, especially where higher risk and more complex investment products are concerned. Hence, this recommendation is not expected to present any particular concerns from a practical perspective. Moreover, it is worth noting that, although the FCA has previously resisted any involvement in the pre-approval of products on a market-wide basis,[67] the recommendation being made here is less intrusive in nature since the FCA would be opining on the complexity of the product only following an assessment which would have already been made by the investment firm, rather than explicitly approving or disapproving it.

C. Introducing a 'Retail Investor Charter'

The basic notion that retail investors should feel responsible for their investment decisions is part of the strategy of all conduct regulators. Irrespective of the degree of intrusiveness of conduct regulation, however, the intention is not to pursue a zero-failure regime that eliminates all risks and absolves retail investors from taking responsibility for their own investment decisions. In this sense, the regulatory system cannot be envisaged as a substitute for a reasonable degree of vigilance on the part of the retail investor and cannot be expected to guarantee an investment against loss in all circumstances and to the fullest extent.[68] In furtherance of this approach, the UK has opted to legislate in favour of investor responsibility by specifically including a general principle of consumer responsibility in the main statute regulating, inter

[66] In the context of discussions on the Draft Financial Services Bill, which took place between 2010 and 2012, Consumer Focus had proposed the establishment of a Trusted Products Board to 'set common standards for a suite of mass market financial services consumer products', which standards were considered to also help retail consumers to easily distinguish complex products from simpler ones. At the time, the Joint Committee had dismissed this idea, observing that, although this was an attractive proposition, the role that was being proposed for this Board should be undertaken voluntarily by the sector (Joint Committee on the draft Financial Services Bill, *Draft Financial Services Bill* (HL 236 HC 1447, 2010–12) paras 259–63).

[67] The regulator viewed such an engagement as excessively resource-intensive, which would increase the cost of regulation and potentially stifle innovation (see eg FCA, 'A response to Journey to the FCA: Your questions answered' (2013) 6–7).

[68] See further Molony Committee, *Final Report of the Committee on Consumer Protection* (Cmnd 1781, 1962) para 896; JUSTICE Committee, *The Protection of the Small Investor* (1992) para 1.12.

alia, investment services. This statutory consumer responsibility principle, which was introduced in Section III of chapter two, is to be contrasted with the less formal approach adopted by regulators in overseas jurisdictions, which have chosen to instill a sense of responsibility amongst retail investors through the promulgation of guidance rather than statutory provisions, which guidance is intended to transcend a series of 'sensible actions' for investors to consider.[69]

A regulator is expected to communicate its expectations with regard to mis-selling 'clearly and consistently'[70] to all stakeholders, including investment firms and retail investors. The lack of prescriptive guidance on what constitutes 'investor responsibility' has arguably enabled the UK regulator to interpret this notion in a broad manner, which has shifted depending on the circumstances and the audience it was addressing. In so doing, the regulator has also created uncertainty amongst the industry and retail investors as to which party can be held responsible, to what extent, in what circumstances and on what legal basis.[71] More importantly, the regulator itself acknowledged that striking a balance between the duty of care towards investors, the duty of responsibility of investors for their decision, the role of firms, and the role of the regulator, is an 'inherently difficult question … [that] has not been adequately answered'.[72]

Amidst this ambiguity, the FSA's Sustainability Group favoured a 'cross-stakeholder statement of consumers' legal responsibilities'.[73] This proposal never gained traction and it is being revived and moulded by this book into what is here being defined as a 'Retail Investor Charter'. The idea is for this Charter to replace the current consumer responsibility principle set out in FSMA, thereby abolishing the statutory principle pursuant to which any regulatory action would have to be guided by the extent to which investors can be held responsible for 'mis-buying'. This Charter is foreseen to play a crucial role in educating investors on the steps they should be taking to safeguard their interests so as to make more informed and rational investment decisions. In seeking redress against an investment firm for its breach of duties, retail investors

[69] See eg AMF, 'News Release: The Autorité des Marchés Financiers calls for extreme vigilance regarding non-standard investments proposed to the public' (2012); BaFIN, 'We need even more transparency' Speech by Dr Elke König (Frankfurt am Main, 13 March 2013): www.bafin.de/SharedDocs/Veroeffentlichungen/EN/Fachartikel/2013/fa_bj_2013_03_interview_koenig_verbraucher_en.html, accessed 11 December 2014; CMVM, 'Policy on complex financial products' (2012); FMA '10 Commandments of Investing Money': www.fma.gv.at/en/the-basics-the-financial-market/the-basics-consultations-with-advisers/, accessed 15 December 2014; Financial Consumer Agency of Canada (FCAC) guidance to investors: www.fcac-acfc.gc.ca/Eng/resources/educationalPrograms/ft-of/Pages/home-accueil.aspx, accessed 15 December 2014; FINRA Guidance: www.finra.org/industry/guidance, accessed 15 December 2014.

[70] NAO, 'Financial services mis-selling: regulation and redress' (HC 851, 2015–16) 11.

[71] The FSA Consumer and Practitioner Panels had attempted to agree on the respective responsibilities of investment firms and investors in the context of an advised sale. Whilst there was substantial agreement as to the nature of investment firms' responsibilities and a high-level understanding about what was sensible for investors to do to protect their own interests, the consensus of the Panels began to fray when they discussed: (1) whether or not sensible consumer actions could, or should, be described as 'responsibilities'; and (2) the consequences if a consumer fails to do these things.

[72] FCA, 'Chief Executive speaks at APM about recent work and future challenges' Speech by Andrew Bailey (Annual Public Meeting, The QEII Centre, London, 19 July 2016): www.fca.org.uk/news/chief-executive-apm-speech-2016, accessed 25 July 2016.

[73] FSA, 'Discussion Paper DP07/01, A Review of Retail Distribution' (2007) para 3.43.

would also be able to use the proposed Charter to gauge the extent to which they would have followed the recommended actions set out in such a Charter and adjust their expectations accordingly.

The biases that corporate retail investors suffer from represent an access problem for these investors and undermine the general statutory principle that investors should take responsibility for their own decisions.[74] To this end, the proposed Charter obviates the need for a statutory consumer responsibility principle, by recognising that the investment firm is ultimately best-placed to bear most of the responsibility for the investment transaction when the counterparty is a retail investor. It is not intended for the Charter to have a basis in statute but, rather, its main objective is to serve as a guide for retail investors as well as raising awareness amongst these investors and instill an inquisitive attitude that should sensitise them to the importance of enquiring about key issues not just before undertaking the transaction but also throughout the lifetime of the investment.

In line with the regulatory emphasis on the afore-mentioned 'non-zero failure' regulatory regime, investors should be engaged and made aware of the limitations of regulation, including that the optimum level of regulation 'falls short of eliminating all possibility of consumers making the wrong choices in financial contracts', which hence requires investors to exercise 'due care'.[75] It follows, therefore, that investors' first safeguard must always be 'an alert and questioning attitude'[76] and the proposed Charter encourages retail investors to embrace this. Notably, this Charter is suitable for all retail investors, irrespective of whether they are individuals or corporate entities, and is hence conducive towards securing an equal level of protection across the retail investor category, whilst being sufficiently flexible to suit the different circumstances of the diverse pool of such retail investors. It is being recommended that this Charter is endorsed by the government, the FCA, the FOS, the FSCS, and FCA Panels representing the interests of the industry and of investors,[77] and that it falls within the auspices of the new money guidance body that shall be replacing the MAS, given that it will be entrusted with responsibilities around, inter alia, improving the financial capabilities of retail investors.

The proposed Charter is split into three main sections to reflect the end-to-end thought-process that retail investors follow when making an investment decision. As outlined in the table that follows, the Charter purports to address pre-transaction, transaction-based, and ongoing, considerations. For each of these stages, a set of questions and observations that the retail investor may wish to reflect upon are being suggested hereunder.[78]

[74] FCA, 'Occasional Paper 17: Access to Financial Services in the UK' (2016) 34.

[75] David T Llewellyn, 'Consumer protection in retail investment services: Protection against what?' (1995) 3 *Journal of Financial Regulation and Compliance* 43, 52–53.

[76] Molony Committee, *Final Report of the Committee on Consumer Protection* (Cmnd 1781, 1962) para 896.

[77] These panels include the FCA Practitioner Panel (FSMA s. 1N), the FCA Smaller Business Practitioner Panel (FSMA, s 10) and the FCA Consumer Panel (FSMA, s 1Q).

[78] The actions listed in the Charter include a collation of sensible actions put forward by regulators and consumer bodies, as well as best practices adopted in other jurisdictions, whilst also being supplemented by the author's own views.

Issues to be considered	*Pre-transaction*
	• Understand your risk tolerance and the range of products that fit your investment needs.[79] • Request and read prospectuses, promotional material and information documents, paying particular attention to risk disclosures and how these fit in with your risk appetite.[80] • Do not buy something you do not understand.[81] • Be wary of promises of excessive returns and do not be tempted by cold calling.[82] • Do not rely exclusively on verbal assurances given by the investment firm but seek an independent opinion. • Seek assistance from an advice service body or an investment firm (refer to FCA website to check the authorised status of the investment firm);[83] • Be alert to warnings issued by the FCA concerning particular investment professionals or investment products; • Display a healthy scepticism[84] – beware of attractive high yields on investments as the reward typically reflects the inherent high risks involved.
	Transaction-based
	• Be clear and honest about your investment goals and the amount of risk you are comfortable taking.[85] • Answer questions factually and fully to the best of your knowledge.[86] • Volunteer further information that seems relevant.[87] • Discuss fees and related expenses with your investment service provider (these may include sales commissions, administrative and management charges, and costs associated with the sale or redemption of an).[88] • Pay money on time.[89]

(continued)

[79] FCA Practitioner Panel, 'Consumer Responsibility: Identifying and closing the gap' (2013); ASIC's Money Smart: www.moneysmart.gov.au/investing/investing-basics, accessed 15 December 2014; FMA '10 Commandments of Investing Money': www.fma.gv.at/en/the-basics-the-financial-market/the-basics-consultations-with-advisers/, accessed 15 December 2014.

[80] FSA, 'Discussion Paper DP08/5, Consumer Responsibility' (2008) Annex I; FINRA Guidance: www.finra.org/industry/guidance, accessed 15 December 2014.

[81] FSA, 'Discussion Paper DP08/5, Consumer Responsibility' (2008).

[82] FMA '10 Commandments of Investing Money': www.fma.gv.at/en/the-basics-the-financial-market/the-basics-consultations-with-advisers/, accessed 15 December 2014.

[83] FSA, 'Discussion Paper DP08/5, Consumer Responsibility' (2008) Annex I; FMA '10 Commandments of Investing Money': www.fma.gv.at/en/the-basics-the-financial-market/the-basics-consultations-with-advisers/, accessed 15 December 2014.

[84] BaFIN: www.bafin.de/SharedDocs/Veroeffentlichungen/EN/Fachartikel/2014/fa_bj_1403_grauer_kapitalmarkt_en.html?nn=3698804#empfehlung, accessed 15 December 2014.

[85] FINRA Guidance: www.finra.org/industry/guidance, accessed 15 December 2014.

[86] FSA, 'Discussion Paper DP08/5, Consumer Responsibility' (2008) Annex I.

[87] ibid.

[88] FINRA Guidance: www.finra.org/industry/guidance accessed 15 December 2014.

[89] FSA, 'Discussion Paper DP08/5, Consumer Responsibility' (2008) Annex I.

(Continued)

	• Vet and read carefully the documents before signing – point out any errors and ask for clarification if you do not understand any of the terms or product features.[90] • Read suitability letters and ensure they reflect discussions.[91] • Insist on a copy of all documentation when purchasing a product, including the client profile and file notes, and ensure that you read them thoroughly.
	Ongoing
	• Use cooling off periods to consider whether to go ahead.[92] • Alert the investment professional to any changes in your financial circumstances as soon as reasonably possible.[93] • Monitor the performance of your investment portfolio and read and retain periodic statements.[94] • Keep personal data safe.[95] • React promptly when issues arise[96] by first raising a complaint with the investment firm and subsequently complaining to the FOS and/or seeking legal advice.
Questions to ponder upon	*Pre-transaction*
	• Why am I investing? • Which amounts do I want to invest? • For how long do I want to tie up my money? • Do I want to be able to access funds at any time? • Are any major expenses planned in the near future? • Do I have financial reserves for a contingency which can be readily accessed? • What does my investment portfolio look like and how does this particular investment fit in? Will my new portfolio still reflect my investment objectives and risk disposition?
	Transaction-based
	• Do I have clear visibility of the nature of the service being provided by the investment professional? • Do I need to obtain supplementary legal or financial advice? • Am I comfortable with the 'small print' in the agreement? • Am I fully aware of all the potential fees which I might incur in relation to this engagement, including those related to liquidating the investment prior to maturity?

(continued)

[90] ibid.

[91] FSA, 'Treating Customers Fairly: Towards Fair Outcomes for Consumers' (2006) para 2.21.

[92] ibid.

[93] FSA, 'Discussion Paper DP08/5, Consumer Responsibility' (2008) Annex I.

[94] ibid; FCA Practitioner Panel, 'Consumer Responsibility: Identifying and closing the gap' (2013) 15; FINRA Guidance: www.finra.org/industry/guidance, accessed 15 December 2014; FMA '10 Commandments of Investing Money': www.fma.gv.at/en/the-basics-the-financial-market/the-basics-consultations-with-advisers/, accessed 15 December 2014.

[95] FSA, 'Discussion Paper DP08/5, Consumer Responsibility' (2008) Annex I; FCA Practitioner Panel, 'Consumer Responsibility: Identifying and closing the gap' (2013) 15.

[96] FSA, 'Discussion Paper DP08/5, Consumer Responsibility' (2008) Annex I.

(Continued)

	Ongoing
	• Do I have any particular concerns about my investment portfolio in general? • Is there anything untoward in the periodic statements which I was not expecting or which I do not understand? • Is the investment performing as expected? If not, am I aware of the circumstances giving rise to such negative results? • Do I have any particular concern about the manner in which the investment firm is treating me as a client?

The abolition of the statutory consumer responsibility principle in favour of the introduction of the proposed Charter is believed to eliminate the ambiguity around the nature and extent of investors' duties and liabilities that this statutory principle has implanted and which has made its application unpredictable and inconsistent.[97] Further, as a result of the removal of this principle, the court will no longer seek to super-impose this statutory provision onto common law duties, although it may well be the case that the Charter is referred to by the court in deciding the degree of contributory negligence, if any, exhibited by the retail investor. In respect of the latter point, however, the court would have no statutory obligation to do so and, therefore, the courts would be allowed greater flexibility and discretion.

D. Extending FSMA, Section 138D

The FSMA, section 138D right of action discussed in Section IIC of chapter three was originally introduced by the FSA 1986, section 62, which formalised and established the right of action for breaches of regulatory rules for any person, irrespective of whether such person was an individual or a corporate entity.

The FSA 1986 represented a wide-ranging overhaul of the financial services regulatory framework in the UK and, in order to give an opportunity to the industry to familiarise itself with its provisions, section 62 was not brought into force for six months. During this 'grace period' the market expressed its concern that the open-ended provision for claims by any investor may encourage tactical litigation, which could disrupt the markets by hindering healthy competition and growth, as well as by creating a higher risk of legal action for minor breaches of regulations.[98]

[97] Whilst the operation of the consumer responsibility principle should not cut across the statutory or common law rights that retail investors would expect to enjoy, and should not be abridging their rights thereon, there have been instances where the courts have directly drawn upon the consumer responsibility principle to the detriment of investors, thereby weakening these investors' rights in court.

[98] DTI, 'Defining the Private Investor: Consultative Document' (1990) para 2.2; Iain MacNeil, 'FSA 1986: does s. 62 provide an effective remedy for breaches of Conduct of Business Rules?' (1994) 15 *Company Lawyer* 172, 174; Gerard McMeel and John Virgo (eds), *McMeel and Virgo on Financial Advice and Financial Products: Law and Liability* (Oxford University Press, 2001) para 2.08; Christa

Consequently, section 62A was later introduced as an addendum to section 62[99] to limit rights of action under section 62 only to 'private investors'. As a result of the insertion of section 62A, non-individuals, including corporate retail investors, lost their section 62 rights in relation to any form of business, since a 'private investor' was defined as:

> an investor whose cause of action arises as a result of anything he has done or suffered—
>
> (a) in the case of an individual, otherwise than in the course of carrying on any investment business; and
>
> (b) in the case of any other person, otherwise than in the course of carrying on business of any kind,
>
> but does not include a government, local authority or public authority.[100]

According to Sir David Walker, then Chairman of the SIB, the FSA 1986, section 62 had a 'serious adverse effect on the SIB rulebook' and led to 'long and complicated provisions'.[101] The FSA 1986, section 62A was, therefore, welcomed by the SIB as an 'important change' and 'a significant encouragement' in its quest for a more principle-based structure.[102] At the time, the stated objective of section 62A was 'to avoid the financial markets becoming excessively litigious, and in doing so to remove one obstacle widely perceived as inhibiting the simplification of the FS Act rulebooks'.[103] Yet, the reasons underpinning the introduction of section 62A, namely the avoidance of tactical claims against investment firms, have been described as 'exaggerated',[104] since it was the perception that litigation would increase dramatically that led to increased demands for specification as to what the particular rule required and exemptions from its scope, rather than actual proceedings being initiated.[105] Even so, however, the priority of the UK Government at the time was to avoid any risk of US-like 'floodgates' and litigiousness.[106]

When the FSMA regime came into force in the year 2000, the right of action provision was retained under FSMA, section 150, thereby combining the earlier FSA 1986, section 62 and section 62A. The current version of the FSMA (as considerably amended by the FSA 2012) retains the same right of action provision, which is now established under FSMA, section 138D. The definition of 'private person' contained in the present Rights of Action Regulations, was therefore brought

Band and Karen Anderson, 'Selling complex financial products to sophisticated clients: JP Morgan Chase v Springwell: Part 2' (2009) 24 *Journal of International Banking Law and Regulation* 233, 235.

[99] This was done by virtue of s 193 of the Companies Act 1989.

[100] Financial Services Act 1986 (Restriction of Rights of Action) Regulations 1991 (SI 1991/489), Reg 2.

[101] David Walker, 'Financial Services: The Principles Initiative' (1989) 4 *Journal of International Banking and Financial Law* 51, 51.

[102] ibid.

[103] DTI, 'Defining the Private Investor: Consultative Document' (1990) para 4.1.

[104] Eva Z Lomnicka, 'Curtailing section 62 actionability' (1991) *Jul Journal of Business Law* 353, 354.

[105] See further ibid; Arthur Selman, 'Regulation of UK retail investment business' (1996) 3 *European Financial Services Law Journal* 331, 332.

[106] In furthering its agenda, a proposal to facilitate investor litigation against investment funds in the Financial Services Bill 2010 was also dropped by the government in the final version of the ensuing Act (see further Mads Andenas and Iris H-Y Chiu, *The Foundations and Future of Financial Regulation: Governance for Responsibility* (Routledge, 2014) 166, 223).

forward from one decade to another notwithstanding that the current environment is now very different to that preceding the introduction of section 62A. In the present circumstances, the limited scope of FSMA, section 138D is, in effect, shielding investment firms from claims lodged by corporate retail investors, the majority of which lack experience and knowledge and would therefore have relied on investment firms to guide them on the most appropriate investment pathway. This suggests that the basic premise underlying the restriction on the right to take private action is arguably no longer defensible and neither is it appropriate.[107]

IRHP mis-selling claims that have made their way through the English courts in recent years, and discussed throughout this book, show that the narrow scope of FSMA, section 138D undermines the position of corporate retail investors in the context of litigation.[108] The broad interpretation of the courts of the terms 'in the course of carrying on business of any kind' has meant that corporate retail investors failed to meet the definition of 'private person' for the scope of Regulation 3 of the Rights of Action Regulations simply because they were involved in a business of some sort, even though investing in financial instruments was clearly not part of the day-to-day business of these investors (in fact, most of these corporate retail investors had not elected to transact in IRHPs at their own initiative but were forced to do so in order to obtain the necessary funding). Hence, apart from not discriminating between individual 'professional' experienced investors and 'retail' amateurish investors, the definition of 'private person' also scopes out a considerable number of corporate retail investors, which typically lack expertise in the field of complex investments.[109] Further, the circumstances under which 'non-private persons' are able to bring a private right of action under Regulation 6 of the Rights of Action Regulations are equally of limited relevance to corporate investors. The right of action provisions thus give rise to a situation where individuals are able to make claims under FSMA, section 138D in their own personal capacity, but those same individuals would be unable to do so if they were to incorporate a company and opt to invest in an investment product through that company. In this sense, an investment firm's liability for exactly the same advice can be radically altered by the way in which the retail investor decides to structure the transaction.

The definition of 'private investor' would seem to have distorted the intended effect of the original section 62A, which was to ensure that the section 62 action

[107] Iain G Mitchell, 'Written Evidence made to the Parliamentary Commission on Banking Standards' (16 October 2012).

[108] This limitation was also evident in cases presented for judicial review to challenge the manner in which the regulator reached its decision on IRHP-related redress. In this context, Maynard argues that *Holmcroft* could be considered a further example of the judiciary abiding by Parliament's intention in terms of corporate entities not being entitled to sue for breach of statutory duty for breach of the COBS (Lloyd Maynard, 'Holmcroft Properties: will a contractual phoenix rise from its ashes?' (2016) 31 *Journal of International Banking and Financial Law* 356, 358).

[109] JUSTICE Committee, *The Protection of the Small Investor* (1992) para 2.19.

is available only to those for whom it is most suitable. This has led to an apparent mismatch between the regulatory protection given to corporate retail investors by the rules contained in the COBS that implement the MiFID framework and the statutory right of the same investors to make a claim in respect of breaches of the COBS. Additionally, the many restrictions in the UK civil liability regime mean that it no longer has any practical role in the investor protection framework, particularly where corporate retail investors are concerned, thereby possibly contributing to a breach of MiFID II, Article 69(2).

i. Proposal for a Revised Definition of 'Private Person' under FSMA, Section 138D

This book has shown that corporate retail investors do not have access to fair and concrete redress opportunities, and, it is therefore here argued that reforms to FSMA, section 138D are necessary to complement the additional measures that are being proposed in this chapter. More specifically, this book contends that corporate retail investors should not be denied a private right of action by virtue of the 'private person' definition since these investors are 'just as 'deserving' as their private investor counterparts'.[110] To apply a blanket bar to any corporate investor thus 'provides profoundly iniquitous consequences', which consequences are not necessarily commensurate with the original intentions of policymakers.[111]

It is hence being proposed that the statutory right of action should be open to all retail investors by adopting a definition of 'private person' which is reflective of the MiFID categories and which therefore distinguishes between 'retail' and 'professional' investors.[112] An extension to the statutory right of action to all retail investors is also reasonable on the basis that it would offer a viable route of redress to investors which should already be benefitting from regulatory protection as a consequence of the MiFID regime transposed in the COBS. Further, the proposed extension is also sensible in light of the assumed purpose of FSMA, section 138D, which is that of protecting vulnerable consumers from unfair or prejudicial conduct perpetrated by the more sophisticated investment firms. The unfair consequences resulting from the application of FSMA, section 138D were also acknowledged by English courts in, for example, *Suremime Limited v Barclays Bank Plc*,[113] where the

[110] Julian Pritchard, 'Investment Protection Sacrificed: The New Settlement and s 62' (1992) 13 *Company Lawyer* 171, 211.

[111] Stevie Loughrey and Charles Enderby Smith, 'Banking litigation: a changing landscape?' (2015) 9 *Journal of International Banking and Financial Law* 563, 564.

[112] The Law Commission contemplated an extension to the rights to sue for breach of statutory duty under FSMA, s 138D to also enable businesses to sue, which right could not be excluded by contract. It however concluded that no such reform was necessary as the effect of this change would be uncertain and potentially disruptive (also because the FCA can decide which of its rules are actionable and hence fine-tune the scope of the liability) (see further Law Commission, 'Consultation Paper 215, Fiduciary Duties of Investment Intermediaries: A Consultation Paper' (2013) paras 14.66–14.70; Law Commission, 'Fiduciary Duties of Investment Intermediaries' (Law Com No 350, 2014) paras 11.14–11.35).

[113] [2015] EWHC 2277 (QB) [32]–[39].

court observed that unless private law rights of action are vested into corporate customers (including corporate retail investors), there remains a gap in available remedies for which the rationale of according statutory rights of suit under FSMA, section 138D to individuals only does not cater. Further, Kitchin LJ, in granting the claimants in *Bailey*[114] permission to appeal, agreed that precluding companies from being considered as 'private persons' 'rob(s) the provision of its substance because most companies will be in business of some kind'.

In light of the uniform treatment of the retail category of investors being promoted by this book, and the arguments presented to demonstrate that corporate retail investors suffer from vulnerabilities and hence are in need of protection, it is contended here that the legislators' approach to carve out corporate retail investors from the rights accorded by FSMA, section 138D is unjustified. It is therefore being proposed that the definition of a 'private person' in the Rights of Action Regulations is revised as follows:

(a) any person who is classified as a retail client in terms of COBS 3.4.1(R), unless the loss in question is suffered in the course of carrying on any regulated activity or any activity which would be a regulated activity; and
(b) any other person who is not classified as a retail client in terms of COBS 3.4.1(R), unless he suffers the loss in question in the course of carrying on business of any kind.

Notably, the proposed definition attempts to establish a co-extensive relationship, as discussed in chapter six, between the common law and the regulatory framework insofar as corporate retail investors are concerned. Moreover, this amendment is directed at improving the redress opportunities available to corporate retail investors since, unless FSMA, section 138D is revisited as proposed above, 'the judiciary will not repair what parliament broke and the FCA cannot fix'.[115] It follows, therefore, that it is only pursuant to an extension to the statutory definition of 'private person' to cover corporate retail investors, that English courts can have a direct means of assessing mis-selling allegations raised by corporate retail investors. Further, the proposed extension in the scope of the right of action under FSMA, section 138D ensures that corporate retail investors are also able to rely on the rights of action in terms of, inter alia, the client's best interest rule (COBS 2.1.1(R)), rules surrounding information disclosure (COBS 2.2A(R)), the requirement for an authorised investment firm's communication to be fair, clear and not misleading (COBS 4.2(R)), and the regulatory prohibition on excluding liability (COBS 2.1.2(R)). The proposed amendment also extends relief to corporate retail investors, not just individuals, provided that these are not in the business of carrying on a regulated activity as defined in the RAO. Further, the second limb of the definition retains the right of action for non-retail individuals (including

[114] *Bailey* [12].
[115] Lloyd Maynard, 'Holmcroft Properties: will a contractual phoenix rise from its ashes?' (2016) 31 *Journal of International Banking and Financial Law* 356, 358.

individuals who are classified as professional investors), as long as the damages claimed by them are not borne in the course of carrying on business of any kind.

III. A Side-note on Unregulated Complex Products

The areas discussed in this book are by no means comprehensive insofar as complex investment products are concerned. Corporate retail investors are exposed to the risk of mis-selling from other sources, such as those related to unregulated complex products, which, whilst similar in nature to IRHPs, open up a novel range of concerns that merit further consideration and are hereby being acknowledged by this book.

The optimal fixing of the regulatory perimeter remains a major concern for regulators. In fact, the FCA acknowledges that, in practice, 'the lines between regulated and unregulated activities have become blurred', pursuant to which it has attributed many of the problems that we have seen in the market since the global financial crisis to 'regulated firms undertaking activities which are outside … [the] "regulatory perimeter"'.[116] One such example relates to concerns around the selling practices in connection with what are known as 'Tailored Business Loans' (TBLs). Like IRHPs, TBLs contain interest rate hedging features, yet, rather than being a standalone derivative contract (as is the case with IRHPs), these features are embedded within the contract of the loan itself. Due to the embedded nature of these hedging products, TBLs are categorised as 'corporate lending', which makes them an unregulated product.

Although TBLs and IRHPs have very similar complex features and economic functions, legally, TBLs are a very different product to standalone IRHPs.[117] Fundamentally, standalone IRHPs are covered by the perimeter of regulation but TBLs are not. The former are classified as CFDs for the purposes of RAO, Article 85, since they include rights under a contract the purpose of which is to secure a profit or avoid a loss by reference to fluctuations in, for example, interest rates. In contrast, TBLs are not CFDs because the purpose of the loan is not to secure a profit or avoid a loss by reference to interest rate fluctuations but, rather, the purpose of the loan from the customer's perspective is to borrow money on the specified terms in the loan. Since extending corporate loans, such as

[116] FCA, 'Our Future Mission' (2016) 4.

[117] A number of submissions have been made to this effect as part of oral and written evidence heard and received by the Treasury Committee in its review of conduct and competition in SME lending (see eg Treasury Committee, *Conduct and competition in SME lending: Minutes of evidence* (17 June 2014) response of David Thorburn (in his capacity as Chief Executive, Clydesdale and Yorkshire Banks) to Q425; Letter from Martin Wheatley to Rt Hon Greg Clark MP (9 May 2013); Treasury Committee, *Conduct and competition in SME lending: Minutes of evidence* (1 July 2014) response of Chris Woolard (in his capacity as Director of Policy, Risk and Research, FCA) to Q678). See also Toby Riley-Smith, 'FCA regulation of interest rate hedging products: one rule for some?' (2015) 30 *Journal of International Banking and Financial Law* 425.

TBLs, is not listed as a regulated activity in the RAO, the FCA has extremely limited powers to regulate, investigate, or bring enforcement actions in respect of the sale of TBL-type products. Equally, English courts may struggle to determine whether or not any deficiencies can be attributed to banks in respect of the provision of TBLs to corporate retail investors, given the lack of regulatory powers in this area.

On this basis, this area appears to represent a 'lacuna in the law'[118] insofar as issues of consumer protection are concerned, particularly in the light of statements made by the banks themselves indicating that these products were specifically created to avoid regulation,[119] as well as the fact that, despite their complex nature, TBLs have allegedly been sold using standard terms and conditions, which, as demonstrated by the experience with IRHPs, make it difficult for SME customers to fully understand the specific risks and features of TBLs.[120]

The FCA itself admitted that, since the features of TBL-type products are very close to IRHPs, it would be beneficial for retail businesses if the regulator had the ability to regulate such products.[121] Similarly, other commentators argued for the regulatory perimeter to 'be expanded to include more lending and selling of financial products to SMEs',[122] particularly since these businesses may not fully understand the extent to which they are entitled to regulatory protection. This notwithstanding, certain authorities, as well as banks, expressed concerns about the consequences of a widening of the regulatory perimeter, highlighting the potential for this further inhibiting SMEs' access to credit as well as the likely increase in costs of compliance.[123] Equally, the government pronounced itself against an extension of the regulatory perimeter to business lending, stating that 'there is not an appetite for general business lending to come under regulation'.[124]

[118] Treasury Committee, *Conduct and competition in SME lending: Written Evidence* (27 January 2015) Jonathan Fisher Written submission SME0162.

[119] Treasury Committee, *Conduct and competition in SME lending: Minutes of evidence* (17 June 2014) response of David Thorburn (in his capacity as Chief Executive, Clydesdale and Yorkshire Banks) to Q410 and Q392.

[120] Banks selling these TBLs acknowledged that most SME customers have very limited financial sophistication and TBLs were in fact sold to SMEs 'who did not always understand what they were getting into in a falling interest rate environment' (Treasury Committee, *Conduct and competition in SME lending: Minutes of evidence* (17 June 2014) response of David Thorburn (in his capacity as Chief Executive, Clydesdale and Yorkshire Banks) to Q410 and Q396).

[121] Treasury Committee, *Conduct and competition in SME lending: Minutes of evidence* (1 July 2014) response of Chris Woolard (in his capacity as Director of Policy, Risk and Research, FCA) to Q701.

[122] Treasury Committee, *Conduct and competition in SME lending: Written Evidence* (29 April 2014) Prof Mark Watson-Gandy Written submission SME0061.

[123] See eg Treasury Committee, *Conduct and competition in SME lending: Written Evidence* (10 June 2014) Shawbrook Bank Limited Written submission SME0123; Treasury Committee, *Conduct and competition in SME lending: Written Evidence* (2 September 2014) Lloyds Banking Group Written submission SME0157; Treasury Committee, *Conduct and competition in SME lending: Written Evidence* (22 July 2014) Royal Bank of Scotland Written submission SME0150; HM Treasury, 'Conduct and Competition in SME Lending: Letter to the Treasury Select Committee' (2015).

[124] Treasury Committee, *Conduct and competition in SME lending: Minutes of evidence* (1 July 2014) response of Andrea Leadsom (in her capacity as MP, Economic Secretary, HM Treasury) to Q741.

These conflicting observations led the Treasury Committee to recommend an assessment of the 'feasibility, benefits and costs of adjusting the perimeter of regulation to cover loans with features of interest rate hedging products'.[125] This statement, together with the observations made throughout this book specifically around the vulnerabilities of corporate retail investors and the risks they face when transacting in complex products, portend that scope for further research into this area is desirable.

IV. Concluding Remarks

The main value of this book lies in its critical assessment of the investor protection framework applicable to corporate retail investors. This book has shown that corporate retail investors remain in a vulnerable position as they are not only exposed to the risk of mis-selling due to the inexperience, lack of knowledge and behavioural biases they face, but also because they encounter a number of hurdles in attempting to obtain adequate redress for the financial detriment they suffer as a result of mis-selling. These obstacles exist not only because corporate retail investors are excluded from applying for redress in the first place (for example when attempting to pursue a private right of action under FSMA, section 138D), but also since these investors are seen as 'sophisticated' parties that are able to take independent and well-informed decisions (particularly in cases where they have been the subject of regulatory redress schemes or when attempting to pursue a civil claim in English courts), such that they are presumed to have access to the required professional advice. This perception has been challenged throughout this book by arguing that corporate retail investors should not be distinguished from individual retail investors and that the uniformity which the MiFID regime attempts to establish (in that it does not distinguish between 'individual' and 'corporate' investors that fall within the scope of the 'retail' category) should not be threatened by discrimination at a national level between individual and corporate retail investors.

The current landscape of consumer protection is aimed at addressing concerns around mis-selling, but remains 'tempered by the resilient language of consumer responsibility',[126] especially insofar as corporate retail investors are concerned. This book has concluded that post-mis-selling and post-crises regulatory initiatives have been mostly targeted at protecting individual retail investors, hence failing to consider the needs of corporate retail investors, even though these investors exhibit similar behavioural biases and limitations. To this end, the recommendations presented in this chapter purport to secure a more robust regulatory protection framework for corporate retail investors, which is preventative in

[125] Treasury Committee, *Conduct and competition in SME lending* (HC 204, 2015) Eleventh Report para 151.

[126] Lorna Fox O'Mahony, Christian Twigg-Flesner and Folarin Akinbami, 'Conceptualizing the Consumer of Financial Services: a New Approach?' (2015) 38 *Journal of Consumer Policy* 111, 112.

nature and which supplements the traditional regulatory tools by making investment firms more accountable. These proposals have been informed primarily by the historical shifts in investment services regulation as well as the extent to which past regulatory reforms have been effective in securing an adequate level of protection for all retail investors. Insights from behavioural law and economics have also been considered by this book in arguing that corporate retail investors are deserving of a more intrusive and protective framework.

More specifically, it is contended here that the requirement for a suitability assessment for all retail investors transacting in complex products as proposed in Section IIA, coupled with the implementation of a Retail Investor Charter (and, consequently, the elimination of the FSMA consumer responsibility principle) suggested in Section IIC, will equip these investors with a sound basis for making investment decisions which are in their own best interests, whilst also protecting them against any improper conduct by investment firms. Particularly in the case of corporate retail investors, the proposed measures should ensure that these investors are better-placed to persuasively defend their actions in court, should any dispute over the transaction arise. In addition, establishing a clear structure for the assessment of complexity by the FCA, as proposed in Section IIB, would introduce a much-needed element of objectivity. Finally, the recommended extension to the scope of the private right of action arising from FSMA, section 138D to cover all retail investors including corporate entities (pursuant to the revised definition of 'private person' proposed in Section IID), is seen as being conducive towards creating a level playing field amongst retail investors. Whilst encouraging a more investor-centric approach, these recommended measures have still been designed in a manner that allows flexible implementation without unnecessarily inhibiting product innovation.

Collectively, the recommended measures, complemented by the supplementary research in the areas being highlighted in this chapter, are considered essential to strengthen the regulatory regime for corporate retail investors. The proposals seek to provide these investors with an added layer of protection, both from a regulatory and legislative perspective, whilst also having spin-off benefits for individual retail investors. Additionally, these proposals are intended to promote adequate redress mechanisms for retail investors.

In conclusion, the suggested reforms aim to reduce the likelihood of retail investors falling victim to mis-selling prior to undertaking the transaction, to foster a greater understanding of the risks associated with complex products amongst retail investors, to secure adequate redress mechanisms on an ex-post basis, and, importantly, to promote greater trust in the financial system amongst all retail investors.

BIBLIOGRAPHY

Books and Book Chapters

Ackert L and Deaves R, *Behavioral Finance: Psychology, Decision-Making, and Markets* (Cengage Learning, 2010)

Andenas M and Chiu I, *The Foundations and Future of Financial Regulation: Governance for Responsibility* (Routledge, 2014)

Aspinwall R, 'Conflicting Objectives of Financial Regulation' in Robert Guttmann (ed), *Reforming Money and Finance* (M E Sharpe, 1997)

Atiyah P, *The Rise and Fall of Freedom of Contract* (Clarendon Press, 1979)

Austin L and Klimchuck D (eds), *Private Law and the Rule of Law* (Oxford University Press, 2014)

Avgouleas E, 'Reforming Investor Protection Regulation: The Impact of Cognitive Biases' in Michael Faure and Frank H Stephen (eds), *Essays in the Law and Economics of Regulation in Honour of Anthony Ogus* (Intersentia, 2008)

—— 'What Future for Disclosure as a Regulatory Technique? Lessons from Behavioural Decision Theory and the Global Financial Crisis' in Iain MacNeil and Justin O'Brien (eds), *The Future of Financial Regulation* (Hart Publishing, 2010)

Baisch R and Weber R, 'Investment Suitability Requirements in the Light of Behavioural Findings: Challenges for a Legal Framework Coping with Ambiguous Risk Perceptions' in Klaus Mathis (ed), *European Perspectives on Behavioural Law and Economics* (Springer International Publishing, 2015)

Baker K and Nofsinger J (eds), *Behavioral Finance: Investors, Corporations, and Markets* (John Wiley & Sons, Inc, 2010)

Baldwin R, 'Better Regulation: The Search and the Struggle' in Robert Baldwin, Martin Cave, and Martin Lodge (eds), *The Oxford Handbook of Regulation* (Oxford University Press, 2010)

Barr M, Mullainathan S, and Shafir E, 'The case for behaviourally informed regulation' in David Moss and John Cisternino (eds), *New Perspectives on Regulation* (The Tobin Project, 2009)

Beale H (ed), *Chitty on Contracts*, 32nd edn (Sweet & Maxwell Ltd, 2015)

—— and Lando O (eds), *Principles of European Contract Law: Parts I and II* (Kluwer Law International, 2000)

Beaston J, 'The relationship between regulations governing the financial services industry and fiduciary duties under the general law' in Ewan McKendrick (ed), *Corporate aspects of trusts and fiduciary obligations* (Clarendon Press, 1992)

Benston G, *Regulating Financial Markets: A Critique and Some Proposals* (Institute of Economic Affairs, 1998)

Bentham J, *The Works of Jeremy Bentham* published under the Superintendence of his Executor, John Bowring (William Tait, 1838–43)

Black J, *Rules and Regulators* (Clarendon Press, 1997)

—— 'Law and Regulation: The Case of Finance' in Christine Parker and others (eds), *Regulating Law* (Oxford University Press Inc, 2004)

—— 'Financial Markets' in Peter Cane and Herbert M Kritzer (eds), *The Oxford Handbook of Empirical Legal Research* (Oxford University Press, 2010)

—— 'The Role of Risk in Regulatory Processes' in Robert Baldwin, Martin Cave, and Martin Lodge (eds), *The Oxford Handbook of Regulation* (Oxford University Press, 2010)

—— 'The rise, fall and fate of principles-based regulation' in Kern Alexander and Niamh Moloney (eds), *Law Reform and Financial Markets* (Edward Elgar Publishing, 2011)

—— and Scott C, *Cranston's Consumers and the Law*, 3rd edn (Butterworths, 2000)

Busch D, 'Agency and Principal Dealing under MiFID I and MiFID II' in Danny Busch and Guido Ferrarini (eds), *Regulation of the EU Financial Markets: MiFID II and MiFIR* (Oxford University Press, 2017)

—— and Ferrarini G, 'Who's Afraid of MiFID II?' in Danny Busch and Guido Ferrarini (eds), *Regulation of the EU Financial Markets: MiFID II and MiFIR* (Oxford University Press, 2017)

Cane P, *Tort Law and Economic Interests* (Clarendon Press, 1996)

Cardozo B, *Paradoxes of Legal Science* (Columbia University Press, 1928)

Cartwright P, *Consumer Protection in Financial Services* (Kluwer Law International Ltd, 1999)

Chen-Wishart M, 'Regulating Unfair Terms, in English and European Perspectives on Contract and Corporate Law' in Louise Gullifer and Stefan Vogenauer (eds), *Essays in Honour of Hugh Beale* (Hart Publishing, 2014)

Cherednychenko O, *Fundamental Rights, Contract Law and the Protection of the Weaker Party: a comparative analysis of the constitutionalisation of contract law, with emphasis on risk financial transactions* (European Law Publishers, 2007)

—— 'Conceptualising unconscionability in the context of risky financial transactions: how to converge public and private law approaches?' in Mel Kenny, James Devenney, and Lorna Fox O'Mahony (eds), *Unconscionability in European Private Financial Transactions: Protecting the Vulnerable* (Cambridge University Press, 2010)

—— 'Full Harmonization of Retail Financial Services Contract Law in Europe: A Success or a Failure?' in Stefan Grundmann and Yeşim M Atamer (eds), *Financial Services, Financial Crisis and General European Contract Law – Failure and Challenges of Contracting* (Kluwer Law International BV, 2011)

Cheshire C and Fifoot C, *Law of Contract*, 4th edn (Butterworths, 1965)

Clarke M, *Citizens' Financial Futures: The regulation of retail investment financial services in Britain* (Ashgate Publishing Ltd, 1999)

Colaert V, 'MiFID: Picking Up the Crumbs of a Piecemeal Approach' in Danny Busch and Guido Ferrarini (eds), *Regulation of the EU Financial Markets: MiFID II and MiFIR* (Oxford University Press, 2017)

Collins H, *Regulating Contracts* (Oxford University Press Inc, 1999)

—— 'Regulating Contract Law' in Christine Parker and others (eds), *Regulating Law* (Oxford University Press Inc, 2004)

Colombi Ciacchi A, 'Freedom of contract as freedom from unconscionable contracts' in Mel Kenny, James Devenney, and Lorna Fox O'Mahony (eds), *Unconscionability in European Private Financial Transactions: Protecting the Vulnerable* (Cambridge University Press, 2010)

D'Agostino E, *Contracts of Adhesion Between Law and Economics: Rethinking the Unconscionability Doctrine* (Springer International Publishing, 2015)

Davies H, 'Reforming Financial Regulation: Progress and Priorities' in Eilís Ferran and Charles Goodhart (eds), *Regulating Financial Services and Markets in the Twenty First Century* (Hart Publishing, 2001)

Douglas M and Wildavsky A, *Risk and Culture* (University of California Press, 1982)

Elliott N, Hewetson C and Warne D (eds), *Banking Litigation*, 3rd edn (Sweet & Maxwell Ltd, 2011)

Enriques L and Gargantini M, 'The Overarching Duty to Act in the Best Interests of the Client in MiFID II' in Danny Busch and Guido Ferrarini (eds), *Regulation of the EU Financial Markets: MiFID II and MiFIR* (Oxford University Press, 2017)

Fawcett A, 'Examining the objectives of financial regulation – Will the new regime succeed? A practitioner's view' in Eilís Ferran and Charles Goodhart (eds), *Regulating Financial Services and Markets in the Twenty First Century* (Hart Publishing, 2001)

Feintuck M, 'Regulatory Rationales Beyond the Economic: In Search of the Public Interest' in Robert Baldwin, Martin Cave, and Martin Lodge (eds), *The Oxford Handbook of Regulation* (Oxford University Press, 2010)

Ferran E, 'Principles-based, risk-based regulation and effective enforcement' in Michel Tison and others (eds), *Perspectives in Company Law and Financial Regulation: Essays in Honour of Eddy Wymeersch* (Cambridge University Press, 2009)

—— 'Crisis-driven regulatory reform: where in the world is the EU going?' in Eilís Ferran and others (eds), *The Regulatory Aftermath of the Global Financial Crisis* (Cambridge University Press, 2012)

Ferrarini G and Busch D (eds), *Regulation of the EU Financial Markets: MiFID II and MiFIR* (Oxford University Press, 2017)

Finn P, 'The Fiduciary Principle' in TG Youdan (ed), *Equity, Fiduciaries and Trusts* (Law Book Company, 1989)

—— 'Fiduciary Law and the Modern Corporate World' in Ewan McKendrick (ed), *Corporate Aspects of Trusts and Fiduciary Obligations* (Clarendon Press, 1992)

Fridman G, *The Law of Contract in Canada*, 5th edn (Carswell, 2006)

Friedman L, *Contract Law in America* (University of Wisconsin Press, 1965)

Frith S, *Derivatives: Law and Practice* (Sweet & Maxwell Ltd, 2003)

Giudici P, 'Independent Financial Advice' in in Danny Busch and Guido Ferrarini (eds), *Regulation of the EU Financial Markets: MiFID II and MiFIR* (Oxford University Press, 2017)

Goodhart A, *Hamlyn Lectures: English Law and the Moral Law* (Stevens & Sons Ltd, 1953)

Goodhart C, 'The Costs of Regulation' in Arthur Seldon (ed), *Financial Regulation – or Over-Regulation* (Institute of Economic Affairs, 1988)

—— 'How should we regulate bank capital and financial products? What role for 'living wills'?' in *The Future of Finance: The LSE Report* (London School of Economics and Political Science, 2010)

—— and others, *Financial Regulation: Why, how and where now?* (Routledge, 1998)

Graham P, 'The Statutory Regulation of Financial Services in the United Kingdom and the Development of Chinese Walls in Managing Conflicts of Interest' in Ewan McKendrick (ed), *Corporate aspects of trusts and fiduciary obligations* (Clarendon Press, 1992)

Gray J and Hamilton J, *Implementing Financial Regulation: Theory and Practice* (John Wiley & Sons Ltd, 2006)

Gunningham N, 'Enforcement and Compliance Strategies' Robert Baldwin, Martin Cave, and Martin Lodge (eds), *The Oxford Handbook of Regulation* (Oxford University Press, 2010)

Haar B, 'From public law to private law: market supervision and contract law standards' in Stefan Grundmann and Yeşim M Atamer (eds), *Financial Services, Financial Crisis and General European Contract Law – Failure and Challenges of Contracting* (Kluwer Law International BV, 2011)

Hackenthal A, 'Financial Advice' in Ester Faia and others (eds), *Financial Regulation: A Transatlantic Perspective* (Cambridge University Press, 2015)

Hartkamp A, Tillema M and ter Heide A, *Contract Law in the Netherlands*, 2nd edn (Kluwer Law International, 2011)

Hill J, 'Why did Australia fare so well in the global financial crisis?' in Eilís Ferran and others (eds), *The Regulatory Aftermath of the Global Financial Crisis* (Cambridge University Press, 2012)

Holland T, *Elements of Jurisprudence*, 12th edn (Oxford University Press, 1917)

Horowitz D, *The Courts and Social Policy* (Brookings Institution Press, 1977)

Hudson A, *The Law of Finance*, 2nd edn (Sweet and Maxwell, 2013)

Jackson R, Stewart R and Powell J (eds), *Jackson & Powell on Professional Liability*, 7th edn (Sweet & Maxwell Ltd, 2012)

Jebens K, *LAUTRO: A Pioneer Regulator 1986 to 1994* (CE Jebens, 1997)

Jones M (ed), *Clerk & Lindsell on Torts*, 21st edn (Sweet & Maxwell Ltd, 2014)

Kahneman D, *Thinking Fast and Slow* (Penguin Books Ltd, 2011)

—— and Slovic P and Tversky A (eds), *'Judgment under Uncertainty: Heuristics and Biases'* (Cambridge University Press, 1982)

—— and Tversky A (eds), *'Choices, Values, and Frames'* (Cambridge University Press, 2000)

Kingsford Smith D and Dixon O, 'The Consumer Interest and the Financial Markets' in Niamh Moloney, Eilís Ferran, and Jennifer Payne (eds), *The Oxford Handbook of Financial Regulation* (Oxford University Press, 2015)

Köndgen J, 'Rules of Conduct: Further Harmonisation?' in Guido Ferrarini (ed), *European Securities Markets: The Investment Services Directive and Beyond* (Kluwer Law International Ltd, 1998)

—— 'Policy responses to credit crisis: does the law of contract provide the answer' in Stefan Grundmann and Yeşim M Atamer (eds), *Financial Services, Financial Crisis and General European Contract Law – Failure and Challenges of Contracting* (Kluwer Law International BV, 2011)
Kruithof M, 'Policy responses to credit crisis: does the law of contract provide the answer' in Stefan Grundmann and Yeşim M Atamer (eds), *Financial Services, Financial Crisis and General European Contract Law – Failure and Challenges of Contracting* (Kluwer Law International BV, 2011)
Langevoort D, *Selling Hope, Selling Risk: Corporations, Wall Street, and the Dilemmas of Investor Protection* (Oxford University Press, 2016)
Lloyd R, *Williston on Contracts*, 4th edn (Lawyers Cooperative Publishing, 2012)
Lomnicka E, 'The Impact of Rule-Making by Financial Services Regulators on the Common Law: The Lessons on PPI' in Louise Gullifer and Stefan Vogenauer (eds), *English and European Perspectives on Contract and Corporate Law: Essays in Honour of Hugh Beale* (Hart Publishing Ltd, 2014)
MacNeil I, *An Introduction to the Law on Financial Investment*, 2nd edn (Hart Publishing, 2012)
—— and O'Brien J (eds), *The Future of Financial Regulation* (Hart Publishing, 2010)
Mathis K (ed), *European Perspectives on Behavioural Law and Economics* (Springer International Publishing, 2015)
Mayer C, 'Regulatory Principles and the Financial Services and Markets Act 2000' in Eilís Ferran and Charles Goodhart (eds), *Regulating Financial Services and Markets in the Twenty First Century* (Hart Publishing, 2001)
McKendrick E, *Contract Law: Text, Cases and Materials* (Oxford University Press, 2004)
—— *Contract Law*, 3rd edn (Oxford University Press, 2007)
McMeel G and Virgo J (eds), *McMeel and Virgo on Financial Advice and Financial Products: Law and Liability* (Oxford University Press, 2001)
Mill J, *Principles of Political Economy* (D Appleton and Company, 1868)
Moloney N, *How to Protect Investors: Lessons from the EC and the UK* (Cambridge University Press, 2010)
—— 'Financial Services and Markets' in Robert Baldwin, Martin Cave, and Martin Lodge (eds), *The Oxford Handbook of Regulation* (Oxford University Press, 2010)
—— 'Regulating the Retail Markets: Law, Policy and the Financial Crisis' in George Letsas and Colm O'Cinnéide (eds) *Current Legal Problems* (Oxford University Press, 2010)
—— 'The legacy effects of the financial crisis on regulatory design in the EU' in Eilís Ferran and others (eds), *The Regulatory Aftermath of the Global Financial Crisis* (Cambridge University Press, 2012)
—— *EU Securities and Financial Markets Regulation*, 3rd edn (Oxford University Press, 2014)
—— 'Financial Market Governance and Consumer Protection in the EU' in Ester Faia and others (eds), *Financial Regulation: A Transatlantic Perspective* (Cambridge University Press, 2015)
—— 'Regulating the Retail Markets' in Niamh Moloney, Eilís Ferran, and Jennifer Payne (eds), *The Oxford Handbook of Financial Regulation* (Oxford University Press, 2015)
—— 'Conduct Rules and Investor Protection: The Evolution of the EU's Approach' in Matthias Casper and others (eds), *Festschrift für Johannes Köndgen* (RWS Vlg Kommunikationsforum, 2016)
—— and Alexander K (eds), *Law Reform and the Financial Markets* (Edward Elgar Publishing Ltd, 2011)
—— and Ferran E and Payne J (eds), *The Oxford Handbook of Financial Regulation* (Oxford University Press, 2015)
Monti A, 'Formation of Contracts' in Luisa Antoniolli and Anna Veneziano (eds), *Principles of European Contract Law and Italian Law: A Commentary* (Kluwer Law International, 2005)
Moss D and Cisternino J (eds), *New Perspectives on Regulation* (The Tobin Project, 2009)
Mülbert P, 'The Eclipse of Contract Law in the Investment Firm-Client Relationship: The Impact of MiFID on the Law of Contract from a German Perspective' in Guido Ferrarini and Eddy Wymeersch (eds), *Investor Protection in Europe: Corporate Law Making, the MiFID and Beyond* (Oxford University Press, 2007)
Nelken D and Örücü E (eds), *Comparative Law: A Handbook* (Hart Publishing, 2007)
Ogus A, *Regulation: Legal Form and Economic Theory* (Oxford University Press, 1994)

—— 'Regulatory Paternalism: When is it Justified?' in Kalus J Hopt and others (eds), *Corporate Governance in Context: Corporations, States, and Markets in Europe, Japan, and the US* (Oxford University Press, 2005)
Padoa-Schioppa T, *Regulating Finance: Balancing Freedom and Risk* (Oxford University Press, 2004)
Page A and Ferguson R, *Investor Protection* (Weidenfeld and Nicolson, 1992)
Parry D, *The Sanctity of Contracts in English Law* (Stevens & Sons London, 1959)
Posner R, *How Judges Think* (Harvard University Press, 2008)
Pothier R, *A Treatise on the Law of Obligations, or Contracts* (A Strahan, 1806)
Powell J, *Essay upon the Law of Contracts and Agreements* (J Johnson and T Whieldon, 1790)
Ramsay I, *Consumer Law and Policy: Text and Materials on Regulating Consumer Markets*, 3rd edn (Hart Publishing, 2012)
—— and Williams T, 'The crash that launched a thousand fixes: Regulation of consumer credit after the lending revolution and the credit crunch' in Kern Alexander and Niamh Moloney (eds), *Law Reform and the Financial Markets* (Edward Elgar Publishing Ltd, 2011)
Reid M, *All-Change in the City: The Revolution in Britain's Financial Sector* (Macmillan Press, 1988)
Reimann M and Zimmermann R (eds), *The Oxford Handbook of Comparative Law: Part II* (Oxford University Press, 2008)
Reynolds F, 'Unfair Contract Terms: A Comment' in Alan C Neal (ed), *Law and the Weaker Party* (Professional Books, 1981)
Riesenhuber K, 'Policy responses to credit crisis: does the law of contract provide the answer' in Stefan Grundmann and Yeşim M Atamer (eds), *Financial Services, Financial Crisis and General European Contract Law – Failure and Challenges of Contracting* (Kluwer Law International BV, 2011)
Rose N, *Powers of Freedom: Reframing Political Thought* (Cambridge University Press, 1999)
Scott C, 'Standard-Setting in Regulatory Regimes' in Robert Baldwin, Martin Cave, and Martin Lodge (eds), *The Oxford Handbook of Regulation* (Oxford University Press, 2010)
Sibony A, 'Can EU Consumer Law Benefit From Behavioural Insights? An Analysis of the Unfair Practices Directive' in Klaus Mathis (ed), *European Perspectives on Behavioural Law and Economics* (Springer International Publishing, 2015)
Skidelsky R, *Keynes: The Return of the Master* (Allen Lane, 2009)
Stiglitz J, 'Regulation and Failure' in David Moss and John Cisternino (eds), *New Perspectives on Regulation* (The Tobin Project, 2009)
Sunstein C, *Why Nudge? The Politics of Libertarian Paternalism* (Yale University Press, 2014)
—— and Thaler R, *Nudge: Improving Decisions About Health, Wealth and Happiness* (Penguin Books, 2008)
Tafara E, 'Foreward' in Eilís Ferran and others (eds), *The Regulatory Aftermath of the Global Financial Crisis* (Cambridge University Press, 2012)
Tanzi V, *Regulating for the New Economic Order: The Good, the Bad and the Damaging* (Politeia, 2008)
Tison M, 'Conduct of Business Rules and Their Implementation in the EU Member States' in Guido Ferrarini, Klaus J Hopt, and Eddy Wymeersch (eds), *Capital Markets in the Age of the Euro: Cross-Border Transactions, Listed Companies and Regulation* (Kluwer Law International, 2002)
Tomasic R, 'Regulation of British Banks after the Financial Crisis' in Iain MacNeil and Justin O'Brien (eds), *The Future of Financial Regulation* (Hart Publishing, 2010)
Treitel G, *The Law of Contract*, 11th edn (Sweet & Maxwell Ltd, 2003)
Waddams S, 'Protection of weaker parties in English Law' in Mel Kenny, James Devenney, and Lorna Fox O'Mahony (eds), *Unconscionability in European Private Financial Transactions: Protecting the Vulnerable* (Cambridge University Press, 2010)
Wilken S and Ghaly K, *The law of waiver, variation and estoppel* (3rd edn, Oxford University Press, 2012)
Williams T, 'Open the Box: An Exploration of the Financial Services Authority's Model of Fairness in Consumer Financial Transactions' in Mel Kenny, James Devenney, and Lorna Fox O'Mahony (eds), *Unconscionability in European Private Financial Transactions: Protecting the Vulnerable* (Cambridge University Press, 2010)

Wood P, *Regulation of International Finance* (Sweet & Maxwell Ltd, 2007)
Yeung K, 'The Regulatory State' in Robert Baldwin, Martin Cave, and Martin Lodge (eds), *The Oxford Handbook of Regulation* (Oxford University Press, 2010)

Articles and Papers

Afghan S, 'Should private opt-out collective redress actions be introduced for the resolution of widespread consumer financial services claims? Part 1' (2016) 31 *Journal of International Banking Law and Regulation* 194
—— 'Should private opt-out collective redress actions be introduced for the resolution of widespread consumer financial services claims? Part 2' (2016) 31 *Journal of International Banking Law and Regulation* 249
Ahonen Z, 'The Recent Financial crisis and its Impact of Interest Rate Swaps: A Road to Recovery Through the Frustration of Corporate Purpose Doctrine' (2014) 24 *Indiana International and Comparative Law Review* 429
Akerlof G, 'The Market for "Lemons": Quality Uncertainty and the Market Mechanism' (1970) 84 *The Quarterly Journal of Economics* 488
Akinbami F, 'Financial services and consumer protection after the crisis' (2011) 29 *International Journal of Bank Marketing* 134
Alcock A, 'Are financial services over-regulated?' 24 (2013) *Company Lawyer* 132
Alexander K, 'Principles v rules in financial regulation: re-assessing the balance in the credit crisis' (2009) 10 *European Business Organization Law Review* 169
Andenas M, 'Liability for Regulators and Public Authorities' (2007) 18 *European Business Law Review* 1
Arora A, 'Unfair contract terms in international banking contracts' (2001) Sep *Journal of Business Law* 553
Avgouleas E, 'The Global Financial Crisis, Behavioural Finance and Financial Regulation: In Search of a New Orthodoxy' (2009) 9 *Journal of Corporate Law Studies* 23
Awrey D, 'Regulating Financial Innovation: A More Principles-Based Alternative?' (2011) 5 *Brooklyn Journal of Corporate, Financial and Commercial Law* 273
—— 'Complexity, Innovation and the Regulation of Modern Financial Markets' (2012) 2 *Harvard Law Business Review* 235
—— 'The Limits of Private Ordering Within Modern Financial Markets' (2014) 34 *Review of Banking and Financial Law* 183
Baldwin R, 'From Regulation Behaviour Changes: Giving Nudge the Third Degree' (2014) 77 *The Modern Law Review* 831
Balling M, 'Objectives and theoretical foundations of the European Commission's 1999 action plan concerning the framework for financial markets' (2004) 5 *Journal of International Banking Regulation* 256
Band C, 'Selling complex products to sophisticated clients: JP Morgan Chase v Springwell: Part I' (2009) 24 *Journal of International Banking Law and Regulation* 71
—— and Anderson K, 'Selling complex financial products to sophisticated clients: JP Morgan Chase v Springwell: Part 2' (2009) 24 *Journal of International Banking Law and Regulation* 233
Bar-Gill O, 'Seduction by Contract: Law, Economics and Psychology in Consumer Markets – Introduction' (2012) NYU Center for Law, Economics and Organization, Law and Economics Research Paper Series, Working Paper No 12–33
—— and Epstein R, 'Consumer Contracts: Behavioral Economics vs Neoclassical Economics – An exchange between Oren Bar-Gill and Richard A Epstein' (2007) NYU Center for Law, Economics and Organization, Law and Economics Research Paper Series, Working Paper No 07–17
Barnett R, 'Consenting to Form Contracts' (2002) 71 *Fordham Law Review* 627
Basedow J, 'The Optional Instrument of European Contract Law: Opting-in through Standard Terms – A Reply to Simon Whittaker' (2012) 8 *European Review of Contract Law* 82

Bazley S, 'The Financial Services Authority, risk-based regulation, principles based rules and accountability' (2008) 23 *Journal of International Banking Law and Regulation* 422

—— 'Further pressure on UK banks' (2012) 33 *Company Lawyer* 257

Beale H, 'The Impact of the Decisions of the European Courts on English Contract Law: The Limits of Voluntary Harmonization' (2010) 18 *European Review of Private Law* 501

Beaumont M, 'How do you solve a problem like mis-selling?' [2015] Recovery 21

Ben-Shahar O, 'The Myth of 'Opportunity to Read' in Contract Law' (2009) 5 *European Review of Contract Law* 1

Benjamin J, 'The Narratives of Financial Law' (2010) 30 *Oxford Journal of Legal Studies* 787

—— and Raffan M, 'Wholesale Markets and the Limits of Regulation' (2015) 40 *International Financial Law Review* 1

Benston G, 'Consumer Protection as Justification for Regulating Financial Services Firms and Products' (2000) 17 *Journal of Financial Services Research* 277

Black B, 'Behavioural Economics and Investor Protection: Reasonable Investors and Efficient Markets' (2013) 44 *Loyola University Chicago Law Journal* 1493

Black J, 'Decentring Regulation: Understanding the Role of Regulation and Self Regulation in a "Post Regulatory World"' (2001) 54 *Current Legal Problems* 103

—— 'Critical reflections on regulation' (2002) 27 *Australian Journal of Legal Philosophy* 1

—— 'Enrolling actors in regulatory systems: examples from UK financial services regulation' [2003] *Public Law* 63

—— 'Involving Consumers in Securities Regulation' (2006) Prepared for the Taskforce to Modernize Securities Regulation in Canada

—— 'Forms and paradoxes of principles-based regulation' (2008) 3 *Capital Markets Law Journal* 425

—— 'Seeing, Knowing, and Regulating Financial Markets: Moving the Cognitive Framework from the Economic to the Social' (2013) LSE Law, Society and Economy Working Paper No 24/2013

—— 'Learning from Regulatory Disasters' (2014) LSE Law, Society and Economy Working Paper No 24/2014

—— and Baldwin R, 'Really Responsive Regulation' LSE Law, Society and Economy Working Papers (2007)

—— and Hopper M and Band C, 'Making a success of Principles-based regulation' (2007) 1 *Law and Financial Markets Review* 191

—— and Nobles R, 'Personal Pensions Misselling: The Causes and Lessons of Regulatory Failure' (1998) 61 *The Modern Law Review* 789

Bolgár V, 'The Contract of Adhesion – A Comprehension of Theory and Practice' (1972) 20 *The American Journal of Comparative Law* 53

Bonavita J, 'Case comment: The regulation of "speculative interest-rate bets" by the German Federal Court of Justice – new dimensions of market intervention hidden behind the old information model' (2012) 13 *European Business Organization Law Review* 271

Bowen A, 'Investment mis-selling and Breach of Statutory Duty' (2013) Greens Business Law Bulletin Issue 127

Bradley M, 'Three years post-Rubenstein: causation and loss revisited' (2015) 8 *Journal of International Banking and Financial Law* 513

Braithwaite J, 'Rules and Principles: A Theory of Legal Certainty' (2002) 27 *Australian Journal of Legal Philosophy* 47

Braithwaite J P, 'OTC derivatives, the courts and regulatory reform' (2012) 7 Capital Markets Law Journal 364

—— 'The origins and implications of contractual estoppel' (2016) 132 *Law Quarterly Review* 120

Braucher J, 'Form and Substance in Consumer Financial Protection' (2013) 7 *Brooklyn Journal of Corporate, Financial and Commercial Law* 107

Brooks-Gallerani A and Fox A, 'Case comment – Swaps litigation update: Green v Royal Bank of Scotland' (2014) 27 *Insolvency Intelligence* 14

Brunnermeier M and others, 'The Fundamental Principles of Financial Regulation' (2009) *Geneva Reports on the World Economy* 11

Bubb R and Pildes R, 'How Behavioral Economics Trims its Sails and Why' (2014) 127 *Harvard Law Review* 1593

Busch D, 'The private law effect of MiFID: the Genil case and beyond' (2017) 13 *European Review of Contract Law* 70

Camerer C and others, 'Regulation for Conservatives: Behavioral Economics and the Case for "Asymmetric Paternalism"' (2003) 151 *University of Pennsylvania Law Review* 1211

Campbell D, 'The absence of negligence in Hedley Byrne v Heller' (2016) 132 *Law Quarterly Review* 266

Campbell J and others, 'Consumer Financial Protection' (2011) 25 *Journal of Economic Perspectives* 91

Cartwright P, 'The Vulnerable Consumer of Financial Services: Law, Policy and Regulation' (2011) Financial Services Research Forum

—— 'Understanding and Protecting Vulnerable Financial Consumers' (2015) 38 *Journal of Consumer Policy* 119

Casey K, 'Banker-customer: contracts regulation' (1995) 10 *Journal of International Banking Law* N99

Cerchia RE, 'Interest Rate Swaps' Contract and "Excessive Onerousness": An Italian Viewpoint' (2015) 23 *European Private Law Review* 121

Chang E, Tang D, and Zhang M, 'Suitability Checks and Household Investments in Structured Products' (2015) 50 *Journal of Financial and Quantitative Analysis* 597

Chen Chao-hung C, 'The resolution of the structured notes fiasco in Hong Kong, Singapore and Taiwan' (2013) 34 *Company Lawyer* 119

Chen-Wishart M, 'Undue Influence: Vindicating Relationships of Influence' (2006) 59 *Current Legal Problems* 231

Cheng A and Young A, 'Lack of legal safeguards for investors when buying financial investment products: the need for legal reforms in Hong Kong' (2015) 30 *Journal of International Banking Law and Regulation* 267

Cherednychenko O, 'European Securities Regulation, Private Law and the Investment Firm-Client Relationship' (2009) 17 *European Review of Private Law* 925

—— 'Freedom of Contract in the Post-Crisis Era: Quo Vadis?' (2014) 10 *European Review of Contract Law* 390

—— 'Contract Governance in the EU: Conceptualising the Relationship between Investor Protection Regulation and Private Law' (2015) 21 *European Law Journal* 500

Chew C, 'Statutory aspects of unjust banking contracts: a legal analysis' (2014) 29 *Journal of International Banking Law and Regulation* 312

Chiu I, 'The nature of a financial investment intermediary's duty to his client' (2008) 28 *Legal Studies* 254

—— 'Does the Retail Distribution Review protect consumers?' (2012) 33 *Company Lawyer* 225

Choi S and Gulati C, 'Contract as Statute' (2006) 104 *Michigan Law Review* 1130

Ciro T, 'Game theory in financial markets litigation' (2005) 20 *Journal of International Banking Law and Regulation* 315

Coffee J, 'The Mandatory/Enabling Balance in Corporate Law: An Essay on the Judicial Role' (1989) 89 *Columbia Law Review* 1618

Coleman R, 'Compensating customers who have been missold interest rate hedging products' (2013) 8 *Journal of International Banking and Financial Law* 507

Connelly K, 'The Suitability Rule: Should a Private Right of Action Exist?' (1981) 55 *St John's Law Review* 493

Cooper JC and Kovacic WE, 'Behavioral Economics: Implications for Regulatory Behavior' (2012) 41 *Journal of Regulatory Economics* 41

Cover R, 'Nomos and Narrative' (1983) 97 *Harvard Law Review* 4

Cunningham L, 'A Prescription to Retire the Rhetoric of "Principles-Based Systems" in Corporate Law, Securities Regulation and Accounting' (2007) 60 *Vanderbilt Law Review* 1411

Curzon Price T and Andrews P, 'The game of caps and nudges' (*Insight: Opinion and Analysis from the FCA*, 27 July 2017)

Darby M and Karni E, 'Free Competition and the Optimal Amount of Fraud' (1973) 16 *Journal of Law and Economics* 67

Darling A, 'Government and the Financial Services Industry' (1994) 2 *Journal of Financial Regulation and Compliance* 107
Dastis J, 'Change of Circumstances (Section 313 BGB) Trigger for the Next Financial Crisis?' (2015) 23 *European Review of Private Law* 85
Davies H, 'FSA's Strategy in Applying its Powers under the New Regime' (1999) 1 *Journal of International Financial Markets* 51
—— 'Law and Regulation' (1999) 3 *Company Financial and Insolvency Law Review* 1
Davies J, 'What is misselling?' (2004) 19 *Journal of International Banking Law and Regulation* 1
Davies P, 'Protecting investors proves tricky' *Financial Times Fund Management* (London, 20 March 2011)
De Geest G, 'The Death of Caveat Emptor' (2014) University of Chicago Law School, Law and Economics Workshop
DeBondt W and others, 'What can behavioural finance teach us about finance?' (2010) 2 *Quantitative Research in Financial Markets* 29
Donnelly M, 'The Financial Services Ombudsman: asking the "existential question"' (2012) 35 *Dublin University Law Journal* 229
Doyle C, 'Self Regulation and Statutory Regulation' (1997) 8 *Business Strategy Review* 35
Eaglesham J, 'Making the Watchdogs Come to Heal' *Investors Chronicle* (London, 9 December 1994)
Ebers M, 'Information and Advising Requirements in the Financial Services Sector: Principles and Peculiarities in EC Law' (2004) 8.2 *Electronic Journal of Comparative Law* 1
Edelman J, 'When Do Fiduciary Duties Arise?' (2010) 126 *Law Quarterly Review* 302
Ellison R, 'Time to revisit caveat emptor? What has regulation ever done for us?' (2008) 13 *Pensions* 123
Evans D, 'Why Now Is Not the Right Time to Revamp Consumer Financial Protection' (A paper based on remarks made during Panel III at New York University-New York Federal Reserve Conference on Regulating Consumer Financial Products, 6 January 2010)
—— and Wright J, 'How the Consumer Financial Protection Agency Act of 2009 would change the law and regulation of consumer financial products' (2009) 2 Bloomberg Law Reports: Risk and Compliance
Fernández J, 'Interest Rate Swap and *Rebus sic Stantibus* Clause' (2015) 23 *European Private Law Review* 133
Ferran E, 'Regulatory lessons from the payment protection insurance mis-selling scandal in the UK' (2012) 13 *European Business Organization Law Review* 247
Ferrarini G, 'Contract Standards and the Markets in Financial Instruments Directive (MiFID): an Assessment of the Lamfalussy Regulatory Architecture' (2005) Institute for Law and Finance Working Paper Series No 39
Finn P, 'Common Law Divergences' (2013) 37 *Melbourne University Law Review* 511
Fong A, 'Fiduciary duty in the context of providing investment services' (2013) 28 *Journal of International Banking Law and Regulation* 390
Ford C, 'New Governance, Compliance, and Principles-Based Securities Regulation' (2008) 45 *American Business Law Journal* 1
—— 'Principles-based Securities Regulation in the Wake of the Global Financial Crisis' (2010) 55 *McGill Law Journal* 1
Forner J, 'Spain: corporate law – consumer protection' (2000) 11 *International Company and Corporate Law Review* N31
Fox A and Arthurs C, 'Negligence: Don't bank on it: borrowers, lenders and the duty of care' (2013) 52 *Corporate Litigation Journal* 4
—— and Davies E, 'All is not lost?' (2016) 166 *New Law Journal* 14
Fox O'Mahony L, Twigg-Flesner C, and Akinbami F, 'Conceptualizing the Consumer of Financial Services: a New Approach?' (2015) 38 *Journal of Consumer Policy* 111
Frase D, 'Conflicts of interest' (2012) 97 *Compliance Officer Bulletin* 5
Furse C, 'Comment: Sox is Not to Blame – London is Just Better as a Market' *Financial Times* (London, 17 September 2006)

Gazal-Ayal O, 'Economic analysis of standard form contracts: the monopoly case' (2007) 24 *European Journal of Law and Economics* 119

Gennaioli N, 'Contracting in the Shadow of the Law' (2006) Institute for International Economic Studies, Stockholm University

Georgosouli A, 'The debate over the economic rationale for investor protection regulation: a critical appraisal' (2007) 15 *Journal of Financial Regulation and Compliance* 236

—— 'The nature of the FSA policy of rule use: a critical overview' (2008) 28 *Legal Studies* 119

—— 'Regulatory Interpretation: Conversational or Constructive?' (2010) 30 *Oxford Journal of Legal Studies* 361

—— 'The revision of the FSA's approach to regulation – an incomplete agenda?' (2010) 7 *Journal of Business Law* 599

Gilad S, 'Accountability or Expectations Management? The Role of the Ombudsman in Financial Regulation' (2008) 30 *Law and Policy* 227

—— 'Exchange without capture: the UK Financial Ombudsman Service's struggle for accepted domain' (2008) 86 *Public Administration* 907

—— 'Juggling conflicting demands: the case of the UK Financial Ombudsman Service' (2008) 19 *Journal of Public Administration Research and Theory* 661

Gilligan G, 'Historical Touchstones in the Regulation of the Financial Services Sector: The Evolution of Financial Services Regulation' (1992) 1 *Journal of Financial Regulation and Compliance* 63

—— 'The origins of UK financial services regulation' (1997) 18 *Company Lawyer* 167

Goh N, 'Non-reliance clauses and contractual estoppel: corporately sensible or anomalous?' (2015) 7 *Journal of Business Law* 511

Golden J, 'The courts, the financial crisis and systemic risk' (2009) 4 *Capital Markets Law Journal* 141

Goodhart C, Hartmann P, and Llewellyn D, 'Reflections on Financial Regulation' (1997) 3 *Bank of England and SIB Financial Stability Review* 51

Gossé J and Plihon D, 'The future of financial markets and regulation: what strategy for Europe?' (2014) 16 *Foresight* 95

Grant J, 'Bernanke Calls for US to Follow UK's "Principles-based" Approach' *Financial Times* (Washington, 16 March 2007)

—— and Guha K, 'Paulson Seeks British-Style Flexibility in Capital Markets' *Financial Times* (London, 21 November 2006)

Gray J, 'The Legislative Basis of Systemic Review and Compensation for the Mis-Selling of Retail Financial Services and Products' (2004) 25 *Statute Law Review* 196

—— 'Legal Commentary: *Titan Steel Wheels Ltd v Royal Bank of Scotland Plc*' (2010) 18 *Journal of Financial Regulation and Compliance* 293

Greene S, 'Unfair terms in consumer contracts: implementation in Ireland' (1995) 6 *International Company and Corporate Law Review* 333

Grundmann S, 'The Bankinter Case on MIFID Regulation and Contract Law' (2013) 9 *European Review of Contract Law* 267

Haar B, 'Investor protection through model case procedures – implementing collective goals and individual rights under the 2012 amendment to the German Capital Markets Model Case Act (KapMuG)' (2014) 15 *European Business Organisation Law Review* 83

Hacker P, 'The Behavioral Divide: A Critique of the Differential Implementation of Behavioral Law and Economics in the US and the EU' (2015) 4 *European Review of Private Contract Law* 299

Hamilton J, 'Negligence in the corridor? The interaction between "separate rooms" of regulation and the common law in financial services' (2007) 23 *Professional Negligence* 134

Hamilton W, 'The Ancient Maxim Caveat Emptor' (1931) 40 *Yale Law Journal* 1133

Harding M, 'Equity and the rule of law' (2016) 132 *Law Quarterly Review* 278

Harris J, 'Will the FCA's product intervention strategy work?' (2011) 32 *Company Lawyer* 321

Herbert J and Bordeleau S, 'The application of the economic reality over legal form principle to threshold disclosures' (2009) 1 *International Business Law Journal* 80

Hill C and Maycock W, 'Temporary Product Intervention Rules: transient or intransigent?' (*Compliance Monitor*, 1 June 2012)

Hilton A, 'Lighter touch on regulation needs all-round support' *Evening Standard* (London, 2 December 2005)

Hindle J, 'The future of regulation' (2009) 17 *Journal of Financial Regulation and Compliance* 415

Hirschleifer D, 'Investor psychology and asset pricing' (2001) 56 *Journal of Finance* 1533

Ho L and Mathias T, 'Basis Clauses and the Unfair Contract Terms Act 1977' (2014) 130 *Law Quarterly Review* 377

Hooley R, 'Contractual estoppel and the Misrepresentation Act 1967' (2016) University of Cambridge Legal Studies Research Paper No 57/2016

Hopper M and Stainsby J, 'Principles-based regulation – better regulation?' (2006) 21 *Journal of International Banking Law and Regulation* 387

Horn N, 'Banks' Duties to Inform and to Give Advice under German Law' (1998) 11/12 *European Business Law Review* 367

Hoskins H and Watkins M, 'The Extent of a Bank's Duty of Care in Negligence to its Customer' (2016) 31 *Journal of International Banking and Financial Law* 112

Hughes A, 'The FSA was asleep on the job' (*Money Marketing*, 21 February 2013)

Inderst R, 'Retail finance: thoughts on reshaping regulation and consumer protection after the financial crisis' (2009) 10 *European Business Organisation Law Review* 455

—— and Ottaviani M, 'Regulating financial advice' (2012) 13 *European Business Organisation Law Review* 237

Jansen J, 'Case Note – Judgment of the Bundesgerichtshof (Federal Court of Justice of Germany) of 22 March 2011: Passion to Inform – BGH Expands Banks' Advisory Duties' (2011) 12 *German Law Journal* 1492

Jolls C, 'Behavioral Law and Economics' (2007) National Bureau of Economic Research Working Paper No 12879

—— and Sunstein C and Thaler R, 'A Behavioral Approach to Law and Economics' (1998) 50 *Stanford Law Review* 1471

Jolowicz J, 'The protection of the consumer and purchaser of goods under English Law' (1969) 32 *The Modern Law Review* 1

Jordans R, 'Investor protection in Germany through investment-advice protocol, product-information sheets and extended statute of limitation' (2010) 25 *Journal of International Banking Law and Regulation* 257

—— 'Information duties about payments received for distribution of financial products – an overview of German case law' (2013) 28 *Journal of International Banking Law and Regulation* 14

Joseph D and Brown E, 'Equity set alongside freedom of contract: Deutsche Bank Unitech, round two' (2016) 31 *Journal of International Banking and Financial Law* 393

Kalss S, 'Civil law protection of investors in Austria – a situation report from amidst a wave of investor lawsuits' (2012) 13 *European Business Organization Law Review* 211

Kaplow L, 'Rules versus Standards: An Economic Analysis' (1992) 42 *Duke Law Journal* 557

Kempson E, Collard S, and Moore N, 'Fair and reasonable – An assessment of the Financial Ombudsman Service' (2004) Personal Finance Research Centre, University of Bristol

Kessler F, 'Contracts of Adhesion – Some Thoughts About Freedom of Contract' (1943) 43 *Columbia Law Review* 629

—— 'The Protection of the Consumer Under Modern Sales Law' (1964) 74 *Yale Law Journal* 262

Khalique F, 'Mis-selling: The importance of Crestsign v RBS' *Euromoney Magazine* (London, 17 April 2015)

Kingsford Smith D, 'Regulating investment risk: individuals and the global financial crisis' (2009) 32 *University of New South Wales Law Journal* 514

Klohn L, 'Preventing excessive retail investor trading under MiFID: a behavioural law and economics perspective' (2009) 10 *European Business Organization Law Review* 437

Korobkin R and Ulen T, 'Law and Behavioural Science: Removing the Rationality Assumption from Law and Economics' (2000) 88 *California Law Review* 1051

Kronman A, 'Paternalism and the Law of Contracts' (1983) 92 *The Yale Law Journal* 763

Kovas A, 'UCITS – Past, Present and Future in a World of Increasing Product Diversity' (2006) Institute for Law and Finance Working Paper Series No 44, 02/2006

La Blanc G and Rachlinski J, 'In Praise of Investor Irrationality' (2005) Cornell Law School Research Paper No 05-006

Langevoort D, 'Selling Hope, Selling Risk: Some Lessons for Law from Behavioural Economics about Stockbrokers and Sophisticated Customers' (1996) 84 *California Law Review* 627

—— 'Managing the "Expectations Gap" in Investor Protection: The SEC and the Post-Enron Agenda' (2002) Georgetown University Law Center, Working Paper Series in Business Economics and Regulatory Law No 328080

Lau A, Rajaretnam T, and Young A, 'Mis-selling of financial products in Hong Kong: the problem, limitation and a proposition' (2016) 37 *Company Lawyer* 104

Leece D, 'Inappropriate Sales in the Financial Services Industry: The Limits of the Rational Calculus?' (2000) 21 *Managerial and Decision Economics* 133

Leff A, 'Contract as thing' (1970) 19 *The American University Law Review* 131

Leggatt G, 'Making sense of contracts: the rational choice theory' (2015) 131 *Law Quarterly Review* 454

Levitin A, 'The Consumer Financial Protection Bureau: An Introduction' (2013) 32 *Review of Banking and Financial Law* 321

Llewellyn D, 'The regulation and supervision of financial institutions' (1986) Institute of Bankers

—— 'Regulation of Retail Investment Services' (1995) 15 *Economic Affairs* 12

—— 'Consumer protection in retail investment services: Protection against what?' (1995) 3 *Journal of Financial Regulation and Compliance* 43

—— 'The case for financial regulation' (1999) 1 *Journal of International Financial Markets* 153

—— 'The Economic Rationale for Financial Regulation: FSA Occasional Paper 1' (1999) 26

Llewellyn K, 'What Price Contract? An Essay in Perspective' (1931) 40 *The Yale Law Journal* 704

Lo A, 'Regulatory Reform in the Wake of the Financial Crisis of 2007–2008' (2009) 1 *Journal of Financial Economic Policy* 4

Lodge M and Wegrich K, 'The Rationality Paradox of Nudge: Rational Tools of Government in a World of Bounded Rationality' (2016) 38 *Law and Policy* 250

Loewenstein G and Ubel P, 'Economics Behaving Badly' *New York Times* (New York, 14 July 2010)

Lomnicka E, 'Curtailing section 62 actionability' (1991) *July Journal of Business Law* 353

Loss L, 'The Protection of Investors: The Role of Government' (1963) 80 *South African Law Journal* 53

Loughrey S and Enderby Smith C, 'Banking litigation: a changing landscape?' (2015) 9 *Journal of International Banking and Financial Law* 563

Lowenfels L and Bromberg A, 'Suitability in Securities Transactions' (1999) 54 *The Business Lawyer* 1557

MacDonald J, Phipps S, and Holderness K, 'The Conduct of Business Rules and the Sale of Structured Products to Retail Customers' (2012) 1 *Journal of International Banking and Financial Law* 58

Maclean C, 'Judicial Review of the FCA Review Process on Swap Misselling' (*Banking Disputes Blog*, 10 October 2013): https://mbmcommercial.co.uk/Banking-Disputes-Blog/Banking-disputes/Judicial-review-of-the-fca-review-process-on-swap-misselling.htm, accessed 25 October 2015

—— and Morrison N, 'Hedges: a financial plague' (2014) 59 *The Journal of the Law Society of Scotland* 20

MacNeil I, 'FSA 1986: does s62 provide an effective remedy for breaches of Conduct of Business Rules?' (1994) 15 *Company Lawyer* 172

—— 'The Future for Financial Regulation: The Financial Services and Markets Bill' (1999) 62 *The Modern Law Review* 725

—— 'Uncertainty in commercial law' (2009) 13 *Edinburgh Law Review* 68

—— 'The trajectory of regulatory reform in the UK in the wake of the financial crisis' (2010) 11 *European Business Organization Law Review* 483

—— 'Rethinking conduct regulation' (2015) 30 *Journal of International Banking and Financial Law* 413

Majumdar S, 'Entire agreement, non-reliance clauses and contractual estoppel – what do they prevent and how?' Radcliffe Chambers (undated)

Mak V, 'Standards of Protection: In Search of the "Average Consumer" of EU Law in the Proposal for a Consumer Rights Directive' (2011) 19 *European Review of Private Law* 25

Marinelli N and Mazzoli C, 'Profiling investors within the MiFID: current practice and future prospects' (2010) Research paper for Ascosim

Markesinis B and Fedtke J, 'Authority or Reason? The Economic Consequences of Liability for Breach of Statutory Duty in a Comparative Perspective' (2007) 18 *European Business Law Review* 1

Markham J, 'Protecting the Institutional Investor – Jungle Predator or Shorn Lamb' (1995) 12 *Yale Journal on Regulation* 345

Marshall P, 'Interest rate swaps and the sale of the unknown: blind alleys, an enfeebled equity and the triumph of certainty over fairness' (2014) 29 *Journal of International Banking and Financial Law* 9

—— 'Humpty Dumpty is broken: "unsuitable" and "inappropriate" swaps transactions' (2014) 29 *Journal of International Banking and Financial Law* 679

—— 'Novating mis-sold swaps: the poverty of narrowly contractual analysis' (2015) 30 *Journal of International Banking and Financial Law* 11

—— 'Fault lines in English financial law: Thornbridge v Barclays Bank' (2016) 31 *Journal of International Banking and Financial Law* 266

Martin E, 'High Court backs Principles in PPI battle' (*Compliance Monitor*, 1 May 2011)

Mason A, 'The Place of Equity and Equitable Remedies in the Contemporary Common Law World' (1994) 110 *Law Quarterly Review* 238

Mason L, 'Non-Reliance Clauses: Past, Present (And Futile?)' (2009) 20 *European Business Law Review* 623

—— 'Consumers and Unfair Contract Terms: Inadequate Legal Protection and Suggestions for Reform' (2014) 44 *Hong Kong Law Journal* Part 1

—— 'Precluding liability for pre-contractual misrepresentation: the function and validity of non-reliance clauses' (2014) 4 *Journal of Business Law* 313

—— 'Protecting Consumers from Unfair Terms in Standard Form Contracts: The UK Approach' (2015) 26 *European Business Law Review* 335

Maynard L, 'Holmcroft Properties: will a contractual phoenix rise from its ashes?' (2016) 31 *Journal of International Banking and Financial Law* 356

McMeel G, 'The Consumer Dimension of Financial Services Law: Lessons from the Pension Mis-Selling Scandal' (1999) 3 *Company Financial and Insolvency Law Review* 29

—— 'Documentary Fundamentalism in the Senior Courts: The myth of contractual estoppel' (2011) *Lloyd's Maritime and Corporate Law Quarterly* 185

—— 'International Issues in the Regulation of Financial Advice: A United Kingdom Perspective – The Retail Distribution Review and the Ban on Commission Payments to Financial Intermediaries' (2013) 87 *St John's Law Review* 595

McVea H, 'Financial services regulation under the Financial Services Authority: a reassertion of the market failure thesis?' (2005) 64 *Cambridge Law Journal* 413

—— and Cumper P, 'The Financial Ombudsman Service and disputes involving "wider implications" issues' (2007) Part 2 *Lloyd's Maritime and Corporate Law Quarterly* 246

Merricks W, 'The Financial Ombudsman Services: not just an alternative to court' (2007) 15 *Journal of Financial Regulation and Compliance* 135

Micklitz H, 'The Visible Hand of European Regulatory Private Law: The Transformation of European Private Law from Autonomy to Functionalism in Competition and Regulation' (2008) EUI Working Papers

Millett P, 'Equity's Place in the Law of Commerce' (1998) 114 *Law Quarterly Review* 214

Minor J, 'Consumer protection in the EU: searching for the real consumer' (2012) 13 *European Business Organisation Law Review* 163

Mitchell C, 'Suitability of investments' (*Compliance Monitor*, 11 April 2012)

Mitchell G, 'To advise or not to advise?' (2014) 29 *Journal of International Banking and Financial Law* 686

—— and Knight A, 'Swaps: signs of a shift?' (2015) 260 *Legal Business* 72

Moloney N, 'Building a retail investment culture through law: the 2004 Markets in Financial Instruments Directive' (2005) 6 *European Business Organization Law Review* 341

—— 'Large-Scale Reform of Investor Protection Regulation: The European Union Experience' (2007) 4 *Macquarie Journal of Business Law* 147

—— 'EU Financial Market Regulation after the Global Financial Crisis: "More Europe" or more Risks?' (2010) 47 *Common Market Law Review* 1317

—— 'The Investor Model Underlying the EU's Investor Protection Regime: Consumers or Investors?' (2012) 13 *European Business Organization Law Review* 169
—— 'Brexit, the EU and its Investment Banker: Rethinking Equivalence for the EU Capital Market' (2017) LSE Legal Studies Working Paper No 5/2017
—— 'LSE Law Brexit Special #6: Negotiating a Financial Services Deal' (2017) LSE Law – Policy Briefing Paper No 25-2017
—— 'EU Financial Market Governance and the Retail Investor: Reflections at an Inflection Point' (2018) 37 *Yearbook of European Law* 25
Momberg R, 'Beyond the Risk: Swaps, Financial Crisis and Change of Circumstances; Comparative Case Note: Supreme Court of Portugal – 10.10.2013' (2015) 23 *European Review of Private Law* 81
Morris P, 'The intersection of corporate powers and complaints: the Financial Ombudsman Service, consumer protection and the courts' (2009) Part 3 *Lloyd's Maritime and Corporate Law Quarterly* 344
—— and James R, 'The Financial Ombudsman Services: a brave new world in "ombudsmanry"?' [2002] *Public Law* 640
Nakamoto M, 'Tokyo Eyes Move Towards UK-style Financial Regulation' *Financial Times* (London, 25 October 2007)
Nelson M, 'Behavioural evidence on the effects of principles- and rules-based standards' (2002) 17 *Accounting Horizons* 91
Nelson P, 'Information and consumer behaviour' (1970) 78 *Journal of Political Economy* 311
Newman J, 'Impact of the Financial Crisis on Fixed Rate Swap Payors' (2010) *New England Real Estate Journal*
Nicholas B, 'Rules and Terms – Civil Law and Common Law' (1973–74) 48 *Tulane Law Review* 946
Nobles R, 'Rules, Principles and Ombudsmen: Norwich and Peterborough Building Society v the Financial Ombudsman Service' (2003) 66 *The Modern Law Review* 781
Nolan D, 'Deconstructing the duty of care' (2013) 123 *The Law Quarterly Review* 559
O'Sullivan J, 'Suing in tort where no contractual claim will lie – a bird's eye view' (2007) 23 *Professional Negligence* 165
Ogilvie M H, 'Banks, Advice-Giving and Fiduciary Obligation' (1985) 17 *Ottawa Law Review* 263
Ovey E, 'Balancing the scales: firms v consumers' (2009) 24 *Journal of International Banking and Financial Law* 330
Padfield A, 'The impact on English contract law of the EC Directive on unfair terms in consumer contracts' (1995) 10 *Journal of International Banking Law* 175
Patient J, 'Treating customers fairly: the challenges of principles-based regulation' (2007) 22 *Journal of International Banking Law and Regulation* 420
Philippe D, 'Unforeseen Circumstances in Belgian Law' (2015) 1 *European Review of Private Law* 101
Picciotto S, 'Introduction: Reconceptualizing Regulation in the Era of Globalization' (2002) 29 *Journal of Law and Society* 1
Pimlott G, 'The Reform of Investor Protection in the UK – An Examination of the Proposals of the Gower Report and the UK Government's White Paper of January 1985' (1985) 7 *Journal of Comparative Business and Capital Markets Law* 141
Pistor K and Xu C, 'Incomplete Law – A Conceptual and Analytical Framework and its Application to the Evolution of Financial Market Regulation' (2003) 35 *Journal of International Law and Politics* 931
Poro L, 'Unfair corporate practices in financial services: is the EU legal framework sufficient to protect consumers' (2014) 29 *Journal of International Banking Law and Regulation* 422
Posner R, 'Theories of Economic Regulation' (1974) 5 *The Bell Journal of Economics and Management Science* 335
—— 'Rational Choice, Behavioral Economics, and the Law' (1998) 50 *Stanford Law Review* 1551
—— 'Treating Financial Consumers as Consenting Adults' *Wall Street Journal* (New York, 23 July 2009)
Pritchard J, 'Investment Protection Sacrificed: The New Settlement and s 62' (1992) 13 *Company Lawyer* 171
Proctor C, 'The euro – fragmentation and the financial markets' (2011) 6 *Capital Markets Law Journal* 5
Rachlinski J, 'The Uncertain Psychological Case for Paternalism' (2003) 97 *Northwestern Law Review* 1165

Rakoff T, 'Contracts of Adhesion: An Essay in Reconstruction' (1983)

Ramsay I, 'Consumer law and the search for empowerment' (1991) 19 *Canadian Business Law* 397

Rawlings P, Georgosouli A, and Russo C, 'Regulation of financial services: Aims and methods' (2014) Queen Mary (Centre for Corporate Law Studies)

Raz J, 'Legal principles and the limits of law' (1972) 81 *The Yale Law Journal* 823

Reid K, 'Legislative Comment: Unfair Terms in Consumer Contract Regulations 1994' (1995) 16 *Company Lawyer* 280

Reyes E, 'Roundtable: Financial Mis-selling: Costly business' (2013) *Law Society Gazette* Issue 25

Reynolds P, 'Selling financial products: the interface between regulatory and common law standards' (2014) 29 *Journal of International Banking Law and Regulation* 269

Riley-Smith T, 'FCA regulation of interest rate hedging products: one rule for some?' (2015) 30 *Journal of International Banking and Financial Law* 425

Ring P, 'A critical analysis of depolarisation' (2004) 12 *Journal of Financial Regulation and Compliance* 248

—— 'The retail distribution review' (2016) 24 *Journal of Financial Regulation and Compliance* 140

Robb V, 'The genesis of regulation: How has regulation developed in the UK and what are the new arrangements' (1997) 3 *Bank of England and SIB Financial Stability Review* 29

Roberts S, 'The interest rate hedge mis-selling saga: three recent judgments and a pending appeal' [2015] *Recovery* 38

Rose C, 'The challenges of quantifying investor protection in a comparative context' (2007) 8 *European Business Organization Law Review* 369

Ryley P and Virgo J, 'Mis-selling of personal pension plans: A legal perspective' (1999) 5 *Journal of Pensions Management* 18

Samuel A, 'Consumer financial services in Britain: new approaches to dispute resolution and avoidance' (2002) 3 *European Business Organisation Law Review* 649

—— 'Contract Certainty – the new regulatory battlefield' (*Compliance Monitor*, 1 June 2005)

—— 'Principles-based regulation, MiFID and the new financial promotion rules' (2007) 49 *Compliance Officer Bulletin* 1

—— 'Who is the sophisticated investor?' (*Compliance Monitor*, 10 December 2013)

Schillig M, 'Inequality of bargaining power versus market for lemons: legal paradigm' (2008) 33 *European Law Review* 336

—— 'Legislative Comment: Directive 93/13 and the "price term exemption": a comparative analysis in the light of the "market for lemons" rationale' (2011) 60 *International and Comparative Law Quarterly* 933

Schlag P, 'Rules and Standards' (1985) 33 *UCLA Law Review* 379

Schwarcz S, 'Regulating Complexity in Financial Markets' (2009) 87 *Washington University Law Review* 211

Scott J and Strum S, 'Courts as Catalysts: Re-Thinking the Judicial Role in New Governance' (2006) 13 *Columbia Journal of European Law* 565

Selman A, 'Regulation of UK retail investment business' (1996) 3 *European Financial Services Law Journal* 331

Shafir E, 'A behavioural perspective on consumer protection' (2008) 15 *Competition and Consumer Law Journal* 302

Sharpe A, 'Legislative comment: Australian consumer law on unfair contract terms' (2010) 16 *Computer and Telecommunications Law Review* 128

Shaw S, 'Mifid II: Europe's answer to RDR' (*Money Marketing*, 19 June 2014)

Shleifer A, 'Efficient Regulation' (2010) NBER Working Paper Series, Working Paper No 15651

Simmonds J, 'Bankers' documents and the Unfair Terms in Consumer Contracts Regulations' (2002) 17 *Journal of International Banking Law* 205

Sivathillainathan K, 'Unnatural selection in financial mis-selling' (2017) *New Law Journal*: www.newlawjournal.co.uk/content/unnatural-selection-financial-mis-selling, accessed 24 March 2017

Sivathillainathan S, 'David v Goliath Litigation' (2017) *Solicitors Journal*: www.solicitorsjournal.com/comment/201702/david-v-goliath-litigation, accessed 24 March 2017

Slawson W, 'Standard Form Contracts and Democratic Control of Lawmaking Power' (1971) 84 *Harvard Law Review* 529

Smith J, 'Out with "TCF" and in with "fiduciary"?' (2012) 27 *Journal of International Banking and Financial Law* 343
Speaight A and Hamilton P, 'Restoring the Rule of Law to Financial Services Compensation: The Defects of the FOS and Constructive Proposals for Reform' (2011)
Spindler G, 'Behavioural Finance and Investor Protection Regulations' (2011) 34 *Journal of Consumer Policy* 315
Stanton K, 'Case comment: Andrews v SBJ Benefit Consultants Ltd [2010] EWHC 2875 (Ch)' (2012) 26 *Professional Negligence* 67
Staple G and Anderson K, 'Financial services and markets: Civil rights of action' (2001) 9 *Journal of Financial Regulation and Compliance* 237
Stigler G, 'The Theory of Economic Regulation' (1971) 2 *Bell Journal of Economics and Management Science* 3
Stöhr A, 'Approaches to financial regulation in view of the crisis: Report about the 34th meeting of the German Comparative Law Society' (2015) 23 *Journal of Financial Regulation and Compliance* 73
Stoyanov D, 'Causa and Consideration – A Comparative Overview', Challenges of the Knowledge Society conference, Bucharest, May 2016
Stretton J, 'Regulating Life Assurance: Objectives and Machinery' (1995) 15 *Economic Affairs* 34
Sunstein C, 'Problems with Rules' (1995) 83 *California Law Review* 953
—— 'Deciding by Default' (2013) 162 *University of Pennsylvania Law Review* 1
—— 'Nudging: A Very Short Guide' (2014) 37 *Journal of Consumer Policy* 583
—— 'The Ethics of Nudging' (2015) 32 *Yale Journal on Regulation* 413
—— and Thaler R, 'Libertarian Paternalism Is Not an Oxymoron' (2003) 70 *University of Chicago Law Review* 1159
—— and Thaler R, 'Human Frailty Caused This Crisis' *Financial Times* (New York, 11 November 2008)
Tattersall J, 'Key differences in regulatory approaches: What do they mean in practice?' (1996) 4 *Journal of Financial Regulation and Compliance* 292
Tettenborn A, 'Professional liability and remoteness: contract v tort' (2016) 32 *Professional Negligence* 68
Thomas C, 'What role should substantive fairness have in the English law of contract? An overview of the law' (2010) 6 *Cambridge Student Law Review* 177
Twigger A, 'Sophisticated Investors: do they have any rights?' (2010) 25 *Journal of International Banking and Financial Law* 515
Uff J, 'Standard contract terms and the common law' (1993) 9 *Construction Law Journal* 108
Van Wijck P, 'Protection against Unfair Contracts: An Economic Analysis of European Regulation' (2000) 9 *European Journal of Law and Economics* 73
Vestini L, 'Recent decisions of Italian Courts on Interest Rate Swaps' (2013) 3 *Bankpedia* 7
von Gaudecker H M, 'How Does Household Portfolio Diversification Vary with Financial Literacy and Financial Advice?' (2015) 70 *The Journal of Finance* 489
Walker D, 'Financial Services: The Principles Initiative' (1989) 4 *Journal of International Banking and Financial Law* 51
Walker G, 'UK borrowers collared by interest rate flaws' (2012) 27 *Journal of International Banking Law and Regulation* 321
Warren E, 'Unsafe at any rate' (2007) 8 *Democracy: A Journal of Ideas* 8
—— 'Product safety regulation as a model for financial services regulation' (2008) 42 *The Journal of Consumer Affairs* 452
Weatherill S, 'The Role of the Informed Consumer in European Community Law and Policy' (1994) 2 *Consumer Law Journal* 49
—— 'Consumer protection under EU law 'is not absolute': yes, but be careful!' (2012) 8 *European Review of Contract Law* 221
Welle E, 'Freedom of Contract and the Securities Laws: Opting Out of Securities Regulation by Private Agreement' (1999) 56 *Washington and Lee Law Review* 519
Wheatley M, 'Rethinking investor protection' (2011) 2 *JASSA The Finsia Journal of Applied Finance* 6
White R, 'The Review of Investor Protection. The Gower Report' (1984) 47 *The Modern Law Review* 553

Whittaker A M, 'Better Regulation – Principles vs Rules' (2006) 21 *Journal of International Banking Law and Regulation* 233
Whittaker S, 'A framework of principle for European contract law?' (2009) 125 *Law Quarterly Review* 616
—— 'The Optional Instrument of European Contract Law and Freedom of Contract' (2011) 7 *European Review of Contract Law* 371
Williams M, 'New Targets for Litigation?' (2009) 159 *New Law Journal* 444
Williams T, 'Empowerment of Whom and for What? Financial Literacy Education and the New Regulation of Consumer Financial Services' (2007) 29 *Law and Policy* 226
—— 'Who wants to watch? A comment on the new international paradigm of financial consumer market regulation' (2013) 36 *Seattle University Law Review* 1217
Willett C, 'General clauses and the competing ethics of European consumer law in the UK' (2012) 71 *Cambridge Law Journal* 412
Wood G, 'Too much regulation?' (2001) 9 *Journal of Financial Regulation and Compliance* 350
Wood P, 'Legal Impact of the Financial Crisis' (2008) 11 *Journal of International Banking and Financial Law* 575
—— 'Life after Lehmans: Survey of Changes in Market Practice' (2009) 10 *Journal of International Banking and Financial Law* 579
Wright J, 'Behavioral Law and Economics, Paternalism and Consumer Contracts: An Empirical Perspective' (2007) 2 *NYU Journal of Law and Liberty* 470
—— 'A "Plain Vanilla" Proposal for Behavioral Law and Economics' (*Truth on the Market*, 16 July 2010): http://truthonthemarket.com/2010/07/16/a-plain-vanilla-proposal-for-behavioral-law-and-economics/, accessed 22 January 2015
—— and Ginsburg D, 'Behavioral law and economics: Its origins, fatal flaws, and implications for liberty' (2012) 106 *Northwestern University Law Review* 1033
Wright R and Ward A, 'The liability of UK banks for financial advice – recent developments' (1996) 11 *Journal of International Banking Law* 472
Yeung K, 'Nudge as Fudge' (2012) 75 *The Modern Law Review* 122
—— 'Better Regulation, Administrative Sanctions and Constitutional Values' (2013) 33 *Legal Studies* 312
Zepeda R, 'Derivatives mis-selling by British banks and the failed legacy of the FSA' (2013) 28 *Journal of International Banking Law and Regulation* 209
Zunzunegui F, 'Mis-selling of preferred shares to Spanish retail clients' (2014) 29 *Journal of International Banking Law and Regulation* 174

Policy Documents

AFM, Policy and Priorities for the 2007–2009 Period' (2007)
—— 'Central Focus on Client Interests at banks and insurers' (2011)
—— 'Summary Annual Report for 2012' (2012)
AMF, 'The Challenges of the New Regulatory Environment: How is the French Financial Community Adapting?' (2006)
—— and ACP, 'Marketing of complex financial instruments' (2010) AMF position no 2010-05 and the ACP recommendation no 2010-R-10
—— 'News Release: The Autorité des Marchés Financiers calls for extreme vigilance regarding non-standard investments proposed to the public' (2012)
ASIC, 'Money Smart': www.moneysmart.gov.au/investing/investing-basics, accessed 15 December 2014
—— 'Report 224: Access to financial advice in Australia' (2010)
—— 'Report 377: Review of advice on retail structured products' (2013)
—— 'Regulatory Guide 36, Licensing: Financial product advice and dealing' (2013)
—— 'Report 384: Regulating complex products' (2014)
—— 'Report 427, Investing in hybrid securities: Explanations based on behavioural economics' (2015)

Association of Professional Financial Advisers, 'The Advice Market Post RDR Review' (2014)
Australian Government, 'Design and Distribution Obligations and Product Intervention Power: Proposals Paper' (2016)
BaFIN, 'Retail Investors Protection Act: Improved transparency on the unregulated capital market' (2015)
Bank of England, 'Financial Stability Report' Issue No 37 (2015)
Basic Skills Agency and FSA, 'Adult Financial Capability Framework' (2003)
Beachcroft LLP, 'Opening up, Reaching out and Aiming high – An agenda for accessibility and excellence in the Financial Ombudsman Service' The Independent Review of the Financial Ombudsman Services by Rt Hon Lord Hunt of Wirral MBE (2008)
Better Regulation Commission, *Risk, Responsibility, Regulation: Whose Risk is it Anyway?* (Cabinet Office 2006)
Better Regulation Task Force, *Principles of Good Regulation* (Cabinet Office 2003)
Board of Trade, *Fixed Trusts – Report of the Departmental Committee Appointed by the Board of Trade* (Cmd 5259, 1936)
BVA, 'French Government: Nudge Me Tender' (2014)
Central Bank of Ireland, 'Consultation on the Protection of Retail Investors in relation to the Distribution of CFDs: Consultation Paper 107' (2017)
Centre for Competition Policy and Federation of Small Businesses, 'Small Businesses As Consumers: Are They Sufficiently Well Protected?' (2014)
CESR, 'A Consumer's Guide to MiFID: Investing in Financial Products' CESR/08-003 (2008)
—— 'Questions and Answers: MiFID complex and non-complex financial instruments for the purpose of the Directive's appropriateness requirements' CESR/09-559 (2009)
CFA Institute & Edelman, 'Investor Trust Study' (2013)
Citizens Advice Bureau, 'The experiences of small businesses as consumers in regulated markets' (2014)
CMVM, 'Policy on complex financial products' (2012)
Commission of the Regulation of US Capital Markets in the 21st Century, 'Report and Recommendations' (2007)
Committee on Economic and Monetary Affairs, 'On the proposal for a European Parliament and Council directive on investment services and regulated market, and amending Council Directives 85/611/EEC, Council Directive 93/6/EEC and European Parliament and Council 2000/12/EC (COM (2002) 625 – C5-0586/2002 – 2002/0269 (COD))' Rapporteur Theresa Villiers, A5-0287/2003 (2003)
—— 'Recommendation for Second Reading on the Council common position for adopting a European Parliament and Council directive on markets in financial instruments, amending Council Directives 85/611/EEC and 93/6/EEC and Directive 2000/12/EC of the European Parliament and of the Council and repealing Council Directive 93/22/EEC (13421/3/2003–C5-0015/2004–2002/0269(COD))' Rapporteur Theresa Villiers, A5-0114/2004 (2004)
—— 'Draft Report on Green Paper on Retail Financial Services' (2016/2056(INI))
Commonwealth of Australia Financial System Inquiry, 'Final Report' (2014)
Competition and Markets Authority, 'Unfair Contract Terms Guidance: Guidance on the unfair terms provisions in the Consumer Rights Act, Draft for consultation' CMA37 (2015)
—— 'Retail banking market investigation: Summary of provisional findings report' (2015)
Competition Commission, 'Market investigation into payment protection insurance' (2009)
CONSOB, 'Discussion Paper: Assessing investors' risk tolerance through a questionnaire' (2012)
—— 'Communication on Distribution of Complex Financial Products to Retail Investors, Communication No 0097996' (2014)
Consumer Affairs Victoria, 'Discussion Paper: What do we mean by 'vulnerable' and 'disadvantaged' consumers?' (2004)
Consumer Focus, 'Response to HM Treasury on the Draft Financial Services Bill' (2011)
Consumers International, 'Consumer Rights and Responsibilities': www.consumersinternational.org/who-we-are/consumer-rights, accessed 30 November 2014
Delmas-Marsalet J, 'Report on the marketing of financial products' (2005)

Department for Business, Enterprise, and Regulatory Reform, 'Consumer Law Review: Call for Evidence' (2008)
Department for Business, Innovation and Skills, 'Consumer Law Review: Call for Evidence: Summary of Responses' (2009)
—— 'Empowering and protecting consumers: consultation on institutional changes for provision of consumer information, education, advocacy and enforcement' (2011)
—— 'The Kay Review of UK Equity Markets and Long-Term Decision Making' (2012)
—— 'Enhancing Consumer Confidence by Clarifying Consumer Law: Consultation on the Supply of Goods, Services and Digital Content' (2012)
—— 'Small Business Survey 2012: Businesses with no employees' (2013)
Department for Exiting the European Union, 'The United Kingdom's exit from and new partnership with the European Union' (2017)
—— 'Legislating for the United Kingdom's withdrawal from the European Union' (Cm 9446, 2017)
Department of Trade and Industry, *Financial Services in the UK: A New Framework for Investor Protection* (HMSO, Cmnd 9432, 1985)
—— 'Defining the Private Investor: Consultative Document' (1990)
EBA, 'Technical advice on possible delegated acts on criteria and factors for intervention powers concerning structured deposits under Articles 41 and 42 of Regulation (EU) No 600/2014 (MiFIR)' Op/2014/13 (2014)
ESMA, 'Consultation Paper Guidelines on certain aspects of the MiFID suitability requirements' ESMA/2011/445 (2011)
—— 'Opinion: MiFID practices for firms selling complex products' ESMA/2014/146 (2014)
—— 'Discussion Paper: MiFID II/MiFIR' ESMA/2014/548 (2014)
—— 'Consultation Paper: MiFID II/MiFIR' ESMA/2014/549 (2014)
—— 'Final Report: Technical Advice to the Commission on MiFID II and MiFIR' ESMA/2014/1569 (2014)
—— 'Consultation Paper: Draft guidelines on complex debt instruments and structured deposits' ESMA/2015/610 (2015)
—— 'Guidelines on complex debt instruments and structured deposits' ESMA/2015/1787 (2016)
—— 'MiFID Suitability Requirements Peer Review Report' ESMA/2016/584 (2016)
—— 'Questions and Answers on MiFID II and MiFIR investor protection topics' ESMA35-43-349 (2017)
—— 'Final Report: Guidelines on MiFID II product governance requirements' ESMA 35-43-620 (2017)
—— 'Consultation Paper: Guidelines on certain aspects of the MiFID suitability requirements' ESMA35-43-748 (2017)
—— 'Final Report: Guidelines on certain aspects of the MiFID suitability requirements' ESMA35-43-869 (2018)
ESRC Centre for Competition Policy, 'Behavioural Economics in Competition and Consumer Policy' (2013)
European Commission, 'Communication in Implementing the Framework for Financial Markets Action Plan' (Communication) COM (1999) 232
—— 'Financial Services Action Plan' (1999)
—— 'Initial Report of the Committee of Wise Men on the Regulation of European Securities Markets' ('Lamfalussy Report') (2000)
—— 'The application of conduct of business rules under Article 11 of the Investment Services Directive (93/22/EEC)' (Communication) COM (2000) 722 final
—— 'Proposal for a Directive of the European Parliament and of the Council on Investment Services and Regulated Markets, and amending Council Directive 85/611/EEC, Council Directive 93/6/EEC and European Parliament and Council Directive 2000/12/EC' COM (2002) 625 final
—— 'Communication from the Commission of 12 February 2003 to the European Parliament and the Council – A more coherent European contract law – An action plan' COM (2003) 68 final

—— 'Communication from the Commission to the European Parliament and the Council: European Contract Law and the revision of the *acquis*: the way forward' COM (2004) 651 final
—— 'Financial Services Policy 2005-2010' COM (2005) 629 final
—— 'Green Paper on the Review of the Consumer Acquis' COM (2006) 744 final
—— 'Draft Commission Directive implementing Directive 2004/39/EC as regards organisational requirements and operating conditions' (2006) Background Note 15
—— 'Draft Commission Directive implementing Directive 2004/39/EC as regards organisational requirements and operating conditions' (2006) Background Note 31
—— 'Green Paper on Retail Financial Services in the Single Market' COM (2007) 226 final
—— 'Pre-Contractual Information for Financial Services: Qualitative study in the 27 Member States' (2008)
—— 'Your Questions on MiFID' (2008)
—— 'Guidance on the Implementation/Application of Directive 2005/29/EC on Unfair Corporate Practices' (2009)
—— 'Staff Working Document on the follow up in retail financial services to the consumer markets scoreboard' SEC (2009) 1251 final
—— 'Public Consultation: Review of the Markets in Financial Instruments Directive (MiFID)' (2010)
—— 'Consumer Decision-Making in Retail Investment Services: A Behavioural Economics Perspective, Final Report' (2010)
—— 'Proposal for a Directive of the European Parliament and of the Council on markets in financial instruments repealing Directive 2004/39/EC of the European Parliament and of the Council (Recast)' COM (2011) 656 final
—— 'Impact Assessment accompanying the document: Proposal for a Directive of the European Parliament and of the Council on Markets in Financial Instruments [Recast] and the Proposal for a Regulation of the European Parliament and of the Council on Markets in Financial Instruments [COM (2011) 656 final] and [SEC (2011) 1227 final]' SEC (2011) 1226 final
—— 'Study on the application of Directive 2005/29/EC on Unfair Corporate Practices in the EU, Part 1 – Synthesis Report' (2011)
—— 'Study on the application of Directive 2005/29/EC on Unfair Corporate Practices in the EU, Part 2 – Country Reports' Conducted by Civic Consulting (2011)
—— 'Special Eurobarometer 373, Retail Financial Services Report' (2012)
—— 'Report from the Commission to the European Parliament, the Council and the European Economic and Social Committee: First Report on the application of Directive 2005/29/EC of the European Parliament and of the Council of 11 May 2005 concerning unfair business-to-consumer corporate practices in the internal market and amending Council Directive 84/450/EEC, Directives 97/7/EC, 98/27/EC and 2002/65/EC of the European Parliament and of the Council and Regulation (EC) No 2006/2004 of the European Parliament and of the Council' (2013)
—— 'Applying Behavioural Sciences to EU Policy-making' (2013) EUR 26033 EN
—— 'More transparent and safer financial markets: European Commission welcomes European Parliament vote on updated rules for Markets in Financial Instruments (MiFID II)' Statement 14/129 (2014)
—— 'Emerging challenges in retail finance and consumer policy' Steering Notes: Session II – Behavioural economics and financial services (2014)
—— 'Green Paper on retail financial services: Better products, more choice, and greater opportunities for consumers and businesses' COM (2015) 630 final
—— "Summary of contributions to the 'Call for Evidence': EU regulatory framework for financial services' (2016)
European Parliament, 'Consumer Protection Aspects of Financial Services' (2014)
—— 'Legislative resolution of 24 November 2015 on the proposal for a directive of the European Parliament and of the Council on insurance mediation (recast)' (COM(2012)0360-C7-0180/2012-2012/0175(COD)) (2015)
FCA, 'Occasional Paper No 1: Applying behavioural economics at the Financial Conduct Authority' (2013)

—— 'The FCA's approach to advancing its objectives' (2013)
—— 'A response to Journey to the FCA: Your questions answered' (2013)
—— 'Business Plan 2013/2014' (2013)
—— 'Business Plan 2014/2015' (2014)
—— 'Vulnerability exposed: The consumer experience of vulnerability in financial services' (2014)
—— 'Post-implementation review of the RDR – Phase 1' (2014)
—— 'Consultation Paper CP14/10, Proposals for a price cap on high-cost short-term credit' (2014)
—— 'Consultation Paper CP14/23, Restrictions on the retail distribution of regulatory capital instruments' (2014)
—— 'Guidance Consultation GC14/03, Retail Advice: Clarifying the boundaries and exploring the barriers to market development' (2014)
—— 'Policy Statement PS14/16, Price cap on high-cost short-term credit' (2014)
—— 'Temporary Product Intervention Rules – Restrictions in relation to the retail distribution of contingent convertible instruments' (2014)
—— 'Response to the Eleventh Report of the Treasury Committee, 2014-15 Conduct and Competition in SME Lending' (2015)
—— 'Occasional Paper No 8: Consumer Vulnerability' (2015)
—— 'Business Plan 2015/2016' (2015)
—— 'Consultation Paper CP15/43, Markets in Financial Instruments Directive II Implementation – Consultation Paper I' (2015)
—— 'Discussion Paper DP15/3, Developing our approach to implementing MiFID II conduct of business and organisational requirements' (2015)
—— 'Discussion Paper DP15/7, Our approach to SMEs as users of financial services' (2015)
—— 'Finalised Guidance FG15/1, Retail Investment Advice' (2015)
—— 'Policy Statement PS15/22: General Insurance Add-Ons Market Study – Remedies: banning opt-out selling across financial services and supporting informed decision-making for add-on buyers' (2015)
—— 'Thematic Review TR15/2, Product Development and Governance' (2015)
—— 'Thematic Review TR15/12, Wealth management firms and private banks: Suitability of investment portfolios' (2015)
—— 'Feedback Statement FS15/5, Feedback statement to The FCA's approach to advancing its objectives' (2015)
—— 'Response to the Eleventh Report of the Treasury Committee, 2014-15 Conduct and Competition in SME Lending June 2015' (2015)
—— 'Insistent clients: good and poor practice' (2016)
—— 'The Financial Conduct Authority's response to the European Commission's call for evidence on the EU regulatory framework for financial services' (2016)
—— 'Thematic Review TR16/1, Assessing suitability: Research and due diligence of products and services' (2016)
—— 'Occasional Paper No 13: Economics for Effective Regulation' (2016)
—— 'Occasional Paper No 24: Behaviour and Compliance in Organisations' (2016)
—— 'Business Plan 2016/17' (2016)
—— 'The Financial Conduct Authority's response to the European Commission Green Paper: Retail Financial Services' (2016)
—— 'FCA survey of firms providing financial advice' (2016)
—— 'Occasional Paper 17: Access to Financial Services in the UK' (2016)
—— 'Statement on European Union referendum result' (2016)
—— 'Annual Report and Accounts 2015/16' (2016)
—— 'Consultation Paper CP 16/29, Markets in Financial Instruments Directive II Implementation – Consultation Paper III' (2016)
—— 'Our Future Mission' (2016)
—— 'Consultation Paper CP 16/40: Enhancing conduct of business rules for firms providing contract for difference products to retail clients' (2017)

—— 'Guidance Consultation GC17/4: Financial Advice Market Review (FAMR): Implementation part 1' (2017)
—— 'Our Mission 2017: How we regulate financial services' (2017)
—— 'Business Plan 2017/18' (2017)
—— 'The Assessing Suitability Review – Results' (2017)
—— 'Asset Management Market Study: Final Report MS15/2.3' (2017)
—— 'Annual Report and Accounts 2016/17' (2017)
—— 'Policy Statement PS17/14, Markets in Financial Instruments Directive II Implementation – Policy Statement II' (2017)
—— 'Annual Public Meeting' (2017)
—— 'Consultation Paper CP17/28, Financial Advice Market Review (FAMR): implementation Part II and insistent clients' (2017)
—— 'Consultation Paper CP18/31, Increasing the award limit for the Financial Ombudsman Service' (2018)
—— 'Consultation Paper CP18/37: Product intervention measures for retail binary options' (2018)
—— 'Consultation Paper CP18/38: Restricting contract for difference products sold to retail clients and a discussion of other retail derivative products' (2018)
—— 'Discussion Paper DP18/5, On a duty of care and potential alternative approaches' (2018)
—— 'Policy Statement PS18/21, SME access to the Financial Ombudsman Service – near-final rules' (2018)
—— 'Policy Statement PS19/8, Increasing the award limit for the Financial Ombudsman Service' (2019)
—— and PRA, 'Consultation Paper CP15/9, Strengthening accountability in banking: a new regulatory framework for individuals' (2015)
FCA Practitioner Panel, 'Consumer Responsibility: Identifying and closing the gap' (2013)
FCAC, 'Guidance to investors': www.fcac-acfc.gc.ca/Eng/resources/educationalPrograms/ft-of/Pages/home-accueil.aspx, accessed 15 December 2014
FINRA, 'Guidance to the industry': www.finra.org/industry/guidance, accessed 15 December 2014
FMA, '10 Commandments of Investing Money': www.fma.gv.at/en/the-basics-the-financial-market/the-basics-consultations-with-advisers/, accessed 15 December 2014
FOS, 'The ombudsman and smaller businesses: your guide to the FOS' www.financial-ombudsman.org.uk/publications, accessed 22 October 2014
—— 'The ombudsman and larger businesses: your guide to the FOS': www.financial-ombudsman.org.uk/publications, accessed 22 October 2014
—— 'Case studies – IRHPs': www.financial-ombudsman.org.uk/publications/ombudsman-news/112/112-hedging-products.html, accessed 7 November 2014
—— 'Micro-enterprises and financial services: a review of complaints' (2015)
—— 'Annual Report and Accounts for the year ended 31 March 2016' (HC 309, 2016)
FSA, 'Consumer Research 5: Informed Decisions? How Consumers use Key Features: a synthesis of research on the use of product information at the point of sale' (2000)
—— 'A new regulator for the new millennium' (2000)
—— 'Consumer Research Paper No 5: Informed Decisions? How Consumers use Key Features: a synthesis of research on the use of product information at the point of sale' (2000)
—— 'Regulation of Stakeholder Pensions – Feedback on CP61' (2001)
—— 'Building financial capability in the UK' (2003)
—— 'Reasonable expectations: Regulation in a non-zero failure world' (2003)
—— 'Towards a National Strategy for Financial Capability' (2003)
—— 'FSA advises industry on definition of "mis-selling"' (2003): www.fsa.gov.uk/library/communication/pr/2003/052.shtml, accessed 1 December 2014
—— 'Business Plan 2005/2006' (2005)
—— 'Better Regulation Action Plan: What we have done and what we are doing' (2005)
—— 'Discussion Paper DP 05/3, Wider Range Retail Investment Products: Consumer Protection in a Rapidly Changing World' (2005)
—— 'Implementing MiFID's Client Categorisation requirements' (2006)

—— 'Treating Customers Fairly: Towards Fair Outcomes for Consumers' (2006)
—— 'Financial capability in the UK: Delivering change' (2006)
—— 'Feedback Statement FS06/3, Wider range Retail Investment Products, Consumer protection in a rapidly changing world' (2006)
—— 'Discussion Paper DP07/01, A Review of Retail Distribution' (2007)
—— 'Principles-based Regulation: Focusing on the Outcomes that Matter' (2007)
—— 'Consumer Research Paper 69, Financial Capability, A Behavioural Economics Perspective' (2008)
—— 'Discussion Paper DP08/5, Consumer Responsibility' (2008)
—— 'FSA update on the Treating Customers Fairly initiative and the December deadline' (2008)
—— 'Annual Report 2007/2008' (2008)
—— 'Discussion Paper DP 09/2, A regulatory response to the global banking crisis' (2009)
—— 'Mortgage market review' (2009)
—— 'Financial Risk Outlook' (2010)
—— 'Discussion Paper DP11/1, Product Intervention' (2011)
—— 'Feedback Statement FS11/3, Product Intervention: Feedback on DP11/1' (2011)
—— 'Finalised Guidance FG11/05, Assessing Suitability: Establishing the risk a customer is willing and able to take and making a suitable investment decision' (2011)
—— 'Retail Conduct Risk Outlook' (2012)
—— 'Journey to the FCA: to make financial markets work well so consumers get a fair deal' (2012)
—— 'Consultation Paper CP12/35, The FCA's use of temporary product intervention rules' (2012)
—— 'Consultation Paper CP12/37, The Financial Services Bill: Implementing markets powers, decision, making procedures and penalties policies' (2012)
—— 'Finalised Guidance FG12/10, Simplified Advice' (2012)
—— 'Finalised Guidance FG12/15, Retail Distribution Review: Independent and Restricted Advice' (2012)
—— 'Interest Rate Hedging Products Pilot Findings' (2013)
—— 'Interest rate hedging products: Information about our work and findings' (2013)
—— 'Policy Statement PS13/5, The new FCA Handbook: Feedback on Regulatory Reform proposals relating to the FCA Handbook, including financial Handbook rules' (2013)
—— 'Final Guidance, Risks to customers from financial incentives' (2013)
FSCP, 'Annual Report 2005/2006' (2006)
—— 'Response to FSA Discussion Paper 08/5 on Consumer Responsibility' (2009)
—— 'Response to DP11/1: Product Intervention' (2011)
—— 'Position Paper on Consumer Responsibility' (2012)
—— 'Position Paper on Fiduciary Duty' (2012)
—— 'Position Paper on Advice' (2012)
—— 'The FSA's Conduct Regulation Regime' (2012)
—— 'Advice Gap Research' (2012)
—— 'Annual Report 2012/2013' (2013)
—— 'Incorporating a Duty of Care into the Financial Services and Markets Act' (2015)
—— 'Position Paper – Banking Culture' (2016)
—— 'Consumers and competition: Delivering more effective consumer power in retail financial markets' (2017)
—— 'Position Paper – Consumers and Competition' (2017)
FSUG, 'Making financial services work for financial users, Paper 1: New model financial regulation' (2012)
Farnish C, 'Review of the Money Advice Service' (2015)
Financial Advice Working Group, 'Rules of Thumb and Nudges: Improving the financial well-being of UK consumers' (2017)
—— 'Consumer explanations of "advice" and "guidance"' (2017)
Financial Services Agency of Japan, 'Plan for Strengthening the Competitiveness of Japan's Financial and Capital Markets' (2007): www.fsa.go.jp/en/news/2007/20071221/01.pdf, accessed 28 March 2015
—— 'The Principles in the Financial Services Industry' (2008): www.fsa.go.jp/en/news/2008/20080424/01.pdf, accessed 28 March 2015

Financial Services and Markets Authority, 'Moratorium on the distribution of particularly complex structured products' (2011)

—— 'Communication for undertakings that distribute non-mainstream financial products (such as CFD's, binary options, etc.) online' (2014)

—— 'Regulation of the Financial Services and Markets Authority governing the distribution of certain derivative financial instruments to retail clients' (2016)

Financial Services Board, 'Consumer Finance Protection with particular focus on credit' (2011)

Gower L, *Review of Investor Protection: A Discussion Document* (Cmnd 9125, 1982)

—— *Review of Investor Protection: Part I* (Cmnd 9215, 1984)

—— *Review of Investor Protection: Part II* (1985)

HM Courts and Tribunals Service, 'Guide to the Financial List' (2015)

HM Government, *A Better Deal for Consumers: Delivering Real Help Now and Change for the Future* (Cm 7669, 2009)

HM Treasury, 'Reducing administrative burdens: effective inspection and enforcement: The Hampton Review' (2005)

—— 'Financial Capability: The Government's long-term approach' (2007)

—— 'Thoresen Review on Generic Financial Advice: Interim Report, Annex 4 – Paper on regulatory boundary of generic financial advice' (2007)

—— 'Thoresen Review of Generic Financial Advice: Final Report' (2008)

—— *Reforming Financial Markets* (Cm 7667, 2008)

—— *A new approach to financial regulation: judgment, focus and stability* (Cm 7874, 2010)

—— *A new approach to financial regulation: building a stronger system* (Cm 8012, 2011)

—— *A new approach to financial regulation: the blueprint for reform* (Cm8083, 2011)

—— 'Conduct and Competition in SME Lending: Letter to the Treasury Select Committee' (2015)

—— 'Budget 2016' (HC 901, 2016)

—— *Treasury Minutes – Government responses on the Thirty Fourth to the Thirty Sixth; the Thirty Eight; and the Fortieth to the Forty Second reports from the Committee of Public Accounts: Session 2015–2016* (Cm 9323, 2016)

—— 'Amending the definition of financial advice: consultation' (2016)

—— 'Amending the definition of financial advice: consultation response' (2017)

—— and FCA, 'Financial Advice Market Review: Call for input' (2015)

—— and FCA, 'Financial Advice Market Review: Final report' (2016)

—— and FSA, 'Helping You Make the Most of Your Money: A Joint Action Plan for Financial Capability' (2008)

HMSO, *Financial Services in the UK: A New Framework for Investor Protection* (Cmnd 9432, 1985)

House of Commons, *Sixth Report: The Regulation of Financial Services in the UK, Volume I* (HC 332-I, 1995)

—— *Financial Services Bill – Bill 278 of 2010-12* (Research Paper 12/08, 2012)

—— Committee of Public Accounts, *Forty-First Report: Financial services mis-selling: regulation and redress* (HC 847, 2016)

—— *Common Financial Services Questions* (2016) Briefing Paper No 07262

IOSCO, 'Objectives and Principles of Securities Regulation' (2010)

—— 'Suitability Requirements With Respect To the Distribution of Complex Financial Products' Final Report FR01/13 (2013)

Joint Committee on the draft Financial Services Bill, *Draft Financial Services Bill* (HL 236 HC 1447, 2010–12)

Joint Committee on Financial Services and Markets, *Draft Financial Services and Markets Bill: First Report* (HC 328-I, 1999)

—— *Draft Financial Services and Markets Bill: Minutes of evidence* (18 March 1999)

JUSTICE Committee, *The Protection of the Small Investor* (1992)

Large A, *Financial Services Regulation: Making the two tier system work* (SIB 1993)

Law Commission, 'Exemption Clauses – Second Report' (Law Com No 69, 1975)

—— *The Parol Evidence Rule* (HMSO Working Paper No 70, 1976)

—— *Law of contract: the parol evidence rule* (HMSO Cmnd 9700, 1986)
—— 'Unfair Terms in Consumer Contracts: a new approach?' (2012)
—— 'Consultation Paper 215, Fiduciary Duties of Investment Intermediaries: A Consultation Paper' (2013)
—— 'Fiduciary Duties of Investment Intermediaries' (Law Com No 350, 2014)
Legal Services Consumer Panel, 'Risk and responsibility: Implications for regulating legal services' (2013)
Lord Morris of Borth-y-Gest, Unfair Contract Terms Act Deb 23 May 1977, vol 383 col 1100
Milburn A, Financial Services and Markets Bill Deb 28 June 1999, vol 334 col 40
Mitchell I, 'Written Evidence made to the Parliamentary Commission on Banking Standards' (16 October 2012)
Molony Committee, *Final Report of the Committee on Consumer Protection* (Cmnd 1781, 1962)
Money Advice Trust, 'The cost of doing business: Supporting the self-employed and small businesses' (2015)
NAO, 'Financial services mis-selling: regulation and redress' (HC 851, 2015–16)
—— 'Vulnerable consumers in regulated industries' (HC 1061, 2016–17)
New City Agenda, 'A report on the culture of British retail banking' (2016)
OECD, 'OECD's Financial Education Project, 87 Financial Market Trends' (2004)
—— 'Improving Financial Literacy: Analysis of Issues and Policy' (2005)
—— 'Recommendation of Principles and Good Practices for Financial Education and Awareness' (2005)
—— 'Consumer Policy Toolkit' (2010)
—— 'G20 High-Level Principles on Financial Consumer Protection' (2011)
—— 'Behavioural economics and financial consumer protection' (2017)
OFT, 'Savings and Investments, Consumer Issues: An Occasional Paper to the OFT by J Mitchell and H Weisner' (1992)
—— 'Research Paper No 11: Consumer Detriment under Conditions of Imperfect Information' (1997)
—— 'Unfair contract terms guidance: Guidance for the Unfair Terms in Consumer Contracts Regulations 1999' (2008)
—— 'Guidance on the Consumer Protection from Unfair Trading Regulations 2008' (2008)
—— 'Financial Services Plan' (OFT 1106, 2009)
—— 'What does Behavioural Economics mean for Competition Policy? (OFT 1224, 2010)
Parliamentary Joint Committee on Corporations and Financial Services, 'Inquiry into financial products and services in Australia' (2009)
—— 'Inquiry into financial products and services in Australia: ASIC submissions' (2009)
PCBS, *Changing banking for good: Report of the Parliamentary Commission on Banking Standards, Volume I* (HL Paper 27-I, HC 175-I, 2013)
—— *Changing banking for good: Report of the Parliamentary Commission on Banking Standards, Volume II* (HL Paper 27-II, HC 175-II, 2013)
PFS and CII, 'The FSA's Retail Distribution Review: A Background' (2010)
PIA, 'Pension Transfer and Opt Outs: Review of Past Business' (1995)
SFC, 'Mystery Shopping Programme Findings' (2014)
SIB, 'The Securities and Investments Board's Application for the Designated Agency Status under the terms of the Financial Services Act 1986 and the Revised Rule Book' (1987)
—— 'Review Committee Report' (1990)
—— and LAUTRO, 'Review of Retail Regulation: Consumer Research by Taylor Nelson Financial' SIB Disclosures Research Report (1992)
—— 'Pension Transfers and Opt Outs: Further Safeguards for Future Business' (1994)
—— 'Chief Executive Annual Report for 1996/1997' (1997)
SMSG, 'Advice to ESMA: Investor Protection Aspects of the Consultation Paper on MiFID II and MiFIR' ESMA/2014/SMSG/035 (2014)
Synovate Ltd, 'Consumer Market Study on Advice within the Area of Retail Investment Services – Final Report' (2012) Prepared for the European Commission, Directorate-General Health and Consumer Protection

Treasury and Civil Select Committee, *The Regulation of Financial Services in the UK* (HC 1994–95) Sixth Report Vol I
Treasury Committee, *Conduct and competition in SME lending: Written Evidence* (2014–2015)
—— *Conduct and competition in SME lending: Minutes of evidence* (2014–2015)
—— *Conduct and competition in SME lending* (HC 204, 2015) Eleventh Report
—— *Oral Evidence: Financial Conduct Authority* (HC 515, 2016)

Treasury Select Committee

—— *Banking Crisis – FSA and FSCS: Minutes of Evidence* (25 February 2009)
—— *Treatment of Financial Services Consumers: Oral Evidence* (15 October 2014)
Turner A, 'The Turner Review: A Regulatory Response to the Global Banking Crisis' (2009)
Tyrie A, 'Evidence session on small and medium sized enterprises lending' (2014)
UAE Central Bank, 'Notice No. 3803/2009 – Structured Products' (2009)
World Bank, 'Finance for All: Policies and Pitfalls in Expanding Access' (2008)
—— 'Policy Research Working Paper, Consumer Protection and Financial Literacy: Lessons From Nine Country Studies' (2010)
—— and others, 'The Case for Financial Literacy in Developing Countries: Promoting Access to Finance by Empowering Consumers' (2009)

Speeches and Addresses

ASIC, 'ASIC and behavioural economics: Regulating for real people' Speech by Peter Kell (The Impacts of Behavioural Economics on Financial Markets and Regulations Symposium, Brisbane, 18 October 2016)
BaFIN, 'We need even more transparency' Speech by Dr Elke König (Frankfurt am Main, 13 March 2013)
—— 'Consumer protection and regulation – where we stand and what must still be done' Speech by Dr Elke König (BaFin Annual Press Conference, Frankfurt am Main, 20 May 2014)
ESMA, 'Opening statement of Steven Maijoor' (ESMA Investor Day, Paris, 12 December 2012)
—— 'ESMA and Investor Protection' Speech by Laurent Degabriel (ESMA Investor Day, Paris, 12 December 2012)
European Commission, 'Increasing Financial Capability' Speech by Charlie McCreevy (Increasing Financial Capability Conference, Brussels, 28 March 2007)
—— 'Forging a New Deal between Finance and Society: Restoring Trust in the Financial Sector' Speech by Michel Barnier (European Financial Services Conference, Brussels, 26 April 2010)
—— 'Turning around the telescope – consumers at the centre of financial services policies' Speech by Jonathan Hill (Emerging Challenges in Retail Finance and Consumer Policy Conference, Brussels, 18 November 2014)
FCA, 'Human face of regulation' Speech by Martin Wheatley (London School of Economics, London, 10 April 2013)
—— 'Building on experience' Speech by Martin Wheatley (The future of financial services conference, Lansons, London 17 April 2013)
—— 'Ethics and Economics' Speech by Martin Wheatley (Worshipful Company of International Bankers, London, 4 March 2014)
—— 'Making competition king – the rise of behavioural economics at the FCA' Speech by Martin Wheatley (Australian Securities and Investments Commission, Australia, 25 March 2014)
—— 'Investor protection in the UK: New tools, new challenges' Speech by Maggie Craig (FCA MiFID II Conference, London, 18 September 2014)

—— 'Regulating in a recovery' Speech by John Griffith-Jones (CASS Business School, London, 13 November 2014)

—— 'Using Behavioural Insights to Make Competition Work Well for Financial Consumers' Speech by Peter Andrews (Emerging Challenges in Retail Finance and Consumer Policy Conference, Brussels, 18 November 2014)

—— 'Enforcement and the Wholesale Markets' Speech by Tracey McDermott (13th Annual FX Week Europe, London, 26 November 2014)

—— 'The corporate importance of culture to industry' Speech by Martin Wheatley (FCA Enforcement Conference, London, 2 December 2014)

—— 'Learning the lessons of the past as an industry' Speech by Tracey McDermott (FCA Enforcement Conference, London, 2 December 2014)

—— 'Confidence to crisis and back' Speech by Martin Wheatley (IOSCO Conference, London, 17 June 2015)

—— 'Wholesale Conduct Risk' Speech by Tracey McDermott (British Bankers' Association Conference 'Wholesale Markets and Risk: FEMR and beyond', London, 24 July 2015)

—— 'Investor protection under MiFID II' Speech by David Geale (FCA MiFID II Conference, London, 19 October 2015)

—— 'The rapidity of change' Speech by Tracey McDermott (City Banquet, Mansion House, London, 22 October 2015)

—— 'Tackling the hard questions' Speech by Mark Steward (Thomson Reuters Annual Compliance and Risk Summit, London, 26 April 2016)

—— 'Beyond Economics?' Speech by Peter Andrews (Conference on behavioural finance, London, 14 June 2016)

—— 'Chief Executive speaks at APM about recent work and future challenges' Speech by Andrew Bailey (Annual Public Meeting, The QEII Centre, London, 19 July 2016)

—— 'New thinking in regulatory economics' Speech by Peter Andrews (The European Securities and Markets Authority, Paris, 2 March 2017)

—— 'Conclusions from the Cryptoassets Taskforce' Speech by Christopher Woolard (The Regulation of Cryptocurrencies event, London, 20 November 2018)

FINRA, 'Remarks from the Consumer Federation of America Consumer Assembly' Speech by Richard G Ketchum (Washington DC, 14 March 2013)

Financial Services and Markets Authority, 'Product Intervention' Speech by Jean-Paul Servais (ESMA Investor Day, Paris, 12 December 2012)

FOS, 'Boundaries of responsibility in financial services' Speech by Walter Merricks (Financial Services Research Forum, London, 7 November 2006)

FSA, 'Financial Services and Markets Bill Conference' Speech by Howard Davies (Grosvenor House Hotel, London, 24 September 1998)

—— 'Why Regulate?' Speech by Howard Davies (Henry Thornton Lecture, City University Business School, London, 4 November 1998)

—— 'Financial Regulation: Why Bother?' Speech by Howard Davies (Society of Business Economists lecture, London January 1999)

—— 'Mansion House speech' Speech by Callum McCarthy (London, 20 September 2005)

—— 'What does caveat emptor mean in the retail market for financial services?' Speech by Callum McCarthy (Financial Services Forum, London, 9 February 2006)

—— 'Principles-based regulation and what it means for insurers' Speech by John Tiner (Insurance Sector Conference, London, 20 March 2006)

—— 'Keynote address' Speech by John Tiner (Enforcement Law Conference, London, 16 June 2006)

—— 'Principles based regulation: the EU context' Speech by John Tiner (APCIMS Annual Conference Hotel Arts, Barcelona, 13 October 2006)

—— 'Supervision in a Principles Based World, Speech by Sarah Wilson (FSA Retail Firms Division Conference, London, 27 February 2007)

—— 'Principles-based regulation – moving from theory to practice' Speech by Clive Briault (ABI Conference, London, 10 May 2007), available at
—— 'The Financial Services Authority: looking back, looking forward' Speech by John Tiner (ABI Annual Conference, London, 2 July 2007) as reproduced in House of Commons (SN/BT/3787, 2008)
—— 'The UK approach to regulation' Speech by Hector Sants (Financial Services Seminar, British Embassy, Tokyo, 7 November 2007)
—— 'Regulatory challenges in a principles-based environment' Speech by Clive Briault (The Westminster Forum, London, 8 November 2007)
—— 'Delivering Intensive Supervision and Credible Deterrence' Speech by Hector Sants (Reuters Newsmakers event, London, 12 March 2009)
—— 'Delivering Credible Deterrence' Speech by Margaret Cole (FSA Enforcement Conference, London, 27 April 2009)
—— 'Intensive Supervision: Delivering the Best Outcomes' Speech by Hector Sants (Bloomberg, London, 9 November 2009)
—— 'UK Financial Regulation: After the Crisis' Speech by Hector Sants (Annual Lubbock Lecture in Management Studies, London, 12 March 2010)
—— 'The Future of Banking Regulation in the UK' Speech by Hector Sants (BBA Annual Conference, Guildhall, 29 June 2011)
—— 'My vision for the FCA' Speech by Martin Wheatley (British Bankers' Association, London, 25 January 2012)
—— 'Credible Deterrence: Here to Stay' Speech by Tracey McDermott (FSA Enforcement Conference, London, 2 July 2012)
FSCP, 'The New Financial World – A Better Deal for Consumers' Speech by Adam Phillips (The Building Societies Association Annual Lecture, London 13 October 2009)
—— Panel Discussion, Speech by Sue Lewis, (FCA MiFID II Conference, London, 18 September 2014)
FSUG, 'Ensuring financial education and behavioural economic initiatives are a good use of limited regulatory resources' Speech by Mick McAteer (ESMA Investor Education Day, Paris, 30 October 2014)
Halpern D, 'Inside the Nudge Unit: how small changes can make a big difference' (LSE Public Lecture, 15 September 2015)
Investment Management Association, Panel Discussion, Speech by Guy Sears (FCA MiFID II Conference, London, 18 September 2014)
Lord Chief Justice Thomas of Cwmgiedd, 'Corporate Justice in the Global Village: The Role of the Corporate Courts' (DIFC Academy of Law Lecture, Dubai, 1 February 2016)
OECD Task Force on Financial Consumer Protection, 'Consumer protection deserves a central place' Speech by Theodor Kockelkoren (International Regulators Seminar, London, 28 November 2013)
State Street Global Advisors, 'Behavioural Finance in Quantitative Active Equity Portfolio Management' Speech by Dr Marcus Schulmerich (ESMA Investor Day, Paris, 12 December 2012)

List of Websites

www.behaviouralinsights.co.uk/about-us, accessed 12 October 2016
www.consumerfinance.gov/, accessed 20 May 2016
www.esma.europa.eu/page/esma-short, accessed 12 February 2015
www.fca-consumer-spotlight.org.uk, accessed 20 March 2016
www.fca.org.uk/consumers/interest-rate-hedging-products/background-review, accessed 22 October 2016
www.fca.org.uk/firms/senior-managers-certification-regime, accessed 20 June 2017
www.fca.org.uk/news/press-releases/lloyds-banking-group-fined-£117m-failing-handle-ppi-complaints-fairly, accessed 4 October 2016
www.fca.org.uk/news/national-audit-office-misselling-report, accessed 2 April 2016

www.ombudsman-decisions.org.uk/viewPDF.aspx?FileID=17717, accessed 7 November 2014
www.ombudsman-decisions.org.uk/viewPDF.aspx?FileID=20286, accessed 7 November 2014
www.sfc.hk/sfcPressRelease/EN/sfcOpenDocServlet?docno=08PR171, accessed 15 March 2015
www.sfc.hk/sfcPressRelease/EN/sfcOpenDocServlet?docno=09PR100, accessed 15 March 2015

Other Sources

Allen & Overy, 'FCA rules may inform standard of common law duty of care owed by financial adviser to client' (2015)
BDRC Continental, 'SME Finance Monitor: Q4 2014' (2015)
Berkeley Research Group LLC, 'The Behavioural Regulators' Agenda' (2015)
Berwin Leighton Paisner LLP, 'Emerging Themes 2015: Another turbulent year for financial regulation' (2015) 76
—— 'Trends in the FCA's use of 'hard' and 'soft' powers' (2015)
Bloomberg BNA, 'The EU's MiFID 2: Advising Clients – Independence, Suitability and Appropriateness' (2015) 21 World Securities Law Report 1
—— 'MiFID still happens with "Brexit"' (2016)
Clifford Chance, 'Briefing Note: FSA's Discussion Paper on Product Intervention' (2011)
—— 'Bank succeeds in defending claim for alleged mis-selling of structured products' (2012)
—— 'Hong Kong High Court Confirms the Effectiveness of non-reliance clauses in Bank-Customer Contracts' (2015)
—— 'A crown of thorns: misspelling claim against bank fails' (2015)
—— 'Contractual interpretation: shades of grey' (2015)
—— 'English judiciary establishes a specialist court for the financial markets' (2015)
DLA Piper, 'Recent decisions from the Administrative and Mercantile Courts have stirred things up in the swaps mis-selling arena, potentially opening up two new fronts of litigation' (2015)
de Palma A and Picard N, 'Evaluation of MiFID questionnaires in France: Study for the Autorité des Marchés Financiers' (2010)
Dēmos, 'How Safe Are Your Savings?' (2011)
Edgeworth Economics LLC, 'Deceptive for Whom? The Implications of Behavioral Economics Driven Consumer Financial Services Policy' (2016)
Ernst & Young, 'Product Intervention – Consumer Agenda: Global regulatory reform' (2014)
Europe Economics, 'Retail Distribution Review: post-implementation review' (2014)
FTI Consulting, 'Lessons learnt from Interest Rate Hedging Products' (2014)
Gadens, 'Greater protection for small business afforded by FOS and the ABA? You can bank on that!' (2016)
Herbert Smith Freehills LLP, 'Product Intervention: some thoughts on the FCA's interactions with Europe' (2012)
—— 'Product intervention – what should the future hold' (2012)
—— 'Hong Kong Dispute Resolution Briefing, Investment mis-selling claims: An overview of recent case-law in Hong Kong and Singapore and lessons to be learnt' (2013)
—— 'Hong Kong court dismisses investor's counterclaim against bank for mis-selling of financial products' (2015)
Hogan Lovells, 'Financial Disputes Update – The Law of Mis-Selling with an Asian Twist' (2013)
International Regulatory Strategy Group, 'The EU's Third Country Regimes and Alternatives to Passporting' (2017)
Linklaters, 'Misselling of Financial Products' (2010)
—— 'Large-scale retail misselling claims' (2011)
Mayer Brown JSM, 'Suitability Requirement – Now a Contractual Obligation on Licensed and Registered Persons' (2016)
McKinsey & Co, 'Sustaining New York's and the US' Global Financial Services Leadership' (2007)

NMG Consulting, 'Impact of the Retail Distribution Review on consumer interaction with the retail investments market: A qualitative research report' (2014)
—— 'Retail Investment Advice Assessment of Ongoing Services – A research report' (2014)
—— 'The motivations, needs and drivers of non-advised investments: A qualitative research report' (2014)
Norton Rose Fulbright, 'MiFID II / MiFIR series – investor protection (conduct of business)'
Oxera, 'A framework for assessing the benefits of financial regulation' Prepared for Financial Services Authority (2006)
—— 'Behavioural economics and its impact on competition policy: A practical assessment with illustrative examples from financial services' Prepared for The Netherlands Authority for Consumers and Markets (2013)
RPC, 'Claims for financial misselling under English Law – An overview' (2013)
—— 'The regulatory regime continues to inform the advisory duty in mis-selling claims' (2015)
Radcliffe Chambers, 'Crossing the line – Advising on structured deposits' (2015)
Reed Smith, 'New decision on bank's duties re interest rate swaps' (2016)
Slaughter and May, 'Buyers beware, and sellers be careful: The doctrine of contractual estoppel revisited' (2012)
Weston, 'Brexit: What Does This Mean for MiFID II' (2016)

INDEX

www.ingramcontent.com/pod-product-compliance
Lightning Source LLC
Chambersburg PA
CBHW071258180926
51613CB00001B/68

* 9 7 8 1 5 0 9 9 2 5 8 6 5 *